EAST ASIA DECENTRALIZES

MAKING LOCAL GOVERNMENT WORK

EAST ASIA DECENTRALIZES

MAKING LOCAL GOVERNMENT WORK

THE WORLD BANK
Washington, D.C.

1818 H Street NW
Washington DC 20433
Telephone: 202-473-1000
Internet: www.worldbank.org
E-mail: feedback@worldbank.org

1 2 3 4 08 07 06 05

ISBN-10: 0-8213-6059-0
ISBN-13: 978-0-8213-6059-0
eISBN-10: 0-8213-6060-4
eISBN-13: 978-0-8213-6060-6

Cover photos (left to right): Tran Thi Hoa/World Bank (2002); Hugh Sitton/Getty Images; and Ray Witlin/World Bank (1996).

Library of Congress Cataloging-in-Publication Data

East Asia decentralizes.
p. cm.
Includes bibliographical references and index.
ISBN 0-8213-6059-0 (pbk.)
1. Decentralization in government—East Asia.

JQ1499.A56D424 2005
352.2'83—dc22

2005047796

CONTENTS

LIST OF BOXES, FIGURES, AND TABLES

BOXES

FIGURES

TABLES

PREFACE

Decentralization has gained momentum across East Asia, and it is time to take stock of the experience so far. This study reviews intergovernmental reform in the region, distills key messages, highlights positive experiences, and points out areas where policy makers will need to take priority action to avoid going down the wrong path. Where relevant, the study draws on international experience while recognizing the economic, political, and cultural factors unique to East Asia.

The report has been written primarily for policy makers who are currently making decisions on these issues, but academics, business people, and development practitioners should also find it useful. It does not attempt to provide an exhaustive analysis or a detailed practical manual on decentralization in East Asia. Space limitations do not permit coverage of all facets of decentralization that may be important. Nor is every country in the region included. Instead, the volume focuses on six East Asian countries where decentralization is a major issue: Cambodia, China, Indonesia, the Philippines, Thailand, and Vietnam. The report is intended to be helpful in tracking progress on decentralization in East Asia today and in guiding reforms as they go forward.

This report was produced by a multisector team led by Duvvuri Subbarao and Roland White. Chapter authors are listed on the Contents page. The authors benefited from background papers and input from various specialists, namely Alex Brillantes, Hana Brixi, Jasmin Chakeri, Robert Ebel, James Ford, Kai Kaiser, Bui Duong Ngheim, Barbara Nunberg, Duvvuri Subbarao, Helen Sutch, Charas Suwanmala, Jorge Martinez Vazquez, and Christine P. W. Wong. Team assistance was provided by Muriel Greaves, Gloria Elmore, and Walter Meza-Cuadra. The work was carried out under the overall direction of Homi Kharas.

The report received useful advice from a team of peer reviewers comprising Richard Bird, Roy Bahl, James Hicks, Stuti Khemani, Keith McClean, Ranjana Mukherjee, David Rosenblatt, Dana Weist, and Don Winkler.

Many people both inside and outside the World Bank provided comments on the report during drafting. Valuable contributions were received from Madga Adriani, Mats Anderssen, Naomi Aoki, Philippe Auffret, IIhem Baghdadli, Jitendra Bajpai, Aldo Baietti, Joven Balbosa, Halsey Beemer, Simeth Beng, Kirida Bhaopichitr, Jasmin Chakeri, Songsu Choi, Luis Crouch, Soren Davidsen, Lynnette de la Cruz Perez, Robert Ebel, Wolfgang Fengler, Cyprian Fisiy, James Ford, David Gomez-Alvarez, Philip Gray, Arvind Gupta, Alejandro N. Herrín, Dingyong Hou, Boun Oum Inthaxoum, Emmanuel Jimenez, Kai Kaiser, Wolfgang Koehling, Philip Lam, Qing Lani Wu, Jennica Larrison, Blaine Lewis, Xiaofan Liu, Puti Marzoeki, Stephen Mink, Amitabha Mukherjee, Tariq Niazi, Antonio M. Ollero, Demetrios Papathanasiou, Juan Antonio Perez, Tanaporn Poshyanand, Sjamsu Rahardjs, Merwin Salazar, Rubi Sugana , Bambang Suharnoko, Hioraki Suzuki, Luiz Tavares, Thanh Thi Mai, Jessica Tisch, Roy van der Weide, Minh Van Nguyen, Khuankaew Varakornharn, Emiliana Vegas, Jonathan Walters, Liping Xiao, Bastian Zaini. Despite efforts to compile a comprehensive list, some who contributed may have been inadvertently omitted. The team apologizes for any oversights and reiterates its gratitude to all who contributed to this report.

The team undertook a wide range of consultations including workshops in Cambodia, China, Indonesia, the Philippines, Vietnam, and the Lao People's Democratic Republic. The participants in these workshops included policy makers, academics and nongovernmental organizations.

Book design, editing, and production were coordinated by the World Bank's Office of the Publisher.

1

EAST ASIA DECENTRALIZES

Roland White and Paul Smoke

A fundamental transformation in the structure of government has been taking place across East Asia. Before 1990 most East Asian countries were highly centralized; today subnational governments have emerged as the fulcrum for much of the region's development. They deliver many critical services and account for a significant fraction of total public expenditures (see figure 1.1). Though East Asia's decentralization has come later than in some other parts of the world, it is now here to stay.

From China to Cambodia to Thailand, countries of varying sizes, income levels, and political systems are moving government down this path. Reform processes are under way in almost every country. Demands for accountable government whose services reach the grassroots effectively are on the rise. Thus, a wholesale recentralization of government is unlikely. With all that is invested in successful development of these decentralized public sectors, the key question is no longer whether to decentralize. It is how best to design intergovernmental structures and manage the implementation process to achieve optimal results.

In many countries initial progress is encouraging. Where decentralization "leaps" have been attempted, as in Indonesia and the Philippines, they have gone fairly smoothly. Intergovernmental fiscal systems have been institutionalized. Workers have been transferred from central ministries to local governments without significant disruptions. And local authorities have taken up their service-delivery functions reasonably effectively. Where decentralization has proceeded more gradually, as in Cambodia and Vietnam, it has produced some gains in service delivery and public participation at the local level. Decentralization has also unleashed local initiative and energy. New service-delivery models have begun to emerge, and the potential for continued improvement and innovation has become tangible.

But there have also been problems, and there is a real danger that programs could stall. While East Asian decentralization does not pose the macroeconomic risks confronted in other regions, it does face three distinctive challenges, which play out differently in each country setting. The first challenge relates to the design of sound intergovernmental organizational arrangements. For example, unclear assignments of functions among levels of governments threaten to sidetrack decentralization reforms in some countries. The second challenge concerns the development of robust financial mechanisms for channeling money to subnational governments. In some countries, the failure to allocate sufficient own-source revenues to local governments could hamper their ability to deliver services, for example. The third challenge relates to the accountability of local governments and the capacity of their management systems. Attenuated accountability and weak management—of both financial and human resources—could constrain effective implementation of decentralized

FIGURE 1.1 Subnational Expenditures as a Share of Total Public Spending

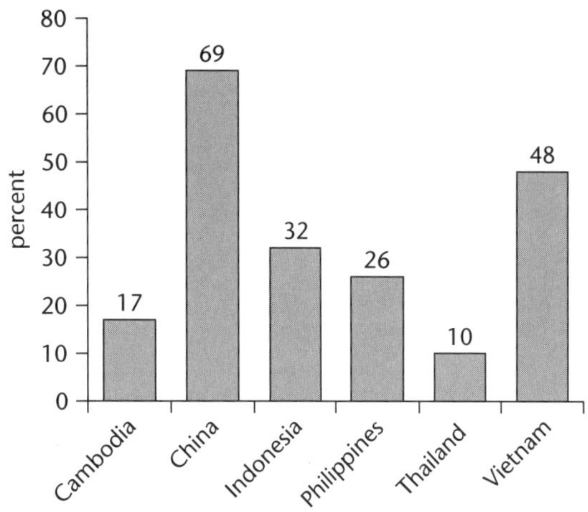

Source: Refer to chapter 5, table 5.1.

functions by subnational entities. In sum, the potential benefits of harnessing the power of subnational government in East Asia are substantial. But national leadership across the region will be critical in responding consistently and systematically to these three broad challenges if decentralization is to live up to its promise.

This Study

Clearly, governments in East Asia have an important stake in getting decentralization right. They will need to develop strategic approaches that fit country conditions but that also benefit from regional and global lessons of decentralization. This study seeks to provide guidance to country reformers by reviewing the East Asian experience so far, and by furnishing an analytic perspective on the design and implementation challenges that face policy makers in the region.

This chapter sets the stage for more detailed discussions in subsequent chapters. It provides an overview of East Asian decentralization. First, it shows why decentralization is an important issue in the East Asian context by highlighting its broad implications for economic, governance, and service delivery outcomes. The discussion then examines the origins of decentralization in East Asia, pointing to structural and political factors that have driven the process. The approaches taken by East Asian governments are discussed, and an early view of the record provided. The chapter proceeds to examine the three main intergovernmental challenges outlined above, looking at the organizational structures, financial mechanisms, and subnational government management and accountability systems that have emerged in East Asian countries engaged in the decentralization process. This discussion touches on themes that will be taken up again in later chapters. Finally, the chapter distills some key messages for East Asian policy makers grappling with decentralization issues.

The ensuing chapters are organized as follows. Chapter 2 delves into greater detail on the frameworks, structures, and processes of decentralization across East Asian countries. Chapters 3 and 4 discuss the macro-fiscal issues of maintaining fiscal sustainability and ensuring interregional equity. Chapters 5 through 7 explore the nuts and bolts of decentralizing public management systems, including public expenditures, revenues, and human resources. Chapters 8 through 10 examine the nexus between decentralization and service delivery in key sectors: health, education, and infrastructure. Chapters 11 and 12 cover governance and citizen empowerment.

Why Does Decentralization Matter for East Asia?

Intergovernmental reforms adopted in the process of decentralization are important because they inevitably affect broader country performance in three critical, interrelated areas: the economy, service delivery, and governance.

The Economy

East Asia's remarkable achievements in economic growth and poverty reduction over the past 30 years can be attributed largely to significant public investment in human capital formation and infrastructure, and to the establishment of a regulatory environment conducive to private enterprise.[1] With decentralization, subnational governments are now at the heart of a range of investment, fiscal, and regulatory activities that affect both the pace and quality of economic growth. For example, they are now responsible for planning and financing economic infrastructure, such as local roads and irrigation schemes, and for regulating and taxing businesses. In some East Asian countries, such as Cambodia, the role of local and regional authorities in these areas is still limited. But in most, including China and Indonesia, it has become crucial.

There are fiscal dangers associated with decentralization. To the extent that newly empowered subnational governments can transfer significant financial liabilities to the center, the expansion of subnational activities could generate macroeconomic risks for national governments. With the possible exception of China, this has yet to emerge as a problem in East Asia. But local off-budget fiscal activity, subnational borrowing, and inadequate local control of contingent liabilities are common throughout the region. These weaknesses, combined with deepening autonomy and expanding access to domestic and international capital markets, could aggravate longer-term risk unless institutional, regulatory, and monitoring systems improve.

Service Delivery

While many East Asian countries have strengthened the delivery of public services in recent years (chapters 8, 9, and 10), profound problems remain. It is precisely in the areas where these difficulties are concentrated—such as primary health, education, and potable water supply—that subnational governments in East Asia have assumed most of their responsibilities. As discussed in later chapters, performance in these sectors has been mixed. In addition, subnational governments have been required to assume regulatory roles in areas (such as environmental protection) for which they are poorly structured and have little technical capacity. The concern is that if local and intergovernmental systems do not function well, countries are unlikely to sustain positive service-delivery trends, or to reverse negative ones.

The equity of service delivery is also a concern. Wide divergences in natural resource endowments and economic concentration, combined with the design of frameworks for own-source revenues at the subnational level in most countries, have produced pronounced horizontal fiscal inequalities in East Asia. In China, the per capita own-revenue of the richest province is 16 times that of the poorest region. In Indonesia, the Philippines, and Vietnam, own-source revenues are even more skewed. Such disparities can be mitigated by fairly designed systems of intergovernmental transfers. In the absence of such mechanisms, decentralization may reinforce inequitable distribution of services across jurisdictions, potentially posing serious concern for both subnational and national political leaders in the region.

Governance

While the successes that came to be known as the Asian Miracle were partly attributed to well-performing public sectors, serious deficiencies in public sector governance were evident in many countries by the time the 1997 financial crisis hit East Asia (World Bank 2000). Low levels of government accountability, transparency, and probity contributed to the calamity. Despite postcrisis efforts to reform these governance weaknesses, problems persist. In particular, institutions of public financial accountability often diverge strongly from internationally accepted standards, especially with respect to procurement, accounting and auditing, and performance management and information systems in government (Mountfield 2001).

Perception surveys suggesting that corruption runs deep and wide across East Asia are particularly vexing. Transparency International's 2003 Corruption Perceptions Index ranks the six countries covered in this report in the bottom half of the 133 countries surveyed, ranging from China at 66 to Vietnam at 100 (Transparency International 2003). The World Bank's Governance Research Indicators for 2002 show East Asia's control of corruption in a steady decline since 1996 (Kaufmann et al. 2003). Country-specific diagnostic surveys in Cambodia, Indonesia, and Thailand also point to the high costs of corruption for households and enterprises alike.[2] Recent Investment Climate Assessments in Cambodia and the Philippines provide further evidence that graft—pervasive in the justice sector and revenue administration—is a major obstacle to doing business.[3]

Decentralization magnifies these governance challenges for subnational governments. Opportunities to strengthen grassroots accountability are paired with risks that, absent tight central controls, corrupt practices could proliferate (Bardhan and Mookherjee 2000). Chapter 11 discusses these issues at length, emphasizing the importance of intergovernmental reform design to ensuring good governance in decentralized contexts.

What's Driving Decentralization?

Decentralization is a process, not an event, and stipulating a starting point in any country is a difficult and sometimes controversial exercise. But there is broad consensus that, for most countries in East Asia, intergovernmental reform gained significant momentum in the 1990s. The evolution of intergovernmental reform has been distinctive for each country, but common dynamics can be identified. For the most part, long-run structural transformations—mainly economic and demographic—have created an environment conducive to decentralization, while powerful political imperatives have precipitated and shaped it.

Structural factors. In most East Asian countries, decentralization has been preceded by significant and continuous periods of economic growth and urbanization, broadly suggesting a relationship among these three phenomena (see table 1.1).

As nations develop and urbanize, there is growing pressure to provide services to rapidly expanding and increasingly concentrated populations (World Bank 2000). The challenges facing national governments in effectively administering services create demands to empower subnational governments to meet the burgeoning needs. Indeed, for developing and developed countries alike, evidence shows that growth in per capita income is associated with a declining central government share in public investment (World Bank 2000).

Urbanization rates in the region are particularly informative. With the exception of Thailand in recent years, urban growth rates over the last quarter-century have been high for the six countries under consideration here, particularly during earlier periods in China, Indonesia, the Philippines, and Thailand. Although Cambodia and Vietnam began urbanizing later, their urbanization rates have accelerated and are projected to be substantial up to 2015. The interplay between economic growth, urbanization, and intergovernmental reform in East Asia is not clearly understood. But, as in other parts of the world, the basic economic and demographic transformations in East Asia seem to have created an environment conducive to decentralization, raising the stakes for intergovernmental systems to function effectively (World Bank 2000).

Political factors. While these structural changes have generated pressures for decentralization, political factors appear to have been the more proximate and powerful drivers of the process.[4] Democratization appears sometimes to have been an important trigger. In the Philippines and Indonesia, decentralization was adopted after the sudden collapse of authoritarian regimes (Marcos in 1986 and Soeharto in 1997, respectively) fueled demand for legitimate, local representation. Thailand's prodemocracy movement in the 1990s paired protests against the inordinate role of the military in politics with the development of an initial decentralization framework. Explicit moves toward pluralism have not figured in China and Vietnam. But in both cases, more audible demand for citizen participation and good government at the local level has driven decentralization. Certainly, the impediments that China's sheer physical size poses to effective central control has reinforced these tendencies through the refinement of an intergovernmental framework that has long had quasi-federal features (World Bank 2002a).

Political dynamics have also shaped the nature of decentralization arrangements. In Indonesia, the need to minimize the probability of provincial separatism in the fragile post-Soeharto era produced a system that favored subprovincial governments. Central political elites have also sought to prevent the emergence of regional provincial rivals by pushing authority and resources down to less powerful city and district levels of government. Faced with calls for grassroots "People's Power," post-Marcos regimes in the Philippines created multilayered systems that diffused subnational power among different jurisdictions, for example. In contrast, low levels of party competition in China and Vietnam may explain the relative administrative power of the provinces, as these don't act as platforms for rival political interests.

TABLE 1.1 Economic and Demographic Trends in East Asia, 1975–2002

	Population 2002 (millions)	GDP per capita, PPP, 2001 (in 1995 US$)	Compound annual rates of growth, current/constant PPP			Urban population, % of total population		Urbanization rate		
			1975–1983	1984–1994	1995–2002	1980	2000	1975–1980	1985–1990	1995–2000
World	6,199	6,837	7.6/1.3	4.1/1.3	3.3/1.8	39.2	47.1	2.72	2.72	2.22
Cambodia	12	1,747	—	—	5.4/—	12.4	16.9	2.25	3.65	6.25
China	1,281	3,796	11.2/5.1	10.9/7.9	7.8/6.1	25.7	35.8	3.39	4.09	2.84
Indonesia	212	2,768	11.1/4.5	7.3/4.4	1.9/0.2	22.1	42.0	4.90	5.00	4.74
Philippines	80	3,672	8.5/2.1	2.1/−0.7	2.4/0.9	37.5	58.5	3.75	4.87	3.64
Thailand	62	5,932	10.8/4.3	9.7/6.8	2.1/0.0	26.8	31.1	4.71	2.36	1.61
Vietnam	81	1,956	—	7.3/4.8	6.2/4.7	19.4	24.3	2.56	2.85	3.22

Sources: World Bank (SIMA); United Nations 2004, tables A.2 and A.6.
Note: PPP = purchasing power parity.

BOX 1.1 Variants of Decentralization: Pros and Cons

Deconcentration refers to decentralization of central government ministries and arrangements whereby subnational governments act as agents of the center. Sometimes regional branches of central offices and agent governments have some authority to make independent decisions, usually within central guidelines. Often, though, deconcentrated local government lacks authority over the scope or quality of local services and how they are provided.

Under *delegation*, subnational governments rather than branches of central government are responsible for delivering certain services, subject to some supervision by the central government. Delegation may improve efficiency when subnational governments can better administer programs of national interest—including certain aspects of education, water, and health—in ways that better reflect local circumstances. The center, or sometimes intermediate government, determines what should be spent, and may also set minimum service standards, while subnational governments define the details. The design of intergovernmental fiscal transfers, and the degree and nature of central monitoring, influence the balance between central and local decision making under delegation.

Devolution is the most complete form of decentralization. Independent or semi-independent and, typically, elected subnational governments are responsible for delivering a set of public services and for imposing fees and taxes to finance those services. Subnational governments have considerable flexibility in selecting the mix and level of services they provide. Other levels of government may provide intergovernmental transfers. For devolution to work, the central and local governments must act as partners, with the former keeping its commitment to devolve functions, and local officials agreeing to make difficult choices and develop the capacity to exercise their powers effectively.[a]

Intergovernmental systems usually have some elements of each of these variants. In principle, devolution should improve efficiency by giving citizens more influence over the mix and level of services, and by giving local governments greater incentives to mobilize resources. The associated efficiency gains—combined with the ability to mobilize untapped revenues at the subnational level (from the formal and informal sectors)—may prove particularly significant in countries with diverse economies, cultures, geography, or tastes for services. Indeed, assigning some local control over expenditure and tax decisions can be key to nation building.

a. Bahl 1999.

How Are Governments Approaching Decentralization?

In response to these structural and political drivers, East Asian governments have taken different approaches to decentralization, combining standard elements of delegation, deconcentration, and devolution found in many intergovernmental reforms around the world (see box 1.1). Country approaches can be divided into three broad categories: fast starters, incrementalists, and cautious movers.

The *fast starters* (the Philippines and Indonesia) have rapidly introduced major structural, institutional, and fiscal reforms in response to a sudden and far-reaching political stimulus. Sweeping decentralization reforms were introduced in the late 1980s after the fall of Marcos in the Philippines, and through a "Big Bang" decentralization in the aftermath of Soeharto's fall and the 1997 financial crisis in Indonesia. These *fast starters* introduced the basic elements of a decentralization framework, subnational democratic elections, and substantial resource sharing swiftly. Considerable follow-up policy and legislative work to create a fully coherent and functional system remains.

The *incrementalists* (China and Vietnam) have taken a more piecemeal approach to decentralization. In China, the government made ad hoc policy decisions and passed legislation directly affecting subnational governments (some decentralizing, some recentralizing), but decentralization is not an officially documented policy. Instead, it is anchored in historical realities and broader political and economic reforms. In Vietnam, decentralization policy has been more formal than in China, involving a sequence of specific legislative measures. But with the exception of a few bolder, asymmetric experiments in some of the major cities, decentralization in Vietnam has been limited and incremental. In both cases, decentralization has focused on administrative and fiscal reform, with modest political change and the retention of considerable central control over subnational governments (in law and policy if not always in practice).

Cautious movers (Cambodia and Thailand) have established significant elements of decentralization at the formal policy and legislative levels, but there has been limited progress with implementation. In Thailand, the ambitious decentralization framework developed in the wake of the 1997 Constitution has been only partly implemented. In Cambodia, elected commune councils have limited functions and receive only modest resources. The provincial system is stronger but heavily managed by national line ministries and centrally appointed governors. Only recently has the government undertaken further work on devolution policy. In both countries, the commitment to extensive decentralization appears to be limited.

Cross-Country Trends

The broad categories outlined above describe a cluster of characteristics related to the pace and timing with which different countries have introduced decentralization. Other features of decentralization in the region defy straightforward classification. There is an ongoing unevenness in the way in which decentralization is being planned and implemented across countries.

For example, the degree to which countries utilize consistent and intentional policy frameworks to guide reform varies considerably and appears unrelated to the pace or appetite for reform. Indonesia decentralized faster than any other country in the region, but the Big Bang took place in the absence of a comprehensive policy framework. While recent revisions of the key Indonesian framework laws (Laws 22 and 25 of 1999, now Laws 32 and 33 of 2004) have clarified outstanding issues in the governmental transfer system, many other policy elements—such as the regulatory frameworks for subnational borrowing—have yet to be defined. China lacks even the incomplete policy framework of the Indonesian case but has gradually developed one of the most decentralized intergovernmental structures in the region (World Bank 2002a). In contrast, countries with well-developed, more comprehensive policy frameworks have yet to implement decentralization reforms. Thailand's decentralization framework is elaborated in great detail in the Constitution, in law, and through parliamentary and cabinet decisions, but the country has been slow in carrying out reforms.[5]

Decentralization in East Asia is a complex blend of characteristics in other respects as well. Decentralized subnational governments have, for the most part, been assigned substantial functional mandates and responsibility over large fractions of total public spending. And even where limited recentralization has taken place (such as in China in 1994), this was a temporary move to improve system performance. So the trend has been mainly toward greater local autonomy—albeit at varying rates. The difficulty, however, is that this trend coexists with weak intergovernmental institutional environments and a record of generally poor (while in some instances improving) performance of core mandates by most subnational governments. In some countries (Indonesia, the Philippines) centralized, top-down systems for economic investment and service delivery have weakened. Oversight and regulation of the emerging intergovernmental arrangements are undeveloped. And local systems—lacking appropriate bottom-up incentives and human resource capacity—are not in place to take up the slack.

The result is a kind of "institutional limbo" which typifies decentralizing environments internationally. In East Asia, it has two main features. First, whether by design or as a result of slippages in the implementation process, intergovernmental structures have substantial internal inconsistency. The functions of different levels of government overlap. Bottom-up accountability of locally elected bodies is dampened by top-down methods for appointing key officials. And the discretion given to local authorities in spending unconditional fiscal transfers is effectively curtailed by central government control over human resources. The aforementioned substantial capacity constraints—both local and central—compound these policy and design deficiencies.

Second, the decentralization process itself has slowed, even among countries that had been on the more accelerated, "fast starter" path described above. For example, repeated attempts to revise aspects of the Local Government Code in the Philippines have borne little fruit, and there are few signs of significant advances in implementing other key policy initiatives (e.g., the reform of the Internal Revenue Allotment grant system). In China, recent intergovernmental reform has become more modest, restricting its focus to introducing equalizing adjustments to the existing central-provincial fiscal transfer system. Reforms that would address more fundamental problems, such as those of subnational debt, do not seem to be on the immediate horizon. In Indonesia, aspects of Law 32 of 2004 represent a tightening of central control over local budgeting and own-source revenue decisions, altering the more deliberate move toward subnational autonomy present in the initial phases of the Big Bang reforms.

Of course, policy and design inconsistencies, along with stop-and-start progress, characterize institutional reform processes in developing countries around the world. Progress is rarely monotonic, and policy reconsideration and reformulation can even be sensible and salutary. To the extent that such fits and starts reflect problematic aspects of the decentralization process in East Asia, however, they are mainly explained by political and bureaucratic conflicts, which break down into three broad types.

First, conflicts between national agencies and subnational governments—usually over the pace of decentralization and resource questions (such as revenue allocations)—have been gaining importance. Some conflicts are explicit and formal, such as public disputes between central and local government officials over jurisdictional issues. Some are informal and implicit, such as disputes between local and central authorities over local tax bases and the regulatory powers of subnational governments. The latter are particularly prevalent in countries where the law remains unclear. In Indonesia, local authorities have increasingly begun to assert themselves in competition with central and provincial government in local business regulation. In China, local governments have disputed centrally imposed fiscal constraints and raised local revenues outside the regular budget in response.

Second, in most East Asian countries, conflicts among central agencies themselves over the leadership and direction of decentralization are widespread:

- In Indonesia, the recently completed modification of Laws 22 and 25 (now Laws 32 and 33 of 2004) was complicated, and hence delayed, by policy disagreements between the ministries of Finance and Home Affairs. In fact, these laws now provide for simultaneous regulatory jurisdiction of both ministries over a number of subnational fiscal and financial matters.
- In Cambodia, responsibility for policy development and implementation of decentralization is divided across a number of key interministerial agencies, and coordinated progress has proven difficult. Only recently has the central government attempted to institute a single process of policy development on issues related to deconcentration and decentralization, backed by a program of joint donor support.
- In the Philippines, it appears that opposition from major government banks has played a role in ensuring that the legal and regulatory environment for local borrowing continues to place private investors at a competitive disadvantage (World Bank and Asian Development Bank 2003; Pellegrini and Ma 2002).
- In contrast to other regions, finance ministries in East Asia are less active in managing decentralization than are ministries of Interior, Home Affairs, or Planning, which have strong incentives to limit local autonomy. These central ministries often prevail, as those who would champion decentralization tend to be less powerful.

Third, in some countries, conflicts over the scope of decentralization have become an issue between elected political leaders and administrative bureaucracies. For example, the Indonesian Parliament developed its own bill to reform Law 22, as an alternative to the legislative drafting efforts of the ministries of Finance and Home Affairs. Similar dynamics appear to have slowed attempts to reform aspects of the intergovernmental transfer system in the Philippines.

While these conflicts may be no more pronounced in East Asia than in other decentralizing regions, it does appear that they have seriously impeded progress on key reforms in some countries (Cambodia, Indonesia, and the Philippines).

Even where agreement has been reached among central agencies on intergovernmental frameworks, the arrangements that have been struck tend to fix in place confusion over functional mandates that perpetuate interagency squabbles which, in turn, slow implementation. Moreover, in a number of countries, the absence of clear intergovernmental reform policies, combined with weak management capacity at the center, has generated incentives and opportunities for local authorities to work outside the formal system. Indeed, almost half of Chinese subnational government revenue is, by some estimates, not captured in formal local budgets (Ahmad et al. 2000). With decentralization, local payrolls for temporary workers have expanded in the Indonesia, the Philippines, Thailand, and Vietnam. Indonesian businesses are increasingly subject to regulation and taxation imposed by local ordinances that have not been harmonized with existing central government legislation. These practices are largely the unintended result of inadequately designed reform programs, and illustrate the difficulties countries face in trying to systematize decentralization policies.

Early Impacts

Despite initial anxiety in many countries, the effects of decentralization in East Asia appear to have been largely benign so far. In particular, there seems not to have been a systematic deterioration in the delivery of key services, a major preoccupation in many countries. Indeed, while subnational governments have had difficulties with service delivery, so have some central governments. These are still early impressions. Comprehensive assessment of the effects of decentralization is yet to be done. But initial trends can be detected in three broad areas: resources (particularly fiscal resources), outputs and outcomes, and propoor service delivery.[6]

Spending Envelopes

Overall, decentralization seems to have had a positive effect on aggregate fiscal spending. In health, average annual expenditure in Indonesia and Vietnam remained constant as a proportion of gross domestic product (GDP) during the most intense decentralization reforms, from 1997 to 2001. In the Philippines, health spending at the local level exceeded that at the national level by 2001, while total health spending remained in line with other East Asian countries. In education, the positive trend is more pronounced. In China, education spending nearly tripled as a share of total expenditure from 1978 to 2001 (from 6.7 to 18 percent). In the Philippines, total government spending on education grew from just over 2.5 percent to well over 4 percent of GDP between 1991 and 1998. In Indonesia, the share of spending on education has risen to 4 percent of GNP from only 1.4 percent before decentralization. The subnational share of education resources has also increased, partly because funds and functions have been transferred to the local level, and partly because local governments are expected to mobilize additional resources to perform these functions.

The record on infrastructure is mixed. Local infrastructure investment in China has recently been sustained at high levels, but an initial postdecentralization spending surge in the Philippines has given way to a slow but steady decrease in spending since 1995. There are some indications that horizontal disparities in spending in some sectors have widened during decentralization (education in China). But this has not been widely found and is not entirely consistent with the evidence on service-delivery outcomes.

Outputs and Outcomes

The positive trends in health outcomes in East Asia that began in the 1980s have been broadly sustained through the period of decentralization reform. During the period of intensive intergovernmental reform in Indonesia, the Philippines, and Vietnam, infant mortality rates (IMRs) fell and life expectancy grew steadily, albeit slowly. In some countries, gaps in health status between rich and poor local governments have narrowed markedly. In the Philippines, the difference in IMRs between the richest and poorest regions was further reduced in the 1990s, and by 2000 the IMR of the poorest area was lower (Eastern Visayas, at 10.7 per 1,000 live births) than that of the richest (Manila, 19.4 per 1,000) (chapter 8). This favorable trend was due, in part, to improved health outputs and service coverage that extended its subnational reach: the proportion of births attended by trained health personnel, and the share of the population with access to water or sanitation, rose discernibly over the postreform period. Similar trends were evident in education during periods of intergovernmental reform. As China decentralized, literacy rates rose from 1982 to 1999, most dramatically in the poorer regions. (Further examples of service-delivery trends can be found in chapters 8, 9, and 10.)

Service Delivery to the Poor

The impact of decentralization on the poor is not well understood. National decisions related to decentralization (fiscal equalization, nationally mandated service levels) affect the poor. So do local processes (budgetary allocations, planning decisions, and service mix and quality). In 2001, predecentralization survey data on perceptions among Indonesian households of service delivery suggested that the poor knew less about programs and policies affecting them than did other groups. A postdecentralization follow-on survey is under way to understand these issues more deeply. Better monitoring and evaluation—and more data—are needed to get a fuller picture of service delivery performance in poor communities throughout the region.

Intergovernmental Systems: What Challenges Do East Asian Countries Face?

As countries in the region continue to decentralize, they will need to design and implement reforms of their intergovernmental systems in the three broad areas touched upon earlier in this chapter. These include the organizational arrangements that constitute a country's basic intergovernmental structure; the financial resources that subnational governments can mobilize and the way they are distributed; and the management and accountability systems that govern resource allocation and control at the subnational level. The following discussion highlights the key characteristics of these challenges. It draws on international experience to stimulate thinking about pitfalls to avert and innovative approaches that might be adapted to each country's circumstances.

Organizing the Intergovernmental System

The first broad challenge faced by decentralizing East Asian governments is how to design the organizational structures of the intergovernmental system. This section examines how functions and expenditure responsibilities are assigned, explores issues related to coordination among intergovernmental structures and subnational entities, and examines questions of special configuration and subnational boundaries.

Functional and Expenditure Assignments. Substantial functions have been assigned to subnational governments in East Asia (see table 1.2). But in most countries, specific responsibilities are unclear, and overlaps among the different levels of government are common. In Indonesia, despite recent legal revisions (Law 32 of 2004), a lack of clarity regarding central and subnational functions

TABLE 1.2 Expenditure Shares and Functional Allocations in East Asia

Country	Subnational expenditure (% of total)[a]	Functional allocations[b]		
		Education	Health	Social welfare
Cambodia	17	Provincial	Provincial	Provincial
China	69	Local	Local	Local
Indonesia	32	Local	Local	Local
Philippines	26	Central, provincial, local	Central, provincial, local	Central, provincial, local
Thailand	10	Central, provincial	Central, provincial	Central, provincial
Vietnam	48	Provincial, local	Provincial, local	Provincial, local

Sources: Various country case studies prepared for this report and World Bank statistics.
a. 2001, except for China, Indonesia, and Vietnam (2002).
b. "Provincial" refers to the level immediately below the central or national level; "local" refers to all levels below the provincial level. Classifications vary across countries; municipalities, for example, can be at either the intermediate level (as in Cambodia and Vietnam) or the local level (as in the Philippines and Thailand).

TABLE 1.3 Vertical Organization of Intergovernmental Systems in East Asia

Country	Levels of subnational government[a]	Number of first-tier subnational governments	Average population of first-tier subnational governments (millions, 2002)
Cambodia	2	24	0.5
China	4	32	40.0
Indonesia	3	32	7.0
Philippines	4	149	0.5
Thailand	3	76	0.8
Vietnam	3	61	1.3

Sources: Various country case studies prepared for this report and World Bank statistics.
a. "Level" refers to an organ of government with some degree of formal budget (expenditure) authority. In some cases (such as Indonesia), this can be highly circumscribed, particularly at the lowest levels.

remains, as do a number of inconsistencies between Law 32 and various sectoral laws (such as Law 31 of 2004, which assigns all fisheries functions to the central government). In the Philippines, some clauses in the 1991 Local Government Code appear to distribute functions unambiguously across levels of government, but this clarity is diluted by other clauses allowing both national government agencies and local government units to initiate devolved activities. In China, there is no national law that clarifies the functions of each level of local government; expenditure assignments are decided by the provinces and thus differ across regions (World Bank 2002a).

Achieving greater de jure clarity on functional mandates will not entirely eliminate vertical interagency conflict, and even mature intergovernmental systems are characterized by some dynamic tension over jurisdictional issues. But East Asia may be able to learn from countries that have faced these questions in other parts of the world. As with many other issues, solving these problems is usually about overcoming political obstacles more than technical challenges, and an ongoing dialogue involving various stakeholders will be necessary to resolve these challenges in most countries.

Organization of Intergovernmental Structures and Coordination among Subnational Entities. The character of decentralization varies considerably across East Asian countries, ranging from deconcentration to devolution, and encompassing different levels of subnational government. The intergovernmental structures in turn have varying implications for the scope of intergovernmental coordination, both among subnational governments and between subnational governments and the center.

All East Asian countries have multiple levels of subnational administration or government, but the structures vary widely (table 1.3 and chapter 2). These variations make simple cross-country comparisons difficult, but a rough pattern of vertical organization is evident. Intergovernmental structures in Indonesia and the Philippines are oriented toward the subprovincial level, though interprovincial variations in size, wealth, and influence are wide. In both, however, countries now have limited powers and functions relative to subprovincial governments—perhaps to the point that being precluded from oversight, coordination, and regulation of city and district governments has become dysfunctional for the intergovernmental system as a whole. Subnational structures in China and Vietnam focus more on the intermediate level. These are "nested hierarchies," in which central government determines the overall character of the system and deals directly only with provincial administrations; provinces oversee subprovincial levels; and so on (World Bank 2002). This has allowed the development of significant variation in fiscal and institutional arrangements below the provinces.

Cambodia and Thailand are at the other end of the spectrum, with the most centralized structures in the region. In both, there are elected subprovincial governments, but they have not been assigned significant resources, authority, or functional mandates. In Cambodia, provinces operate fully under the control of the center. In Thailand, provinces have some independent functions in principle, but their realization in practice has been limited.

When planning and budgetary authority is dispersed laterally and devolved downward, there is a need for horizontal coordination across subnational entities and vertical coordination among levels of government. As the responsibilities of local authorities expand, the effects of their activities can spill over into neighboring jurisdictions, intensifying the need for horizontal cooperation across boundaries. This area has not yet been well studied, but initial indications are that horizontal cooperation has generally been weak in the region. There are some examples of progress in some sectors, such as the Joint Health Councils in Yogyakarta, Indonesia (chapter 8), but these tend to be exceptions. Some donor projects are attempting to introduce incentives to stimulate such cooperation—in China, for example—but systematic initiatives are not common in the region.

Vertical coordination between central and subnational governments is also critical for major planning and investment activities. In Indonesia, provinces are reportedly encountering difficulties in facilitating cooperation across local governments, leading to underperformance in tasks with large spillover effects and significant economies of scale, such as ocean management. An ongoing tug-of-war between the center and the regions on investment approval and land has cooled local investment (World Bank 2003b). These difficulties are related in part to the underlying lack of clarity in the division of functions and powers among the different levels of government—and in part to the changing scope and diminishing authority of national planning agencies under decentralization. To maintain efficient planning, budgeting, and regulation of infrastructure investment, governments need to make conscious efforts to develop models of vertical and horizontal cooperation that can function in a more complex institutional landscape.

There are many international examples of successful intergovernmental cooperation. A number of these lie in the area of tax administration. In the United States, the sovereignty accorded the states by the constitution has created a highly independent system of tax administration and generated the need for cooperative arrangements between state and federal tax authorities. These arrangements aim primarily to improve tax compliance and enforcement, including the exchange of personal and corporate information between federal and state levels and across states. This exchange may be accomplished either through a voluntary uniform exchange of information or through separate bilateral exchange agreements. At present, 45 states use the uniform exchange of information agreement as a framework for exchanging this kind of taxpayer information—and for cooperative activities to combat tax avoidance (Duncan and McLure 2005; Ebel and Taliercio 2004).[7]

In Estonia, localities have the authority to levy local gross receipts taxes and then verify taxpayer reports by checking reported gross receipts against the central government's VAT declarations. To enforce the tax payment, localities may choose to deny operating licenses to businesses that have not paid the tax and/or they may choose to contract with the National Tax Board for collection of the tax (Sootla et al. 2000). Mexico presents a special case of cooperative administration whereby the central government may enter into agreement with states to audit and otherwise verify compliance with federal laws in exchange for a portion of the federal revenues. States thus reduce costs of administration by using their knowledge of the local economic activity, which the central government might not possess (Mikesell 2003).

Spatial configuration and boundaries of subnational entities. The wide variation in the structure of subnational governments across East Asia is consistent with the political and geographic diversity in the region. As decentralization has progressed, two important concerns have emerged for the spatial organization of local authorities. First, there is the question of the administrative efficiency and capacities of subnational units. In Cambodia, studies have raised issues about the ability of communes to operate effectively given their very small sizes (1,600 communes serve 12 million people) (Rusten et al. 2004). In Indonesia, where around 400 *kabupaten/kota*[8] governments serve well over 200 million people, the limited political connectivity between decision makers and constituents in large districts is often considered problematic.

Second, there is more fragmentation of subnational jurisdictions. In Indonesia, the number of *kabupaten* and *kota* increased from 292 to 434 between 1998 and 2003; in Vietnam, the number of provinces expanded from 61 to 64 during 2003. This fragmentation raises questions about whether the process for creating new subnational units creates incentives for increasingly inefficient local government structures. Recent research on Indonesia, for example, indicates that "perverse fiscal and bureaucratic rent-seeking initiatives also may be at work in the creation of new regions" (Filtrani et al. 2004, p. 3). Proliferation often introduces substantial instability in local institutional frameworks, discouraging economic investment and possibly undermining the institutional consolidation needed for effective government administration.

East Asia has much in common with other regions here. Decentralization in a number of African, Central European, and Latin American countries has been characterized by a proliferation of local governments, sometimes to the point where the average unit has become inefficiently small (Bird et al. 1995). In some of these instances, fragmentation has been followed by a later phase of consolidation, in others not. These dynamics are to some extent intrinsic to decentralization. But international experience provides examples of transparent processes that force a more objective examination of technical factors—such as the impact of boundary changes on the fiscal position and administrative capacities of local authorities—and that appear to lead to more rational outcomes. South Africa is worth examining in this regard. In 2000 it rationalized a wasteful and dysfunctional system of more than 800 local authorities into 284 municipalities and districts by introducing legislation and establishing an independent, nonpolitical body to scrutinize local government boundaries on the basis of detailed, technical criteria. While the final boundary determinations were not without controversy, the overall streamlining of the system is widely regarded as having laid the platform for a major improvement in local government efficiency and operations (Glasser and White 2004).

Accessing and Distributing Financial Resources

The second common challenge in East Asia's intergovernmental reform relates to access by subnational governments to financial resources. This discussion covers fiscal resources such as own-source revenues and intergovernmental transfers, as well as local government borrowing activities and the extent to which they are subject to hard budget constraints.

Own-source revenues. East Asian decentralization has been characterized by a relative lack of own-source revenue autonomy, in both the range of local revenue sources assigned to subnational governments and their authority to determine the tax base and rate. As in other areas, comprehensive data on fiscal arrangements are not available for most countries in the region, but table 1.4 presents an informed impressionistic overview of key features of the intergovernmental fiscal structure, including own-source revenues (see chapter 6).

TABLE 1.4 Subnational Fiscal Structure of Selected East Asian Countries

Country	Own-source revenues	Shared taxes	Unconditional transfers	Conditional transfers	Informal revenues
Cambodia	Low	Low	High[a]	n.a.[b]	High
China	Moderate	High	Low	High	High
Indonesia	Low	Moderate	High	Low	Moderate
Philippines	Moderate	Moderate	High	Low	Moderate
Thailand	Low	High	Moderate	Moderate	Low
Vietnam	None	High	Low	High	Moderate

Sources: Subsequent chapters and unpublished country case studies prepared by World Bank staff for this report.
Note: "Low," "moderate," and "high" refer to the rough proportions of total subnational revenues attributable to each revenue source relative to international experience.
a. Refers only to the commune level.
b. Most "provincial" agencies are deconcentrated arms of central ministries, so the term "transfer" does not apply.

A brief survey of typical own-source revenues in East Asia demonstrates the overall lack of subnational autonomy. Among the six countries considered in this study, none permits personal income taxes or general sales taxes at the subnational level. The real property tax on land or on land and building improvements is effectively a national tax in Indonesia, Vietnam, and Thailand. Real estate (property) taxes are a potentially robust source of local revenue, but they are either permitted only on a very narrow base, as with unused land in Cambodia, or subject to maximum rates set by the center, as in China and the Philippines. Business receipts taxes are also underused, except in the Philippines and China, where they constitute about a third and a fifth of local revenues, respectively. Some decentralization laws allow the imposition of modest excises and fees, including those on motor fuel in Indonesia, vehicle and vessel use in China, markets in Cambodia and Indonesia, and public transportation in Thailand.

One result of this limited authority over subnational tax policy is increasing informality, through which subnational governments seek "unofficial" sources of revenue. Allowing subnational governments to enact new taxes and fees has generated some productive entrepreneurial behavior in several countries, but it has simultaneously created problems. Chinese subnational governments have developed an abundance of "illegal" extrabudgetary fees, with distortionary effects. In Indonesia, a proliferation of "nuisance" taxes yields limited revenues, imposes high administrative costs on subnational governments and compliance costs on taxpayers, and, in some cases, impedes interregional trade. Subnational governments in the Philippines have created a complex variety of taxes, fees, and charges, many of which are uncollected or undercollected.

Weak local revenue authority creates dependency on higher levels of government, restricts subnational autonomy, and undermines the link between services and finance needed for strong local accountability—a key factor in successful decentralization. Combined with the incentives for poor collection of allowable taxes and fees and the proliferation of "illegal" taxes, this contributes to a culture of noncompliance and undermines the integrity of the fiscal system. Although political dynamics pose serious challenges in this area, there is significant scope—and an imperative—for most East Asian countries to empower and encourage subnational governments to generate revenues.

Intergovernmental transfers. Subnational governments are invariably in a better position to spend resources than to raise them, so intergovernmental transfers form a substantial part of the public sector fiscal structure in most countries. In OECD countries, subnational governments depend on transfers to finance about 40 percent of their expenditures, on average, with the numbers for Eastern Europe and Central Asia, and for Latin America and the Caribbean, slightly lower, and those for Africa closer to 60 percent (Ebel and Yilmaz 2002).[9]

East Asia follows this pattern, with transfers accounting for significant but widely varying proportions of total local revenue, ranging from nearly 100 percent in Cambodia to about 34 percent in Thailand. Local fiscal dependence on transfers is about 70 to 80 percent in Indonesia and the Philippines and 50 percent in Vietnam. In addition, in countries such as China, Thailand, and Vietnam, subnational governments obtain much of their income from shared taxes, a form of intergovernmental transfer. These vary widely across the region, and have important additional implications for the dependence of local governments on non–own-revenue sources of funding (see chapter 2).

Many East Asian countries have recently been moving toward internationally accepted "best practice" norms by simplifying complex intergovernmental transfer systems, improving the transparency and predictability of allocations, and increasing subnational government discretion over the use of these resources (Schroeder and Smoke 2003). This is particularly true in Cambodia, Indonesia, and the Philippines, where transfers are formula-driven and largely not earmarked. Thailand and Vietnam have also begun to move in this direction, though central control over the use of transferred resources remains tighter than in other countries. China's transfer system is less transparent, having developed piecemeal over the years; recent efforts have focused on improving horizontal equalization.

These trends are positive, but the increase in local discretion over how transfers are spent often masks important constraints in local decision making. There is a degree of internal inconsistency in the design of intergovernmental transfer systems. While transfer policies seem to favor local expenditure discretion, human resource policy tightly restricts it. For example, the Internal Revenue Allotment in the Philippines and the *dana alokasi umum* in Indonesia are not earmarked transfers. But because they are used primarily to cover local wage costs, and because the central government retains significant control over local civil service staffing and employment conditions, local discretion over the use of these grants is limited. The actual amount of intergovernmental transfer funds that can be spent on truly local priorities in the region is much smaller than first appears.

Subnational borrowing and hard budget constraints. Subnational borrowing varies widely across East Asia (see chapter 3). Such borrowing is virtually nonexistent in Cambodia, highly restricted in Indonesia, moderate in the Philippines and Vietnam, and extensive but indirect in China. The frameworks that regulate local borrowing and the actual practices of subnational governments are complex. In China, for example, subnational borrowing is illegal except when financed by higher levels of government. However, local authorities effectively raise credit (and hence incur liabilities) through special-purpose vehicles created for investment and financing. Therefore, while local borrowing is legally more constrained in China than in many other countries, it is in reality both widespread and unregulated.

The emergence of sustainable subnational borrowing in East Asia is hampered by a number of serious problems. First, while the economic and demographic growth of cities is propelling significant latent demand for financing for subnational loans, policy and regulatory frameworks are poorly developed. Thus, while the larger cities and towns in East Asia are in need of increased financing flows (primarily to fund infrastructure investment) and are expanding their capacity to service debt, the lack of reliable financial data, constrained borrowing authority, and the absence of rules in the event of default interact to undermine the de facto creditworthiness of subnational governments and make them unattractive investment propositions.

Second, private lending to subnational governments remains low throughout the region, even where central governments have attempted to stimulate it. This situation arises from the weak creditworthiness of subnational governments, as well as the public sector–dominated character of the banking industry and the regulatory advantages typically conferred on state-owned banks. As a result, lending to subnational authorities, and the associated credit risk, tends to concentrate in the public sector even in countries such as the Philippines where greater private participation in the subnational debt market is an explicit policy goal.[10]

Third, there are questions about the extent to which subnational governments are subject to hard budget constraints (see box 1.2). China is the only East Asian country in which soft local budget constraints may pose a major problem at the macroeconomic level, largely because of the significant off-budget expenditures of local governments and their widespread—albeit indirect—borrowing. Cambodia is at the other extreme, as communes are responsible for only about 2 percent of total public spending and cannot borrow. While Cambodian provinces account for more spending (17 percent), 80 percent of that is under the direct control of the central government. Provincial off-budget activities are minor, and provinces may not borrow, leaving little scope for accumulating contingent liabilities. The other countries lie between these two extremes, although data weaknesses, the complexity of regulatory frameworks, and the opacity of local accounting systems make the situation unclear. In Indonesia, where subnational governments are usually entitled to borrow, but where these powers are currently restricted,[11] regulatory weaknesses and a poor record of loan repayment indicate potential concern in the medium and long term. Whether local borrowing will become a problem will depend on whether these restrictions are relaxed, as well as on reform of the subnational borrowing framework and the evolution of the intergovernmental transfer system, among other factors.

The degree to which subnational governments are subject to hard budget constraints depends on several aspects of the intergovernmental system, especially the regulatory environment surrounding subnational borrowing. Ultimately, if East Asian countries wish to expand sustainable private investment at the subnational level without misaligning incentives and risking undesirable macroeconomic impacts, they need to develop much more thorough policies and regulations and devote significant efforts to implementing them. This will require a fundamental reassessment of the

BOX 1.2 Hard Budget Constraints

The ability of subnational entities to borrow funds is fundamental to the concept and practice of fiscal decentralization and local fiscal autonomy. Subnational borrowing can be an effective tool for local development, if limited to financing capital investment expenditure. When structured well, it can improve both economic efficiency, in which the cost of debt repayment matches the flow of benefits over time, and intergenerational equity, so that future generations who benefit from investments also share the responsibility for payment.

The key to making subnational borrowing work is the presence of hard budget constraints. These ensure that subnational governments cannot transfer the liabilities they accrue to higher levels of government, either by shifting debt service obligations upward or other means such as expenditure deferrals or the accumulation of contingent or implicit liabilities. The best way to enforce a hard budget constraint is to establish procedures that clearly signal that local governments will bear the costs (and accrue the benefits) of their fiscal decisions.

When this message is conveyed to creditors, asset owners, and voters, the market mechanism comes into play. First, creditors will demand sound fiscal decisions by withholding credit. Second, knowing that local fiscal decisions can directly affect property values and rents, asset owners will have a strong incentive to lobby against imprudent borrowing and debt buildup. Third, political factors may also be important in countries with local elections, where voters can oust underperforming local officials.

In well-established intergovernmental systems, the fiscal discipline of the capital market suffices. Yet markets work only when good information is available on local fiscal performance and risk, when the central government makes a credible commitment that it will not provide bailouts, and when accountability systems are robust. Where these conditions are not in place, as in many developing countries, two reinforcing strategies can help. First, it is important to ensure that subnational entities do not "pay down" debts by borrowing from their own banks, or from a central financial authority that provides additional funding, without accompanying—and severe—consequences for default.

The problem with a subnational entity borrowing from itself is clear. A pattern of central government bailouts may also be costly. Not only will this undermine the center's own credit standing, but it can also lead to selective allocation of credit across subnational governments according to political, ethnic, or religious favoritism. Capital investment can become inefficient, and national cohesiveness may be jeopardized.

The second strategy is to establish a fiscal framework that ensures subnational budget discipline. Central or higher-level governments may limit local borrowing to capital expenditures only, as in Argentina, Latvia, and Poland. They may place statutory limitations on local debt, as in Italy, Portugal, and Canadian provinces. And they may provide for a municipal bankruptcy law, as have Hungary, South Africa, and many member countries of the Organisation for Economic Co-operation and Development. Other rule-based approaches include prohibitions on foreign borrowing in Ethiopia and Ireland, and the establishment of intergovernmental coordinating committees. For example, the Australian Loan Council provides information to the financial markets on local government fiscal positions, and the French Regional Chambers of Accounts may establish remedial fiscal measures if a deficit appears.

A range of sanctions may also be established. In Austria, an explicit Domestic Stability Pact sets overall fiscal targets for municipalities as a group, and allows the transfer of surplus/deficit obligations and rights across subnational governments if the group target is not met. In Brazil, partly in reaction to sharp increases in subnational debt levels (up to 17 percent of GDP in 1996), the central government not only restricts debt service levels but also penalizes governors and mayors for irresponsible performance through impeachment or imprisonment.

objectives of subnational borrowing, close study of the local borrowing environment, a broad framework conducive to disciplined subnational credit activity, and the central capacity to monitor local credit activities, including collection and dissemination of better credit data. East Asia could draw on the experiences of other countries that have begun—and in some cases successfully completed—such exercises, including Hungary, Mexico, Brazil, and South Africa.

Some East Asian governments are beginning to tackle at least some aspects of this agenda. For example, the Department of Finance in the Philippines has recently begun developing mechanisms to measure and monitor subnational liabilities, and the department intends to create an early warning system to identify impending local debt defaults. In the rest of the region, however, efforts appear to address much narrower concerns. Indonesia has focused on developing a regulatory system for the onlending of donor-sourced investment funds within the public sector (KMK 35). Notwithstanding the positive steps mentioned above, the Philippines has invested significant effort in restructuring the Municipal Development Fund Office into a nonbank financial institution that—like two government banks (the Land Bank and the Development Bank)—will cater to the subnational market. Governments have devoted much less attention to broader policy and regulatory issues surrounding subnational borrowing.

Creating Sound Management and Accountability Systems

Management and accountability systems often determine the performance of intergovernmental mechanisms. Designing and implementing systems that work on the ground are not easy tasks. This is where decentralization often falters. The following section examines three key elements of this third common challenge: human resource management; planning, financial management, and information at local and national levels; and local accountability systems.

Human resources. East Asian countries have started down the path of decentralizing human resources (see chapter 7). In most cases, subnational governments have the authority to hire and assign junior staff, but the central government retains control over the aggregate number and pay levels of local staff.[12] Under these arrangements, the overall management of the civil service effectively remains largely centralized.

To compensate for this limited local formal autonomy, subnational practices in some countries have tended to circumvent formal systems. In the Philippines and Thailand, local managers have avoided central guidelines by hiring contractual workers. In Indonesia and the Philippines, local governments have often relied on nontransparent allowances to boost civil service pay. In China, where subnational governments return budget surpluses to the central government, local civil service employment has swelled in the absence of incentives to local managers to keep staffs lean.

The design of decentralization has also had important impacts on the accountability, incentives, and capacity of local civil servants. Unclear policies have sometimes created confusion concerning accountability relationships. In Indonesia, for example, conflicting laws have produced inefficient overlaps in authority. In China, the Philippines, and Vietnam, "double subordination" to central authorities and local assemblies conflates the accountability of local staff.

Though some East Asian countries have established formal mechanisms for merit-based recruitment and performance management, these tend to lack teeth in reality, and civil servants are rarely held accountable for their behavior. Seniority and party loyalty have frequently trumped performance in promotion decisions. In China, the awarding of across-the-board performance bonuses has undercut their ability to leverage civil service quality. In the Philippines, where staff performance has not, until recently, been rigorously evaluated, patronage and nepotism have figured prominently in recruitment and promotion. In countries where wages are low and absenteeism is endemic, service delivery quality cannot be maintained. Throughout East Asia, less well-resourced local governments are often unable to attract enough staff to fill the required number of spots or to fund centrally set wages. For local governments that manage to staff their civil services despite poor incentives, the lack of strong systems for career management also dampens the incentives of local functionaries to perform.

International experience shows that countries often neglect the details of administrative decentralization. In Central and Eastern Europe, confusion about the role of the postcommunist state prompted many governments to decentralize tasks without providing adequate resources (Verheijen 2002). In Latin America, local authority to control personnel costs was critical in enhancing macroeconomic management under decentralization (Burki et al. 1999). Yet even when far-reaching on paper, decentralization of human resource management has usually been quite limited in practice. Governments tend to decentralize the civil service in similar ways, giving local governments autonomy to hire and fire staff and supplement centrally set salaries, while the center retains control over wage rates and interregional mobility (Evans and Manning 2004). Concerns about local capacity, interregional equity, and national unity can spur recentralization of the civil service and threaten the decentralization agenda.

Despite the relative inattention to administrative decentralization, a few interesting experiences in local civil service management provide lessons for East Asian countries. In Uganda, independent District Service Commissions manage the recruitment of local civil servants. The commissions have experienced some growing pains, such as limited ability to discipline and dismiss staff, but they can still serve as a useful model. In Pakistan, reforms envision organizing lower-echelon staff into cadres to facilitate their mobility across districts, while provinces will officially employ more senior staff to allow vertical movement into central government service. In this case, the challenge has been to ensure that district governments rather than provinces hold civil servants accountable for performance. Personnel exchange programs in Japan enhance the career prospects of local civil servants by transferring them between subnational governments and the center. Broadly, international experience suggests that some central controls on wages and civil service mobility, combined with local autonomy over hiring and promotion of more junior staff, have been the preferred policies for most countries moving from centralized to decentralized human resource management systems. These experiences show how important human resource arrangements can be to making intergovernmental systems work.

Planning and financial mangement. As is common in newly decentralizing environments, local planning in East Asia is fairly weak (see chapter 5). Though the Local Government Code of the Philippines prescribes a participatory approach to planning, less than a third of subnational governments accounted for external inputs in creating development plans, according to one survey (Azfar et al. 2000). Indonesia has also begun to introduce a participatory planning process at the *kabupaten* level, but project affordability is not a factor in expenditure choices, so this process creates "wish lists" that do not inform the budget in a meaningful way. In China and Vietnam, insufficient coordination between planning and budgeting means that plans typically far outstrip resources.

The budgeting process is often inefficient and only loosely scheduled. In China, the budget process often starts only two months before the fiscal year begins, creating delays throughout the system as each level of government must wait for information from the previous tier before creating its own expenditure and transfer plans. In Indonesia and the Philippines, poor estimates and unpredictable release of transfers over the budget year distort budget execution.

Difficulties with local financial management systems are also common. In China, Indonesia, the Philippines, and Vietnam, programs to modernize financial management systems are in their infancy, particularly at the subnational level. Though management information systems in the Philippines and Vietnam produce general reports, they cannot do so in a timely or accurate way. Year-end accounts are thus not available in Vietnam until 18 months after the end of the fiscal year. In the Philippines, local financial management is still based mainly on manual systems.

Internal and external auditing of expenditures at the subnational level are of extremely low quality, suffering from low capacity and confused mandates. In Indonesia, the legal framework is unclear with regard to the authority of various auditors in examining local budgets. In the Philippines, internal auditing is nonexistent among most local governments, and the regional offices of the Commission on Audit, which have the power to audit local governments, are overstretched. In Thailand, only a few large-scale local authorities have internal auditors, and two external auditing units—the Office of the Auditor General and provincial auditing teams—have considerable credibility but limited capacity to provide services to all local authorities.

Decentralization implies a shift rather than a weakening of systems and capacity at the center. In fact, as the intergovernmental structure becomes more complex, central ministries need to develop new systems to monitor and manage it effectively. Two challenges are typical of East Asian countries. First, development of the systems connecting different layers of government often lags far behind the policy decisions and institutional arrangements they are meant to support. Cambodia is an extreme case: grant disbursements to provinces are so consistently late and so divergent from initially budgeted amounts that budgets themselves have become virtually meaningless. But similar difficulties with the timely release of intergovernmental transfers are fairly widespread in the region.

Second, central governments face growing problems in monitoring the activities of local governments. China's deficiencies in managing subnational liabilities have already been mentioned. The Philippines and Vietnam have a limited ability to monitor and control the addition of "temporary" or "informal" workers to local establishments. In Indonesia, decentralization has undermined data systems in sectors such as education, for which local authorities are now responsible. As a result, the central government is less able to measure service delivery in these sectors than before decentralization (see chapter 9).

Accountability systems. A number of interlocking factors constrain local accountability in East Asia. Upward accountability—or central oversight of local administrations—tends to be stronger than other forms of accountability but suffers from a lack of clarity in functional allocations, incomplete flow of information, and inadequate monitoring. Horizontal accountability—the monitoring of local bureaucrats by local politicians, and of local government by local legislatures and courts—is diluted by clientelist politics and a serious lack of capacity among local countervailing powers. Downward accountability, or responsiveness to citizens, is often interrupted by a tendency to focus on compliance rather than performance.

East Asian countries have historically emphasized top-down, ex ante control of subnational expenditures. As decentralization evolves and local governments gain greater financial autonomy, both ex post review processes (such as external audits) and horizontal and bottom-up systems inevitably become more important in deepening accountability. For any of these to work, local data must be produced, shared, and maintained. In Vietnamese communes, poor record keeping makes monitoring the use of funds extremely difficult. In China, local reliance on extrabudgetary funds has reduced transparency, and thus accountability, in public spending. Thailand and Vietnam have experimented with mechanisms to shift from central control of expenditures to performance-based accountability, but these are in the early stages.

Low capacity within oversight bodies challenges horizontal accountability at the subnational level. Local legislatures and judicial institutions often lack the financial and human resources to hold local administrations accountable. In some cases, political corruption prevents local politicians from exercising oversight of local bureaucrats. In May 2004, 43 of 55 members of Indonesia's West Sumatra legislative council were found guilty of corruption. Though this experience highlights widespread corruption in local administrations in Indonesia, it also provides a successful example of judicial oversight and prosecutorial effectiveness.

Civil society groups, including the media, can also raise awareness of the extent and costs of weak governance, in terms of monitoring government performance and giving citizens a voice to demand accountability from their leaders (see chapter 12). The importance of civil society grows as decentralization expands citizens' access to government actors. In the Philippines, the Social Weather Stations produced a *Report Card of Pro-Poor Services* to share citizen feedback on public services. Vietnam is launching a similar initiative. In China, some localities have introduced Citizens' Charters through which service users rate how government agencies and public utilities perform against their stated commitments. However, although civil society organizations are growing rapidly in most East Asian countries, they tend to concentrate in national capitals and are therefore less influential at subnational levels. Where they do exist, local civil society groups are constrained by insufficient financial and human resources, political interference, and weak links to central organizations.

International experience shows that accountability stems from numerous processes and relationships, including those outside the formal public sector. Enhancing access to information is a critical step in bringing external pressure to bear on governments. In Mexico, the government has established a System of Evaluation of Municipality Transparency to measure how much information municipal governments are offering their citizens and to encourage greater transparency. In Uganda, after a Public Expenditure Tracking Survey revealed that schools had received only 13 percent of per-student grants, the central government launched a massive information campaign, spreading the word through the media and on notice boards outside schools and district offices. Four years later, a repeat survey showed that over 90 percent of resources were reaching schools. Community report cards have produced similar successes, notably in Bangalore, India, where citizens rated public services and the media widely disseminated results. Workshops allowed providers and clients to interact, and some agencies took steps to improve their service delivery systems.

Finally, citizens need opportunities to hold local governments accountable. In the Brazilian city of Porto Alegre, an experiment in participatory budgeting improved public service delivery considerably and has since expanded to over 80 cities. The *gram sabha* public forum in Indian local governments and community oversight committees in Bolivia allow citizens to monitor government expenditures and help make decisions regarding future activities. Across the spectrum, the most successful mechanisms tend to be those that link information, capacity, and opportunities for participation.

Conclusion: Key Messages and Challenges

As the preceding discussion has shown, East Asia's decentralization process—like the region itself—is characterized by heterogeneity as well as a set of shared features, many of which are common to the decentralization experience of other countries around the world. As elsewhere, the thrust of decentralization in the region has been determined largely by structural and political factors. These factors suggest that decentralization is likely to be a pivotal fact of East Asian life for the foreseeable future. It is already affecting prospects for economic development, possibilities for "good governance" in country institutions, and the quality of service delivery, especially for the poor. Some early indicators give reason to hope that outcomes in these areas are trending in the right direction—that is, that the benefits of decentralization in improving access and voice for local constituencies will outweigh the costs of disruption and inefficiency that overhauling formerly centralized institutions inevitably bring. But the decentralization process has been uneven and, in some countries, may actually have stalled. International experience suggests that progress in moving decentralization forward is rarely monotonic; programs proceed in fits and starts. But there is cause for concern in East Asia that a low-level equilibrium has set in, with only minimal reforms proceeding at a glacial pace.

Recognizing the importance of national requirements in developing decentralization approaches, this report does not offer specific recommendations on the way forward. These must be developed at the country level. But the paramount need to make decentralization work broadly across the region may warrant general guidance to policymakers as they think about the strategies needed to advance the range of intergovernmental reforms appropriate to their particular contexts. Drawing on the earlier sections of this chapter, and previewing the themes that will recur in later chapters of this report, the following three broad substantive imperatives merit priority attention in decentralization:

Improving the organization of the intergovernmental system will usually require focused attention on policy and, often, legislative development in three core areas:

- *Clarifying the expenditure assignments and functional roles* of the various levels of government with a view to eliminating (or greatly narrowing) jurisdictional overlaps and reducing the gaps between mandates and funding.
- *Rationalizing the vertical and horizontal organization of the intergovernmental system* to ensure an appropriate balance in the roles of central, intermediate, and local authorities, and to inject greater transparency and objectivity into the processes that determine the size and geographic boundaries of subnational entities.
- *Developing systems to facilitate lateral and vertical cooperation* between subnational governments and central government agencies, particularly in the areas of planning and investment.

Strengthening local fiscal and financial structures involves expanding the financial resources available to subnational governments while improving their incentives to use these resources efficiently. Three focus areas are evident: *own-source revenues, subnational borrowing, and intergovernmental transfers.* Substantial progress has been made in East Asia with respect to intergovernmental transfer policy and systems, but this dynamic area will require ongoing attention. In the other two instances, the picture is more problematic. Throughout the region, policy environments are not conducive to the emergence of enhanced own-source revenue or vibrant and disciplined borrowing systems. Little serious policy work is under way, and current solutions tend to be at odds with emerging international best practice. The problems that arise in these areas, including the lack of hard budget constraints at the local level, often stem more from enforcement failures than from poor policy. Rules need to be well designed and effectively enforced. And local authorities need to have incentives to raise revenues and control expenditures. Serious efforts are needed in this area.

Developing the functional systems that underpin the effectiveness of intergovernmental structures has three important dimensions:

- *Deepening and enhancing accountability*. Effective accountability systems required to reap the potential developmental benefits of decentralized government are consistently weak across the region. Substantial improvements are needed in formal and informal bottom-up processes of accountability at the local level, and in top-down systems for generating information and effectively monitoring local performance by the center. National and local governments alike need better data on all aspects of the local and intergovernmental system, particularly subnational finance and local government performance in delivering services. Systems must therefore be developed to ensure regular and accurate production and distribution of basic local government data.
- *Improving the performance of intergovernmental functional and management systems*. As intergovernmental structures evolve, systemic "plumbing" needs to be built to allow these structures to function properly. Intergovernmental transfers need to be disbursed, local financial statements need to be produced and audited, and budgets need to be produced in a timely manner. In many East Asian countries, these systems have not kept pace with the evolution of the intergovernmental structure, and local performance has suffered.
- *Building capacity*. The best-designed intergovernmental system in the world will not function effectively without sufficient capacity, particularly in the area of human resources. While capacity limitations have surfaced as an important issue in decentralization processes throughout the developing world, two aspects require particular attention in the East Asian environment. First, insufficient capacity at the local level is not the only issue; central governments also require improvements in their ability to administer the intergovernmental system and drive the decentralization process effectively. Second, capacity-building efforts that focus purely—or even predominantly—on the supply side are likely to bring limited success. For capacity to expand and endure, reform efforts need to generate effective and ongoing demand for enhanced capacity at the local level, and to create systems for responding to that demand. Reforming subnational human resource systems will be critical to this endeavor.

Finally, in addition to these substantive challenges, three messages on the nature of the decentralization *process* are important:

- Given varying conditions within countries, intergovernmental frameworks will need to be crafted with enough flexibility to allow for appropriate asymmetries in the design and implementation of decentralization structures and processes.
- The inevitably uneven pace of reforms and the need to capitalize on political opportunities as they arise call for a reform process that is more piecemeal than comprehensive. International experience suggests that focusing on a few key areas where change is possible and getting these right is likely to yield greater success than trying to accomplish too much simultaneously on too many reform fronts.
- While the inevitably long-term nature of the decentralization process must be understood, each country's policymakers should take stock of progress on intergovernmental reforms and assess whether the pace and energy of reforms are sufficient to meet the important challenges discussed in this report. Mindful of the magnitude of problems that are likely to accumulate if local and intergovernmental structures remain weak and incentives are not in place, governments need to combine political capital, strategic focus, and technical effort to ensure consistent progress on decentralization in the region.

Endnotes

1. In 2001, central government spending on capital in East Asia and the Pacific was 3.6 percent of GDP, compared with 3 percent in Eastern Europe and Central Asia and 1.6 percent in South Asia. (Figures are derived from the World Bank's *World Development Indicators* and World Bank 2004b.)
2. In Indonesia, households perceived corruption as the top national problem. In Cambodia, urban citizens and foreign firms called corruption the leading problem, while rural citizens called it the second most serious problem (after the high cost of living), as did domestic firms (after street crime). In Thailand, respondents called it the third most serious national problem, after the poor economy and high cost of living. See World Bank, Partnership for Governance Reform in Indonesia 2002b; World Bank 2000; and Phongpaichit et al. 2000.
3. For example, in Cambodia, 82 percent of firms reported some level of bribe payments, and 71 percent of large firms suggested that such payments are frequent (World Bank 2004a).
4. This view is consistent with earlier regional analyses of decentralization by the World Bank in Latin America and East and Central Europe (Burki al. 1999; World Bank 2001).
5. To date, only 172 of the 245 functions specified for devolution in the Master Plan have been or are in the process of being devolved, and the rate of devolution has declined over the past two years. The Nine Policy Measures to improve local revenue mobilization, approved by the Cabinet in 1994, have made slow progress toward legal enactment (chapter 2).
6. These assessments are based on initial data that will need to be reviewed over time. Attributing impact to intergovernmental reform is also problematic, as decentralization has occurred in parallel with other policy changes.
7. A review of intergovernmental tax administration in E. Asia is provided in Ebel and Taliercio 2004.
8. *Kabupaten* are districts; *kota* (or *kotamadya*) are cities.
9. These figures are based on a limited sample of countries in each region.
10. Borrowing from private sector sources typically constitutes less than 1.5 percent of total annual subnational revenues in the Philippines, despite the 1996 Local Government Unit Financing Framework, which stresses private lending to local governments as a core objective.
11. The Finance Ministry has imposed a temporary freeze on subnational borrowing, but indications are that this will expire in 2005.
12. There are many legitimate reasons for the center to retain some authority over civil service management, such as to maintain minimum standards for the working conditions and professional qualifications of public servants, to broaden their career paths, and to unify a fragmented nation. On the other hand, as shown by Vietnam's experiment with block grants to districts and departments in Ho Chi Minh City, service delivery and operational efficiency can be improved by extending autonomy over budget allocations to civil service managers and allowing them to keep the savings.

Bibliography

Ahmad, E., Li Keping, and Thomas Richardson. 2000. "Recentralization in China?" Paper presented at International Monentary Fund conference on fiscal decentralization, Washington, DC, November 2000.

Azfar, Omar, Tugrul Gurgur, Satu Kähkönen, Anthony Lanyi, and Patrick Meagher. 2000. "Decentralization and Governance: An Empirical Investigation of Public Service Delivery in the Philippines." Washington, DC: University of Maryland IRIS Center and the World Bank.

Bahl, Roy. 1990. "Implementation Rules for Fiscal Decentralization." Working Paper 99-1. International Studies Program, School of Policy Studies, Georgia State University, Atlanta, Georgia.

Bardhan, Pranab, and Dilip Mookherjee. 2000. "Capture and Governance at Local and National Levels." *American Economic Review* 90 (2):135–9.

Bird, R., R. Ebel, and C. Wallich, eds. 1995. "Decentralization of the Socialist State." Washington, DC: World Bank, Intergovernmental Finance in Transition Economies.

Burki, S. J., G. Perry, and W. Dillinger. 1999. "Beyond the Center: Decentralizing the State." Washington, DC: World Bank.

Duncan, H., and C. E. McLure, Jr. 2005. "Tax Administration Mechanisms for Intergovernmental Cooperation." In Cordes, Joseph J. Cordes, Robert D. Ebel, and Jane G. Gravelle, *The Encyclopedia of Taxation and Tax Policy.* Washington, DC: Urban Institute Press.

Ebel, R. D., and R. Taliercio. 2004. "Subnational Tax Policy and Administration in Developing Economies." *Tax Notes International* March: 919–936.

Ebel, R., and S. Yilmaz. 2002. "Globalization and Localization: Decentralization Trends and Outcomes." Washington, DC: World Bank, Regional and Sectoral Studies.

———. 2003. "On the Measurement and Impact of Fiscal Decentralization." In *Public Finance in Developing and Transitional Countries: Essays in Honor of Richard M. Bird,* eds. Jorge Martinez-Vazquez and James Alm. Cheltenham, UK: Edward Elgar Press.

Evans, A., and N. Manning. 2004. "Decentralization: A Review of Staffing Practices in Eight Countries." Manuscript.

Filtrani, F., B. Hofman, and K. Kaiser. 2004. *Unity in Diversity? The Creation of New Local Government in a Decentralizing Indonesia.*

Freire, M., and J. Petersen. 2004. *Subnational Capital Markets in Developing Countries: From Theory to Practice.*" Washington, DC: World Bank.

Glasser, M., and R. White. 2004. "South Africa." In *Subnational Capital Markets in Developing Countries: From Theory to Practice,*" ed. Mila Freire and John Petersen. Washington, DC: World Bank.

Kaufmann D., A. Kraay, and M. Mastruzzi. 2003. "Governance Matters III: Governance Indicators for 1996–2002." Policy Research Working Paper No. 3106. Washington, DC: World Bank.

Mountfield, E. 2001. "Special Focus: Public Financial Accountability in East Asia." Washington, DC: World Bank.

OECD (Organisation for Economic Co-operation and Development). 2002a. "The Fiscal Decentralization Initiative for Central and Eastern Europe (Budapest) and the Organization for Economic Cooperation and Development." Paris: OECD.

———. 2002b. "Fiscal Design Surveys across Levels of Government." Tax Policy Study #7. Paris: OECD.

Pellegrini, A., and Cecilia Soriano Ma. 2002. "A Study to Revisit the LGU Financing Framework and Its Implementation." Manila: Department of Finance.

Phongpaichit, P., N. Treerat, Y. Chaiyapong, and C. Baker. 2000. "Corruption in the Public Sector in Thailand: Perceptions and Experiences of Households."

Rusten, C., K. Sedara, E. Netra, and P. Kimchoeun. 2004. "The Challenges of the Decentralisation Design in Cambodia." Monograph.

Schroeder, L., and Paul Smoke. 2003. Intergovernmental Fiscal Transfers: Concepts, International Practice and Policy Issues. In *Intergovernmental Transfers in Asia: Current Practices and Challenges for the Future.* Ed. P. Smoke and Y. H. Kim. Manila: Asian Development Bank.

Sootla, G., et al. 2000. "Local and Regional Tax Administration in Estonia." In Mihaly Hogye, ed, *Local and Regional Tax Administration in Transitional Countries.* Budapest: Local Government and Public Service Reform Initiative/Open Society Institute.

Steffensen, J., E. Sewankambo, and P. Tidemand. 2004. "A Comparative Analysis of Decentralization in Kenya, Tanzania, and Uganda." Draft Country Study. World Bank, Washington, DC.

Transparency International. 2003. "Corruption Perceptions Index 2003."

United Nations. 2004. *World Urbanization Prospects 2003.* New York: United Nations.

Verheijen, A. J. G. 2002. "Removing Obstacles to Effective Decentralization: Reflecting on the Role of Central State Authorities." In *Mastering Decentralization and Public Administration Reforms in Central and Eastern Europe.*

World Bank. 2000. "Cambodia Governance and Corruption Diagnostic: Evidence from Citizen, Enterprise, and Public Official Surveys, 2000." *World Development Report: Entering the 21st Century.* Washington, DC: World Bank; and New York: Oxford University Press.

———. 2001. "Decentralization in the Transition Economies: Challenges and the Road Ahead." Washington, DC: World Bank.

———. 2002a. "China National Development and Subnational Finance: A Review of Provincial Expenditure." Washington, DC: World Bank.

———. 2003a. "Decentralization and Poverty Indonesia." Washington, DC: World Bank.

———. 2003b. "Decentralizing Indonesia." Washington, DC: World Bank.

———. 2004a. "Seizing the Global Opportunity: Investment Climate Assessment and Reform Strategy for Cambodia." Washington, DC: World Bank.

———. 2004b. *World Development Report 2003–2004: Making Services Work for Poor People.* Washington, DC: World Bank; and New York: Oxford University Press.

World Bank and Asian Development Bank. 2003. "Philippines: Decentralization and Service Delivery." Washington, DC: World Bank.

World Bank, Partnership for Governance Reform in Indonesia. 2002b. "A National Survey of Corruption in Indonesia". Washington, DC: World Bank.

2

THE RULES OF THE INTERGOVERNMENTAL GAME IN EAST ASIA: DECENTRALIZATION FRAMEWORKS AND PROCESSES

Paul Smoke

Although political forces have largely driven decentralization in East Asia and most countries face similar reform challenges, their decentralization experiences are far from uniform. Countries have adopted different intergovernmental structures, proceeded at uneven paces, and adopted a wide range of implementation strategies. This diversity is not surprising, as East Asian countries vary greatly in geographical size, population, history, economic structure, and political and institutional dynamics, all of which influence the form that decentralization can and should take.

This chapter provides expanded context for the analysis presented in chapter 1 and lays a foundation for later chapters. After reviewing the origins of decentralization, it compares the basic intergovernmental frameworks, structures, and processes evolving in Cambodia, China, Indonesia, the Philippines, Thailand, and Vietnam.[1] The chapter focuses, in turn, on enabling frameworks, the governance environment, fiscal decentralization, and the management and implementation of decentralization reforms.

The Basics of Decentralization in East Asia

This section briefly examines the origins and paths of decentralization in the region. It also outlines the levels and structures of government, compares the thrust of decentralization policy in various countries, and describes the enabling frameworks.

The Origins and Evolution of Decentralization Reforms

Some East Asian countries, such as China, have a long tradition of limited decentralization, while the concept is more recent in countries such as Cambodia. Crisis sparked decentralization in Indonesia and the Philippines, while in China and Vietnam it is part of a gradual process of market and public sector reform. In a few cases, decentralization is essentially complete (in structure if not in practice), such as in the Philippines, or heavily in process, such as in Indonesia. In other cases reforms are less advanced, either with limited policy development, as in

Cambodia, or a substantial but only modestly implemented framework, as in Thailand.

The Philippines has the strongest history of democratic decentralization in the region. The country's colonial heritage established limited democratic roots, and a series of presidential decrees enacted under the autocratic Marcos government—including the Local Tax Code, the Real Property Tax Code, and the Local Fiscal Administration Code—laid the institutional foundation for decentralization. The country reestablished democracy after the fall of Marcos in 1986, and decentralization and local autonomy were among the fundamental principles embodied in the 1987 Constitution. The Aquino administration launched a pilot decentralization project and established autonomous regions in Muslim Mindanao and the Cordilleras. But not until 1991 did constitutional provisions begin to take robust shape through the Local Government Code, which mandated significant devolution to local governments. Today a formal decentralization framework is essentially complete, but much effort remains to realize full implementation.

Although China's lack of democratic institutions may be seen as an impediment to decentralization, the country has some history of subnational authority because its size has made central control difficult. The provinces, in particular, have long enjoyed a degree of administrative and fiscal autonomy. The market transition that began in the late 1970s enhanced the subnational role. As economic reform progressed, changes in the composition of expenditures and relative prices moved the burden of public spending to subnational governments. These adjustments led to further modifications of government operations, but the country never adopted a formal decentralization policy. Still, by 1993, the central government was collecting only 20 percent of public revenues. This prompted the substantially recentralizing Tax Sharing System reforms in 1994. Public demand for more responsive government and greater entrepreneurial freedom has also shaped central-subnational relations, but formal intergovernmental political reforms have been limited.

Indonesia—also a large country and spread over thousands of islands—had elements of decentralization during its Dutch colonial period. As in many ethnically diverse countries colonized by European powers, building national unity through greater centralization was the goal after independence. Weak attempts to decentralize in the 1970s and 1980s did not gain political momentum. The East Asian economic crisis in 1997 hastened the fall of the Soeharto regime. Around that time, a successful independence referendum in the former province of East Timor and growing complaints from resource-rich provinces about insufficient revenue autonomy increased pressure for reform. The 1999 decentralization legislation was a direct response to this political crisis and a perceived need to hold the diverse and tenuously unified country together. The reform devolved power primarily to subprovincial governments, largely because of fear among national leaders that empowered provinces could fuel regional ethnic and political conflicts, leading to further separatism or federalism. The government revised the initial decentralization framework legislation in 2004. This increased higher-level control but left unresolved important aspects of the intergovernmental system. Local capacity is deficient in many areas, and citizens and government officials, both elected and appointed, are still learning to function in the evolving democratic environment.

Vietnam, which became a centrally planned communist state after the Vietnam War, has increasingly formalized the subnational government framework since the mid-1990s. As in China, economic reforms (*doi moi*) spurred initial progress on intergovernmental reform. The center still exerts substantial control, but subnational governments have some discretion. Provinces have greater powers, including considerable authority over lower levels. Popular participation and grassroots demand for political voice have grown, but Vietnam remains a one-party state and a fairly centrally driven system. The country has moved forward with its decentralization framework and conducted some successful policy experiments, but implementation is uneven and additional reforms are required.

Thailand has been modestly enhancing the role of subnational entities for some time, but decentralization has been a priority only since the Seventh National Economic and Social Development Plan (1991–96). The plan emphasized developing local infrastructure, providing credit to expand and improve local services, and helping local authorities mobilize capital and pursue development projects. The May Five democracy movement emerged in the mid-1990s to demand stronger democratic institutions more insulated from the military, which has long played a pivotal role in Thai politics. The Eighth Plan (1997–2002) advocated stronger local institutions, the 1997 Constitution formally enshrined decentralization, and later legislation detailed it. The country has formally adopted many reforms but implemented few of them, and political consensus on further progress remains unclear.

Cambodia's decentralization is relatively unique. Following elections brokered by the United Nations (UN) in 1993, the center reclaimed power from provincial governors—who had previously ruled with a free hand—in order to impose discipline on the intergovernmental system. The UN-funded Cambodia Resettlement and Reintegration (CARERE) Project of the early 1990s, particularly its second stage known as Seila, experimented with sweeping local institutional and governance reforms in many areas. Seila's success in delivering development projects made its formal integration into the government system attractive to the ruling party. Reforms adopted in 2001 led to the election of commune councils and provided them small intergovernmental transfers without formal service responsibilities or own-source revenues. This approach focuses on meeting immediate community needs and developing trust between citizens and the government as a first step in decentralization. Provincial reforms have been limited, except for the adaptation of Seila mechanisms to provide provincial support to communes and a few ad hoc reforms by individual sectoral ministries. A program to build capacity is under way and the country is planning further reforms, but it is unclear how the system will evolve.

Structures of Subnational Government

The structure of subnational governments in the region varies considerably (see table 2.1). Most countries have three or four levels of administration. In China, the Philippines, and Vietnam, each

TABLE 2.1 Levels of Government Administration

Country	Subnational levels of government
Cambodia	Two levels in two parallel systems: • Provincial administrations (20) and municipalities (4) with provincial status divided into districts and *khans* • Elected commune and *sangkat* (urban commune) governments (1,621) divided into villages
China	Four levels: • Provinces (22), autonomous regions (5), and large cities (4) • Prefectures and cities (300) • Counties (2,100) • Townships (44,000+)
Indonesia	Three levels (*de jure*): • Provinces (33), special regions (2), and capital city (1) • Local governments: *kotamadya* (cities) and *kabupaten* (districts) (440) • *Desa* (villages)
Philippines	Four levels: • Provinces (79) • Cities (112) • Municipalities (1,496) • *Barangays*/villages (41,944)
Thailand	Four levels with top three formally empowered: • Provinces (75) • Districts and municipalities (811) • *Tambons* (subdistricts) (6,744) • Villages (67,000+)
Vietnam	Three levels: • Provinces (58) and municipalities (3) • Districts (600) • Communes (10,000+)

Source: Compiled by the author from multiple sources.

level is an active player. In Thailand, all but the lowest level have formal authority. In Cambodia and Indonesia, two levels have independent powers, while other levels perform mostly subsidiary administrative and political functions. In Indonesia, the lower tiers have no formal functions or independent budgets, but centrally managed—often donor-funded—community development schemes have channeled substantial resources to them (see chapter 12). In Cambodia, the provinces (with district subdivisions) and communes (with village subdivisions) have functional mandates, although with a different relationship to the center.

A few countries also have ad hoc subnational institutional arrangements such as special status for the capital and other major cities. These include Jakarta in Indonesia and the Bangkok Metropolitan Administration and Pattaya City in Thailand. China, Indonesia, and the Philippines have created a number of autonomous regions, often in areas of special political, historical, or ethnic significance. A few countries have interjurisdictional structures designed to meet specific needs. The Philippines, for example, has designated 16 planning regions, each with a Regional Development Coordinating Council composed of provincial governors, city mayors, and representatives from national agencies and the private sector.

Decentralization Policy

East Asian countries also vary in the extent to which their decentralization policy emphasizes deconcentration, delegation, or devolution of functions and revenue authority (see box 1.1). Some countries such as China and Vietnam have seen legal or de facto deconcentration of functions to subnational entities that remain substantially accountable to the center, though elements of delegation and devolution have emerged. Thailand is gradually shifting its focus from deconcentration to devolution, but reform remains at a relatively early stage. Indonesia, the Philippines, and, to a certain extent, Cambodia have emphasized devolution of responsibilities to more autonomous subprovincial entities, but specific approaches differ (see table 2.2).

China's decentralization is unusual in that economic reform rather than specific deconcentration or devolution policies has shaped its evolution. During the last two decades China has transitioned from a largely deconcentrated system to one that incorporates elements of delegation and devolution. Subnational governments have become more responsible for financing their expanding functions from their own revenue, both formal and informal, giving them more autonomy except in

TABLE 2.2 Decentralization Policy

Country	Policy orientation
Cambodia	Hybrid case, with deconcentration to provinces and devolution to communes; commune system new and given greater emphasis, but provinces are more significant in terms of public expenditures.
China	Main focus on deconcentration to provinces and larger cities, although lower levels have larger public expenditure role and elements of de facto devolution have emerged in some areas; provinces have considerable regulatory control over lower levels.
Indonesia	Focus on substantial devolution to cities and districts, which replaced earlier emphasis on deconcentration to provinces; limited formal role at lowest levels; 2004 reforms increased the role of higher levels.
Philippines	Focus on devolution to subprovincial units, but provinces still play a significant role.
Thailand	Historical focus on deconcentration to provinces and districts, but 1997 framework shifts toward devolution to municipalities, districts, and subdistricts; implementation has been limited.
Vietnam	Focus mainly on deconcentration with stronger role for provinces, including regulatory control over subprovincial levels; subnational governments have been allocated rights over specific functions, approaching devolution.

Source: Compiled by the author from multiple sources.

sectors with mandated service standards (see chapters 1, 6, and 10).

In Vietnam, decentralization policy blends a deconcentration of service responsibilities with an allocation of rights that resembles devolution. The latter, however, is much less developed than the former, although provinces have considerably more power and autonomy than subprovincial entities. Even provinces are subject to minimum expenditure requirements in some sectors, and the central government still sets rates on major sources of revenue.

Thailand has long-established deconcentration policies but enacted a decentralization law in 1999. The country has drafted action plans for devolving specific functions to subnational governments, but has assigned relatively few functions thus far. The most significant devolution has occurred in infrastructure, quality of life, and natural resources and the environment. Decentralization of health and education has not yet occurred, though the ministries of Public Health and Education have proposed deconcentrating some responsibilities to area health boards and local education authorities until local governments can meet "readiness" criteria for full devolution. The country plans to enhance decentralization of revenues, which are now under substantial central control.

Decentralization reforms in Indonesia include both devolution of authority and, to a lesser extent, deconcentration of functions. Deconcentration to provincial authorities was the dominant form of decentralization before 1999, when the emphasis shifted to devolution to city and district governments. Local governments have broad functions and receive substantial intergovernmental transfers, but have limited revenue authority. The country has increasingly developed the legal framework (most recently through Laws 32 and 33 of 2004), but functional responsibilities and subnational revenues require further elaboration and regulation.

In the Philippines, deconcentration was historically important. The Integrated Reorganization Plan of 1972 divided the country into 11 (later 16) regions, each with administrative authority. In 1991 the center devolved many responsibilities, personnel, and resources to local governments. These governments have some revenue authority, but most resources are subject to central control. Provincial departments continue to be major providers of national services, though the country has not emphasized formally deconcentrating more responsibilities to them.

Both devolution and deconcentration reforms are occurring in Cambodia. The decentralization to elected commune councils is a limited form of devolution, while the central government is planning to deconcentrate responsibilities to provinces and municipalities. Progress with devolution—albeit modest—has been more rapid than with deconcentration, owing largely to the Seila Program's significant influence over institutional reform since the mid-1990s. Deconcentration reform is at an earlier stage and more fragmented, although a few central ministries, such as Agriculture, Education, and Health, have experimented with limited functional deconcentration. Communes have relative autonomy in pursuing small-scale local priorities with the modest resources they receive, but their fiscal roles are limited.

The Formal Basis for Decentralization

The formal basis for decentralization varies widely throughout East Asia (see table 2.3). A few countries have a constitutional basis for subnational governments, and most have at least a law or set of laws that defines the decentralization framework. The formal basis and extent of this framework do not seem to be closely associated with decentralization performance, as highlighted in chapter 1. Still, the nature and depth of enabling provisions could become more important as challenges to decentralization arise.

Thailand and the Philippines have both a constitutional and a legal basis for decentralization. Thailand's 1997 Constitution clearly specifies principles of local autonomy and elected representation, and establishes specific intergovernmental reform objectives. A National Commission on Public Sector Reform includes a subcommittee to implement decentralization policy. The cabinet approved a Local Fiscal Master Plan in 1997, which defined the framework for Decentralization Act of 1999 reforms. Yet the country needs further legal and regulatory instruments to define the subnational system more fully. The constitutional and

TABLE 2.3 Decentralization Frameworks

Country	Formal basis for decentralization
Cambodia	*Legal and administrative basis:* Provincial Budget Law (1997) gives limited functions to provinces; Law on Commune/*Sangkat* Administrative Management (2001) and Election Law (2001) establish commune system; all legislation clarified in numerous administrative decrees.
China	*No constitutional or dedicated legal basis:* Comprehensive Fiscal Reform (1994), Budget Law (1995), and Tax Sharing System (1994) relevant for roles of subnational governments.
Indonesia	*Legal basis and constitutional amendment:* Law 22 on Regional Government (1999) amended as Law 32 (2004), Law 25 on Fiscal Balance between Central Government and Regions (1999) amended as Law 33 (2004), and Law 34 on Regional Taxes/Levies (2000) (to be amended) provide a framework for decentralization; constitutional amendment (2000) strengthens basis for decentralization.
Philippines	*Constitutional and legal basis:* Constitution (1987) provides for local government autonomy; Local Government Code (1991) and various Marcos-era and post-Marcos laws define aspects of the intergovernmental system.
Thailand	*Constitutional and legal basis:* Constitution (1997) specifies principles of local autonomy and elected local government; Provincial Administration Act (1997) codifies deconcentration policies; Decentralization Act (1999) defines functions and decentralization process.
Vietnam	*Legal and administrative basis:* Law on Organization (1994), Ordinance on Concrete Tasks (1996), Budget Law (1998), and revised Budget Law (2002) assign functions and resources to subnational governments.

Source: Compiled by the author from multiple sources.

legal basis for local government is stronger and more specific in the Philippines. Articles II and X of the 1987 Constitution establish the autonomy of local governments and give them the power to create their own sources of revenue. The Local Government Code of 1991 codifies existing laws on local government, provides for substantial devolution of services, and creates local institutions, such as school boards, development councils, health boards, and peace and order councils.

Most other East Asian countries have a legal but not a constitutional basis for decentralization. Cambodia does not have a unified decentralization framework. However, the Provincial Budget Law of 1997 provides for modest provincial fiscal powers, and the Commune/*Sangkat* Administrative Management Law and the Commune Election Law of 2001 broadly define the functions and structures of commune councils and procedures for electing them. No legislation deconcentrates powers to provincial and district governments, but the country is developing such a law within the framework of the National Program for Administration Reform.

Two main laws established decentralization in Indonesia. Law 22 on Regional Government of 1999 eliminated hierarchical relationships between cities and districts and higher levels of government, granting the former autonomy and broad responsibilities. This legislation has been revised as Law 32 of 2004, which allows for the direct election of subnational leaders beginning in 2005, reestablishes central control over the hiring and firing of civil servants, and requires ex ante approval of subnational budgets. Law 25 on Fiscal Balance of 1999 modified the intergovernmental transfer system and provided for limited local revenue authority. This law has been updated as Law 33 of 2004, which further defines aspects of the intergovernmental fiscal system. Law 34 on Regional Taxes and Levies of 2000 modestly enhances local revenue authority and the government has plans to expand these powers in future legislation. Constitutional amendments passed in 2000 consolidated certain decentralization reforms and make it more difficult for the National Assembly and the president to substantially reverse them.

Vietnam has no constitutional basis for decentralization, but a 1994 Law on Organization and a 1996 Ordinance on Concrete Tasks assign functions to provinces and districts. Decentralization is an important part of the Public Administration Reform Program launched in 1995. Budget laws in 1996 and 1998 also formalized fiscal arrangements among levels and assigned budgeting responsibilities to subnational governments, particularly provinces. More recent legislation, including the revised Budget Law of 2002, provides more details on subnational functions and revenue sources.

China has the weakest formal basis for decentralization. Because intergovernmental changes in China have occurred mostly through economic reform, they have no constitutional or dedicated legal framework. Intergovernmental fiscal relations rest largely on a complex system of bargaining between higher-level and lower-level authorities. Since 1994 a number of reforms and legislative changes have clarified the fiscal responsibilities of different levels of government somewhat, although important areas remain undefined. The most relevant reforms include the 1994 Tax Sharing System, the 1994 Comprehensive Fiscal Reform, and the 1995 Budget Law.

The Governance Environment

This section reviews key aspects of the governance environment in East Asian countries; subnational elections, autonomy, and transparency; and the role of civic participation mechanisms and civil society organizations. These factors, among others, help determine governance quality in a decentralizing environment (chapters 5 and 11).

The National Political Environment

East Asian countries exhibit a broad spectrum of political environments. China and Vietnam are single-party states. In Cambodia a single party dominates, while Indonesia, the Philippines, and Thailand have multiple competitive parties. All of these countries have some type of national and subnational assemblies. Table 2.4 summarizes key features of their political systems.

China is a popular republic with a single official political party, the Chinese Communist Party. Minority parties are extremely small and play no role in the political process. The executive branch encompasses a state council, which includes the prime minister. The president serves as head of state. The legislative body—the National People's Congress—is elected by representatives of lower-level legislatures and designates the president and prime minister. The Chinese Communist Party plays a pivotal role through its power to designate senior officials throughout the governmental system. Vietnam is also a one-party state, with the Communist Party the leading force. Party organizations at all levels must operate within the constitutional and legal framework, but they have great power in determining who can run for elected office. The main legislative body is the National Assembly, which localities elect directly. As in China, National Assembly delegates elect the president and prime minister.

Cambodia is a constitutional monarchy under a democratic regime established in the 1991 peace accord. The executive branch includes the king, as head of state, and the prime minister, who holds the real power as head of government. The legislative branch includes a National Assembly and a Senate. The Cambodia People's Party has dominated recent elections, but other parties have won national and subnational seats. Opposition parties did well enough in July 2003 elections that negotiations to form a new government took a full year. Like Cambodia, Thailand is a constitutional monarchy with a unitary democratic government. A directly elected Parliament selects a prime minister. The country has a multiparty system with a history of unstable coalition governments and military intervention. Under the 1997 Constitution, however, the country is evolving into a two-party system dominated by the incumbent Thai Rak Thai Party and the opposition Democrat Party, with the latter advocating decentralization.

Indonesia and the Philippines are both democratic republics. Indonesia's governmental structure is particularly complex. The main legislative body is the largely elected People's Assembly (DPR). In 1999 the electoral system included hybrid proportional and district elements based on closed party lists (voters could not vote for individuals). Most of the 500 DPR members were elected, but 38 were appointed by military and police factions. The People's Consultative Assembly (MPR), which included the DPR plus 135 members selected by provincial

TABLE 2.4 Basic Features of Political Systems

Country	Governmental system	Political competition	Legislative branch	Executive branch
Cambodia	Constitutional monarchy	Multiparty; Cambodia People's Party dominates	National Assembly and Senate with direct elections	King (head of state); prime minister (head of government) designated by National Assembly
China	Popular republic	Single party: Chinese Communist Party	National People's Congress elected by lower-level congresses	President, vice president, and state council (15 members, including prime minister) all designated by National People's Congress
Indonesia	Democratic republic	Competitive multiparty system	People's Assembly (DPR) directly elected; largely consultative Regional Representative Council (DPD) created in 2004; People's Consultative Assembly (MPR) composed of DPR and DPD manages constitutional reform	President elected by the People's Consultative Assembly until direct election in 2004
Philippines	Democratic republic	Competitive multiparty system	House of Representatives and Senate largely directly elected	President elected directly by the people
Thailand	Constitutional monarchy	Multiparty: two dominate	Parliament with direct elections	King (head of state); prime minister (head of government) designated by Parliament
Vietnam	Popular republic	Single party: Vietnamese Communist Party	National Assembly elected by lower-level assemblies	President and state council (including prime minister) designated by National Assembly

Source: Compiled by the author from multiple sources.

legislatures and 65 members representing other groups, met only as needed to elect the president and reform the Constitution. The country adopted major changes for 2004 elections. Political representation by the military, police, and special interest groups ceased, and Indonesians directly elected the president. A new, territorially based, and largely consultative body, the Regional Representative Council (DPD), was also elected, and the DPR and the DPD now together constitute the MPR, which retains only its as-needed constitutional reform function. Until the 1998 collapse of the Suharto regime, Indonesia was effectively a one-party state run by the Golkar Party. Golkar still plays a major role and did well in the 2004 elections, but other parties, particularly the nationalist Democratic Party and the United Development Party, an Islamic party, have become more powerful. The resounding defeat of former President Megawati Sukarnoputri by former army chief Susilo Bambang Yudhoyono in the 2004 direct elections signals a new era in Indonesia's democratization, and has raised expectations of the national leadership.

The Philippines also has a multiparty system, and competition typically requires parties to form a coalition government. The country relies on direct elections to fill all elective offices, including the president and members of the House of Representatives and the Senate. The exception is the provision for a limited number of special party-list representatives

TABLE 2.5 Subnational Assemblies and Elections

Country	Subnational assemblies and elections
Cambodia	Subnational representative bodies elected through universal suffrage only at the commune level.
China	People's Congresses in China exist at all levels of government, but only the village level is directly elected.
Indonesia	Regional People's Assemblies elected at local and provincial levels.
Philippines	Directly elected bodies exist at all subnational levels of government.
Thailand	Different types of subnational governments have directly elected councils of different sizes.
Vietnam	People's councils at all levels of government are directly elected and ratified by the immediately superior council.

Source: Compiled by the author from multiple sources.

of marginalized sectors, where people vote for parties rather than individuals.

Subnational Elections

All East Asian countries reviewed here have subnational government assemblies, but they vary considerably in whether and how they elect those assemblies (see table 2.5). The number of levels, the size of jurisdictions, whether the elections are direct or indirect, the degree of political competition, and the relationship between elected councils and subnational executives all influence the degree of genuine subnational representation and accountability.

At one extreme are China and Vietnam, where the Communist Party heavily influences subnational elections, reinforcing upward accountability. In China, People's Congresses exist at all levels of government, but voters elect delegates only at the village level, which is not a formal unit of local government. Subordinate congresses elect delegates to higher-level congresses from party lists. In Vietnam, People's Councils are elected through universal suffrage at all levels, but leaders are elected by council members and ratified by the People's Council at the next level.

Other countries hold more freely contested elections, but not at all levels. Cambodia holds subnational elections with universal suffrage only for commune councils. These are elected with a five-year mandate on a proportional basis, such that the councils can include representatives of more than one political party. The council chief is the individual receiving the most votes on the majority-party list. The Cambodia People's Party dominated the first local elections in 2002, but other parties also won seats on many councils. Indonesia directly elects the Regional People's Assemblies (DPRD) at local and provincial levels. Under Law 32 of 2004, subnational leaders (governors and mayors) will be directly elected and can be removed with cause by the DPRD, subject to higher-level approval.

Thailand holds subnational elections every four years at all but the lowest (village) tier. The Local Election Act of 2002 shifted responsibility for conducting local elections from the Ministry of the Interior to the Election Commission, a new independent constitutional agency. Various levels of subnational government have councils of differing sizes that are directly elected. Council members have elected the chair of subnational councils, except in the Bangkok Metropolitan Administration, where the governor is popularly elected. Broader direct election of subnational executives (although not provincial governors) is intended for the future. Among countries with multiple political parties, only the Philippines conducts elections at all levels. Per the 1991 Local Government Code, the country holds subnational elections every three years, except at the *barangay* level, where they occur every five years. The Local Government Code also created special-purpose representative bodies such as Local Development Councils, which formulate and ratify development plans.

Subnational Autonomy in Budgetary and Personnel Decisions

The autonomy of subnational governments varies considerably across East Asian countries (see table 2.6). This section characterizes their independence in making budgeting and personnel decisions

TABLE 2.6 Subnational Budgetary and Personnel Autonomy

Country	Degree of subnational autonomy
Cambodia	Commune governments have their own budgets, whereas provincial budgets are linked to the national budget; strong central civil service control.
China	Subnational governments have their own budgets but are hierarchically integrated with higher levels and subject to central civil service regulations; control is weaker in practice and off-budget activity is considerable.
Indonesia	Subnational governments initially had complete budget autonomy, with next-higher level having legality review, and national civil service regulations allowed a reasonable degree of subnational discretion; Law 32 of 2004 significantly expanded higher-level control over budgeting and the civil service.
Philippines	Subnational governments prepare budgets with legality review by next-higher level; national civil service regulations allow subnational discretion.
Thailand	Local governments prepare budgets subject to certain central mandates and follow civil service regulations; major reforms planned.
Vietnam	Subnational governments have their own budgets, but these are hierarchically integrated and approved by higher levels; this is being phased out, and major cities have been permitted to experiment with greater autonomy.

Source: Compiled by the author from multiple sources.

(see also chapters 1, 5, and 7). Subnational governments in some countries are subject to significant control by higher levels, although such control is not always exercised effectively. In other cases, subnational governments are more independent.

Official autonomy is generally weak at the subnational level in China and Vietnam. In China, subnational budgets are approved by People's Congresses at the same level, but hierarchical linking of budgets, a lack of local tax autonomy, higher-level directives, and earmarked funding offset this discretion somewhat. Most subnational officials are also appointed by People's Congresses at the same level, but higher levels appoint top officials. These senior officials increasingly come from lower-level ranks rather than the central bureaucracy, which may improve local accountability. Management of the subnational civil service closely follows national regulations, although local leaders exercise some discretion.

Although subnational People's Councils in Vietnam have their own budgets, they are integrated into a hierarchical system that requires higher-level approval. Provinces have more expenditure autonomy than subprovincial levels. As of January 2004, provincial budgets no longer require approval from the National Assembly, and Provincial People's Councils have some authority to assign expenditure and revenue functions among subordinate levels of government. Central rules and regulations govern staffing of the People's Councils, but each level of subnational government now has limited discretion in managing local personnel. Pilot schemes in Hanoi and Ho Chi Minh City allow even more local discretion in managing budgets and personnel.

The Philippines has established fairly strong local autonomy, in principle. Local governments prepare their own budgets, which are reviewed at the national level in the case of provinces and cities, and by provinces in the case of municipalities and *barangays*. This review is intended to ensure that budgets meet regulatory requirements, not to interfere in composing the budgets. Civil service regulations, particularly regarding salary, are national, but local chief executives exercise some discretion. Salaries of local officials may vary widely, as some local governments lack the funds to meet national standards.

Indonesia, Thailand, and Cambodia fall in the middle of the autonomy spectrum. Indonesia's Laws 22 and 25 of 1999 originally provided for strong regional autonomy in principle. Local governments had authority over their budgets, subject to national legality review, and technically controlled their staff subject to national regulations. On the other hand, local governments did not select many of their staff, who were transferred under the 1999 decentralization, along with substantial intergovernmental transfers to support them. As noted, recent revisions to Law 22 (Law 32 of 2004) expanded central control over budget and civil service decisions. Subnational budgets require formal approval rather than legality review, and authority to hire and fire subnational civil servants has been significantly recentralized.

In Thailand, local governments prepare and execute their own budgets, but they are subject to central direction. A significant share of local expenditures is centrally mandated, with the largest portion devoted to personnel expenses (representing 30 percent of local budgets, on average). Central directives govern staff numbers, salaries, and benefits. Major reforms, however, are intended to eventually move this highly centralized civil service to one where local governments have considerable authority over personnel management.

Cambodia is a more unusual case, as its system is new and the gap between provincial and local procedures is significant. Centrally appointed provincial governors have some power and influence in coordinating budgets, but provincial line departments are primarily accountable to parent ministries. Commune councils have greater autonomy, in principle: they have some discretion in preparing plans and budgets if they follow basic guidelines. Under nascent decentralization, however, centrally appointed key staff limit local autonomy. For example, the Ministry of Interior appoints the commune clerk (though council members can request a replacement if they show cause), and the commune treasurer is a member of the Provincial Treasury (though officially required to follow the instructions of the commune council).

Subnational Transparency

East Asian countries have all made some attempts to improve transparency and expand access to information at the subnational level, but intent has often been more substantial than practice (see table 2.7). Some countries, such as the Philippines, provide extensive public documentation of and access to subnational government budgets and other information, while other countries, including China, do not. Audits do generally occur—internally in some cases, both internally and externally in others—but countries usually do not monitor subnational budget performance comprehensively.

Transparency in China and Cambodia is low. In China, a finance director for each subnational government provides an annual report to the People's Congress on budget implementation and the main features of the current budget. This is the only document on subnational budgets and includes only highly aggregated data. Substantial off-budget funding also limits transparency. Internal audits are relatively strong in the Chinese system. Local audit bureaus conduct external audits, but these fall under the direct authority of the subnational government. External auditing by higher levels is infrequent. There is no system for evaluating budgets, although the central government does focus on meeting targets in priority areas such as family planning and tax collection. Cambodia has a legal framework for budget review, including the 2000 Audit Law. However, the capacity to implement this system is not in place, and public access to documentation is limited.

TABLE 2.7 Subnational Transparency

Country	Mechanisms for subnational transparency
Cambodia	Evolving commune reporting requirements provide public information in some areas; National Audit Authority weak.
China	Limited publishing of official subnational government documents; strong internal audit; external audit weak and not independent from executive.
Indonesia	Various public reporting requirements but weaker in practice; Commission on Audit has mandate to review subnational governments but limited in practice.
Philippines	Several subnational public reporting requirements; Audit Commission review of budgets; internal audit generally weak.
Thailand	Subnational governments required to generate significant public financial reports; external audit hampered by capacity limitations; internal audit generally weak.
Vietnam	Well-defined system of reporting but weaker in practice; State Audit reviews subnational governments, but not independent from executive; weak internal audit.

Source: Compiled by the author from multiple sources.

The Philippines, Indonesia, Thailand, and Vietnam have adopted transparency frameworks, but they do not always function well. In the Philippines, budget documents—including reports on implementing the previous budget and an annual financial report—are made public. The Department of Budget and Management and the Commission on Audit require regular accountability reports, and the financial transactions of local governments are subject to ex post review by the Commission on Audit. In Indonesia, budget documents are supposed to be public and external audits are conducted, although not always on schedule because of capacity constraints in higher-level departments. The revised Constitution guarantees freedom of information, and a new anti-corruption law requires access to information. However, bureaucratic barriers make exercising these civic rights difficult.

Thailand has been improving transparency. The 1997 Constitution guarantees freedom of information, although the country has not yet passed laws implementing that freedom. Local governments must submit budget plans, financial reports, and procurement reports to the Department of Local Authority Promotion, the Bureau of the Budget, and the Auditor General. All are publicly disclosed, and some local authorities prepare publications and Web sites. Internal auditing is weak except in large cities. The auditor general and provincial audit units are credible but do not have the capacity to audit all subnational governments. Vietnam has a well-defined system of reporting from lower to higher levels, and governments must make certain budget data public. Internal auditing is seriously deficient, primarily because of capacity constraints. The State Audit of Vietnam must audit all subnational governments, but the agency is not independent of the executive. Subnational budgets include no performance measures.

The Role of Civic Participation and Civil Society

Most East Asian countries officially require civic participation, and civil society organizations generally exist, but their development and influence vary substantially (see table 2.8). This section focuses on how central governments engage citizens in decision making and support and regulate civil society organizations. In countries with limited democratic institutions, such as China and Vietnam, mechanisms for civic participation tend to be weak, and civil society less independent of the state. The roles of nongovernmental organizations (NGOs) also differ greatly across East Asia, with some taking direct responsibility for providing

TABLE 2.8 Subnational Civic Participation and Civil Society

Country	Subnational civic participation	Subnational civil society
Cambodia	Civic participation introduced in the context of emerging commune system, but weak in many areas.	Some active civil society groups emerged from the period of civil war.
China	No formal government mechanisms for civic participation.	Civil society organizations permitted but heavily regulated, creating disincentives.
Indonesia	Civic participation encouraged and sometimes required by donors, but no official mechanism.	Emerging civil society, but complex and limited in some respects.
Philippines	Civic participation framework in Local Government Code (1991), but no formal mechanism.	Relatively active civil society.
Thailand	Strong constitutional and legal basis for civic participation; much weaker in practice.	Civil society groups limited but growing.
Vietnam	Civic participation mechanisms encouraged under Grassroots Democracy Decree (1998), but new and unfamiliar.	Many civil society organizations, but major groups are under state control.

Source: Compiled by the author from multiple sources.

services. Cambodia, Indonesia, and Thailand, for example, boast many active NGOs, but they tend not to interact extensively with local governments.

Civic participation mechanisms are most developed, and civil society the most organized and dynamic, in the Philippines. Civil society grew during the Marcos dictatorship, when antigovernment sentiment was high and focused on "people's empowerment." After the democratic transition, civil society organizations became more active. The 1987 Constitution and Bill of Rights ensure the rights of independent NGOs and facilitate popular consultation. The 1991 Local Government Code requires public participation in *barangay* development plans and certain local functions. A *Barangay-Bayan* Network assists *barangays* in developing plans and projects, and the Local Government Code Network supports governance. Despite these positive features, the country has room for improvement. The country has not implemented key constitutional provisions on the representation of marginalized groups and local referenda, and civil society includes armed left-wing groups that threaten national stability.

The official framework for civic participation and civil society is relatively strong in Thailand and Indonesia. Thai military regimes discouraged NGOs, but civil society is now officially considered important for good governance. Thailand's 1997 Constitution requires the state to promote popular participation in preparing policies and plans, making public decisions, and monitoring the exercise of state power. The Constitution also enshrines the right to petition and receive a response from the state, and to peacefully resist unconstitutional attempts to acquire power. The Eighth Development Plan (1997–2001) supported the emergence of local civil society, but slow progress on decentralization has constrained the development of civil society organizations.

Neither Indonesia's Constitution nor its recent Bill of Rights mentions popular participation. However, the country does have some local tradition of community consultation. For decades, repression and state-organized unions weakened social participation. Thousands of NGOs have sprung up since the late 1980s, but the Internal Security Law limited their development. The movement that overthrew Suharto dissipated without developing into strong civil society organizations, but those that attained formal status have moved into advocacy on key policy issues. Examples include attempts by the Forum for Popular Participation to push amendments to Law 22 of 1999, and the support of citizen forums by the Indonesian Partnership in Local Governance Initiatives, a network of local NGOs.

China and Vietnam do not emphasize civic participation and do not have vibrant civil societies. Formal NGOs have a shorter history in China than in other East Asian countries, and social welfare is considered the responsibility of central government. In the late 1970s and 1980s, government departments at all levels approved and managed social organizations. As these groups proliferated, the Ministry of Civil Affairs took control of this process in 1988. In 1989, after the Tiananmen incident, new regulations were applied retroactively and became even stricter and more extensive in the late 1990s. Social organizations—official, semiofficial, and popular—must register and win sponsorship of a government agency. Only a minority of grassroots organizations has been able to register legally. Many are financed by international agencies, but support is scarce in less-developed areas. In the late 1990s, a government campaign to regularize NGOs required reregistration at the Ministry of Civil Affairs. The number of NGOs fell from 180,000 in 1995 to 160,000 in 2000.

According to Vietnam's 1992 Constitution, the Communist Party is the leading organ of the state, which includes civil society and mass organizations. Economic reform, however, has encouraged the development of civil society. The country enacted a Law on Co-operatives in 1997 and issued a Grassroots Democracy Decree a year later, establishing a legal framework for citizen participation at the commune level. The Law on Complaints and Denunciations is now under revision to expand opportunities for citizens to register complaints against the civil service. State-sponsored mass organizations, however, are still the major form of social organization. Representatives of the Women's Union, Youth Union, Farmer's Union, and General Confederation of Labor—whose memberships include a large proportion of citizens—sit on national and local committees that discuss policies affecting their constituencies. Strictly speaking, state-sponsored mass organizations are not part of civil society, although they have become somewhat more like NGOs. A growing number of community-based organizations, such as water users' associations, medical volunteers, and village development committees, have formed and are enhancing Vietnamese civil society. A 2003 decree on NGOs recognizes their importance, but some of its provisions raise concerns about how freely they can function.

Cambodia's decentralization legislation requires participatory planning at the commune level, although the extent to which this is genuine and inclusive varies considerably. Though weak in many parts of the country, civil society groups played an important role in providing community services in the absence of local government. Initially hostile to government-related local institutions, NGOs in Cambodia have since offered important expertise and capacity building under Seila, and some are partnering with new commune councils. With little tradition of popular participation in local governance beyond religious-based community development, effectively incorporating civil society participation in local public sector decision making will remain a challenge for the foreseeable future.

Fiscal Decentralization

This section outlines the fiscal functions of subnational governments in East Asia, focusing on assigned roles and own-source and intergovernmental revenues. (See chapter 6 for more detail on own-source revenues, and chapters 1 and 3 for information on subnational borrowing.)

Distributing Functions among Levels of Government

The distribution of functions among levels of governments is far from uniform in East Asia, with subnational roles ranging from modest to dominant (see table 2.9). Although subnational governments have substantial functions in most countries, incomplete implementation of legal authority has resulted in low subnational expenditure shares in some cases. The pattern of assignments also varies across government levels and sectors, and the magnitude of subnational expenditures is not clearly related to autonomy.

At one extreme is Cambodia, where provinces account for less than 20 percent of public expenditures and act primarily as agents of the center. Elected communes have few mandatory functions and account for only about 2 percent of public expenditures, although enabling legislation provides for the eventual formal transfer of specific functions to them. Other East Asian countries have assigned, at least in broad legal terms, relatively significant responsibilities to subnational governments, although legal provisions are not always operationally defined and implemented. An interesting contrast to Cambodia is Thailand, where the 1999 Decentralization Act calls for the transfer of six major functions to local administrations. Because the country has implemented these legal provisions only partially, Thai subnational governments account for only about 10 percent of public expenditures, although that figure is expected to grow sharply.

The Philippines and Indonesia have gone further in defining and implementing functional assignments. The 1991 Local Government Code in the Philippines devolved substantial responsibilities to the various types of local governments, which currently account for about 20 percent of public spending. They also have some regulatory powers, including land reclassification. Indonesia's Law 32 of 2004 reserves only national defense, foreign policy, security, justice, monetary and fiscal policy, and religion for the center. Local governments must perform a wide range of obligatory functions under Law 22 of 1999 and Law 32 of 2004. The province played a smaller role in many functions under the 1999 legislation, focusing mainly on regional coordination and the backstopping of underperforming local governments. Many of the provincial functions assigned under Law 32 of 2004 are similar to those assigned to local governments, raising concerns about clarity and redundancy. Subnational governments account for just over 30 percent of total spending, and that figure is expected to continue growing.

China and Vietnam emphasize the sharing of responsibilities. China's Budget Law defines a broad division of functions between central and local governments, but does not disaggregate local categories. The result is concurrent assignment and significant variation across regions. Subnational governments have heavy safety net responsibilities, including pensions, unemployment, and social welfare, which are unusual subnational responsibilities. The center sets broad expenditure guidelines,

TABLE 2.9 Subnational Functional Assignments and Expenditure Shares

Country	Subnational functions (*see chapter 5*)	Subnational share of expenditures
Cambodia	Provinces dominate subnational service delivery; communes have few mandatory functions, but legal provision for eventual transfer of more functions.	Around 20% overall; 2% at commune level, the rest at provincial level (2001).
China	Broad legal division of responsibility between levels without disaggregation; in practice, multiple levels perform many functions concurrently.	Around 70% overall; 40% at the county level (2002).
Indonesia	Obligatory local functions include health, education, environment, and infrastructure, among numerous others; provinces were originally assigned mainly coordination and gap-filling roles, but Law 32/2004 increases their role and raises concern about lack of functional clarity.	Around 32% for all levels; expected to increase (2002).
Philippines	Substantial functions devolved to subnational governments, particularly health, social services, environment, agriculture, public works, education, tourism, telecommunications, and housing.	Around 20% at subprovincial level (2002).
Thailand	Six broad functions to be devolved to local governments: infrastructure, quality of life, community and social order, planning and investment and promotion of trade and tourism, management of natural resources and the environment, and culture, values, and local wisdom; slow progress on implementation.	Around 10% for all levels; expected to increase (2001).
Vietnam	Main functions remain centralized but different levels share responsibilities in practice; subnational governments dominate in agriculture, forestry, irrigation, fisheries, power, water, education, and health.	Around 50% for all levels (2003).

Source: Compiled by the author from multiple sources.

at least in principle. Subnational governments account for around 70 percent of public spending, with the county level accounting for more than 40 percent. In Vietnam, intergovernmental responsibilities are more specific on paper, but the center and subnational levels share functions in practice. Still, subnational governments have been playing a more dominant role in some sectors, including agriculture, forestry, irrigation, fisheries, power, water, education, and health. Their share of public expenditures stands at around 50 percent.

Subnational Revenues: Own-Source and Shared

Most East Asian countries have few productive own-sources of local revenue (see table 2.10 and chapter 6). Even where local revenue shares are relatively high, most are centrally defined and/or managed taxes over which subnational governments have little control, with the proceeds fully assigned or shared locally. These are in fact intergovernmental transfers, but are included here with own-source revenues because of the lack of disaggregated data to clearly distinguish between the two in some countries. Informal, off-budget revenue is a major issue in some countries (see chapters 1 and 6).

China, Vietnam, and Thailand rely primarily on shared taxes. As economic reforms proceeded and subnational governments came to dominate public sector revenues, China introduced the recentralizing 1994 Tax Sharing System noted above and further refinements in 2002. Subnational revenue includes shared taxes—the relative proportions of which are sometimes negotiated—and several exclusive subnational taxes. Provinces have nearly

TABLE 2.10 Subnational Revenues

Country	Own-source revenues (*see chapter 6*)	Shared sources
Cambodia	Subject to strong central control. *Provincial sources:* taxes on transportation, unused land, markets, business licenses, parking, slaughter; fees and charges. *Commune sources:* administrative fees and contributions required for transfer-funded development projects (current); land and property tax and user fees/charges (authority not implemented).	Most revenue sharing occurs through line-ministry budget allocations to provinces, and intergovernmental transfers to communes (see table 2.11).
China	No formal subnational own-source revenues, except for a limited set of user fees/charges. Some national revenues fully shared with subnational governments (see next column).	Value added tax (25% share). Income tax on enterprises (40% share). Taxes on personal income, natural resources, nonplan construction, salt, security and exchange (50% share). Taxes on non–VAT-sector businesses, urban maintenance and construction, urban land use, rural markets, vehicle use, property, entertainment; also various business-related taxes (100% share). Taxes shared with provinces, which control sharing to lower levels.
Indonesia	Subject to some central control. *Provincial sources (substantially shared with local level):* taxes on motor vehicles, fuel, groundwater extraction and use. *City/district sources (modestly shared with lower level):* taxes on hotels and restaurants, entertainment, advertisement, street lighting, limited mineral exploitation, parking; limited locally designed taxes under Law No. 34 (2000). User fees and charges at both levels. 35% of provincial and 6% of subprovincial revenue (2002).	Main revenue sharing is through formula transfers (see table 2.11) rather than shared taxes. Selected taxes and state-owned enterprise revenues shared with both provinces and cities and districts: property, natural resources, and personal income tax. 32% of provincial and 20% of subprovincial revenue (2002). Revenue sharing, especially for natural resources, expanded under Law 34 of 2004 and is not reflected in above percentages.
Philippines	Subject to some central control. *Main sources:* taxes on real property, proceeds from public enterprises, local business turnover. *Other sources:* taxes on transfer of real property, quarries, amusement; many fees and charges. Cities can impose full set of taxes; fewer in provinces/municipalities. Cities and provinces must share portions of revenues with municipalities and *barangays*. ± 30% of subnational revenue (2002).	Central revenue sharing occurs mostly through intergovernmental transfers (see table 2.11). National wealth composite (based on a set of national revenues derived from related bases) and the tobacco excise tax are shared with subnational governments.
Thailand	Largely centrally defined. *Provincial:* petroleum sales tax; tobacco sales tax; hotel tax. *Subprovincial:* taxes on vehicles, houses and land, land development, signboards, slaughter. Various permits, licenses, and fees at all levels. ± 12% of subnational revenue (2001).	Value added tax (30% share). Natural resources (60% share). Sales, special business, excise taxes (10% share). ±54% of subnational revenue (2001).

Country	Own-source revenues (*see chapter 6*)	Shared sources
Vietnam	No formal subnational own-source revenues, except for a limited set of user fees. Some national revenues are fully shared with subnational governments (see next column).	Taxes on natural resources (except petroleum), transfer of land-use rights, agriculture, land and housing, licenses, state dwelling leases, lottery revenues (100%). Value added tax, taxes on enterprise and personal income, special consumption, remittances, gas and oil fees (partial). Taxes shared with provinces, which control sharing with lower levels. ±46% of subnational revenue (2003).

Source: Compiled by the author from multiple sources.

complete freedom to assign revenue to lower levels, resulting in a variety of practices across the country.

Strictly speaking, Vietnam has no subnational taxes. The central government controls tax bases and rates completely, and the Department of Tax Administration collects all nontrade revenue. Subnational taxes are either assigned 100 percent to the local level or shared among levels. Under 2002 reforms, provinces formally receive the proceeds of all shared taxes and assign portions to districts and communes subject to central standards. Fully and partially shared taxes have recently provided around 46 percent of subnational revenues, in roughly equal proportions.

In Thailand, subnational revenues include own-collected taxes and nontax revenues, centrally collected taxes, and shared taxes. In 2001, locally collected revenues accounted for only 11–12 percent of subnational revenues, while shared revenues accounted for about 54 percent, including about 18 percent from the value added tax. The recent Property Tax Act—which combines the land and building tax and the land development tax—could provide subnational governments with more local revenue.

Indonesia and the Philippines take a different approach. Both have tax sharing, but they pool a high proportion of shared resources into a consolidated fund allocated by formula as an intergovernmental transfer (see below). Indonesia also assigns to provincial and district and city governments a share of revenues from selected taxes. Provinces have uniform tax rates and share the revenues with lower levels. Shared taxes account for about 32 percent of provincial and 20 percent of local income, but Law 33 of 2004 increases tax sharing, particularly on selected natural resource bases. Local governments exercise control—within national ceilings—only over a limited set of taxes, many of which are holdovers from the prereform era. Both provinces and local governments collect user charges. Law 34 of 2000 allows new local sources, but it led to the adoption of some problematic local tax and nontax revenues and is slated for revision. Overall, own-source revenues account for about 35 percent of provincial and about 6 percent of local income, although the latter average masks stronger performance in larger urban areas. In the Philippines, only cities may impose the full set of local taxes, while provinces and municipalities have less taxing power. Cities and provinces must often share portions of their tax revenues with municipalities and *barangays*.

As a newly decentralizing country, Cambodia has established few official subnational own-source revenues. As noted above, the government centralized revenues after the 1993 elections to impose discipline on provinces. The 1998 Provincial Budget Law reinstated limited provincial revenues, but most provincial resources continue to flow through central sectoral budgets. The 2001 Law on Commune/*Sangkat* Administrative Management grants revenue sources to communes, including a land and property tax, but the law requires follow-up legislation. The central government has formally assigned only a few nonproductive fees for civil registration to communes. Some communes also collect minor user fees, but these are extralegal as no enabling regulation exists. The new Department of Local Finance in the Ministry of Economy and Finance has made developing commune own-source revenues a priority.

Intergovernmental Transfers

Intergovernmental transfer systems in East Asia range from substantial to modest in terms of both central and subnational government budgets, from complex to simple in structure, and from relatively transparent to highly nontransparent (see table 2.11). In most cases the central government provides significant intergovernmental transfers, which represent a large share of subnational resources.

The intergovernmental transfer system in China is the most complex and least transparent among the countries considered here. During the past two decades, the government has added components designed to address newly recognized problems without removing or altering existing elements. Beyond shared taxes (discussed above), which account for some 40 percent of transfers, there are a variety of specific-purpose grants. These include quota subsidies (left over from an earlier scheme that subsidized deficits on approved expenditures), transfers to offset the impacts of the 1994 Tax Sharing System, final account subsidies, and a few minor programs. Subnational governments rely on

TABLE 2.11 Intergovernmental Transfers

Country	Unconditional transfers	Conditional transfers
Cambodia	Communes receive largely unconditional transfers via formula allocation from Commune/*Sangkat* Fund.	Provinces receive line-ministry allocations, not transfers; decentralization law allows for conditional transfers to communes.
China	Tax Sharing System (1994) assigns shares of certain taxes (table 2.10) to subnational governments' general revenue, but they are officially subject to some expenditure guidelines.	Complex accumulation of old and new systems; conditional grants account for more than half of all transfers; dominated by social security, wage increase, and fiscal stimulus grants.
Indonesia	Certain taxes shared with lower levels (table 2.10); formula-driven *dana alokasi umum* revenue sharing accounts for at least 26% of domestic revenues; provincial/subprovincial shares based on responsibilities (Law 33 of 2004).	Minor; special-purpose transfers—*dana alokasi khusus*—under development; 10 percent subnational matching requirement under Law 33 of 2004.
Philippines	Internal Revenue Allotment shares by formula account for 40% of internal revenues; 23% each to provinces and cities, 34% to municipalities, 20% to *barangays;* the IRA accounts for 94% of transfers.	Modest categorical grants, including the Municipal Development Fund, the Local Government Empowerment Fund, and the Calamity Fund.
Thailand	Substantial shared tax revenues (table 2.10); "general" transfers for fiscal equalization and other purposes; some, such as the transfer for devolution of compulsory functions, are not truly unconditional.	Specific grants are mostly for capital expenditures, with one type earmarked for education and other types less restricted, so not heavily conditional; some "general" transfers (see left column) subject to conditions.
Vietnam	Certain taxes fully assigned to or shared with subnational governments (table 2.10); equalization transfer distributed by formula to jurisdictions where approved expenditure budgets (based on minimum standards) exceed the sum of shared taxes.	Before 2002, no conditional grants, only national program budget allocations; Budget Law (2002) recast these as specific transfers and provides for more types of conditional transfers.

Source: Compiled by the author from multiple sources.

transfers to finance nearly half their budgetary expenditures in the aggregate.

Thailand and Vietnam also have complex transfer systems, but they are generally more transparent. Thailand has two main forms of intergovernmental transfers besides shared tax revenues. The central government devotes the bulk of seven types of so-called "general" grants to fiscal equalization, devolution of compulsory functions, and tax promotion. Grants fulfilling the first goal are allocated by formula, those fulfilling the second goal are based on the number of beneficiaries, and those fulfilling the third goal are based on past tax performance. Specific grants—largely discretionary—are mostly for capital expenditures; one program is earmarked for education, and larger programs are broader. Subnational governments depend on transfers for about 34 percent of their revenues, not including the 54 percent derived from shared taxes.

Vietnam provides two types of intergovernmental transfers: equalization transfers and specific-purpose transfers. In the past, the central government negotiated transfers with subnational governments mostly to fill budget gaps. As of 2003, the government distributes the equalization transfer by formula to jurisdictions whose approved budgets (based on minimum standards) exceed the sum of "100 percent shared" and partially shared taxes. The formula must remain in place for three to five years. These reforms have improved the transparency and stability of intergovernmental transfers. Line ministries have also long used transfers to support national priority programs, and the 2002 Budget Law formalizes these resources as conditional transfer programs. As noted above, just under half (46 percent) of the revenues of subnational governments come from 100 percent and partially shared taxes; the other 54 percent takes the form of intergovernmental transfers.

Indonesia's Law 25 of 1999 significantly altered the transfer system. The *dana alokasi umum* (DAU) combined substantial transfers for local civil service wages and the fragmented general program Inpres into a revenue-sharing fund financed by at least 25 percent of central domestic net revenues, with 2.5 percent assigned to provinces and 22.5 percent to cities and districts. Under Law 33 of 2004, the pool increased to at least 26 percent of domestic revenues, and provincial/subprovincial shares now depend on functions. The DAU is formula-driven, so the allocation of transfers is more transparent than in the past, and the formula attempts to consider expenditure needs and revenue capacity. Law 25 of 1999 and Law 33 of 2004 also provide for special-purpose transfers: the *dana alokasi khusus* (DAK). These are expected to be mainly sectoral conditional (matching) transfers designed in consultation with line ministries, but the Ministry of Finance has only begun to experiment with DAK on a small scale. Given the weak devolution of revenue powers, subnational governments rely on transfers (exclusive of shared taxes) for more than 65 percent of their revenues, with provinces averaging 34 percent and local governments averaging 74 percent.

The main intergovernmental transfer program in the Philippines is the Internal Revenue Allotment (IRA). The Local Government Code requires that this program share 40 percent of gross national internal revenues (with a three-year lag), and the program accounts for 94 percent of total transfers. Subnational levels share the IRA pool, with 23 percent going to provinces and cities, 34 percent to municipalities, and 20 percent to *barangays*. A simple formula based on population, equal share, and land area allocates the appropriate pool share among units at each level. Two modest revenue-sharing schemes—the national wealth share (national revenues derived from certain taxes) and the tobacco excise share—and a few small categorical grants also exist. Subnational governments rely heavily on transfers, which account for over 80 percent of provincial budgets and around 70 percent of municipal budgets. Cities are more financially independent, relying on the IRA for just over 40 percent of their income.

Cambodia's intergovernmental transfer program is modest, reflecting its early stage of decentralization. The country launched the Commune/*Sangkat* Fund (CSF) in 2002 to coincide with the first election of commune councils. The CSF relies on both domestic and external sources. The central budget contributed 1.2 percent of recurrent domestic revenue in 2002, and that share grew to 2.5 percent in 2004. The Commune/*Sangkat* Law requires that the Cambodian government devote a share of its budget to the CSF, but how to determine this percentage and ensure that it will grow is unclear. CSF transfers are divided into general administration and local development components, with no less than 70 percent allocated to the

TABLE 2.12 Responsibility for Managing Decentralization

Country	Institutional responsibility
Cambodia	The interministerial National Committee to Support the Communes (chaired by the Ministry of Interior) in charge of developing and implementing decentralization involving communes; Council for Administrative Reform in charge of deconcentration involving provinces; generally weak coordination between the two. Single integrated, interministerial process created in 2004 to develop consistent decentralization and deconcentration strategies.
China	No formal decentralization policy, so intergovernmental issues managed through regular government institutions.
Indonesia	High-level Regional Autonomy Review Board initially in charge of decentralization policy but process now dominated by the Ministry of Home Affairs, with specific matters formally under the Ministry of Finance or other ministries; generally weak interministerial coordination and some problematic competition.
Philippines	Interagency oversight committee to monitor implementation of Local Government Code; National Economic and Development Authority, Department of Budget and Management, and Department of Interior and Local Government also play important roles.
Thailand	National Decentralization Committee, with broad representation from national and subnational governments as well as the nongovernmental arena, charged with making, implementing, and monitoring decentralization policy.
Vietnam	No formal decentralization-specific body; regular government institutions such as Ministry of Finance and Ministry of Planning and Investment manage reform.

Source: Compiled by the author from multiple sources.

latter. The central government allocates the general administration share to communes and *sangkats* in proportion to the number of councilors, and the local development share based on a formula with three components: equal share, a share proportional to population, and a share proportional to relative poverty. Given the weak development of local resources, Cambodian communes depend on the center for almost 100 percent of their funds.

Managing Decentralization Reforms

Chapter 1 highlighted the importance of moving beyond the decentralization structure to consider the decentralization process. This section provides a more in-depth, country-specific look at key aspects of this process, focusing on responsibility for designing and managing decentralization, the strategy for implementing it, and the capacity-building activities designed to support it.

Responsibility for the Decentralization Process

In some East Asian countries, regular government institutions manage decentralization. In others, special bodies manage the process, but these differ in composition and role. All countries experience tensions between reformists and defenders of the status quo, and various political parties and institutions may hold different visions of decentralization. Table 2.12 summarizes arrangements for designing and managing decentralization in the region.

Because decentralization is not a formal policy in China, central ministries "manage" decentralization through routine interactions with subnational governments. Existing institutions similarly manage the decentralization process in Vietnam. The Ministry of Finance and Ministry of Planning and Investment, and their provincial counterparts, are particularly important. The Philippines has also relied on existing national institutions, supported by an interagency committee responsible for monitoring implementation of the Local Government Code. Key players include the National Economic and Development Authority, the Department of Budget and Management, and the Department of Interior and Local Government. Besides cities and a few provinces, associations of local governments also play important roles in the Philippines' decentralization process.

Indonesia, Thailand, and Cambodia all established special bodies to guide decentralization.

Indonesia's Regional Autonomy Review Board (DPOD), composed of minister-level members, played a significant role in setting the initial direction of decentralization policy. With a basic legal and institutional framework for decentralization now in place, key national ministries have assumed principal responsibility for detailing and implementing broad policy parameters. The Ministry of Home Affairs plays the strongest official role, and the Ministry of Finance and the national planning agency (Bappenas) provide key inputs in specific areas. Sectoral ministries help develop regulations for decentralizing services, but Home Affairs is attempting to assert leadership. Weak coordination and interministerial competition remain significant problems. Although Home Affairs is technically in charge, it has limited authority over other ministries with important decentralization roles.

In Thailand, the National Decentralization Committee serves as the strategic unit for decentralization policy. Its members include local governmental and nongovernmental officials as well as representatives of central government. This committee, like the Indonesian Regional Autonomy Review Board, was instrumental in designing decentralization, and is now also charged with monitoring and implementing reforms and providing policy recommendations to the cabinet. National agencies, particularly the Ministry of Interior, also engage in the day-to-day management of decentralization.

Responsibility for decentralization policy in Cambodia is fragmented, with the Ministry of the Interior, the Ministry of Economy and Finance, and the Ministry of Planning particularly involved. The government established the National Committee to Support the Communes, chaired by the Ministry of Interior, to develop and implement decentralization to the communes. The Seila task force and its secretariat are also helping integrate the donor-initiated Seila Program with the deconcentrated and decentralized systems as they develop. The Council for Administrative Reform, attached to the Council of Ministers and responsible for overall public sector administrative reform, has been the main player in deconcentration, although the Ministry of Interior has recently taken a stronger role in developing the required legislation. In 2004 the Cambodian government established an integrated process overseen by an interministerial committee to develop decentralization and deconcentration policy in an integrated way.

Strategies for Implementing Decentralization

East Asian countries have generally not implemented decentralization strategically or systematically (see table 2.13). The tendency toward ad hoc approaches is not surprising, given the variety of political rationales for decentralization and the differing nature of regimes in the region. Decentralization is mostly occurring within highly centralized systems. National agencies often lack serious commitment to reform, slowing progress even in countries with reasonable frameworks. The overall environment is not conducive to well-planned and

TABLE 2.13 Decentralization Strategies

Country	Nature of strategy
Cambodia	Limited elements of a strategy for commune system, but weakly developed and short term.
China	No formal strategy; some asymmetric treatment of subnational governments.
Indonesia	No formal strategy; some attention to key reforms after "Big Bang," such as defining functional assignments more clearly, but approach largely fragmented.
Philippines	Broad three-stage strategy for implementing Local Government Code, now in last phase; unclear how carefully the country followed the strategy.
Thailand	Detailed master plan with three phases approved by Parliament in 2002; progress modest (phase one finished in 2004 without meeting key goals).
Vietnam	Ad hoc strategy in that reform has been slow and controlled; some asymmetric treatment of larger cities through pilot programs.

Source: Compiled by the author from multiple sources.

carefully executed implementation, the consequences of which are highlighted in chapter 1.

Because decentralization in China was essentially a by-product of economic reform, it lacks a real strategy. The central government treats various types of subnational governments differently, but there is not a developed asymmetric decentralization strategy. Because of the nature of the administrative hierarchy and the diversity of the country, however, provinces make decisions about subprovincial roles, perhaps in some cases reflecting strategic attempts to improve subprovincial performance. The lack of an overall strategy is also manifested in ad hoc central government steps to define the intergovernmental system, resulting in disjointed revenue and expenditure assignments and an inconsistent intergovernmental transfer system.

Indonesia and Cambodia also have weak implementation strategies. Decentralization was adopted quickly and with little debate in both cases. In Indonesia this occurred in a crisis situation, while Cambodia's efforts might be characterized as a case of political opportunism. Because Indonesia's reforms emerged from crisis, the general framework was pushed urgently, without much thought given to how to make it work. The country's decentralization is often referred to as a "Big Bang" because significant resources and functions were devolved so quickly. A substantial portion of the resources, however, are used to pay for staff who were transferred to local governments, suggesting a possible conscious effort to reduce the effects of major reform shocks. Operational details on many of the legally devolved functions still have to be specified, and the above-noted weak coordination of the national agencies involved constrains the development of a genuine strategy.

Cambodia has limited elements of a strategy. As many of the newly elected communes had little or no capacity or political credibility, the early design included initially modest functional expectations, simple structure and staffing of councils, and classification of communes into two categories based on capacity, with differential funding awarded on that basis. As the system matures, communes are to be assigned greater responsibilities. Unfortunately, there is no strategy for making further progress. The classification system has been abolished without any assessment of the extent of capacity development in weaker communes. There is no clear vision of where the overall system is headed, the plan for fully folding Seila into the formal government system is incompletely developed, and, as in Indonesia, coordination of the key actors is inadequate. The new interministerial effort noted above is intended to provide direction and facilitate coordination, but how successful it will be is unclear.

Though decentralization in the Philippines also emerged from crisis, the country did attempt to develop a strategy, at least on paper. A Master Plan for the Sustained Implementation of the 1991 Local Government Code (1993–98) provided the blueprint for reform. The plan included three phases. Phase one (1992–93) involved the transfer of functions, which varied by type of local government. Phase two (1994–96) gave local governments time to adjust to their formal responsibilities. Phase three (1997 onward) expected a more stable system to focus on building local capacity, with technical assistance from national agencies. The interagency oversight committee noted above was charged with monitoring implementation. The extent to which this phasing was followed is not clear, and decentralization continues to face political difficulties, instability in some regions, and limited resources. Some central agencies have held on to functions they were supposed to devolve, and development of local revenue has been slow.

Thailand and Vietnam are closest to having a decentralization strategy, but both have implemented it slowly. In 1997, after the new Thai Constitution mandated decentralization, a Local Fiscal Master Plan identified 17 measures to enhance local revenues, clarify responsibility for expenditure, reform the intergovernmental transfer system, establish mechanisms for monitoring local fiscal systems, promote new methods of mobilizing capital for local investment, and develop local capacity. Parliament did not approve a more comprehensive plan to decentralize administrative power to local administrations until 2002. The plan includes a general framework, objectives, and guidelines for decentralizing administrative power in three stages. During the first stage (2001–4), the country was supposed to transfer 245 tasks, improve local and regional administrative systems, eliminate overlapping functions, and strengthen local capacity to manage functions, personnel, revenue, and assets. Unfortunately, these goals were not fully achieved, the coordinating National Decentralization Committee (NDC) is understaffed and inadequately financed, and the strength of political support is unclear. Thus, the NDC has not been able to operationalize what appears to be an atypically carefully conceived implementation strategy.

In Vietnam, the movement to give greater responsibility to subnational governments has progressed in stages. Expenditure and revenue assignments have been changed gradually, and the transparency and stability of the intergovernmental transfer system have improved. The central government has also gradually introduced autonomy measures, removing the requirement that the National Assembly approve provincial budgets, and giving provinces more authority over lower levels. Pilot programs have also accorded some urban areas greater autonomy. However, these elements may reflect the conservatism of a highly centralized government in a one-party state more than a strategic effort to decentralize.

Building Subnational Capacity

As chapter 1 notes, capacity building is an important part of any decentralization strategy. This is true not only for subnational governments but also for central agencies, which must learn new ways of doing business and new skills in developing local systems, strengthening subnational actors, and monitoring the implementation of decentralization. Although most East Asian countries have relied on technical assistance and provided training to central employees involved in decentralization, they have paid limited attention to ensuring that national staff can meet their shifting obligations and to realign relationships in the way required.

Local level capacity building under decentralization is generally of two types. The first type involves training to ensure that subnational staff can perform their technical functions. The second type involves building governance mechanisms that are required for a decentralized system to work effectively. Either of these two types can be supply-driven (by the central government) or demand-driven (by subnational governments). The latter type is considered good practice based on the recognition that a lack of demand for reforms and the capacity needed to make them work undermines their chances of being realized and sustained. Most countries in the region have focused on traditional supply-driven technical capacity building, and most governance training has also been supply-driven (table 2.14).

Cambodia faces the greatest challenges. Capacity is weak in many communes, which had no real functions before the first elections in 2002, even as part of provincial administrations. Regions that participated in the Seila Program developed reasonable capacity, but other communes generally lag far behind. Even Seila communes must adjust to new systems and procedures under official decentralization policy, posing significant challenges. The Ministry of Interior and the Ministry of Economy and Finance have conducted most commune-level training, and technical staff at the provincial level help communes implement new procedures. This training, however, has barely laid a foundation, and much work remains at both the commune and

TABLE 2.14 Building Decentralization Capacity

Country	Capacity-building provisions
Cambodia	Massive, basic program run by central government for developing commune system.
China	No specific decentralization-related training; most is organized at subnational level; some temporary posting of higher-level staff to lower levels.
Indonesia	Significant transfer of staff to lower levels; much capacity building driven by central government, although some demand from lower levels.
Philippines	Significant transfer of staff to lower levels; subnational governments responsible for training, which typically focuses on councilors rather than civil servants.
Thailand	Some transfer of staff to lower levels; subnational capacity building driven by national agencies.
Vietnam	Training programs for subnational staff driven by central government.

Source: Compiled by the author from multiple sources.

higher levels. Deepening and institutionalizing capacity takes time, and the prominent role of donors in providing and financing decentralization capacity-building efforts in Cambodia raises concerns about sustainability.

Subnational governments elsewhere in the region have greater capacity, but the levels and mechanisms for building it vary. In China, where decentralization is not official policy, capacity building has focused on improving overall government performance. All ministries and departments receive an annual training budget, and most training is organized locally. The central government also posts its own mid-career staff to subnational administrations for six months to a year, which may boost the capacity of those governments. Although Vietnam has also long been heavily centralized, its decentralization program is more formal. Subnational capacity is generally strongest in provinces and larger cities. Staff from higher levels of government provide most training of subnational staff. Neither China nor Vietnam has made training of citizens to interact with local governments a priority.

In Indonesia, the Philippines, and Thailand, local governments have benefited from the transfer of higher-level staff. Indonesia has decentralized more than 2 million officials since 1999. The Philippines transferred some 70,000 employees from central ministries to local governments following the Local Government Code of 1991. Given its more incremental approach to decentralization, Thailand has made more limited transfers involving about 4,000 central employees so far. In all these cases, the help local governments receive is not always the type they need. Capacity levels vary widely within these countries and are generally higher in urban areas, with significant gaps in smaller urban and rural areas. In Indonesia and Thailand, higher-level agencies drive local capacity building. In the Philippines, local governments are formally responsible for building capacity, but training focuses on councilors rather than staff, and the central government, international agencies, and NGOs often assist with the provision of such training.

Summary and Conclusions

The various historical and political roots of decentralization in East Asia are reflected in the observed diversity in the paths it has taken, the enabling frameworks that define it, and the ways in which it is structured. In Indonesia and the Philippines, the focus quickly shifted from deconcentration to decentralization, and this is happening in Thailand as well. The focus remains on deconcentration in China and Vietnam, but there are emerging elements of delegation and devolution. Cambodia makes a stark division between deconcentration and devolution. Within their basic policy thrust, all countries have multiple tiers of government or administration, but exact forms and responsibilities vary. In Thailand, most levels have a role, while the focus has been on provinces and urban governments in China and Vietnam. In Cambodia, Indonesia, and the Philippines, subprovincial units have been the main targets of decentralization reforms.

Decentralization enabling frameworks differ significantly. The Philippines and Thailand have robust constitutional and legal foundations, and Indonesia adopted constitutional reforms to institutionalize decentralization. Indonesia and Vietnam have legal frameworks, although not fully developed. Weaker laws underpin the system in Cambodia, but additional legislation is in process. China has the weakest framework, with only a few laws that refer to subnational roles. The nature and degree of development of the enabling framework do not seem to affect decentralization progress or quality, but all countries eventually need to define the roles of relevant actors in a framework that protects their rights and provides a basis for accountability.

Although far from complete, governance is improving in the region through political, institutional, and fiscal decentralization reforms. All countries considered here have subnational elections, ranging from Vietnam at all levels to Cambodia at one level. Subnational councils usually have an element of direct election, but in some cases there are higher-level appointments or party list voting. In the Philippines, council leadership is directly elected, and this will soon occur in Indonesia and Thailand. Political competition varies from one-party states in China and Vietnam to the nearly chaotic multiparty system of Indonesia. Cambodia has multiple parties, but one dominates, while political competition is somewhat more robust in the Philippines and Thailand.

Autonomy differs in complex ways across countries. Thailand and Vietnam have higher-level controls over subnational budgeting and personnel decisions, although they are not always exercised and are being relaxed. Philippine subnational governments are more independent in principle, if not always in practice, while new laws curtail autonomy in Indonesia. On transparency, the Philippines and Thailand provide extensive public access to subnational budgets and minimally acceptable auditing, while China and Vietnam do not. Incorporating citizen input into local decisions is a priority only in a few cases, and civil society varies, from relatively free and robust in the Philippines to heavily controlled in China and Vietnam.

Expenditure and revenue assignments vary considerably. In most cases there is some formal assignment, but details typically need clarification. In the Philippines and Indonesia, the process is substantially or moderately advanced. Cambodia has a very long way to go, and China has no clear interest in formalizing assignments. Own-source revenues are generally weak, so subnational governments rely heavily on shared taxes and intergovernmental transfers. In China, Thailand, and Vietnam, national taxes are shared on a tax-by-tax basis, often by origin. In Indonesia and the Philippines, most shared revenues are pooled into a consolidated fund for distribution as a formula-based transfer. Cambodia has little formal tax sharing; provinces are funded primarily through national sectoral budgets, and the commune transfer pool is determined on an ad hoc basis. Transfers vary widely in significance, structure, complexity, and transparency. China's system is highly complex and nontransparent. Other countries have somewhat simpler and more transparent systems, especially for general revenue sharing, but there are commonly less transparent conditional transfers, often for capital expenditures.

Although often neglected, the institutional structures and processes for defining and managing decentralization are critical for success. In most East Asian countries, decentralization is primarily overseen by regular government agencies. Special decentralization bodies exist in some countries, but their composition and role differs. Indonesia has a high-level policy body that influences major design decisions. An interministerial body in the Philippines has primary responsibility only for monitoring implementation. Interministerial bodies in Cambodia and Thailand play broader roles in both design and implementation. In no case are coordination or enforcement of decentralization activities adequate.

Many decentralization problems result from the lack of an implementation strategy. Given China's context, the conspicuous lack of strategy is understandable. Both Indonesia and Cambodia are struggling to deal with the consequences of poor planning prior to rapid, politically driven decentralization. The Philippines, Thailand, and Vietnam have more considered implementation strategies, with articulated phases and timelines. In the Philippines, the final phase of the 1991 decentralization effort is in process, but the phasing does not seem to have been systematically followed, and problems persist. Vietnam, out of an abundance of caution expected in a centralized one-party system, has moved in an atypically structured way. Thailand has a well-articulated strategy, but implementation has been slow. None of these countries has a clear strategy in the sense of using graduated, asymmetric functional assignments and capacity-building support consistent with the performance of individual local governments.

Political factors elaborated in chapter 1 complicate the development of decentralization frameworks and strategies, and the pitfalls of trying to be too normatively comprehensive in designing and implementing decentralization are well known. It is also clear, however, that the costs of ignoring the problems that have often emerged as decentralization has unfolded in East Asia are potentially very high. With a basic decentralization vision and a degree of leadership, East Asian countries should find it possible to accommodate political realities and strategically use opportunities to build more effective decentralization frameworks, structures, processes, and outcomes. This is the significant challenge facing all countries in the region.

Endnote

1. The information in this chapter is largely derived from country reviews prepared as background papers for this volume. These and other key country-specific citations are included in the references at the end of the chapter. David Gomez Alvarez supplied considerable research assistance for this chapter. Some data and clarifications on particular countries were provided by Robert Ebel, Amanda Green, Bert Hofman, Kai Kaiser, Blane Lewis, Ed Mountfield, Amitabha Mukherjee, Duvvuri Subbarao, Rob Taliercio, Dana Weist, Roland White, and Christine Wong.

Bibliography

Alm, James, and Roy Bahl. 1999. "Decentralization in Indonesia: Prospects and Problems." Atlanta, GA: Georgia State University, Andrew Young School of Policy Studies. www.gsu.edu/~wwwsps/publications/1999/990601_IndonesiaReport.pdf.

Alm, James, Jorge Martínez-Vázquez, and Sri Mulyani Indrawati, eds. 2004. *Reforming Intergovernmental Fiscal Relations and the Rebuilding of Indonesia.* Cheltenham, UK, and Northampton, MA: Edward Elgar Press.

Bird, Richard, Jennie Litvack, and M. Govinda Rao. 1995. "Intergovernmental Fiscal Relations and Poverty Alleviation in Vietnam." Washington, DC: World Bank.

Brilliantes, Alex. 2003. "EAP Flagship Country Review of Decentralization in the Philippines." Washington, DC: World Bank.

Hofman, Bert, and Kai Kaiser. 2004. "The Making of the Big Bang and Its Aftermath: A Political Economy Perspective." In *Reforming Intergovernmental Fiscal Relations and the Rebuilding of Indonesia.* Ed. James Alm, Jorge Martínez-Vázquez, and Sri Mulyani, Indrawati. Cheltenham, UK, and Northampton, MA: Edward Elgar Press.

Hofman, Bert, and Kai Kaiser. Forthcoming. "Decentralization, Democratic Transition, and Local Governance in Indonesia." In *Decentralization in Developing Countries: A Comparative Perspective,* eds. D. Mookkerjee and P. Bardham.

Hutchcroft, Paul D. 2003. "State Formation, State Reformation: Deciphering Decentralization in the Philippines and Thailand." Working Paper. Madison, WI: University of Wisconsin, Department of Political Science.

Iszatt, Nina T. n.d. "Legislating for Citizens' Participation in Local Governance: The Philippines Experience." www.ipd.ph/logolinksea/resources/Frameworks%20Phil%20experience.pdf.

King, Dwight Y. 2004. "Political Reforms, Decentralization, and Democratic Consolidation in Indonesia." In *Reforming Intergovernmental Fiscal Relations and the Rebuilding of Indonesia.* Ed. James Alm, Jorge Martínez-Vázquez, and Sri Mulyani, Indrawati. Cheltenham, UK, and Northampton, MA: Edward Elgar Press.

Lewis, Blane D. 2002. "Indonesia." In *Intergovernmental Fiscal Transfers in Asia: Current Practice and Challenges for the Future,* eds. Paul Smoke and Yun-Hwan Kim. Manila: Asian Development Bank.

Lewis, Blane D. 2003a. "Property Taxation in Indonesia: Measuring and Explaining Administrative (Under-) Performance." *Public Administration and Development* 23 (3): 227–39.

———. 2003b. "Tax and Charge Creation by Regional Governments under Fiscal Decentralization: Estimates and Explanations." *Bulletin of Indonesian Economic Studies* 39 (2): 177–97.

Lewis, Blane D. 2004. "Indonesian Local Government Spending, Taxing and Saving: An Explanation of Pre- and Post-Decentralization Outcomes." Jakarta: World Bank.

Lewis, Blane D., and Jasmin Chakeri. 2004. "Decentralized Local Government Budgets in Indonesia." Jakarta: World Bank.

Liang, Sharon. 2003. "Walking the Tightrope: Civil Society Organizations in China." *China Rights Forum* 3. iso.hrichina.org/download_repository/2/Sharon%20Liang.pdf.

Logo Link Southeast Asia. n.d. "Learning Initiative on Citizen Participation and Local Governance." www.ipd.ph/logolinksea/index.html.

Martínez-Vázquez, Jorge, and James Alm, eds. Forthcoming. *Reforming Intergovernmental Fiscal Relations and the Rebuilding of Indonesia.* Cheltenham, UK, and Northampton, MA: Edward Elgar Press.

McLure, Charles E., Jr., and Jorge Martinez-Vazquez. 1998. "Intergovernmental Fiscal Relations in Vietnam." Working Paper 98–2. Atlanta, GA: Georgia State University, Andrew Young School of Policy Studies. isp-ysps.gsu.edu/papers/ispwp9802.pdf.

Nghieu, B.D. 2003. "EAP Flagship Country Review of Decentralization in Vietnam." Washington, DC: World Bank.

Rasyid, M. Ryaas. 2004. "The Policy of Decentralization in Indonesia." In *Reforming Intergovernmental Fiscal Relations and the Rebuilding of Indonesia.* Ed. James Alm, Jorge Martínez-Vázquez, and Sri Mulyani, Indrawati. Cheltenham, UK, and Northampton, MA: Edward Elgar Press.

Rocamora, Joel. 2003. "Legal and Policy Framework for 'Participation' in Southeast Asia." www.ids.ac.uk/logolink/resources/downloads/regionalreports/RegionalReportSouthEast Asia%20final.pdf.

Sidik, Machfud, and Kadjatmiko. 2004. "Combining Expenditure Assignment, Revenue Assignment and Grant Design in Indonesia's Fiscal Decentralization." In *Reforming Intergovernmental Fiscal Relations and the Rebuilding of Indonesia.* Ed. James Alm, Jorge Martínez-Vázquez, and Sri Mulyani, Indrawati. Cheltenham, UK, and Northampton, MA: Edward Elgar Press.

Smoke, Paul. 2002. "Decentralization and Deconcentration in Cambodia." Background paper prepared for *Cambodia Integrated Fiduciary Assessment and Public Expenditure Review.* Washington, DC: World Bank.

Smoke, Paul. 2004. "Expenditure Assignment under Indonesia's Decentralization: A Review of Progress and Issues for the Future." In *Reforming Intergovernmental Fiscal Relations and the Rebuilding of Indonesia.* Ed. James Alm, Jorge Martínez-Vázquez, and Sri Mulyani, Indrawati. Cheltenham, UK, and Northampton, MA: Edward Elgar Press.

Smoke, Paul, and Yun-Hwan Kim. 2002. *Intergovernmental Fiscal Transfers in Asia: Current Practice and Challenges for the Future.* Manila: Asian Development Bank.

Suwanmala, Charas. 2003. "EAP Flagship Country Review of Decentralization in Thailand." Washington, DC: World Bank.

Wong, Christine. 2003. "EAP Flagship Country Review of Decentralization in the People's Republic of China." Washington, DC: World Bank.

Wong, Susan, and Scott Guggenheim. 2003. "Community-Driven Development and Decentralization in the East Asia Region." Washington, DC: World Bank.

World Bank. 2000a. "Thailand Public Finance Review: Public Finance in Transition." Washington, DC: World Bank.

———. 2000b. "Vietnam Public Expenditure Review: Managing Public Resources Better." Washington, DC: World Bank.

———. 2001. "The Filipino Report Card on Pro-Poor Services." Process case studies. www.worldbank.org/participation/Filipino%20Reportcard.htm.

———. 2002a. "China Sub-National Expenditure Review." Washington, DC: World Bank.

———. 2002b. "Implementing Decentralization in Thailand: The Way Forward." Washington, DC: World Bank.

———. 2002c. "Vietnam: Delivering on Its Promise." Washington, DC: World Bank. www.worldbank.org.vn/topic/vdr2003.htm.

———. 2003a. "Cambodia Integrated Fiduciary Assessment and Public Expenditure Review." Washington, DC: World Bank.

———. 2003b. "Cambodia Poverty Reduction Strategy Paper." Washington, DC: World Bank.

———. 2003c. "Cambodia Rural Investment and Local Governance Project." Washington, DC: World Bank.

———. 2003d. "Decentralizing Indonesia: Regional Public Expenditure Review." Washington, DC: World Bank.

———. 2003e. "Indonesia Public Expenditure Review: Fiscal Challenges in a New Era." Washington, DC: World Bank.

———. 2003f. "Philippines: Decentralization and Service Delivery: From Promise to Performance." Washington, DC: World Bank.

———. 2003g. "Philippines: Improving Government Performance—Discipline, Efficiency, and Equity in Managing Public Resources." Washington, DC: World Bank.

———. n.d. "Participation and Civic Engagement in Poverty Reduction Strategy. Washington, DC: World Bank. www.worldbank.org/participation/PRSP/alp.htm.

———. n.d. "Vietnam Process Case Study." Washington, DC: World Bank. www.worldbank.org/participation/web/webfiles/vietnam.htm.

Ye, Zhang. 2003. "China's Emerging Civil Society." Washington, DC: Brookings Institution. www.brook.edu/fp/cnaps/papers/ye2003.htm.

3

ACHIEVING FISCAL SUSTAINABILITY

Sudarshan Gooptu

A well-designed system for fiscal decentralization promises many benefits, including enhanced economic growth and macroeconomic stability. If, however, decentralization is designed badly or implemented and monitored improperly, such a system can foster "soft" budget constraints—loosened controls on the fiscal activities of subnational governments—that may undercut the spectacular economic growth occurring in East Asia today.

This chapter highlights the challenges of decentralization in the context of macroeconomic management, especially in achieving fiscal sustainability and providing a medium-term environment for sustained growth. The focus is twofold. First, the chapter highlights the critical need for central governments to monitor subnational fiscal and quasi-fiscal activities through well-designed reporting, auditing, and financial management institutions, as well as information databases. Second, the chapter addresses the need to institutionalize incentives for subnational governments to publicly and regularly report relevant financial information.

Most East Asian countries are at the early stages of this twofold process. Unless the process keeps pace with decentralization, the result will be subnational arrears and pressures for central bailouts—the latter occurring through ad hoc financial transfers, or accounting "adjustments" that take significant tax and spending activity off-budget. Once countries abandon the discipline of hard budget constraints, systematic budget planning and execution at central and subnational levels will yield to uncertain intergovernmental flows, capricious revenue policies, and a lack of medium-term fiscal planning.

Much is at stake in getting this decentralization system right. East Asian countries have recovered rapidly from the 1997 financial crisis, posting high growth rates. Regional output grew by 6.7 percent in 2002 and 7.9 percent in 2003 and an estimated 7.8 percent in 2004. Growth is expected to reach 7.1 percent in 2005—the strongest record since the start of the global and regional recession in late 2000. The number of people living below US$2 per day is estimated to have fallen to around 34 percent in 2004, amounting to some 636 million people—down from 50 percent as recently as 1999, representing 890 million people (World Bank 2004, 2005 table 1.1).

The policy challenge for each country is to maintain its high growth rate while strengthening its fiscal health through intergovernmental coordination and monitoring. Unfortunately, this task is far from straightforward. For a start, whether developing countries experience a causal relationship between decentralization, macroeconomic stability, and economic growth is unclear. The reasons are twofold. First, the data for measuring the extent to which a country has fiscally decentralized are simply not available—a worldwide problem that also exists in East Asia. Second, the line is not always clear between formal and informal institutional arrangements for enforcing hard budget constraints. Even if the right data and definition were available to measure decentralization, tracking fiscal risks can be difficult when subnational governments have hidden, off-budget expenses and funds, as in some East Asian countries.

Still, the elements of responsible fiscal management, and the criteria for maintaining fiscal discipline in a decentralizing environment, are well known. This chapter therefore focuses on empirical conclusions regarding the links between fiscal decentralization and growth, the role of budget constraints in fostering fiscal discipline, the relationship between subnational borrowing and a country's overall fiscal sustainability, and the resulting need for managing financial risk.

Links between Fiscal Decentralization and Economic Growth

In theory, devolving fiscal responsibilities can improve public sector efficiency, boost competition among subnational governments in delivering public services, and stimulate economic growth (Bird and Wallich 1993). These potential benefits reflect the belief that subnational governments can best make growth-promoting public expenditures in sectors such as education, health, and infrastructure, because they have better information on local circumstances and interregional differences (Oates 1993).[1]

East Asia's spectacular precrisis growth and postcrisis rebound have depended significantly on prudent macroeconomic management. However, empirical research has been inconclusive regarding any causal relationship between decentralization and growth in developing countries.

In a study of 46 countries from 1970 to 1989, Davoodi and Zou (1998) found a negative relationship between fiscal decentralization and economic growth in developing countries, and no relationship in developed countries.[2] The authors explain that "conventional wisdom points towards positive growth effects of capital and infrastructure spending and negative growth effects of welfare and current spending." This implies that in developing countries where subnational entities spend a larger proportion of their budgets on wages and salaries and social welfare—decentralized systems exhibit slower long-term growth per capita.[3] The time frame for assessing the impact of different types of public spending is also important. Analysts see health and education spending, for example, as an investment in human capital with a long-term payoff, resembling physical investment.[4]

Ebel and Yilmaz (2003) reproduced this analysis by weighing degrees of revenue autonomy. They found that tax autonomy and nontax autonomy have a positive correlation with economic growth, while tax sharing has a negative relationship (see chapter 6). These results suggest that a country's economic performance partly reflects the degree to which subnational governments control their revenues.

In a study of the United States, Xie et al. (1999) showed that further fiscal decentralization with the aim of boosting efficiency and economic growth would in fact harm growth. Akai and Sakata (2002) refuted that finding, incorporating a more elaborate definition of fiscal decentralization. Their study examined the growth impact of giving subnational governments the authority to raise taxes and spend public funds.[5] Since local governments do not necessarily spend locally collected revenues locally, the authors found that they may not in fact have tax autonomy (Zhang and Zou 2001).

Martinez-Vazquez and McNab (2001) confirmed the inconclusive relationship between fiscal decentralization and economic growth and the importance of individual country circumstances—including noneconomic ones—in determining causality. Lin and Liu's analysis of China (2000), using provincial-level data from 1970 to 1993, suggests that fiscal decentralization has helped spur that country's impressive growth over the past 20 or 30 years.[6] However, Zhang and Zou (2001) found a negative relationship between fiscal decentralization and economic growth in China.[7]

Subnational Fiscal Discipline and Budget Constraints

Determining the degree of fiscal discipline among subnational governments in East Asia requires identifying the budget constraints they face. Doing so in countries like Cambodia—where subnational governments have little spending and revenue authority and rely almost entirely on transfers from the center—is relatively easy. At the other extreme, about half or more of the resources available to China's subnational governments come from off-budget sources, over which they have virtually total control.[8] In Vietnam, off-budget accounts such as the Social Security Fund, the Health Insurance Fund, and the National Development Fund constrain the budget autonomy of subnational governments.

In some East Asian countries, state-owned enterprises at the subnational level receive off-budget resources in the form of deferred taxes or arrears accruals on debt service and other contractual payments. This is a particular concern in China and Vietnam. In Thailand, this problem is mitigated by the fact that subnational governments do not typically own enterprises, and by the inclusion of all state-owned enterprises in the "consolidated public sector's" budgetary accounts.

Extrabudgetary revenues and expenditures among subnational authorities make their true budget constraints difficult to ascertain. This is especially problematic when data are not reported in a timely manner and are often incomplete, as in most East Asian countries. Thus, when governments rely substantially on extrabudgetary funds, national budgets give only a partial picture of fiscal realities.

Enforcing hard budget constraints among subnational governments requires clear expenditure assignments, formula-based transfer systems, local revenues, prudent subnational borrowing rules, and good financial reporting (see box 1.3 in chapter 1). None of the East Asian countries examined here meet these prerequisites. Such a situation can lead to perverse incentives to overspend, accumulate arrears, and overborrow. Key among such incentives is the prevailing practice of higher-level financial bailouts for subnational governments that are already in or even heading toward default. This is of particular concern if the subnational government is large, as is often the case with soft budget constraints.[9]

A country's system of intergovernmental fiscal management (or lack thereof) may also motivate subnational authorities to keep their transactions off-budget—especially richer provinces that do not want to cede part of their revenue base to the center for tax sharing. Effective fiscal decentralization requires an institutional structure that minimizes such adverse expectations. In China, "fee-to-tax" reforms aim to bring some off-budget subnational revenues within the budgetary umbrella, but much remains to be done in most East Asian countries. Information on these quasifiscal transactions remains weak, and work on improving this information base is just beginning, even in China.

Finally, subnational governments in many countries have faced difficulties in planning their activities and managing their finances owing to delays in allocation decisions and a lack of predictability regarding intergovernmental transfers. In Thailand, other than knowing with certainty that their nongrant revenues will equal those of the previous fiscal year, local governments find it difficult to predict their shared tax revenue allocations. This is mainly due to delays in establishing the criteria for distributing the allocations from the center to local governments.[10]

Subnational Borrowing and Fiscal Sustainability

Fiscal sustainability means that a subnational government covers its expenditures out of its own revenues, reducing its dependence on borrowing and transfers from the center (Bird 2003). To determine whether a subnational government's plans are fiscally sustainable, analysts need accurate information on revenues and expenditures at the central, regional, and local levels. Analysts also need to understand the interplay between intergovernmental grants and government borrowing—that is, how hard the subnational budget constraint truly is. Careful analysis of country-specific intergovernmental relations, and the resulting incentive framework, should accompany any analysis of fiscal sustainability.

Subnational governments in most of the East Asian countries examined here rely heavily on intergovernmental transfers. The large bailouts during the 1997 financial crisis and since, such as the recent recapitalization of Chinese state-owned banks in 2004, have undermined fiscal sustainability in East Asia by softening the budget constraints imposed on subnational governments. Discretionary transfers to deficit subnational governments in China, Indonesia, and Vietnam, and unclear assignment of responsibilities throughout the region, have compounded this result.

Many subnational governments in East Asia also have access to onlending from the central government and donors. Such lending is typically in the form of sovereign guaranteed external loans that the central government contracts but channels to subnational entities at different interest rates. Onlending interest rates and terms vary across countries. In China, the final borrower bears the entire foreign-exchange risk associated with these loans, while in other countries the center assumes some or all of this risk. Most subnational borrowing in Indonesia has occurred through central government onlending mechanisms on terms that are highly favorable to the center. However, the repayment record of Indonesian subnational borrowers has been poor.[11] Thailand allows subnational governments to borrow from domestic banks and bond markets, subject to legal ceilings in any given budget year. In Indonesia, the Ministry of Finance sets the aggregate limits to regional borrowing for a particular fiscal year in August of the previous year, and no direct borrowing from foreign sources is permitted. Instead, all such borrowing occurs through onlending arrangements with the ministry. Subnational governments in Vietnam may not borrow at all (see table 3.1).

International experience since the early 1980s, especially in Latin America, suggests that without appropriate accountability and transparency mechanisms, decentralization can encourage dangerous opportunistic behavior by state and local authorities. If left unchecked, such opportunism could undermine macroeconomic stability. The most vivid manifestation of this phenomenon is the softening of subnational budget constraints (Rodden 2000a; World Bank 2002). Avoiding this risk depends on the ability of the central government to prevent subnational authorities from passing their liabilities to higher-level governments.[12] This, in turn, requires institutional mechanisms to discipline borrowing by state and local governments.

Examining experiences in Argentina, Brazil, and India, Rodden et al. (2003) show that unsustainable subnational deficits emerge when provinces have powerful representatives, when they depend heavily on intergovernmental transfers, and when they have autonomous access to sources of deficit financing. The latter can include bonds, loans from domestic banks (which may themselves be state-owned, as in China), nonpayment of employee wages, and contingent liabilities. If these exist where the central government cannot commit to a no-bailout policy, or cannot limit subnational borrowing, subnational governments have incentives to run unsustainable deficits.

Fiscal, political, and financial institutions that strengthen competition at the local level, especially for capital, can promote hard budget constraints.[13] If institutions directly or indirectly suggest that the central government will step in to cover subnational liabilities in the case of default, they may encourage subnational governments to "overborrow, overspend, or undertax" (Rodden 2000a).

The Latin American experience suggests that subnational governments that are subject to hard budget constraints are more likely to tax and spend prudently (Bird 2001). Fiscal sustainability is also a forward-looking concept, in that it requires accurate assumptions about revenues and expenditures and key economic variables. Making meaningful assumptions that are palatable to policy makers and their constituents requires a good understanding of institutional and country-specific details.

In Indonesia, for instance, only after it passed Laws 22 and 25 on intergovernmental fiscal relations in 1999 and issued implementing regulations (PP107) in 2000 could regions borrow without strict approval from the center.[14] Subnational domestic borrowing is now subject to a rule-based approach and central government approval. Foreign borrowing is not allowed, except through onlending from the central government or donors.

In view of Indonesia's public debt burden, however, and as the country establishes local financial management structures, a ministerial decree temporarily banned any subnational borrowing until the intergovernmental fiscal relations Law 25/99 was revised. This ban has been in effect since 2000 but was to be lifted at the end of fiscal year 2004, after the implementation regulations of the revised Law 25 are in place. The goal is to maintain fiscal discipline by strengthening both market and rule-based mechanisms—highlighting the fact that countries may sometimes require strong, centrally imposed fiscal constraints, especially in the early stages of decentralization. Subnational governments may rely on short-term borrowing (with maturities of less than 12 months) to manage their cash flow. In theory, as in China, the Indonesian central government can intercept general grant funds if a region fails to meet its debt service obligations.

TABLE 3.1 Subnational Borrowing Practices

Summary of practices	Cambodia	China	Indonesia	Philippines	Thailand	Vietnam
Borrowing power and practices (excluding borrowing from central government)	LGs cannot borrow. Stipulated according to central government regulations.	LGs may not borrow against general revenues or issue bonds. LGs can and do borrow through asset-holding or project companies.	LGs can borrow or issue bonds in domestic market subject to rules and central government approval. Temporary freeze on all borrowing up to 2005.	LGs can borrow or issue bonds; some prudential restrictions.	LGs cannot borrow, domestically or from abroad, without prior approval from CG.	Provinces and cities with provincial status can borrow within prudential limits and as approved by CG.
Borrowing from the government/ donor onlending	LGs may not borrow.	Borrowing by LG (mainly special service units) from China Development Bank; commercial bank loans to "off-budget" funds.	LGs borrow mainly from CG through donor onlending and from budget. 50% of latter loans in arrears; 63% of loans to LGs in arrears. New onlending terms being negotiated. Under new PP107, CG can intercept DAU.	LGs borrow exclusively from government financial institutions; largely donor onlending. GFIs monopolize depository bank business, so de facto IRA intercept has led to good LG repayment history. Terms of onlending loans by GFI to be in line with those of local commercial banks, but in practice GFI often sets a lower rate.	LGs not allowed to borrow without prior approval from CG.	

(Continued)

TABLE 3.1 (continued)

Summary of practices	Cambodia	China	Indonesia	Philippines	Thailand	Vietnam
Banking sector	Not much banking sector–related activity; basically a cash economy. Most banks foreign-owned. National Bank of Cambodia opened dollar-denominated accounts for commercial banks in 1998; deposits with the bank are remunerated at 7/8 of SIBOR.	LG-owned companies borrow primarily from commercial banks, mostly 3–5 years; sometimes 10. Interest rates regulated by PBC. Banking sector is burdened by high rate (40%) of nonperforming loans; concern for the ability of LG companies to depend on rollover of bank loans.	LGs borrow short term from banks to cover cash flow. Banking sector still under restructuring; 22 of 27 BPDs recapitalized.	Private commercial bank lending to LGs virtually nonexistent. Land Bank of the Philippines, the largest provider of credit to LGs, now uses its own resources (as well as donor funds): 5 years. Privatized Philippines National Bank still lends to LGs (eligible to be an LG depository): 4–7 years. New GFI players in LG credit.	LGs are only now exploring opportunities to borrow from local commercial banks and public revolving funds. LGs mainly borrow from local development funds monitored by Ministry of Interior.	LG-owned companies borrow from banks to finance infrastructure projects. Commercial banks purchased HCMC private placement bond. Gradual liberalization of interest rate since 1996; State Bank of Vietnam (SBV) removed lending-rate ceiling. SBV launched banking-sector restructuring program in 2001, phasing in SOCB recapitalization.

Capital markets	LG-owned companies cannot issue bonds. Credit to the private sector is 7 percent of GDP, loans are mostly short term. Mainly providing import/export financing and working capital to trade and service sectors.	Defaults of municipal bonds in early 1990s led to ban on LG bond issuance. LG companies issue bonds (Shanghai: 8 years); strict procedures for the issuing corporate bonds (single A or better for issues greater than Y 100 million).	6 LG banks: West Java, East Java, Central Java, North Sulawesi, West Sumatra, and PT Bank DKI issued 12 bonds (1991–2000); 3–7 years.	13 LG bond issues since 1991: 4 issues guaranteed by Home Guarantee Corp. (government agency), 8 issues guaranteed by LGUGC; mostly 7-year. LGUGC established in 1998, owned 51% by Bankers Association and 49% by Development Bank of the Philippines.	LGs cannot go directly to capital markets. Debt financing by LGs has been limited (some revenue bonds issued).	HCMC issued GO bonds in 1995 (D 30 billion, 3-year, private placement) for toll-road project; is preparing another. (Decree 93/2001 allowed HCMC bond issuance.) Ministry of Finance approval required for bond issues; market-rate pricing unlikely. HCMC Securities Exchange established in 2000; bond is 10% of transaction volume; the Hanoi exchange opened in early 2005.
Monitoring of local government credit	Financial accounting centralized in National Treasury and provincial branches. Main financial statement for LG expenditure management produced by Ministry of Finance Budget Dept.	Government financial information system being piloted. LG credit not assessed. Credit-rating agencies exist.	Regional financial information system being prepared; Ministry of Finance starts mapping LG fiscal capacity?	Ministry of Finance pilots new system for LG fiscal/ financing reporting. GFI appraises central government transfer and LG tax base. LGUGC has internal credit-rating system.	Ministry of Information monitors subnational borrowing from local development funds and public revolving funds.	Central budget guidelines. City budget information not disclosed. SOCB evaluates large-scale projects.

Source: World Bank.

Note: BPD = state-owned commercial banks; DAU = *dana alokasi unam,* the main intergovernmental fiscal transfer mechanism in Indonesia; HCMC = Ho Chi Minh City; GO = government order; IRA = Internal Revenue Allotment; PBC = People's Bank of China; LG = local government; CG = central government; GFI = government financial institution; LGUGC = local government unit guarantee corp.; SOCB = state-owned commercial bank.

In Thailand, local governments may borrow domestically and internationally, with prior authorization from the cabinet. These governments may issue debt securities and borrow from official, external bilateral creditors for development projects. In practice, local debt financing is somewhat limited, including from domestic capital markets. The primary source of borrowing has been local development funds managed by the Ministry of Interior. Subnational governments have more recently borrowed from commercial banks and public revolving funds.

In Vietnam, subnational governments may not run fiscal deficits. Provinces may borrow, but only domestically, by issuing project investment bonds, or by borrowing from the Development Assistance Fund.[15] Provinces may use these funds only for projects with prior approval from the Provincial People's Council under the five-year provincial Public Investment Plan. The province must also allocate funds for debt service in future budgets until the debt matures.[16] Local state-owned enterprises that provide essential services, such as waste disposal, water, electricity, and transportation, may borrow from both external and domestic sources. All external borrowing is subject to approval by the central government, which provides a sovereign guarantee.

To promote responsible subnational borrowing, some East Asian governments have disseminated well-defined, transparent fiscal rules. The rationale is that all borrowing decisions should take into account the fiscal implications for future generations.[17] The issue of implementation remains to be addressed, however.

In Indonesia, regulations implementing the decentralization framework limit the debt-to-revenue ratio to 75 percent of the previous year's general revenue, and the debt service-to-revenue ratio to 40 percent in any given budget year. Regulations also govern onlending to the regions.[18] In the Philippines, the central government limits transfers to local governments to 40 percent of their *internal* revenues from three years before.[19] Since the ratio of revenue to gross domestic product has been falling, this rule implies that some local governments may receive higher transfers than intended, or than the central government can afford. Declining trade taxes also build upward bias into the revenue share of local governments. If policy makers do not intend such an outcome, or if local governments do not use the allocated resources efficiently, the resulting trends will undermine fiscal sustainability.

For such rules to be credible and sustainable, they must be part of a well-articulated fiscal framework that improves the government's position over the long term. Such a framework includes clear intergovernmental fiscal relations, appropriate subnational tax structures, and public pensions.[20] The central government needs to clearly define accountability and establish financial management practices to enforce these rules.[21] In fact, the temporary ban on subnational borrowing in Indonesia is a prudent interim measure until the country establishes a more solid framework for regional borrowing and a regional financial information system. A more solid framework for subnational borrowing must include procedures for handling regional default. Otherwise, without a credible legal or regulatory threat, the center will end up paying the bill.[22]

Managing Fiscal Risks

Rules and administrative controls can help reduce the risks of subnational borrowing. Key measures include strengthening the intergovernmental fiscal system and, when the situation warrants, requiring ex ante authorization and ex post monitoring. For instance, the central government could set annual limits on the debt of individual local governments, review individual loans, including their terms and conditions, and centralize all borrowing, with onlending to local governments.[23] Other measures to encourage fiscally sustainable borrowing include prohibiting subnational authorities from issuing guarantees (see table 3.2 for the kinds of explicit and implicit guarantee mechanisms that may exist at subnational levels), and imposing ceilings on the net worth or loan portfolio of borrowers. Indonesia and Thailand have established ceilings on debt or debt service as a share of local revenues. Other countries, such as Vietnam, require local governments to balance their budgets and restrict their borrowing to specific purposes, such as capital investment.

Countries can also rely on the market to regulate subnational borrowing. A market-based system requires minimum legal and regulatory structures,

TABLE 3.2 Subnational Fiscal Risks

Liabilities	Direct (obligation in any event)	Contingent (obligation if a particular event occurs)
Explicit Government liability is recognized by law or contract.	Local government debt. Arrears (if legally binding). Nondiscretionary budgetary spending.	Local government provides guarantees for debt and other obligations of financial and nonfinancial enterprises and other entities. Local government insurance schemes (such as crop insurance).
Implicit A "moral" obligation on the part of the government that mainly reflects public expectations and pressure by interest groups.	Capital and recurrent costs of local public investment projects. The cost of future benefits under local social security schemes.	Claims arising from local government letters of comfort. Claims by failing local financial institutions and other entities. Claims related to enterprise restructuring and privatization. Claims by beneficiaries of failed social security or other funds, beyond any guaranteed limits. Claims related to local crisis management, such as public health, environment, and disaster relief.

Source: Brixi and Mody 2002.

such as supervision and disclosure practices; guidelines for issuing, settling, and repaying debt; bankruptcy procedures (including creditor remedies); protection against disruption of essential public services; and measures to prevent moral hazard. East Asian countries are only now establishing these institutional structures.

Another market instrument for reducing the credit risk of subnational borrowing is regular monitoring of creditworthiness. Private sector entities can help investors by rating the likelihood that subnational governments will default. Such credit ratings should reflect both the capacity and the willingness of debt issuers to make timely payments on both principal and interest. Key elements of creditworthiness include the subnational government's economic base (net worth), revenue autonomy and stability, revenue-expenditure balance, intergovernmental fiscal relations, the subnational debt burden, and contingent liabilities. Financial management practices in the region matter, as do guarantees, insurance, and other mechanisms to enhance the credibility of subnational borrowing. However, credit ratings of subnational entities are not yet available in most East Asian countries.

Subnational governments that relax their budget constraints contribute to public sector deficits and threaten national solvency. Hidden budget channels include off-budget borrowing; arrears on civil service wages and payments to suppliers and other levels of government; indirect liabilities through public enterprises or publicly owned banks, which are often insolvent; and other contingent liabilities such as unfunded pension and provident funds. Soft budget constraints and the expectation of central bailouts contribute to moral hazard. Data on these "hidden deficits" in East Asia are just becoming available (Kharas and Mishra 2001). Thus central governments lack the information they need to monitor the fiscal risks of subnational governments. In most East Asian countries, the Ministry of Finance typically receives regular reports on budgetary revenues and expenditures on a cash basis from subnational governments. The ministry does not, however, have access to timely information on many extrabudgetary and off-budget capital expenditures and borrowing, or on local guarantees, financial institutions, pension funds, employment insurance funds, and other transactions that could generate liabilities (Ma and Brixi 2002). Anecdotal evidence on provincial-level off-budget and contingent liabilities abounds in some countries.

In China—where direct and indirect support of expanded investment and credit to subnational entities has driven much recent growth—reliance on banking and off-budget funds has been important.[24] Poor monitoring of such investment implies that the health of the financial sector is at risk. Significant investment in industries such as cement, steel, and aluminum seems even riskier, given substantial excess capacity.

Table 3.2 outlines typical sources of contingent liabilities, which can be explicit or implicit. For instance, the explicit fiscal burden from rising safety net expenditures may generate liabilities for the central or provincial government. Also, what may be "contingent" for the central government may be a direct liability for a provincial or subnational government. Cataloguing such liabilities is an essential first step in establishing a system to assess the obligations and fiscal risks of local governments.[25] China, Indonesia, Thailand, the Philippines, and Vietnam are now embarking on this important endeavor.

As provincial and municipal governments gain greater authority to tap domestic and international financial markets, the financial risk at subnational levels will also grow—and will need managing. Weaknesses in regulation and oversight have led to the proliferation of off-budget financing, government guarantees, and other contingent liabilities. Decentralization has given subnational governments a greater role in managing and delivering public services, and more budgetary responsibility for civil service pensions and provident funds. All these factors exert a significant impact on the quality of services and expenditure mix of local governments.

Countries need to estimate the costs of delivering devolved responsibilities so they understand the potential fiscal risks. For example, if Thailand allocates 20 percent of revenues to local authorities but does not devolve commensurate responsibility for expenditures, then the central government bears a significant risk of assuming the resulting deficit.[26] These risks will grow if service delivery declines owing to capacity constraints among subnational governments. In China and Indonesia, where subnational governments have more expenditure responsibilities than revenue-raising authority, subnational borrowing and off-budget financing vehicles that carry explicit or implicit guarantees from the central government raise the latter's risk. Yet estimating the scope of the contingent liabilities that subnational spending and borrowing impose on the central government is difficult, especially if no one government agency is cataloguing these transactions. East Asian countries are just beginning to undertake this task, at least for large contingent liabilities. China and Thailand have been building the capacity of the central government to manage overall public debt.

Early warnings, such as those used in Brazil, Colombia, and the United States, can provide a good starting point for monitoring the fiscal risks of subnational borrowing, but such indicators may not reliably reflect future financing pressures.[27] Ma (2001) has proposed a composite indicator that reflects both fiscal pressures and the current fiscal position of subnational governments. Information on their assets and liabilities, exposure to market and rollover risks, capacity for managing these finances, and the compatibility between revenue and spending responsibilities will enable informed judgment concerning fiscal risks that may need immediate attention. Without sound fiscal reporting and auditing at the subnational level, even the best-designed early-warning system will not be effective. Countries need clear rules for dealing with debt-distressed subnational governments. Vietnam is examining the fiscal risks of borrowing by state-owned enterprises, but most East Asian countries are just beginning to tackle this issue.

Conclusions

A piecemeal approach to intergovernmental fiscal reform is unlikely to succeed because it will not take into account the interdependence between transfers and revenue assignments, or between expenditure assignments and own-source revenues and transfers. To enforce hard budget constraints, institutions must clearly and credibly convey the message that local governments will bear the costs and benefits of their fiscal decisions. One such institution is the capital market, which in theory rations access to capital among subnational borrowers based on the soundness of their fiscal decisions. Institutions that ensure that public officials must answer to the needs and aspirations of the local populace are essential as well. However, such institutions can work only if local governments have considerable fiscal autonomy, and when the central government makes a credible commitment that it will not provide bailouts (World Bank 2000b). None of the countries in East Asia now meet these conditions for enforcing hard budget constraints.

East Asian countries need a comprehensive approach to intergovernmental fiscal reform, tackling subnational expenditures and revenues at the same time. Subnational governments must have enough revenues to implement their spending responsibilities (see chapters 5 and 6). Toward this end, incentives that encourage cooperation between officials at different levels are essential. China and Indonesia need such incentives, for example.

Central governments need to carefully monitor subnational borrowing and the resulting fiscal risks in order to maintain fiscal discipline and prudent macroeconomic management. Before countries give subnational governments free rein to borrow—domestically or abroad—they need to make information critical to analyzing subnational creditworthiness available to stakeholders. Appropriate checks and balances must ensure that these data are reliable and consistent across provinces. Domestic and foreign capital markets play an important role in diversifying local government funding sources and tracking subnational creditworthiness. East Asian countries—especially those with weak financial systems—will need to implement a complex set of institutional reforms to support these efforts.

Finally, to achieve fiscal sustainability, countries will also need to reform governance, public enterprises, sectors such as power, and the intergovernmental fiscal structure to ensure hard budget constraints for subnational governments. Central governments also must monitor contingent liabilities to ensure prudent fiscal management. Over the longer term, a database and analytical indicators can form the basis for a credit-rating system for local governments. Such a system is critical to opening up subnational borrowing and developing a municipal bond market.[28] Also important in minimizing future surprises from the decisions of subnational governments is a clear division of responsibilities across levels of government, formal channels for reporting contingent liabilities and analyzing their potential fiscal impact, and appropriate early-warning systems for fiscal risks. East Asian countries have begun work in these critical areas, but success will require consistent effort over the short and medium term.

Endnotes

1. This theory assumes that labor and capital mobility will ensure competition among subnational governments for effective public sector service delivery, as well as a match between the preferences of local citizens and governments.
2. Davoodi and Zou (1998) define fiscal decentralization in terms of spending by subnational governments as a fraction of total government spending. Fiscal decentralization rises if spending by state and local governments expands relative to spending by the central government. The authors use the average growth of real per-capita output over 5-year and 10-year periods as a proxy for long-run growth.
3. Davoodi and Zou (1998) did not use disaggregated subnational data to determine which province or region spent more on capital and infrastructure relative to others. The authors also noted that countries may not realize the efficiency gains of fiscal decentralization if central authorities constrain subnational revenue collection and spending, and if local citizens do not elect local officials. Labor and capital mobility may not be as easy as theory assumes.
4. A significant part of spending in these sectors often occurs under "current expenditure."
5. See chapter 2 in Litvack et al. (1998) for a discussion of the distinction between decentralization, deconcentration, and delegation.
6. Lin and Liu (2000) found that rural reform, development of the nonstate sector, and capital accumulation have also been driving forces in China.
7. In the same study, the authors found a positive relationship between fiscal decentralization and provincial economic growth in India. Questions about the appropriateness of the "decentralization variable" again arise. See Ebel and Yilmaz (2003).
8. See World Bank (2002). Subnational governments in China also often engage in commercial activities to supplement their revenue, using land resources and enterprise assets as their investment capital. Under a model pioneered in Shanghai, many municipalities are creating "corporations" to manage public resources and debt obligations. These corporations may "enhance their debt servicing capacity" by engaging in profit-making activities. The General Corporation of Shanghai Municipal Property Development is one of the first such vehicles, created to help finance the city's enormous need for facilities and infrastructure.
9. Wildasin (1997) showed that a local government's ability to extract a bailout from the central government depends on the former's size. Larger subnational governments thus tend to operate under softer budget constraints, creating incentives for overspending and overborrowing if not adequately monitored by the center.
10. For example, although Thailand's central government set grant allocations well in advance of fiscal year 2002, it did not disburse these grants until the very end of the fiscal year because of delays in establishing the allocation rule.
11. Empirical evidence in Lewis (2003) suggests that local governments have borrowed "well within their fiscal

capabilities to repay," but that they have largely been unwilling to repay these debts. The key issue is therefore one of credit risk rather than fiscal sustainability of subnational borrowing in Indonesia.

12. For example, state-level defaults on debt payments helped trigger Brazil's financial crisis in 2000. See Rodden 2000a.
13. Rodden et al. (2003) draw on the experiences of seven developing and transition economies and four OECD countries in identifying institutional arrangements associated with soft and hard subnational budget constraints. This exercise provides lessons for East Asian countries.
14. States in Indonesia can now borrow for projects that generate a "direct or indirect" financial return, per Implementing Regulation 107 of 2000. However, the central government can restrict borrowing if "general conditions" warrant such a restriction, as in the temporary ban by ministerial decree in 2001.
15. The Vietnamese Budget Law stipulates that, for a given year, a province can borrow up if its outstanding debt will not exceed 30 percent of its capital budget. Until 2003, local governments had issued only two project bonds, both by Ho Chi Minh City (HCMC). In 2003 the central government approved new HCMC urban infrastructure bonds. In September and October 2003, HCMC issued two-year and five-year bonds at annual interest rates of 8.52 percent and 9 percent, respectively. In December 2003, HCMC issued another five-year urban bond at 8.5 percent interest. As of October 2003, provincial borrowing amounted to 0.43 percent of gross domestic product (D 2.5 trillion).
16. The Ministry of Finance closely monitors this commitment each year, requiring all subnational authorities to report their debt, interest and principal payments, and borrowing plans by type of instrument. In practice, subnational governments have delayed providing this information.
17. Hence, these rules are often derived using the fiscal sustainability approach based on the government's "lifetime budget constraint."
18. Decree KMK35 of 2003 in Indonesia stipulates that onlending is allowed only for regional government projects that generate revenue. The decree does not specify how to handle a default by a subnational entity, except in the case of loans from the center, where deductions from the general grant would cover the debt service. KMK35 is currently under review.
19. This means that the intergovernmental transfer equation excludes trade taxes.
20. See Kopits (2001). Adopting fiscal reporting in accordance with the IMF's Code of Fiscal Transparency would signal credibility of rules.
21. These include best-practice accounting standards and effective monitoring and reporting of government liabilities.
22. Where the central government tightly controls local spending decisions, as in Cambodia, China, Vietnam, and to some extent Thailand, local governments are more likely to credibly shift blame for a fiscal crisis to the center (World Bank 2000b).
23. See Burki et al. (1999).
24. The fixed-assets investment is driven by local governments rather than the central government. For the first half of 2003, central government projects amounted to only ¥ 184.8 billion (12.3 percent), a decline of 7.7 percent over the previous year. However, local government projects amounted to ¥ 1,322.4 billion (87.7 percent), an increase of 41.5 percent over the same period in the previous year. Most of this investment is in infrastructure projects.
25. Such a system can potentially be used to generate a ranking of local governments based on their fiscal health, and to enable the central government to decide when to intervene and provide emergency assistance (Ma and Brixi 2002).
26. These risks will be compounded as the local share of revenues grows to 35 percent by 2006.
27. See World Bank (2002). Brazil had imposed limits on subnational borrowing, Colombia had a "traffic light system," and Ohio in the United States has a "fiscal watch program."
28. See Ma and Brixi (2002) for relevant experiences in Australia, Brazil, Colombia, New Zealand, and the United States, and a list of risk indicators for monitoring the contingent liabilities of subnational governments.

Bibliography

Akai, Nobuo, and Masayo Sakata. 2002. "Fiscal Decentralization Contributes to Economic Growth: Evidence from State-Level Cross-Section Data for the United States." *Journal of Urban Economics* 52: 93–108.

Bird, Richard. 2003. "Fiscal Flows, Fiscal Balance, and Fiscal Sustainability." World Bank Institute, Washington, DC.

Bird, Richard, and Christine Wallich. 1993. "Fiscal Decentralization and Intergovernmental Fiscal Relations in Transitional Economies: Towards a Systematic Framework of Analysis." Working Paper. Country Economics Department, World Bank, Washington, DC.

Brixi, Hana Polackova, and Ashoka Mody. 2002. "Dealing with Government Fiscal Risk: An Overview." In *Government at Risk,* ed. Hana Polackova Brixi and Allen Schick. Washington, DC: World Bank.

Burki, Shahid Javed, Guillermo E. Perry, and William R. Dillinger. 1999. "Beyond the Center: Decentralizing the State." *Viewpoints.* Washington, DC: World Bank, World Bank Latin American and Caribbean Studies.

Davoodi, Hamid, and Heng-fu Zou. 1998. "Fiscal Decentralization and Economic Growth: A Cross-Country Study." *Journal of Urban Economics* 43: 244–57.

Ebel, Robert D., and Serdar Yilmaz. 2003. "On the Measurement and Impact of Fiscal Decentralization." In *Public Finance in Developing and Transitional Countries: Essays in Honor of Richard Bird,* ed. Jorge Martinez-Vazquez and James Alm. Cheltenham, UK: Edward Elgar Press.

Kharas, Homi, and Deepak Mishra. 2001. "Fiscal Policy, Hidden Deficits and Currency Crises." In *World Bank Economists' Forum,* ed. S. Devarajan, F. H. Rogers, and L. Squire. Washington, DC: World Bank.

Kopits, George. 2001. "Fiscal Rules: Useful Policy Framework or Unnecessary Ornament?" IMF Working Paper 01/145. Washington, DC: International Monetary Fund.

Lewis, Blane D. 2003. "Local Government Borrowing and Repayment in Indonesia: Does Fiscal Capacity Matter?" *World Development* 31 (6): 1047–63.

Lin, Justin Yifu, and Zhiqiang Liu. 2000. "Fiscal Decentralization and Economic Growth in China." *Economic Development and Cultural Change* 49 (1): 1–21.

Litvack, Jennie, Junaid Ahmad, and Richard Bird. 1998. "Rethinking Decentralization in Developing Countries." Sector Studies Series. World Bank, Washington, DC.

McKenzie, Kenneth J. 2003. "A Note on the Sustainability of Fiscal Policy in Subnational Governments." World Bank Institute, Washington, DC.

Ma, Jun. 2001."Monitoring the Fiscal Risks of Subnational Governments." In *Government at Risk,* ed. Hana Polackova Brixi and Allen Schick. Washington, DC: World Bank.

Ma, Jun, and Hana Polackova Brixi. 2002. "Monitoring the Fiscal Risks of Subnational Governments." *PREM Notes* No. 6. Washington, DC: World Bank.

Martinez-Vazquez, Jorge, and Robert M. McNab. 2001. "Fiscal Decentralization and Economic Growth." Working Paper 01-1. Georgia State University, Andrew Young School of Policy Studies.

Oates, Wallace E. 1993. "Fiscal Decentralization and Economic Development." *National Tax Journal* 42 (2): 237–43.

Rodden, Jonathan. 2000a. "Decentralization and the Challenge of Hard Budget Constraints." *PREM Notes* No. 41. Washington, DC: World Bank.

———. 2000b. "The Dilemma of Fiscal Federalism: Hard and Soft Budget Constraints around the World." Massachusetts Institute of Technology, Cambridge, MA.

Rodden, Jonathan, Gunner Eskeland, and Jennie Litvack, eds. 2003. *Decentralization and Hard Budget Constraints.* Washington, DC: World Bank.

Shah, Anwar. 2004. "Fiscal Decentralization in Developing and Transition Economies: Progress, Problems, and the Promise." Research Working Paper No. 2832. World Bank, Washington, DC.

Ter-Minassian, Teresa, and John Craig. 1997. "Control of Subnational Borrowing." In *Fiscal Federalism in Theory and Practice,* ed. Teresa Ter-Minassian. Washington, DC: International Monetary Fund.

Weist, Dana. 2001. "Thailand's Decentralization: Progress and Prospects." Paper prepared for the King Prajadipk Institute Congress III on Decentralization and Local Government in Bangkok, Thailand.

Wildasin, David E. 1997. "Externalities and Bailouts: Hard and Soft Budget Constraints in Intergovernmental Fiscal Relations." Policy Research Working Paper No. 1843. World Bank, Washington, DC.

World Bank. 2000a. "Thailand: Public Finance in Transition." Report No. 20656-TH. World Bank, Washington, DC.

———. 2000b. "Decentralization and the Challenge of Hard Budget Constraints." *PREM Notes* No. 41. Washington, DC: World Bank.

———. 2000c. "Vietnam: Managing Public Resources Better." Public Expenditure Review Report No. 24469, annex B. World Bank, Washington, DC.

———. 2002. "China: National Development and Subnational Finance: A Review of Provincial Expenditures." Report No. 22951-CHA. World Bank, Washington, DC.

———. 2003a. "Decentralizing Indonesia." Report No. 26191-IND. World Bank, Washington, DC.

———. 2003b. "Philippines: Improving Government Performance: Discipline, Efficiency and Equity in Managing Public Resources." Public Expenditure, Procurement, and Financial Management Review Report No. 24256-PH. World Bank, Washington, DC.

———. 2004. *East Asia Update.* Washington, DC: World Bank.

———. 2005. *Global Economic Prospects.* Washington, DC: World Bank.

Xie, Danyang, Heng-fu Zou, and Hamid Davoodi. 1999. "Fiscal Decentralization and Economic Growth in the United States." *Journal of Urban Economics* 45 (2): 228–39.

Zhang, Tao, and Heng-fu Zou. 1999. "Fiscal Decentralization, Public Spending, and Economic Growth in China." *Journal of Public Economics* 67: 221–40.

———. 2001. "The Growth Impact of Intersectoral and Intergovernmental Allocation of Public Expenditure: With Applications to China and India." *China Economic Review* 12: 58–81.

4

FISCAL DISPARITIES IN EAST ASIA: HOW LARGE AND DO THEY MATTER?

Bert Hofman and Susana Cordeiro Guerra

The decentralization of revenue sources and expenditure responsibilities to subnational levels of government can increase the efficiency of spending, and increase participation in decision making by local constituents. It is also true, however, that decentralization can result in inequities in service delivery among citizens of the same country depending on where they live. While decentralization need not cause these inequities, devolution of revenue sources, combined with disparities in endowments of regions, is likely to lead to disparities in fiscal resources at the subnational level.

If left alone, these disparities could lead to either lower levels of services in fiscally poor regions or higher tax rates for similar levels of government services in those regions. In turn, disparities in service delivery could thwart poverty alleviation efforts, as public services that are usually provided at the subnational level, such as primary health and education, are critical in empowering the poor. Disparities in the level and quality of these services could therefore eventually perpetuate inequalities in income levels, or at least delay conversion of incomes across regions. Large fiscal disparities could also induce migration to regions that have higher revenues and better services, even though the migrants could have been employed more productively elsewhere.[1] Finally, large disparities in public service delivery may cause social unrest in regions that are left behind, and could undermine the sense of unity in a country. Such diversity, coupled with growing disparities across regions, may constitute the basis for regional insurrections such as in the Muslim regions of Mindanao in the Philippines, and in West Papua in Indonesia (Hill 2000).

Most governments take an interest in the level and distribution of public services provided to their citizens, even in a decentralized system. For some countries, this is reason enough not to decentralize the financing or provision of services deemed critical to national goals. Indeed, income redistribution is seen primarily as a central function because central governments are regarded as better able to manage one of the key instruments of this goal: a progressive income tax.[2] Yet, at the same time, services that are likely to affect income distribution, poverty alleviation, or similar national goals *are* decentralized. Moreover, many governments have entered into commitments on the outcomes of services that are routinely at least partially decentralized to subnational levels of government.[3]

So they should be concerned about the level and distribution of fiscal resources among levels of governments, as those resources enable subnational governments to deliver services.

Even if governments care about the distribution of services, they may not take policy action to correct the distribution of fiscal resources among subnational governments—known as horizontal fiscal imbalances. This could occur for two reasons. First, policy makers may count on market adjustments. Thus, for some countries, migration is considered a countervailing, equalizing force, driving people to the constituency that delivers the most beneficial level of public services at tax rates deemed appropriate by the constituents. Second, legitimate policy tradeoffs need to be weighed: an aggressive transfer policy may be seen as dampening needed incentives for increasing own-revenue mobilization by subnational governments. Such a short-term tradeoff deemphasizes equalization to provide for an own-revenue foundation for a future of reduced fiscal disparities and transfer dependency.[4]

Similarly, an equalization-only policy (perhaps just in the early stages of decentralization) may compete with broader considerations of efficiency and growth on the nation's agenda. In China, for instance, the coastal development strategy of the 1980s and 1990s deliberately left more resources in regions with stronger growth prospects. Using data from the 1985 to 1998 period of fiscal decentralization in China, Qiao et al. found that inequality in the distribution of fiscal resources across provinces was positively related to higher economic growth, and that that higher growth, in turn, led to greater inequality (Qiao et al. 2003). Yan found a similar tradeoff between growth and equity in China, and further showed that the fiscal reforms in 1985 and 1994 did not contribute to increased equalization (Yan 2003).

In other countries, governments compensate for horizontal fiscal imbalances not through redistribution, but by centrally providing certain services in poor regions while leaving rich regions to fend for themselves. This approach may indeed also be beneficial from an efficiency point of view, as some evidence suggests that the center is better at some services critical for poverty alleviation, including the targeting of a social safety net (Ravaillion 1998). Finally, redistribution of fiscal resources may remain limited for political reasons: rich regions also tend to be powerful regions, and taking resources away from them to give to poorer regions may simply be politically unfeasible.

Most East Asian governments care about equitable services to their people, and thus take an interest in the distribution of fiscal resources among subnational governments, which deliver many of these services. Countries such as Indonesia have included subnational fiscal equity as an explicit goal in their Constitution.[5] Other countries, such as China and the Philippines, include strong commitments on equal access to services in their Constitution, whereas the delivery of many of these services is devolved to subnational governments.[6] Similarly, international commitments to public service outcomes, such as the Millennium Development Goals, often relate to services delivered at the subnational level. These commitments imply that the state should care about whether subnational governments are capable of delivering such services, and thus a concern about subnational fiscal capacity and its distribution over subnational entities. In fact, most East Asian countries show that they care to some extent by having some form of fiscal equalization mechanism in place.

This chapter reviews the causes and consequences of fiscal inequities among subnational governments in East Asia. It shows that endowments and fiscal capacities among subnational entities are large, and that these inequities translate into large fiscal inequities before equalization. The transfer systems now in place in East Asian countries are only mildly equalizing, so that even after equalization the remaining fiscal disparities are still large. The chapter discusses the possible consequences of these disparities for service delivery inputs, outputs, and outcomes. It concludes with some guidelines on how to increase transparency on inequalities at the subnational level, and how to make transfer systems more equalizing without undermining the incentives for local governments to raise their own revenues and spend their resources efficiently.

Fiscal Disparities in East Asia

East Asian countries show a wide variety of natural endowments, economic opportunities, levels of development, and poverty (see figure 4.1). Indeed, the richest province in Indonesia has 17 times the

FIGURE 4.1 Percentage of Population Living below PPP$2 a Day in 2002, East Asia and Pacific

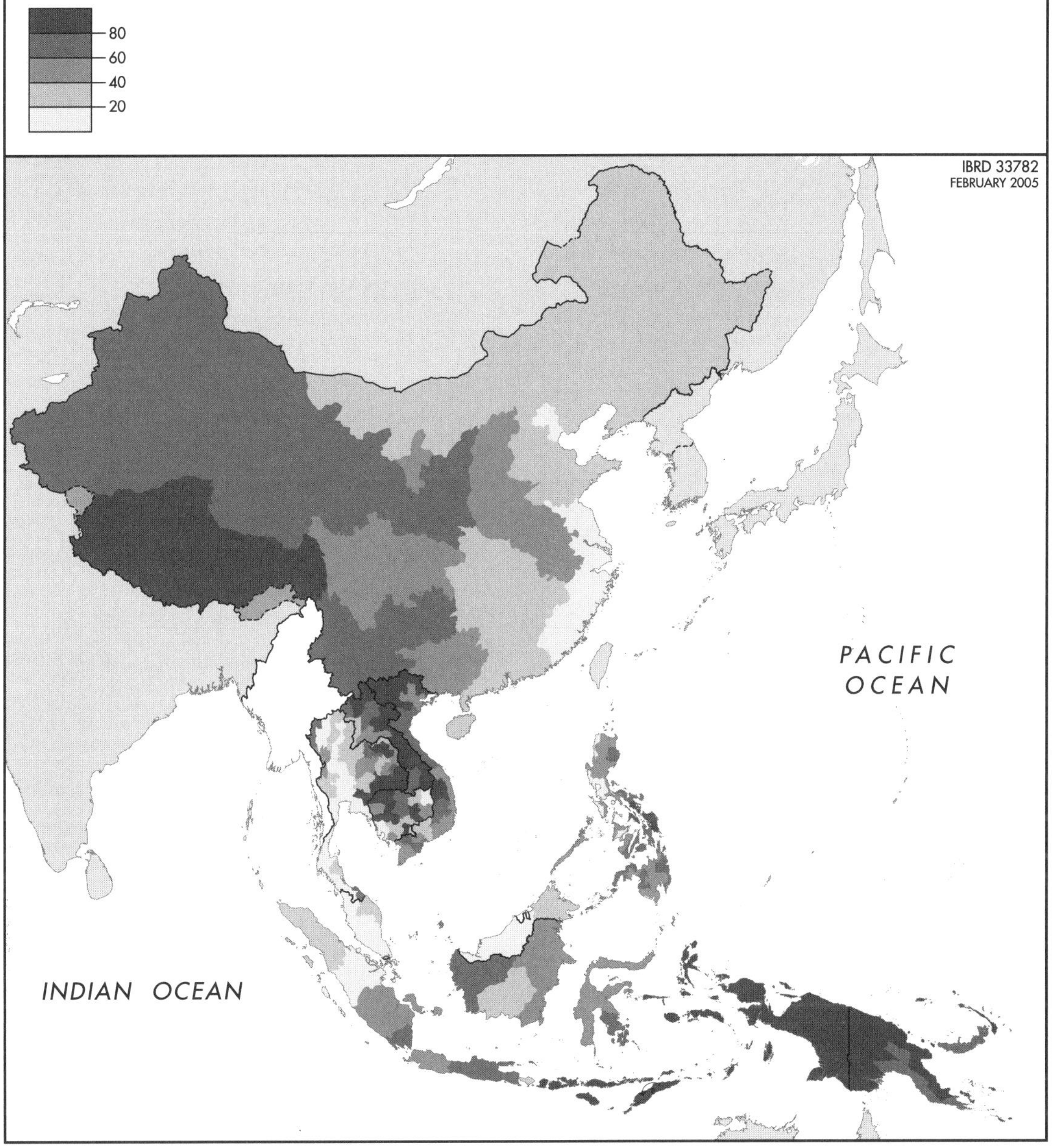

gross domestic product (GDP) per capita as the poorest province; in China that figure is 11, and in Vietnam it is 9.5.[7] These disparities in per capita income have been relatively stable (Hill 2000; Garcia-Garcia and Soehstianingsih 1998). In such an environment, devolving expenditure responsibilities and revenue sources could lead to inequities because of regional disparities in revenue potential and the cost of delivering services.

Indeed, East Asian countries reveal large disparities in subnational revenue-generating capacity (table 4.1). In fact, disparities in own-revenues are larger than disparities in income per capita. In China, for instance, own-revenues per capita of the richest province are 15 times those of the poorest region. These disparities are even higher in Indonesia, the Philippines, and Vietnam.[8] In the latter three countries, natural resource revenues collected

TABLE 4.1 Disparities in Provincial Revenues before Grants, per Capita
(US$, latest available year)

	China	Indonesia	Philippines	Vietnam
Maximum	283.2	59.5	7.6	343.4
Minimum	18.1	3.8	0.2	6.5
Average	55.7	12.1	1.5	36.9
Max./min.[a]	15.7	15.7	35.4	53.0
Standard deviation	54.8	11.6	1.4	61.1
Coefficient of variation[b]	0.98	0.96	0.97	0.79

Sources: SABER Database; Indonesia Regional Fiscal Information System.
Note: The table presents consolidated province-level data. Because of the different nature of the grant systems (see text), the absolute dollar amounts are not comparable. The figures for Indonesia include own-revenues and shared revenues. Since the Internal Revenue Allotment in the Philippines is an equalizing transfer, it is excluded from revenues. A breakdown of revenue for Thailand was not available at a comparable subnational level.
a. The figures represent the ratio in revenues between the province with the highest revenues and the province with the lowest revenues.
b. The coefficient of variation is the standard deviation divided by the average.

TABLE 4.2 Disparities in China's Provincial Fiscal Outcomes, per Capita, 1979–2002
(yuan)

	Revenues		Expenditures	
	1979	2002	1979	2002
Maximum	1,525	4,363	274	5,307
Minimum	−12	274	34	655
Average	143	806	98	1,621
Max./min.	−127	16	8	8
Standard deviation	293.5	939.2	67.4	1,218.4
Coefficient of variation	2.0	1.2	0.7	0.8

Source: Qiao et al. 2003.
Note: The negative minimum value for China reflects the definition of revenues, which counts subsidies that cover losses from state enterprises as negative revenue.

or shared by the center with the regions exacerbates apparent inequalities. Below the provincial level, inequalities grow even larger. In Indonesia, for instance, the richest local government had 50 times the own-revenues of the poorest local government in 2001, and the richest county in Gansu province had 82 times the per capita revenues of the poorest province (World Bank 2003b and World Bank 2002a).[9]

These interregional fiscal disparities are not a recent phenomenon. In China, data show that large fiscal disparities have persisted over time (see table 4.2).[10] Expenditure disparities have risen slightly, with the interprovincial coefficient of variation rising from 0.7 to 0.8; revenue disparities have fallen from 2.0 to 1.2. Yet the latter continue to be large, with Shanghai having almost 16 times the per capita revenue of Tibet. Tibet's per capita expenditure was similarly 8 times that of Hainan in 1979, while Shanghai's is 8 times that of Henna today.

In Indonesia, disparity in total revenues after grants was nearly as large in 2002 as in 1994 (see table 4.3). Disparities in own-revenues across provinces were already rising before decentralization began in 1999. Disparities in own-revenues plus shared revenues have risen since decentralization,

TABLE 4.3 Variation in Revenues across Provinces in Indonesia, 1994–2002[a]

	1994	1999	2000	2002
Own-revenues	0.87	0.88	0.98	0.90
Shared taxes	0.73	0.70	1.28	0.86
Shared nontaxes	0.74	0.74	1.24	1.18
SDO[b]	0.79	0.51	0.64	0.61
INPRES[c]	0.69	0.51	0.68	0.64
Total revenue disparity	0.68	0.51	0.68	0.66

Source: SABER Database.
a. The figures represent coefficients of variation (see table 4.1).
b. SDO (*subsidi daerah otonom*), or Subsidy for Autonomous Region.
c. After 2001, INPRES (*instruksi presiden*), Presidential Instructions (Grant for Regional Development), was made equal to the DAU (*dana alokasi umum*), or General Allocation Grant.

especially because of shared revenues from natural resources.

Equalization Mechanisms

China, Indonesia, the Philippines, Thailand, and Vietnam rely on grant systems to address fiscal disparities (see table 4.4). These systems rely on a formula to determine distribution, and three of the five use a formula to determine the resource pool. Three of the systems take into account both the revenue capacity and the expenditure needs of local governments, whereas the Filipino and Thai systems consider only expenditure needs.

The distribution pools vary greatly from country to country. In Indonesia and the Philippines, equalization grants account for the largest share of grants from the center to local governments, while earmarked grants dominate in Thailand and China. In some countries earmarked grants include equalizing elements, but in others they exert a counter-equalizing effect. Although numbers are hard to come by, the equalization system can also include central spending that exerts a regional impact.

In Indonesia, the equalization grant—*dana alokasi umum* (DAU)—is the mainstay of the intergovernmental fiscal system. DAU funding consists of 25 percent of central revenues after tax sharing with the regions.[11] Of this amount, 10 percent goes to the provincial level, which plays a relatively minor role in public services, while 90 percent goes to local governments. The DAU finances some 70 percent of local government spending and some 50 percent of provincial spending.

The central government distributes the DAU according to a formula that takes both revenue capacity and expenditure needs into account. Revenue capacity is defined as potential own-source revenues plus shared tax revenues, plus 75 percent of shared natural resource revenues.[12] The central government defines expenditure needs based on population, poverty rate, land area, and construction costs as an indicator of "geographical circumstances." Distribution of the DAU is based partly on past spending patterns—largely to accommodate the transitory impact of the 2001 decentralization. A lump sum per region also plays a role in the allocation. The new earmarked grant system (DAK) is still small compared with general grants—amounting to about 3 percent of total grants. However, it also includes an element of equalization. Regions with low fiscal capacity pay only 10 percent in matching funds, whereas those with high fiscal capacity pay up to 50 percent.

In China, the central government dedicates an ad hoc amount to transfers to the 16 poorest provinces. Although the 1994 Tax Sharing System introduced an equalization scheme based on variables such as provincial GDP, student-teacher ratios, number of civil servants, and population density, the scheme is still in "transitional" status.[13] The scheme also remains small: each beneficiary province receives only a fraction of its fiscal needs as determined by the formula, and in 2001 the scheme accounted for only 3 percent of total central transfers (World Bank 2004e). Although the reform marked the first time that the government explicitly budgeted an equalization grant, it may

TABLE 4.4 Equalization in Intergovernmental Transfer Systems

	Indonesia	China	Philippines	Thailand	Vietnam
Equalization grant principles	All regions receive an equalizing general grant.	16 regions receive a small equalizing grant, amounting to only 3% of all transfers in 2001.	All regions receive a fixed share of central government tax revenues known as the Internal Revenue Allotment (IRA).	Allocated based on discretion to Provincial Administrative Organization (PAO), municipalities, and Tambon Administrative Organization (TAO), and then further allocated to individual localities based on formula.	Allocated to jurisdictions where approved expenditure budgets exceed the sum of own-revenues and the 100% retention of all shared revenues.
Formula-based source?	Yes; 25% of actual central government revenues after revenue sharing.	No; level of funding decided by annual budget based on ad hoc principles.	Yes; central government sets IRA of local governments at 40% of average internal tax collections three years before the current year.	No; total amount of different types of grants varies annually. The system is moving to a formula-based system.	Partially; formula based on calculated budget transfer between the center and provinces. Expenditure needs are negotiated.
Main features of formula	Based on expenditure needs and revenue capacity, but 50% determined by transitional elements. Expenditure needs reflect population, poverty rate, land area, and construction cost index. Revenue capacity estimated as standardized own-revenues (based on average efforts), plus shared tax revenues, plus 75% of natural resource revenues.	Expenditure needs and revenue capacity based on formula derived from regression analysis on "standard budget." Relies on variables such as provincial GDP, student-teacher ratios, number of civil servants, and population density. .	IRA divided among provinces (23%), cities (23%), municipalities (34%), and *barangays* (20%). IRA allocated based on population (50%), land area (25%), and equal sharing (25%).	5% reserved for unfunded devolving functions and 95% for local authorities, including PAOs (7%), municipalities (52%), and TAOs (41%). Allocation across local authorities is based on equal share (25%), population (30%), area (5%), invert to local revenues, excluded grants (20%), and invert to specific grants received (20%).	Subnational (SNG) expenditure needs minus total revenue from taxes are shared 100 percent with SNGs. Total revenues shared between central and SNG budgets.

	Indonesia	China	Philippines	Thailand	Vietnam
Equalizing properties (weak, medium, strong)	Weak, owing to transitional elements and imperfections in formula.	Weak, owing to limited resources.	Medium; IRA equalizing effect is not enough to counteract disparities in tax base because it weakly compares expenditure needs and revenue capacity.	Weak; lack of transparency in allocation leads to self-interested politics. Delays in allocation decisions have undermined local planning and financial management.	Medium; improved from ad hoc negotiated transfers. Introduced clear objectives and stability by fixing formulas, decreasing the role of bargaining.
Equalization through specific grants (ad hoc or conditional)?	Yes; special allocations depend on fiscal capacity but are small.	No; special grants deequalizing, such as tax rebates for state enterprise support. Lacks monitoring mechanisms.	No; matching grants from central agencies (augmentation funds) are proportionally small and usually subject to political interests.	Yes; other general grants include tax effort promotion, local good governance promotion, devolution of compensatory functions, train ticket compensation, local development, and education. Specific grants include educational (capital projects) and development projects allocated on a project basis.	No; absence of conditional grants, but targeted national programs function similarly (see below).
Other equalizing elements of fiscal system	Distribution of revenues from natural resources to regions bordering producing regions.	Transitory grants determined on ad hoc basis according to annual budgetary demands.			Targeted "national programs" channeled through provincial budgets in support of poorest communes, reforestation, and national health program.

Sources: World Bank 2000, 2002a, 2003b; Manasan 2002; World Bank background papers on Vietnam and Thailand, 2003.

have only symbolic significance until the government allocates more funds (World Bank 2002a). Earmarked grants—which account for more than 95 percent of all grants—include no equalizing element. Two-thirds are "tax return grants," which amount to revenue sharing on a derivation basis.

In Vietnam, the tax sharing-cum-contracting system equalizes. The revised State Budget Law (2002) gives the equalization transfer to jurisdictions whose approved expenditure needs exceed the sum of own-revenues and 100 percent retention of all shared revenues (World Bank 2004e). According to the equalization formula, the local tax administration branch determines revenue potential based on collections from previous years, factoring in any changes in tax policy and expected economic growth (Martínez-Vázquez 2003). Expenditure needs are based on per capita expenditure norms rather than physical standards as prior to 1996, which were unaffordable. Regions may keep revenues in excess of agreed shares. Beyond the equalization transfer, Vietnam has no other conditional grants except a series of "national programs" aimed at the poorest communes and to fulfill reforestation and health goals. The government channels these programs to recipients through provincial budgets.

In Thailand, general grants include a fiscal equalization grant.[14] Fiscal equalization grants rely on a strict formula based on equal share (25 percent), population (30 percent), area (5 percent), invert to local revenues excluding grants (20 percent), and invert to specific grants received (20 percent). A second type of grant, known as specific grants, covers educational capital investment and development projects based on project criteria. Although grants were the largest source of intergovernmental transfers in 2003—accounting for 38 percent of local revenues—the central government does not determine allocations until well after the fiscal year begins. This leads to a lack of transparency and an extremely politicized system, and creates planning and budgeting difficulties for local governments. Grants do not alleviate the fiscal imbalance between the central and subnational governments.

Under the Local Government Code (LGC) in the Philippines, local governments receive a fixed share of central tax revenues, known as the Internal Revenue Allotment (IRA). The LGC sets the aggregate IRA share at 40 percent of subnational revenues three years before the current year.[15] Of this share, provinces and cities receive 23 percent, municipalities receive 34 percent, and *barangays* receive 20 percent. The share within each tier of government reflects three basic criteria: population (50 percent), land area (25 percent), and equal sharing across provinces (25 percent). Before the LGC, the relative weights of these criteria differed: population (70 percent), land area (20 percent), and equal sharing (10 percent). The greater emphasis on equal sharing (from 10 to 20 percent), coupled with the fall in population weight (from 70 to 50 percent), shows a shift in equity concerns.

Do Grant Systems in East Asia Equalize?

Determining whether these grant systems equalize requires defining "equalization." Common use defines fiscal equality as "the capability of subnational governments to deliver similar levels of services at similar levels of taxes" (Searle 2002). While such a definition points to how an equalization grant might best be designed, determining whether it equalizes requires information on differences in the cost of services—which can be large—among subnational levels of government, and these data are not yet available.[16] This chapter therefore uses a simpler approach, asking whether disparities among subnational revenues drop as a result of intergovernmental grants. The answer is that indeed, for all the countries reviewed, the distribution of revenues per capita becomes more equal after transfers, although their equalizing effect varies significantly, being strongest in Vietnam and weakest in the Philippines (see figure 4.2 and tables 4.1 and 4.5).

Comparing revenues and expenditures per capita against income per capita provides further evidence of the equalization properties of transfer systems. If the income elasticity of expenditures is lower than the income elasticity of revenues, it can be argued that the transfer system is equalizing.[17] This is indeed the case for the East Asian countries for which enough data are available, suggesting that grant systems equalize (see table 4.6).

Even after transfers, though, per capita revenue disparities remain large. The richest province in the Philippines has 28 times more revenues per capita than the poorest one, while the numbers for China, Indonesia, and Vietnam are 8, 10, and 22, respectively. For comparison, in the United States, the

TABLE 4.5 Disparities in Province-Level Revenues after Grants, per Capita
(US$, latest available year)

	China	Indonesia	Philippines	Vietnam
Maximum	444.4	431.4	117.5	393.1
Minimum	42.8	39.8	4.2	25.1
Average	100.7	106.3	14.8	65.9
Max./min.	10.4	10.8	28.1	15.7
Standard deviation	83.1	78.9	13.3	65.2
Coefficient of variation	0.82	0.74	0.92	0.42

Sources: SABER Database; *Indonesia Statistical Yearbook, China Statistical Yearbook; Philippine Statistical Yearbook; Vietnam Statistical Yearbook;* Ministry of Finance (Vietnam); Indonesia Regional Fiscal Information System; Public Expenditure Reviews; Regional Expenditure Reviews; authors' calculations.
Note: The table presents consolidated province-level data. The revenue numbers include own- and shared revenues for Indonesia. A breakdown of revenue for Thailand was not available at a comparable subnational level.

FIGURE 4.2 Disparity in Provincial per Capita Revenues before and after Transfers

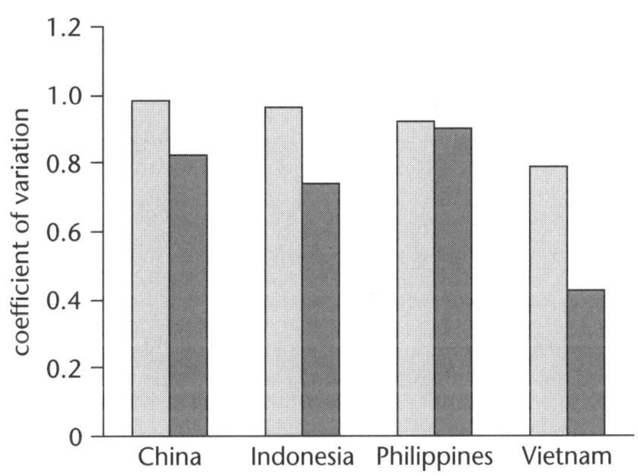

Sources: SABER Database; *China Statistical Yearbook; Finance Yearbook of China;* Indonesia Regional Fiscal Information System; *Philippine Statistical Yearbook; Vietnam Statistical Yearbook;* Vietnam Ministry of Finance; Public Expenditure Reviews; Regional Public Expenditure Reviews; authors' calculations.

TABLE 4.6 Evidence of Equalization

	Income elasticity of revenue	Income elasticity of expenditures
China	1.03	0.61
Indonesia	0.81	0.57
Vietnam	1.26	0.72

Source: Authors' calculations.
Note: The figures are the estimated parameters for the log of income per capita in a regression that regresses the log of revenues (expenditures) per capita against the log of income per capita and a constant. All the reported elasticities are significant at the 1 percent level.

poorest state has about 65 percent of the revenues of the average state. In Germany, the Finanzausgleich subsidizes any state falling below 95 percent of the average level (and taxes any state receiving more than 110 percent). In Brazil, the richest state has 2.3 times the revenues per capita of the poorest state. In Russia, disparities are larger: the richest of 89 regions has revenues per capita some 40 times higher than the poorest (World Bank 2002b; Martínez-Vázquez and Boex 1998). However, Russia's regions are smaller than the average East Asian province, and indications are that the smaller the subnational entity, the larger the measured inequality. In Indonesia, the richest local government had 30 times the revenue per capita of the poorest local government in 2002, while the comparable number for 2001 was more than 50. Within China's Gansu province, the per capita revenues of the richest county were 37 times those of the poorest in 1999 (Hofman et al. 2003; World Bank 2002a). Intraprovincial disparities thus appear to be larger than interprovincial ones.

A number of studies confirm the modest impact on equalization of intergovernmental fiscal systems. A recent study of the Philippines suggests that the IRA's equalizing effect has not countered disparities in tax base across local governments (Manasan 2002). The same study found that the IRA had a counterequalizing effect in provinces from 1995 to 2000, and in municipalities from 1999 to 2000. In Indonesia, Lewis (2003) found the DAU distribution to be equalizing, but less than warranted by revenue capacity and expenditure needs alone, whereas Hofman et al. (2003) elaborated on the DAU's weak equalization performance.

Vietnam's fiscal system seems to be more equalizing: the country redistributes a substantial proportion of revenues collected in wealthier provinces to poorer ones (World Bank 2000). Rao (2001) uses cross-section estimates to show that elasticity is much lower for revenues than for expenditures. This implies a significant degree of equalization, in line with the steep drop in provincial inequality presented here. For China, Yan (2003) shows that fiscal reforms in 1985 and 1994 have not alleviated the unequal impact of market reform, and indeed appear to have exacerbated regional disparities. Indeed, evidence reveals that earmarked grants are mostly flowing to richer provinces (Ahmad et al. 2000; World Bank 1993). Disparities in per capita revenues after grants translate into disparities in per capita expenditures, although not on a one-to-one basis. These disparities may reflect differences in access to borrowing or in the use of reserves.

Do Fiscal Disparities Matter?

Policy makers may focus on fiscal disparities for a number of reasons. However, they matter if they translate into large disparities in service delivery and outcomes. Indicators of service delivery at the subnational level are as scarce as fiscal data, but Human Development Indicators and information on persons per hospital bed, literacy, and life expectancy are available for most countries under review.[18] The first indicator—persons per hospital bed—measures service inputs, whereas the other indicators measure outcomes. These measures show large variation across and within countries, although less than the fiscal indicators reveal.[19] In terms of persons per hospital bed, Indonesia's lowest-ranking province is 7.6 times worse than the best-ranking province, while the same numbers for Vietnam, China, the Philippines, and Thailand—3.3, 3.4, 4.4, and 6.8, respectively—are better but still discouraging.[20] China's highest-ranking province is almost 3 times as literate as the lowest-ranking one, while Indonesia (1.34) and Vietnam (1.9) follow close behind. Human development and life expectancy indicators confirm this trend, with Vietnam's best province ranking nearly twice as high as the lowest province on both indicators. The figures for China and Indonesia are only slightly better (see tables 4.7 to 4.10).

To assess whether there is a systemic relation between fiscal disparities and disparities in service delivery indicators, we used a simple regression approach. We used two specifications (see table 4.11). Specification 1 is a regression of social outcome indicators—HDI, persons per hospital beds, life expectancy, and literacy rates—as a function of a constant and expenditures per capita. In specification 2, we also include per capita GDP as an explanatory variable, to control for potential correlations between provincial per capita income and

TABLE 4.7 Disparities in Province-Level HDI Indices, 1997–2002[a]

	China	Indonesia	Philippines	Vietnam
Maximum	0.85	0.73	0.65	0.84
Minimum	0.52	0.54	0.39	0.49
Average	0.70	0.64	0.56	0.74
Max./min.	1.64	1.34	1.65	1.72
Standard deviation	0.07	0.04	0.11	0.06
Coefficient of variation	0.10	0.06	0.19	0.08

Sources: United Nations Development Programme (UNDP) Human Development Indicators (HDI); Government of Indonesia 2002; National Statistical Coordination Board 2003; Republic of China, multiple years; Republic of Vietnam, multiple years.

a. Data are not available across all provinces for Thailand. Data for the Philippines are at the regional level.

TABLE 4.8 Disparities in Province-Level Persons per Hospital Bed, 1997–2002[a]

	China	Indonesia	Philippines	Thailand	Vietnam
Maximum	650.34	3,969.41	3,502.49	1,114.00	867.93
Minimum	189.73	524.30	796.71	165.00	261.20
Average	405.34	1,862.43	2,125.25	579.65	524.77
Max./min.	3.43	7.57	4.40	6.75	3.32
Standard deviation	105.35	903.95	1,536.92	494.75	152.94
Coefficient of variation	0.26	0.49	0.72	0.85	0.25

Sources: UNDP Human Development Indicators; Government of Indonesia 2002; National Statistical Coordination Board 2003; Republic of China, multiple years; Republic of Vietnam, multiple years.
a. Data are for the most recent year available. Data for the Philippines are from the regional level.

TABLE 4.9 Disparities in Province-Level Life Expectancy, 1996–2002[a]

	China	Indonesia	Philippines	Thailand	Vietnam
Maximum	78.14	71.10	73.70	79.80	95.00
Minimum	64.37	57.80	60.32	61.60	50.00
Average	71.24	66.21	70.79	72.34	81.66
Max./min.	1.21	1.23	1.22	1.30	1.90
Standard deviation	3.19	3.23	3.17	35.76	7.64
Coefficient of variation	0.04	0.05	0.05	0.49	0.09

Sources: UNDP Human Development Indicators; Government of Indonesia 2002; National Statistical Coordination Board 2003; Republic of China, multiple years; Republic of Vietnam, multiple years.
a. Data are for the most recent year available. Data for the Philippines are at the regional level and for males only. Data for Vietnam are for males only.

TABLE 4.10 Disparities in Province-Level Literacy Rates, 1994–2002[a]

	China	Indonesia	Philippines	Vietnam
Maximum	93.55	97.80	98.80	96.90
Minimum	33.82	72.80	73.50	51.30
Average	83.19	89.34	92.27	88.16
Max./min.	2.76	1.34	1.34	1.89
Standard deviation	11.04	6.57	5.92	8.32
Coefficient of variation	0.13	0.07	0.06	0.09

Sources: UNDP Human Development Indicators; Government of Indonesia 2002; National Statistical Coordination Board 2003; Republic of China, multiple years; Republic of Vietnam, multiple years.
a. Data are for the most recent year available. Data are not available across all provinces for Thailand. Data for the Philippines refer to the regional level.

expenditures, and their implications for service outcomes.[21]

Specification 1 suggests a modestly significant correlation between social indicators and subnational expenditures. In China and Vietnam, the indicators usually correlate significantly with expenditures. In China, the only exception is literacy rates: the correlation, although positive, is not significant. The reason may be that education financing still falls partly under the auspices of the central government, given recent efforts to recentralize education expenditures. In Vietnam, the only exception to the correlation between social indicators and subnational expenditures is persons per hospital bed. This

TABLE 4.11 Expenditure Disparities and Service Outputs and Outcomes at the Subnational Level

Dependent variable and specification	China	Indonesia	Vietnam
HDI 1	0.10*	0.01	0.10*
HDI 2	−0.01	0.002	−0.001
Persons per hospital bed 1	−0.48*	−0.29*	0.04
Persons per hospital bed 2	−0.39*	−0.15	−0.15
Life expectancy 1	0.04*	0.02*	0.04*
Life expectancy 2	−0.02*	0.01	−0.02
Literacy 1	0.03	0.02	0.06**
Literacy 2	−0.03	0.01	−0.02

Source: Authors' calculations.

Note: The table presents the results of regression analysis with the output or outcome indicator as a dependent variable. Dependent variables are a constant and expenditures per capita in specification 1 ($y = \alpha + \beta$ * expenditure per capita), and a constant, expenditures per capita, and provincial GDP per capita in specification 2 ($y = \alpha + \beta$ * expenditure per capita + γ * GPP per capita. The average number of observations for each specification: China (28), Indonesia (27), Vietnam (59). China results exclude Chongqing, Tibet, and Qinghai. Indonesia results exclude Aceh, Papua, and Maluku. Vietnam results exclude Ba Ria Vung Tau and Long An).

* indicates significance at the 5 percent level

** indicates significance at the 10 percent level.

reflects the relatively modest government role in financing health care.[22] Given the predominance of private funding for health services, subnational revenues would not make a tangible difference in outcomes. Infant mortality might therefore be a better outcome measure in this case because it relates directly to health services, unlike life expectancy, which may imply other variables such as food source.

In Indonesia, unlike in China and Vietnam, the results are significant only for persons per hospital bed and life expectancy. Such relatively modest results may reflect the fact that the decentralization process is just beginning in these countries.

In specification 2, per capita subnational expenditures do not correlate with service outputs and outcomes. A possible explanation for these ambiguous results may be multicollinearity,[23] which reduces the efficiency of the estimation, although the estimator remains unbiased.[24]

In addition, the outcome indicators used in this chapter are naturally limited in the power of their estimation. Most provinces score highly in literacy and life expectancy rates, for example. Unlike income, most of these outcome indicators are bounded, so convergence over time should be the norm, which presents difficulties with the estimation.

Another possible explanation for the weak correlation between fiscal disparities and service indicators is that the latter change slowly over time. Only China has data that allow for testing the hypothesis that indicators deteriorate in regions with persistently low spending, compared with regions that spend more. In this third set of regressions, we use a longer time series for provincial per capita expenditures (1985–2000) as the explanatory variable for service delivery indicators (see table 4.12). We also add a fifth social indicator—combined student enrollment for primary, secondary, and tertiary schools—to further test our hypothesis.[25] In this case, excluding life expectancy, both specifications 1 and 2 suggest a significant correlation between the four outcome indicators and subnational expenditures across time, suggesting that persistent fiscal inequities do matter.[26]

In sum, although the variation in outcome indicators is much less than the variation in revenues, there is some evidence that outcomes are affected by different levels of subnational revenues across provinces. In the short run, effects seem dominated by differences in income per capita, but evidence on China suggests that persistent fiscal inequalities result in inequalities in social indicators beyond those that can be explained by income per capita.

TABLE 4.12 Fiscal Disparities and Public Services Outputs and Outcomes in China, 1985–2000

Variable and Specification	
HDI 1	0.11*
HDI 2	0.003
Persons per hospital bed 1	−0.50*
Persons per hospital beds 2	−0.40*
Life expectancy 1	0.06*
Life expectancy 2	−0.02
Literacy 1	0.06*
Literacy 2	0.07*
Combined enrollment 1	0.13*
Combined enrollment 2	0.08*

Source: Authors' calculations.
Note: The table presents the results of regression analyses with the output or outcome indicator as a dependent variable. Dependent variables are a constant and expenditures per capita over 15 years in specification 1 ($y = \alpha + \beta$ * expenditure per capita over 15 years), and a constant, expenditures per capita over 15 years, and provincial GDP per capita in specification 2 ($y = \alpha + \beta$ * expenditure per capita + γ * GPP per capita). Results exclude Chongqing, Tibet, and Qinghai.
* indicates significance at the 5 percent level;
** indicates significance at the 10 percent level.

Although public spending can be critical in improving health and education outcomes, there are many reasons why increased public spending does not necessarily translate into better services and better outcomes. How (effectiveness) and where (sector allocation, levels of government, geographical distribution) resources are used determines whether they lead to positive outcomes. For example, Thailand and Peru both increased public spending on primary schooling, yet completion rates fell in Thailand while they rose in Peru. Conversely, health spending in Mexico and Jordan diverged, but child mortality fell in both countries (World Bank 2004a). Indeed, effectiveness in the use of funds varies widely across countries. Studies show that the nonpoor typically receive a disproportionate share of public spending (Filmer 2003). Yet, even if spending is well targeted, it does not always reach frontline service providers (teachers, doctors), and when it does, providers must be both present and effective in their jobs (World Bank 2004a). Services can also fail poor people due to a lack of demand. In this case, the geographical distribution of resources matters because there may be insufficient demand for services in certain regions and locations. Ultimately, whether spending will materialize into better services and outcomes will depend if it is coupled with accountability systems (strong performance management and producer accountability) and appropriate policies (Pritchett 2004).

Conclusions

This chapter shows that fiscal disparities among subnational governments in East Asia are considerable. Equalization mechanisms diminish subnational fiscal disparities, yet they remain large. We find considerable disparities in service outputs and outcomes as well, but data and methodological issues prevent us from establishing a strong link with large fiscal disparities. For the one country with enough data (China), we find that persistent fiscal disparities do seem to affect health and education outcomes.

The reasons why inequalities may persist are numerous. First, expenditure needs may vary significantly. Such variation could reflect differences in costs or the fact that some regions provide more services than others. Persistent inequalities may also reflect the central government's emphasis on revenue mobilization. Too much equalization—if not well designed—could reduce the incentives for subnational governments to mobilize own-revenues, undermining overall tax revenues. Inequalities among regions could also induce people to migrate to regions with better economic prospects. Poor regions may be less capable of handling funds than rich ones, or less concerned with poverty alleviation than the center. Rich regions are also powerful, and they do not like to lose out to poorer regions. Reasons for persisting inequalities in the East Asian context include the coastal development strategy in China, which allowed some provinces to get rich first, and Indonesia's policy of channeling revenues from natural resources to regions with separatist tendencies.

Based on these preliminary findings and the broader implications of interregional inequity, we offer recommendations to address such inequity in four areas: information management, transfer systems, the role of the central government, and further research and analysis.

The policy debate on fiscal inequalities—and intergovernmental fiscal relations more generally—requires more data. Without better information on the size of inequalities and how they have evolved, informed debate over which are acceptable is impossible. Each East Asian country suffers from a dearth of data. Those analyzed here are far from perfect, and we could not include other countries because they lack fiscal data at the subnational level, especially below the first subnational tier. Data on differences in the cost of delivering services are also critical in assessing interregional disparities. Governments must set up monitoring systems—an undertaking that requires significant resources. Indonesia maintains a database that—supported by the legal requirement that regions report—includes fiscal information on most of 410 local governments. In China, subnational governments have fiscal data, but the central government has little of this information. Some countries also need to adjust their accounting and budget classification systems. China, for instance, classifies significant fiscal resources as "extrabudgetary" and information on those funds is even scarcer, even though they fundamentally alter conclusions on fiscal disparities.

More data analysis also needs to inform the policy debate. Countries should aim to regularly review the results of their intergovernmental fiscal systems, including fiscal and service disparities. For example, following the highly successful example of South Africa, Indonesia published the first of what will be a regular intergovernmental fiscal review in March 2004. Such reports will allow policy makers to evaluate the intergovernmental fiscal system.

Regardless of whether more or less fiscal equalization is desirable, countries have significant scope to improve the design of their intergovernmental systems. Central governments must determine their equalization goals and priorities regarding income levels, fiscal capacity, expenditure needs, and per capita revenues (Bahl 2000). The goals of equalization grants are often unclear: some grants embody features of earmarked grants, for example, usually based on temporary considerations. A more comprehensive goal would require each local government to deliver a minimum level of goods and services.

Country-specific recommendations include:

- China's transfer system could aim to reflect local revenue capacity and expenditure needs in a rules-based manner, rather than through ad hoc distribution. Besides a more transparent system, China should also aim for simpler equalization mechanisms—perhaps by combining various equalization grants into one overarching grant. To further enhance both transparency and simplicity, the country could systematically identify total equalization funds, based on tradeoffs between equalization, growth, and incentives for local revenue mobilization and expenditures.
- Although Indonesia's transfer system introduces the notion of expenditure needs and revenue capacity through its equalization grant, it should define a more equalizing DAU by phasing out the transitional elements and the "hold harmless" portion of the allocation. In terms of transparency and simplicity, Indonesia should focus on more consistent treatment of natural resource revenues in revenue sharing and the equalization formula. The country should introduce a selective system of specific grants combined with an onlending window to promote local financing of national priorities.
- In Vietnam, negotiation and discretion remain, primarily for "surplus" provinces and local governments. The central government may wish to consider introducing conditional grants or other transfer instruments—with or without matching provisions—to create incentives and provide financing for expenditures in priority areas such as health and education. Local governments could also use such funding for social assistance programs, along with grants for capital infrastructure.[27]

Our data show that although huge fiscal disparities exist across subnational governments, inequalities in health and education outcomes are relatively modest. Why? What are the countervailing forces within each country or groups of subnational provinces and municipalities? Do people tend to migrate from one region to another? Is there a push for asymmetrical decentralization? What are government preferences, and what role do they play in policy making? Debate regarding the center's role and the impact of its programs is also critical. These and many other questions present challenging lines for further empirical analysis.

Endnotes

1. Migration can be considered excessive in an economic sense, if the marginal productivity of a worker would be higher in his place of origin, or if the congestion costs in the region of destination are larger than the private benefits obtained from the better services; see Ahmad and Craig in Ter-Minassian, ed., 1997.
2. For an extensive discussion of this point, see Tanzi and Shuknecht 1995 and Prud'homme 1995.
3. A review, assessing constitutional rights to education and health care in 187 countries, concludes that of the 165 countries with written constitutions available, 116 made reference to a right to education and 73 to a right to health care (Gauri 2003).
4. In the Philippines, for example, IRA allocations have somewhat detracted from LGUs' incentive to improve the collection of own-source revenues (World Bank 2003a).
5. Art. XVIII (a), sub. 2, of the Indonesian Constitution states, "The relationship in finances, public services, utilization of natural resources and other resources . . . shall be regulated and executed fairly and equitably based on the law."
6. Art, II, sections 9 and 10, of the Philippine Constitution states, "The State shall promote a just and dynamic social order that will ensure the prosperity and independence of the nation and free the people from poverty through policies that provide adequate social services, promote full employment, a rising standard of living, and an improved quality of life for all. The State shall promote social justice in all phases of national development."
7. The figure for Vietnam excludes the oil-producing region of Ba-Ria Vung Tao.
8. Fiscal disparities can differ depending on the indicator of inequality. A future version of this study will also use the population-weighted Theil indicator to calculate fiscal disparities. This will better measure the impact of fiscal disparities from the individual's perspective.
9. The level of fiscal disparities is sensitive to cost differentials across provinces. However, data on provincial cost of living are not readily available for these countries.
10. Data limitations, along with changes in these countries' decentralization processes, make a similar analysis very difficult to perform for other countries in our sample.
11. In principle, the law prescribes this as 25 percent of actual revenues, but the DAU has so far been based on budgeted revenues.
12. For detail, see Hofman et al. 2003.
13. As a result of the 1994 Tax Sharing System, revenue-sharing arrangements changed from a negotiated, mildly equalizing system to one based on strict tax assignments (Wong 2002). For more detail, see Ahmad et al. 2000.
14. Besides fiscal equalization, general grants promote tax effort and local good governance, devolution of compulsory functions, train ticket compensation, local development, and education. Exceptions to the formula-based allocation criteria are local good governance, train ticket compensation, and local development.
15. Although the aggregate IRA share is fixed by law, the central government withheld 5 percent after the 1998 Asian financial crisis without any consultation. Despite a Supreme Court ruling in favor of local governments, disagreement remains on whether the formula should be subject to appropriation or decreased as part of the congressional appropriation process. See Manasan 2002.
16. The United States has seen some success in using these data for grant design. See Rafuse 1992.
17. This ignores the effect of borrowing. However, since richer regions are likely to have more access to borrowing, the conclusions on equalization are likely to hold.
18. This chapter adopts the UNDP procedure for computing HDI. Provincial HDI is based on three indicators: longevity, as measured by life expectancy at birth; education attainment, as measured by a combination of adult literacy (two-thirds weight) and combined primary, secondary, and tertiary enrollment ratios (one-third weight); and standard of living, as measured by real GDP per capita in terms of purchasing power parity (in dollars) (UNDP 1999). We broadly define persons per hospital bed in terms of public hospitals. (In Indonesia, the indicators include both special and general hospitals.) We define literacy rate as the percentage of people aged 15 and above who cannot read and write a short, simple statement about their everyday life (World Bank 2003c). We define life expectancy as the number of years a newborn infant would live if prevailing patterns of mortality remained the same throughout its life (World Bank 2003c).
19. Variation is measured through the coefficient of variation, which is the standard deviation divided by the average.
20. Although maximum-to-minimum ratios within countries capture the same trends as more sophisticated measures (such as the gini coefficient), those ratios are more responsive than other measures to the tail-end of the distribution across countries.
21. Specification 2 aims to address the problem of reverse causality between expenditures (revenues) and outcomes. Otherwise, reverse causality would suggest the possibility that our regression estimates may be upwardly biased. The third set of regressions, which examines a longer time series for China, will address the possible problem of multicollinearity (when two or more independent variables are approximately linearly related) in specification 2.
22. "In 1998, the public expenditure share in aggregate health spending was only about 20 percent, with households accounting for the remaining 80 percent" (World Bank 2000).
23. The problem of multicollinearity is when two or more independent variables are approximately linearly related in the sample data.
24. Indeed, expenditures are highly correlated with GDP for China (.67), Indonesia (.42), and Vietnam (.67) (with significance at the 1 percent level). It would be interesting to see if the same results hold at even lower levels of governments. The only exception to the rule is China.
25. As shown in the previous set of regressions, life expectancy yields ambiguous results, as it is affected by a broad range of factors for which we do not control. Infant or child mortality would therefore be a better indicator. Lacking those data, we have used combined gross enrollment as our fifth outcome indicator in this final set of regressions.
26. The only exception to the results is HDI in specification 2, yet this is understandable, as GDP is one of its components.
27. Martínez-Vázquez argues for the need to structure transfers at the subprovincial level (2004b).

Bibliography

Ahmad, Ehtisham, and John Craig. 1997. "Intergovernmental Transfers." In *Fiscal Federalism in Theory and Practice*, ed. Teresa Ter-Minassian. Washington, DC: International Monetary Fund.

Ahmad, Ehtisham, Li Keping, and Thomas Richardson. 2000. "Recentralization in China?" Conference on Fiscal Decentralization, November.

Bahl, Roy. 2000. "Intergovernmental Transfers in Developing and Transition Countries: Principles and Practice." Washington, DC: World Bank, Urban and Local Government, Municipal Finance.

Bahl, Roy, and Jorge Martínez-Vázquez. 2003. "Fiscal Federalism and Economic Reform in China." Atlanta, GA: Georgia State University, International Studies Program.

Balisacan, Arsenio M., Ernesto M. Pernia, and Abuzar Asra. 2003. "Revisiting Growth and Poverty Reduction in Indonesia: What Do Subnational Data Show?" *Bulletin of Indonesian Economic Studies* 39 (3): 329–51.

Birdsall, Nancy, and Estelle James. 1990. "Efficiency and Equity in Social Spending: How and Why Governments Misbehave." Washington, DC: World Bank; Policy, Research, and External Affairs; Population and Human Resources Operations.

Bourguignon, François. 2003. "Transition of China's Northeast: The Need for Combining Regional and National Policies." Paper for seminar on Development Strategy for Northeast China, Shenyang, Liaoning Province, China, December 3–4.

Brodjonegoro, Bambang. 2000. "Regional Autonomy and Fiscal Decentralization in Democratic Indonesia." *Hitotsubashi Journal of Economics* 41: 111–22.

Buchanan, James M. 1950. "Federalism and Fiscal Equity." *American Economic Review* 40 (4): 583–99.

Ebel, Bob. 2003. "Intergovernmental Transfers." Presentation at workshop on Decentralization and Intergovernmental Fiscal Reform. Washington, DC: World Bank, March 24–26.

———. 2003. "Subnational Revenues and Intergovernmental Relations." Presentation at workshop on Decentralization and Intergovernmental Fiscal Reform. Washington, DC: World Bank, March 24–26.

Filmer, Deon. 2003. "The Incidence of Public Expenditures on Health and Education." Background note for *World Development Report 2004: Making Services Work for Poor People*. Washington, DC: World Bank; and New York: Oxford University Press.

Garcia-Garcia, Jorge, and Lana Soehstianingsih. 1998. "Why Do Differences in Provincial Income Persist in Indonesia?" *Bulletin of Indonesian Economic Studies* 34 (1).

Gauri, Varun. 2003. "Social Rights and Economics: Claims to Health Care and Education in Developing Countries." Washington, DC: World Bank, Development Research Group.

Gill, Nicholas, and Andres Rodriguez-Pose. 2003. "Is There a Global Link between Regional Disparities and Devolution?" *Research Papers in Environmental and Spatial Analysis* 79. London: London School of Economics and Political Science, Department of Geography and Environment.

Government of Indonesia. 2002. *Statistik Indonesia (Statistical Yearbook of Indonesia)*. Jakarta: Badan Pusat Statistik.

Hegedus, Jozsef. 2001. "Creating Change Networks for Local Governance." Presentation for World Bank Institute/United Nations Development Programme, Initiative for Central Asia, Bratislava, July 30–August 3.

Hill, Hal. 2000. "Intra-Country Regional Disparities." Paper presented at Second Asian Development Forum, Singapore, June 6–8.

———. 2002. "Spatial Disparities in Developing East Asia: A Survey." *Asian-Pacific Economic Literature* 16 (1): 10–35.

Hofman, Bert, Kadjatmiko, and Kai Kaiser. 2003. "Fiscal Equalization in Indonesia's 2001 'Big Bang' Decentralization." Paper prepared for conference at Georgia State University, Can Decentralization Help Rebuild Indonesia?, Atlanta.

Jimenez, Emmanuel, and Donald Cox. 1995. "Private Transfers and the Effectiveness of Public Income Redistribution in the Philippines." In *Public Spending and the Poor: Theory and Evidence*, eds. Dominique Van de Walle and Kimberly Nead. Washington, DC: World Bank.

Lewis, Blane. 2003. "Local Government Borrowing and Repayment in Indonesia: Does Fiscal Capacity Matter?" *World Development* 31 (6): 1047–63.

Manasan, Rosario. 2002. "Fiscal Decentralization: The Case of the Philippines." Background Paper for World Bank–sponsored course on Decentralization and Intergovernmental Fiscal Reform in East Asia, Bangkok, June 6–7.

Martínez-Vázquez, Jorge. 2003. "Improving the Design of Fiscal Decentralization in Vietnam." Presentation at Government of Vietnam/World Bank workshop, Ha Tay Province, February.

———. 2004a. "The Design of Fiscal Decentralization: Principles and Best International Practice." Presentation to Public Expenditure Review and Integrated Fiduciary Assessment Mission, Hanoi, April.

———. 2004b. "Improving the Design of Fiscal Decentralization in Vietnam." Prepared for World Bank Vietnam Public Expenditure Review. Washington, DC: World Bank.

Martínez-Vázquez, Jorge, and Jameson Boex. 1998. "Fiscal Decentralization in the Russian Federation: Main Trends and Issues." Washington, DC: World Bank, Economic Development Institute.

Martínez-Vázquez, Jorge, and Robert M. McNab. 2003. "Fiscal Decentralization and Economic Growth." *World Development* 31 (9): 1597–1616.

McLure, Charles E., Jr. 1999. "The Tax Assignment Problem: Conceptual and Administrative Considerations in Achieving Subnational Fiscal Autonomy." Washington, DC: World Bank.

Milanovic, Branko. 2001. "Conflict between Horizontal Equity and Maximum Poverty Reduction: How Best to Allocate Funds to Regions? An Empirical Analysis." Washington, DC: World Bank.

National Statistical Coordination Board. 2003. *Philippine Statistical Yearbook*. Manila: National Economic and Development Authority.

Pritchett, Lant. 2004. "Towards a New Consensus for Addressing the Global Challenge of the Lack of Education." Copenhagen Consensus Challenge Paper.

Pritchett, Lant, and Jonah Gelbach. 2000. "Indicator Targeting in a Political Economy: Leakier Can Be Better." Washington, DC: World Bank.

Pritchett, Lant, Deon Filmer, and Jeffrey Hammer. 1999. "Health Policy in Poor Countries: Weak Links in the Chain." Washington, DC: World Bank.

Prud'homme, Rémy. 1995. "The Dangers of Decentralization." *World Bank Research Observer* 10 (2): 201–21.

Qiao, Baoyun, Jorge Martinez-Vazquez, and Yongsheng Xu. 2003. "Growth and Equity Tradeoff in Decentralization Policy: China's Experience." Atlanta, GA: Georgia State University, International Studies Program.

Rafuse, Robert. 1992. "Representative Expenditure." Washington, DC: U.S. Advisory Commission on Intergovernmental Relations.

Rao, M. Govinda. n.d. "Fiscal Assignment and Service Delivery." Presentation for Institute for Social and Economic Change, Bangalore, India.

———. 2001. "Challenges in Fiscal Decentralization: An Asian Perspective." Paper presented at conference on Public Finance in Developing and Transition Countries, Atlanta, GA.

Rao, M. Govinda, Richard M. Bird, and Jennie Litvack. 1998. "Fiscal Decentralization and Poverty Alleviation in a Transitional Economy: The Case of Vietnam." *Asian Economic Journal* 12 (4): 353–78.

Ravallion, Martin. 1993. "Poverty Alleviation through Regional Targeting: A Case Study for Indonesia." In *The Economics of Rural Organization: Theory, Practice and Policy*, eds. Karla Hoff, Avishay Braverman, and Joseph Stiglitz. Washington, DC: World Bank; and New York: Oxford University Press.

———. 1998. "Reaching Poor Areas in a Federal System." Policy Research Working Paper. Washington, DC: World Bank, Development Research Group.

———. 1999a. "Is More Targeting Consistent with Less Spending?" Washington, DC: World Bank.

———. 1999b. "Are Poorer States Worse at Targeting Their Poor?" *Economic Letters* 65: 373–77.

Ravallion, Martin, and Gaurav Datt. 1990. "Regional Disparities, Targeting, and Poverty in India." Washington, DC: World Bank; Policy, Research, and External Affairs; Population and Human Resources Operations.

Republic of China. Multiple years. *Statistical Yearbook of the Republic of China*. Taiwan: Directorate-General of Budget, Accounting, and Statistics.

Republic of Vietnam. Multiple years. *Statistical Yearbook*. Hanoi: Statistical Publishing House.

Searle, Bob. 2002. "Federal Fiscal Relations in Australia." Torino, Italy: International Centre for Economic Research.

Smoke, Paul. 2001. "Fiscal Decentralization in Developing Countries: A Review of Current Concepts and Practices." Democracy, Governance and Human Rights Programme Paper No. 2. Geneva: United Nations Research Institute for Social Development.

Tanzi, Vito, and L. Shuknecht. 1995. "The Growth of Government and the Reform of the State in Industrial Countries." Working Paper. Washington, DC: International Monetary Fund.

Ter-Minassian, Teresa. 1997. *Fiscal Federalism in Theory and Practice, International Monetary Fund*. Washington, DC: International Monetary Fund.

UNDP (United Nations Development Programme). 1999. *China Human Development Report*. New York: United Nations.

Van de Walle, Dominique. 1995. "Incidence and Targeting: An Overview of Implications for Research and Policy." In *Public Spending and the Poor: Theory and Evidence*, eds. Dominique Van de Walle and Kimberly Nead. Washington, DC: World Bank.

Wong, Christine. 2002. "Issues of Equalization in China." Presentation for workshop on Intergovernmental Fiscal Relations in East Asia. Washington, DC: World Bank.

World Bank. 1993. "China: Budgetary Policy and Intergovernmental Fiscal Relations." Report No. 11094-CHA. Washington, DC: World Bank.

———. 2000. "Managing Public Resources Better." Vietnam Public Expenditure Review. Washington, DC: World Bank.

———. 2002a. "China: National Development and Subnational Finance: A Review of Provincial Expenditures." Washington, DC: World Bank.

———. 2002b. "Brazil: Issues in Brazilian Federalism." Washington, DC: World Bank, Latin America and the Caribbean Region, Poverty Reduction Economic Management Sector Unit, Brazil Country Management Unit.

———. 2003a. "Philippines: Improving Government Performance—Discipline, Efficiency, and Equity in Managing Public Resources." Washington, DC: World Bank, Poverty Reduction Economic Management, East Asia and the Pacific Region.

———. 2003b. "Decentralizing Indonesia." Regional Public Expenditure Review. Washington, DC: World Bank, Poverty Reduction Economic Management, East Asia and the Pacific Region.

———. 2003c. "World Development Indicators." Washington, DC: World Bank.

———. 2004a. *World Development Report 2004: Making Services Work for Poor People*. Washington, DC: World Bank; and New York: Oxford University Press.

———. 2004b. "Chinese 11th Five-Year Plan." Concept note. Washington, DC: World Bank, Development Economic Research Group.

———. 2004c. "2004 Public Expenditure Review and Integrated Fiduciary Assessment." Aide mémoire, Multi-Donor Mission, Hanoi, April 5–16.

———. 2004d. "Inequality in Latin America and the Caribbean: Breaking with History?" Washington, DC: World Bank, Latin American and Caribbean Studies.

———. 2004e. "Managing Decentralization in East Asia." Washington, DC: World Bank, Poverty Reduction Economic Management, East Asia and Pacific Region.

Yan. 2003. "Regional Equalization in China's Public Finance." Unpublished paper.

Zhang, Zhihua, and Jorge Martínez-Vázquez. 2003. "The System of Equalization Transfers in China." International Studies Program Working Paper No. 03-13. Atlanta, GA: Georgia State University, Andrew Young School of Policy Studies.

5

PUBLIC EXPENDITURE ON THE FRONTLINE: TOWARD EFFECTIVE MANAGEMENT BY SUBNATIONAL GOVERNMENTS

Edward Mountfield and Christine P. W. Wong

East Asia has been home to some of the world's most centralized public expenditure management systems. From a macroeconomic perspective, this approach may have had its merits—for example, allowing for a rapid fiscal response during the 1998 crisis. However, such top-down approaches have typically not been conducive to locally responsive service delivery (World Bank 2000d, pp. 31–33). Countries have often achieved fiscal discipline at the expense of effectiveness and efficiency. To accomplish broader national objectives—not only macroeconomic stabilization but also poverty reduction and effective and efficient local service delivery—public expenditure management is moving closer to the frontline.

Intergovernmental reform of expenditure management presents some major opportunities. Local management of spending can support service delivery that is more responsive to the needs and wishes of local people and more efficient given local conditions. Equally, there are significant threats: duplication, poor coordination, growing inequity, and even the collapse of essential services.

Of the five most populous low- and middle-income countries in East Asia—hereafter referred to as the EA5[1]—four are designing programs to transfer expenditure responsibilities to lower-level governments. Indonesia is implementing a "Big Bang" decentralization program. Thailand has committed to implementing a gradual but potentially major decentralization program. Vietnam has recently legislated to shift greater expenditure authority and responsibility to provincial People's Councils. And the Philippines continues to explore policy options for strengthening its comprehensive program of decentralization started a decade ago. The fifth country, China, is alone in moving in the opposite direction: since the late 1990s it has instituted a program to reform public expenditure management that will—at least in the short run—increase central scrutiny of local spending. However, since China has gone furthest among the EA5 in assigning spending responsibilities to subnational governments, the recent changes should be seen as part of a continuing effort to find the right balance between central control and local flexibility, rather than a rejection of decentralization.

Given the EA5's relatively recent moves to decentralize expenditure management, deriving conclusions as to whether these countries have "failed" or "succeeded" in terms of service delivery would be premature. Instead, this chapter reviews experiences so far with decentralizing expenditures in the EA5. The chapter presents some empirics on expenditure decentralization and provides an initial assessment of the nascent expenditure management systems at subnational levels in these countries. Finally, the chapter analyzes the extent to which the incentive framework and institutional environment in each country are likely to foster successful subnational expenditure management.

Subnational Expenditure Management in the EA5: Some Empirics

The extent to which EA5 countries have decentralized public spending varies. By the conventional measure of subnational shares of total spending, China is by far the most decentralized of the five, with subnational spending at 69 percent. It is followed by Vietnam, with 48 percent. At the lower end is Thailand, where subnational spending is just 10 percent of the total. The East Asian archipelago countries are somewhere in the middle: the Philippines is at 25 percent and Indonesia reached 31 percent after Big Bang decentralization. Table 5.1 compares the subnational expenditure shares of the EA5 with those of other countries.

In a study of some 100 countries, Roy Bahl and his colleagues at Georgia State University found the share of subnational expenditures to be positively correlated with per capita gross domestic product (GDP) and land area, and negatively correlated with ethnic diversity.[2] Transition economies as a group also tend to be more decentralized than expected from the other variables. Led by the two transition economies of China and Vietnam, the EA5 have decentralized more than the average 14 percent of total expenditures that Bahl et al. found for developing countries, but have decentralized less than the average of 35 percent in developed countries. Even considering these factors, however, the authors found that China and Vietnam were more decentralized than expected in the 1990s, Indonesia and Thailand less, and the Philippines exactly at the expected level.[3]

TABLE 5.1 Expenditure Decentralization in East Asia in Comparative Perspective

	Subnational expenditure (% of national expenditure)
China 2002	69
Indonesia 2002	32
Philippines 2001	26
Thailand 2001	10
Vietnam 2002	48
Developing countries 1990s	14
Transition countries 1990s	26
OECD countries 1990s	32
Other large countries, 1990s:	
Germany	40
India	46
Japan	61
Pakistan	29
Russia	38
United States	46

Sources: Bahl 2002; World Bank 2003a; staff estimates.
Note: OECD = Organisation for Economic Co-operation and Development.

However, while subnational spending share is a convenient measure for comparing decentralization across countries, it is often misleading when the locus of spending does not coincide with the level of decision making, as has often been the case in East Asia (Bahl 2002). Vietnam is a perfect illustration of this shortcoming. Despite its high subnational spending share, Vietnam was—until it implemented the new State Budget Law in January 2004—formally one of the least decentralized countries in the world. Local governments were essentially carrying out deconcentrated functions at the behest of the central government, which determined service levels and standards.

Another conventional yardstick for measuring decentralization is the pattern of expenditure assignments. Table 5.2 shows expenditure assignments for the EA5 and other countries. China again appears to be the most decentralized of the five. Compared with the other countries, China has transferred a much larger portion of expenditure responsibilities to local governments, including several big-ticket items—not only education and health, which are common local functions in many countries, but also unemployment benefits and pensions. The latter make China highly unusual. Pensions and unemployment benefits often exceed the financing capacity of subnational governments, and their cyclical nature makes them often inappropriate for such governments. In almost all other countries, these responsibilities are either central or shared with state governments. Indonesia and Thailand are also quite decentralized compared with other countries, with education and health assigned solely to local governments. In the Philippines, health is a joint responsibility of state and local governments, while education remains a central government responsibility.

Table 5.2 shows expenditure assignments, but again we must be cautious in interpreting such summary tables. The table identifies only the level of government responsible for providing services, not necessarily the one that finances the services. Indonesia, for example, assigns costly functions like education and health to subnational levels, but finances them through specific transfers from the central government. Subprovincial governments in China, in contrast, receive limited transfers from which to fund their expenditure mandates. Local governments are responsible for not only providing but also financing their service responsibilities, with little support from either earmarked or equalization transfers.

Differences in how countries report the division of responsibilities may also muddy comparisons. Such differences may simply reflect different transfer instruments. A central government that earmarks transfers for education would more likely report education as a joint responsibility than a central government that provides block grants to local governments.

Given the heterogeneity of the EA5, another dimension is worth mentioning: multiple levels of subnational government. China's intermediate level of government is larger than that of most countries: each such government has an average of 45 million people. Prefectural units—mostly municipalities—have an average population of 3.7 million, making them as large as or larger than provinces and states in many countries. Considering the size of countries themselves is also important in drawing inferences about state versus local service provision. Even accounting for size, China is extreme in having transferred so many responsibilities to the lowest levels: municipalities and counties—not provinces or the central government—are responsible for social welfare provision.

Public Expenditure Management Processes in the EA5

East Asian countries have substantially expanded the extent to which subnational levels manage public expenditure. The most critical expenditure management processes, which are nascent and still evolving, include the following:

Policy analysis and planning. The policy responsibilities of government departments and the legislature must be clear, appropriate, and transparent. An effective policy analysis and planning process should identify clear development goals and priorities, provide a realistic fiscal framework for public expenditure rather than encouraging a "shopping list" approach, and inform planning with sound, evidence-based policy analysis. Such a process should also involve sector departments within the subnational government rather than just planning and finance departments; provide a mechanism for the central government to coordinate policy with

TABLE 5.2 Expenditure Assignments in East Asian and Comparison Countries

Country	Defense	Foreign affairs	Environment and natural resources	Unemployment insurance	Industry and agriculture	Education	Health	Social welfare	Police	Highways
EA5 countries:										
China	F	F	F, S, L	L	F, S, L	L	L	L	L	F, S, L
Indonesia	F	F	..	..	L	L	L	L	F	F, S, L
Philippines (1)	F	F	..	..	..	F	F	F	..	..
Philippines (2)	F	F	..	..	..	F, S, L	F, S, L	S, L	S, L	..
Thailand (1)	F	F	..	..	..	L	L	..	L	L
Thailand (2)	F	F	..	..	..	L	L	..	L	L
Vietnam	F	F	F, S, L	..	F, S, L	S, L	S, L	F, S, L	F	F, S, L
Comparison countries:										
India (1)	F	F	F, S	F, S	F, S	F, S	S	F, S	S	F
India (2)	F	F	F, S	F, S	F, S	F, S, L	S, L	F, S	S	F
Japan (1)	F	F	..	..	L	F, L	F, L	F, L	L	..
Japan (2)	F	F	..	..	..	L	F, L	F, L	F, L	L
Malaysia (1)	F	F	L	..	F, S	F	F, S	F, S	F	F
Malaysia (2)	F	F	L	..	F, S	F	F, S	F, S	F	F
Countries that assign constitutional powers:										
Canada	F	F	F, S	F, S	C	S	S(F)	F, S	F, S	S
United States	F, S	F	F, S	F, S	S	S, F	S(F)		F, S	F, S
Switzerland	F	F	C	C	F, S	C, F, S	S, C	F, C	S	F, S
Australia	F, S	F	F, S	C	S, C	F, S	F, S	C	S, F	F, S
Germany	F	F, S	C	C	C	C, S	C, F, S	C	C, S	C
Austria	F	F	F, S	F	F	F, S	C, F, S	C	F, S	F, S

Sources: World Bank 2003a, annex 4; other World Bank information.
Note: 1 = responsibility, 2 = provision, F = federal/national, S = state/province, L = local, C = concurrent, (..) = not identified.

subnational governments; and institute processes that allow for extensive consultation with service users, frontline providers, donors, and civil society. Finally, both the planning framework and the underlying analysis should be made public and widely disseminated, and the planning framework updated regularly—ideally annually, as part of the budget cycle.

Budget formulation. An effective budget cycle should have a logical sequence and timing and build on the planning framework. The budget should also reconcile development goals and policy priorities with a realistic assessment of fiscal constraints. The budget should cover all subnational expenditures, including capital and current expenditures as well as subsidies, transfers, interest, and net lending. The budget should explicitly incorporate the use of extrabudgetary funds, including those financed by donors; minimize earmarking of resources; and clarify the future budget implications of investment decisions. Once again all stakeholders should be involved, with budgets widely disseminated and enough time allowed for consultation and debate before legislative approval.

Budget execution. Budget execution should adhere as closely as possible to the estimates approved by the legislature (although under clearly prescribed circumstances the finance agency may have the authority to change departmental allocations during the fiscal year). Annual cash requirements for each spending unit should be forecast so cash management is efficient and consistent with releases and authorizations to spend. Arrears should not be significant as a proportion of total spending, and planning and control systems should protect against overspending, provide effective crosschecks between human resource management systems and payroll, and establish competitive and transparent procurement.

Monitoring and accounting. National law needs to establish financial reporting and accounting rules for subnational governments that reflect recognized accounting standards. Subnational governments need to collect comparable data, to facilitate policy analysis as well as management of national fiscal targets. In-year and end-year statements should be produced shortly after the end of the fiscal year and made routinely available to all stakeholders. And governments should monitor budget outputs and outcomes to the extent possible.

Auditing and evaluation. A clear distinction should be made between internal and external audit. End-year accounts of subnational expenditures should be audited under a reasonably rapid timetable, ideally by an independent auditor general or under his or her supervision. Audit reports should be scrutinized by the legislature and made public in a timely fashion. When the auditor general issues an adverse report, policy makers need to take appropriate follow-up action. Audits should include budget outputs and outcomes as well as financial inputs to the extent possible. They should also systematically evaluate a sample of projects and programs, with the results drawn upon in planning and budget formulation for subsequent years.

Assessing East Asian Countries

To what extent do the EA5 countries have these core expenditure management processes in place? To answer that question, we reviewed published and unpublished reports on expenditure decentralization in these countries.[4] We found that such processes generally remain weak at the subnational level (see table 5.3). Planning processes are disconnected from fiscal planning and budgeting processes, and poorly coordinated with planning at other levels of government. Budget formulation suffers from major delays and is fragmented, with parallel budgets for investment projects and recurrent expenditures managed by separate institutions. Budget execution is slow, with long delays in effecting appropriations, significant divergence between approved appropriations and outturns, and corruption in procurement. Monitoring and accounting systems often produce data that are neither timely nor accurate. Auditing is typically weak, and evaluation almost nonexistent.

Part of the explanation is that countries such as Indonesia, Thailand, and Vietnam are just beginning to decentralize expenditures. However, time does not automatically solve these problems: China and the Philippines are still struggling to build the institutions they need despite starting one and two decades ago.

We provide further assessment, with country-by-country examples, on the next page.

TABLE 5.3 Strength of Core Expenditure Management Processes at Subnational Levels

	China (1980)	Indonesia (2001)	Philippines (1992)	Thailand (1999)	Vietnam (1994–1996)
Policy analysis and planning	❍	◑	◑	❍	❍
Budget formulation	◑	◑	❍	●	◑
Budget execution	❍	❍	❍	❍	◑
Monitoring and accounting	❍	❍	❍	◑	❍
Auditing and evaluation	❍	❍	❍	❍	❍

Source: Authors' assessment.
Note: ● = strong, ◑ = medium, ❍ = weak. Start date of decentralization in parentheses.

Policy Analysis and Planning. Vietnam has an established tradition of planning at subnational as well as national levels. Provincial Planning and Investment departments coordinate inputs to a Five-Year Plan and a five-year Public Investment Program (PIP). The national Five-Year Plan and PIP then consolidate these plans. However, problems persist. First, under Vietnam's system of "double subordination," reporting arrangements remain confused: the provincial departments of Planning and Investment report not only to the local People's Committee and People's Council, but also to the central Ministry of Planning and Investment, and through it to the National Assembly. Second, the local planning process occurs with little reference to fiscal constraints. Provinces submit investment plans that would typically add up to much more than the resources available. Third, the planning process encompasses only the investment budget (capital projects plus the often donor-funded development projects), paying little attention to the cost implications of development expenditures or the future budgetary implications of new spending commitments. Vietnam has started piloting medium-term expenditure planning, both at national and provincial levels, bringing planning of capital and recurrent expenditures under a single framework. However, establishing this system fully will take some years.

In China, provincial Planning Commissions address the priority areas declared by the central government in its Economic Development Plans. As in Vietnam, capital budgeting is separate from recurrent budgeting at each level of government. For example, a provincial Finance Bureau determines the annual capital provision, but a provincial Planning Commission allocates these resources between projects. These agencies rarely use cost-benefit analysis or other selection techniques.

In Indonesia, the center has traditionally dominated planning processes. These processes have started to evolve since the Big Bang decentralization of 2001, and the government has introduced a number of subnational planning instruments. Participation of civil society at the village level has greatly increased, reflecting new regulations that prescribe this participation. Planning processes are thus both top-down and bottom-up. However, major weaknesses remain. It is unclear how and when the top-down and bottom-up planning processes are integrated, for example. There is a large amount of duplication between these planning processes, as well as some inconsistency. The planning process is largely devoid of considerations of affordability: only the annual regional plan takes fiscal considerations into account. This results in much disappointment at all levels of government: district governments must make difficult choices and sharp cuts in the wish lists of villages, bureaus, and the district as a whole. Also similar to Vietnam is the focusing of planning on the development budget and capital projects rather than on the budget as a whole. Altogether, this situation is inconsistent with Indonesia's plans to require "performance budgets" from regional governments under Government Regulation 105/2000. However, only a few regions, such as Semarang, have prepared to move in that direction. The lack of clarity regarding the postdecentralization role of the national development planning agency, BAPPENAS, further confuses these processes.

In the Philippines, the Local Government Code prescribes a participatory approach to planning, but compliance is poor. The code mandates that each local government have a comprehensive, multisectoral development plan formulated by its Local Development Council (LDC) and approved by its legislature. However, fewer than half of local governments have an LDC in place. According to the code, one-quarter of LDC members should come from nongovernmental organizations (NGOs) and people's organizations. However, one survey found that fewer than one-third of local development plans have benefited from meaningful input from NGOs and people's organizations. The planning that does exist focuses heavily on capital projects. Some cities and provinces report having medium- and long-term development plans. However, most smaller local governments have only an Annual Investment Plan. Project prioritization is usually an ad hoc process, conducted with little reference to costs and benefits. Local officials report that their investment plans are formulated independently of regional and national investment plans, and vice versa.

Budget Formulation. In Vietnam, provincial Departments of Finance manage budget formulation at subnational levels, supervised by the provincial People's Council. Province-level spending units supervised directly by the provincial government submit their spending bids to the provincial Department of Finance. At the district level, Bureaus of Finance filter the spending bids of district-level spending units and communes. The provincial People's Councils previously submitted their budgets to the central Ministry of Finance for review and approval by the National Assembly. Under the new State Budget Law, however, the provincial People's Councils have enhanced authority to approve provincial spending plans, with the National Assembly responsible principally for approving revenue shares and transfers from the center, plus the consolidated budget. Transfers from the center to the provinces for stable periods of three years will also promote local budget planning.

Although seemingly coherent, this subnational budget process has continuing weaknesses. Perhaps the most significant problem is the separate Department of Finance and Department of Planning and Investment at the provincial level, and the relatively weak coordination between these finance and planning functions. This produces a disconnect between planning and budgeting processes, and between recurrent and capital spending, with plans focused on capital investments and little forward planning for recurrent spending. The rural transport sector, for example, has recently attracted major capital investment: only 269 communes now have no road access to district centers. However, a lack of maintenance provisions means that many roads fall into disrepair soon after construction is complete. Requiring communities to contribute to road maintenance places a disproportionate burden on the poor: World Bank staff estimate that such annual contributions equal 9.8 percent of the annual poverty line in the relatively poor Northern Uplands, compared with 4.6 percent in the country as a whole.

In China, the 1994 Budget Law governs the budget formulation process at central and local levels, but major weaknesses in subnational budgeting persist. The period allowed for preparing the budget is too short, often beginning only two months before the start of the budget year in January. This has a cascading effect through the five-tiered system, since each tier has to wait for information from the higher level before it can formulate its own expenditure and transfer plans. Because capital subsidies usually require matching funds, subnational governments have to hold large reserves. Budget formulation occurs on an annual basis, and the budget is not explicitly linked to a medium-term strategy or a multiyear plan. Instead, budgeting is essentially incremental, characterized by passive distribution of resources among existing structures and services. Extrabudgetary funds finance portions of expenditures in most subnational departments, and many local governments finance investments off-budget. The main budget includes considerable earmarking.

Budget formulation in Indonesia's regions remains principally an administrative exercise, largely guided from the center, with district governments and regional councils getting involved late in the process. All spending units submit their budget proposals to the local government's budget committee, which in East Lombok, for example, includes representatives of the regional secretary, the finance bureau, the revenue office, the planning bureau, and the legal bureau. The budget committee reviews revenue estimates and spending plans before finalizing the budget proposal around October for submission to the Regional Council. At least in some provinces, the Regional Council approves the budget before the start of the budget year in January. However, regional budget preparation during the first few years of decentralization has been compressed as a result of late approval of the national budget, which determines transfers from the center.

These processes are further complicated by continuing confusion regarding relationships between national and subnational governments, and between agencies at each level. According to regulation 105/2000, the Ministry of Home Affairs is still in charge of issuing budgeting guidelines, but the Ministry of Finance sets standards for financial management throughout the public sector.

In the Philippines, the integrity of local budgeting is distorted, as in Indonesia, by poor revenue estimates during the budget formulation process. In particular, the Internal Revenue Allotment (IRA) supplied by the central Department of Budget and Management has been highly unreliable: in 1998 the IRA estimate was 9 percent short of actual releases. The shortfall dropped to 2 percent and 6 percent in 1999 and 2000, respectively, but shot up to 15 percent in 2001. Budgeting is largely conducted in an incremental fashion. Community participation is limited: budget hearings are officially open to all interested parties, but local governments often do not circulate the budget document or expenditure statements.

In Thailand, annual budgeting has been relatively well-established in local administrations since it was first instituted. Local authorities prepare their budgets in conformance with central mandates. Executive bodies usually ready their budget documents between May and July and submit them to the local council in August, with final endorsement by provincial governors or district heads by the start of the budget year in October. However, only a small proportion of Thailand's public spending is managed at the local level.

Budget Execution. In Vietnam, provincial People's Councils approve subnational budgets. However, provincial and district branches of the State Treasury Department—part of the central Ministry of Finance—supervise financial execution of the approved budget. Treasury offices are responsible for issuing line-item allotments, approving checks drafted by spending units against those allotments, maintaining records of unspent balances, and compiling periodic financial reports. These mechanisms have proven broadly effective in preventing overspending, helping Vietnam earn its reputation for fiscal prudence. Although procedures exist for reallocating the budget during the fiscal year, divergence between budget plans and outputs is smaller than in most countries at similar levels of development. However, multiple layers of control also contribute to delays in projects and programs. Furthermore, a portion of subnational expenditures—although often eventually accounted for by Treasury—remains outside the budget execution process.

Indonesia has established procedures for apportioning and executing the approved budget. However, delays in issuing warrants pose a significant problem. The main reasons for these delays are lack of information about revenues from the center and lack of clarity of central regulations regarding decentralized funds. In the first year of decentralization, many regional governments were forced to engage in a major budget adjustment. The main cause was a centrally mandated increase in civil service wages announced in July 2001 (although contingency transfers offset the impacts of this increase).

In China, likewise, budget execution at local levels has been characterized by slow disbursement. Late approval of the budget and the long delay in effecting appropriations mean that spending units cannot plan their spending efficiently. A significant portion of expenditures thus occurs during the last months of the year.

Procurement processes remain weak and poorly administered at national and subnational levels in most EA5 countries. In Vietnam, the Ministry of Planning and Investment formally oversees procurement at all levels of government, but its scrutiny is weak and indirect, and a clarifying Procurement

Ordinance has yet to be approved. In Indonesia, Law 25 of 1999 (now Law 32 of 2004) allows regions to establish their own procurement regulations, with upcoming tenders published in local newspapers. However, Presidential Decree 18 of 2000 allows for preferential treatment of local bidders, and many regional officials see procurement as a means to support local contractors rather than a way to obtain the best price. In the Philippines, the Local Government Code decentralized procurement to local governments at a time when the legal and institutional framework was unclear and nontransparent. Although the country has since strengthened the national procurement framework, local policies and practices still raise concerns, including delays, excessive local preference, and contract price negotiation, which often becomes an entry point for corruption. In Thailand, local politicians often intrude in the procurement process.

Monitoring and Accounting. Experience from around the world has underscored the importance of having the central government set and enforce standards for financial reporting. National law needs to provide reporting and accounting rules for both the central and subnational levels. Such provisions help ensure that subnational governments generate financial reports that are comparable with those of other localities. They also help ensure that the central government can generate data for the entire government, for both analyzing policy and managing fiscal targets. Local capacity constraints may also require the central government to lead in this technically complex area. However, under a systematic program, local governments can often quickly develop their capacity to fulfill this task.

China, Indonesia, the Philippines, and Vietnam all have programs to modernize their financial management information systems at national and subnational levels. In the Philippines and Vietnam, the central government has the legal authority to set and enforce financial reporting standards. Both countries also have centrally specified charts of accounts, accounting systems, and reporting procedures. However, while these systems can produce general government reports, they are not timely or accurate. For example, end-year accounts are not available in Vietnam until 18 months after the end of the fiscal year. In the Philippines, local financial management is still based mainly on manual systems. Each country is implementing new financial management information systems that should strengthen overall government reporting.

In China and Indonesia, each budget level maintains its own accounting system. Both countries have established some reporting requirements, but institutional confusion over the powers of central agencies to specify and enforce these requirements has undermined them. In Indonesia, for example, the decentralization law splits subnational responsibility for financial management between two ministries—Finance and Home Affairs. In both countries, the quality of reporting is poor, financial reports are difficult to compare, and consolidating these reports is difficult. This situation reflects poor financial management information systems. For example, in Indonesia, subnational units submit quarterly budget reports and financial accounts to the Ministry of Finance mostly on paper. These two countries are investing in strengthening their financial management information systems. However, success will depend on their ability to resolve issues regarding the authority of central government to impose accounting systems on subnational governments.

Auditing and Evaluation. In Indonesia, local audit arrangements remain confused. Law 25 of 1999 determined that "prevailing regulations" should govern audits of local budgets. These regulations assigned the central government's internal auditor, the Supreme Audit Authority, the Inspectorate General of the province, and the Inspectorate General of Home Affairs as external auditors. Presidential Decree 74 of 2001 has since assigned three internal auditors the right to audit local budgets: the local government's auditor, the province's auditor, and the inspectors general of line ministries on technical aspects. According to Law 5 of 1973, the Supreme Audit Agency—the only external auditor in the country—has the authority to audit all levels of government. However, a draft law submitted to Parliament in September 2000 puts this authority in doubt.

In Vietnam, the State Audit of Vietnam (the external auditor) has existed for less than a decade. The Ministry of Finance recently issued 21 new auditing standards that reflect international standards and strengthened reporting to the National Assembly. Formally, the State Audit of Vietnam includes provinces and has five regional offices. In practice, however, the role of the state auditor at the subnational level has not been established, and most auditing is performed by the State Inspection Office (the internal auditor) and the network of provincial inspection offices.

In the Philippines, the Commission on Audit has the power to audit local governments. However, the internal audit function is nonexistent in most local governments. Until recently, the commission's regional directors were overstretched, personally supervising the audit of all government agencies in the region, although the government took steps in 2002 to address that problem.

Auditing is a weak link in China's subnational expenditure management. Local audit bureaus do ex post audits of local budgets. Audit bureaus may also select particular departments for a more in-depth audit and are also charged with auditing extrabudgetary funds. Each local government at the province level and below has its own audit bureau with similar responsibilities. However, although local audit bureaus also report to the People's Congress, they are under the direct authority of the executive branch, compromising their independence. They are also underresourced and in need of staff training.

In Thailand, only a small number of large-scale local authorities, such as the Bangkok Metropolitan Administration, Pattaya City and Nakorn municipalities, have internal auditors. Two external auditing units—the Office of Auditor General and the provincial auditing teams—have considerable credibility but limited capacity to provide auditing services to all local authorities.

In most EA5 countries, subnational budget evaluation is still in the earliest stages of development. In China, local budget evaluation barely exists. In Vietnam, the government has conducted three provincial expenditure reviews and is planning several more. In Indonesia, the head of a region is required to present an annual accountability report to the Regional Council. However, because the budget documentation does not specify measurable targets, evaluating outputs and outcomes is difficult.

Subnational Expenditure Management: Getting Institutions and Incentives Right

The institutional environment for subnational public expenditure management will play an important part in determining its evolution in the EA5. Central governments have an important role to play. Unless they establish appropriate institutions and incentive frameworks, successful subnational expenditure management processes are unlikely to develop. Key factors include the following:

Clear assignment of responsibilities. Clarity is essential regarding which expenditures each level of government is responsible for. According to Wallace Oates's "decentralization theorem," "each public service should be provided by the jurisdiction having control over the minimum geographic area that would internalize the benefits and costs of such provision."[5] The European Union has adopted the "subsidiarity" principle, which asserts that lower levels of government should have responsibility for spending and delivering services unless there is a convincing case for assigning that responsibility to higher levels.

Matching of resources to responsibilities. The resources available to each subnational government should reflect the costs of the services it must provide. Such a match can occur through some combination of tax and revenue assignment, tax- and revenue-sharing agreements, unconditional grants, conditional block grants (transfers subject to conditions or service standards), targeted grants for specific purposes or projects, and appropriate borrowing authority. These resource flows should be as stable and predictable as possible to facilitate local planning.

Matching of authority to responsibilities. Subnational governments will build stronger expenditure management processes—and deliver services more effectively—if they have the necessary degree of authority over those resources. Central governments sometimes pass functions and resources to subnational governments but then deny them the control they need to deliver responsive and high-quality services. Such overconstrained approaches rest on the often false assumption that central officials have better information and sharper incentives than subnational officials. Such approaches distort expenditure management processes and impede the ability of local governments to innovate. Above all, micromanagement and second-guessing blur the lines of accountability between tiers of government.

Local capacity. Subnational governments need the capacity to develop strong processes for managing expenditures for cost-effective service delivery. In deciding how far to decentralize responsibility for public spending, central governments need to

TABLE 5.4 Do EA5 Countries Meet Conditions for Effective Decentralization of Expenditure Management?

	China (1980)	Indonesia (2001)	Philippines (1992)	Thailand (1999)	Vietnam (1994–96)
Clear assignment of responsibilities	❍	◑	◑	◑	◑
Matching of resources to responsibilities	❍	◑	◑	◑	◑
Matching of authority to responsibilities	◑	◑	◑	❍	❍
Local capacity	◑	◑	◑	❍	◑
Local accountability	❍	❍	❍	◑	❍
National accountability	◑	❍	❍	◑	❍

Source: Authors' assessment.
Note: ● = high, ◑ = medium, ❍ = low. Start date of decentralization in parentheses.

assess local capacity. Nevertheless, substantive capacity is likely to develop only through "learning by doing," in which subnational governments are given some budget to manage. Central government has an important role to play in creating such an environment, as well as in mentoring and training local officials.

Local accountability. If subnational expenditure management is to translate into cost-effective services, local governments need to be accountable to citizens and their institutions. Such accountability includes external auditors and representative local assemblies, public interest bodies and civil society, and individuals with concerns and grievances. Analysts often argue that boosting the share of local expenditures financed by own-revenues enhances local accountability (although this argument has deficiencies in countries where only a small proportion of citizens pay direct taxes).

National accountability. Because subnational administrations draw on transfers and deliver services with national impacts, central governments must find a way to hold them accountable but stop short of micromanagement. Toward that end, central and local governments could create multiyear "contracts" covering both expenditure and revenue assignments that include performance criteria and minimum service standards.

Assessing East Asian Countries

To what extent have EA5 countries established these conditions for success? Once again we reviewed published and unpublished reports on expenditure decentralization. At present, as table 5.4 shows, none of the EA5 countries score highly on any of these conditions. Assignment of responsibility is often fuzzy. Resources and authority over those resources are often poorly matched with responsibilities. Local capacity and accountability—to both local people and central government—are often limited.

The following sections elaborate on this assessment.

Clear Assignment of Responsibilities. A lack of clarity in assigning responsibilities is a common problem in the EA5. In Indonesia, these problems are due mainly to hasty implementation of sweeping changes and the inexperience of reformers. This experience illustrates the difficulty of applying theoretical concepts of decentralization. Based on the subsidiarity principle, the decentralization law (Law 20) of 1999 gave all "authorities" to local governments except those specifically assigned to the center and regions. However, since "authorities" are broader than functions, the result is much confusion over who is responsible for what, from legislation to planning to implementation. Further confounding the assignment of responsibility is the fact that central line ministries still account for a significant amount of local spending. Adding to the confusion and disputes, Law 22 of 1999 called for adjusting sectoral laws and regulations to conform to the new decentralization framework—in effect setting aside the functional responsibilities and operational

TABLE 5.5 Distribution of Expenditures and Revenues in China, by Administrative Level
(percent)

1999	Expenditures					Revenues				
	China	Hebei	Gansu	Hunan	Jiangsu	China	Hebei	Gansu	Hunan	Jiangsu
Province	28.2	26.4	32.8	31.6	25.8	21.2	20.6	16.5	13.6	16.2
Prefecture	30.2	23.7	19.5	22.4	34.7	35.4	23.4	24.9	27.8	43.8
County[a]	41.5	39.2	34.3	37.8	39.5	43.4	35.8	39.9	35.2	40.0
Township		10.7	13.4	8.9	0.0		20.2	18.7	23.4	0.0
Change since 1994/95 (in percentage points)										
Province	1.8	6.8	0.5	5.6	5.8	4.1	0.9	−1.4	−0.4	11.3
Prefecture	−1.1	−1.6	−2.6	1.1	0.1	−5.6	−1.9	−3.0	3.3	−1.8
County[a]	−0.6	5.9	0.2	−2.4	−5.9	1.5	2.5	0.6	0.8	−9.5
Township		−11.0	1.9	−3.8	0.0		−1.5	3.8	−3.6	0.0

Source: World Bank 2002a, table 8.
a. County figures for China include townships.

details that sectoral and ministerial decrees usually contain. Legal battles have ensued, as some central ministries sought to exempt their agencies from decentralization laws, at least until local governments were ready to take on the functions.[6]

In China and Vietnam, the lack of clarity stems from a second dimension of the assignment problem: how to distribute functions among levels of government in a multitiered administrative setting. In both countries, the administrative systems operate as nested hierarchies, in which the central government sets rules only for provinces, which set rules for districts and communes.[7]

China's 1994 Budget Law spells out in broad principles the division of functions between central and subnational governments, but is silent on the division of labor between tiers of subnational government. This leaves essentially all decentralized functions as concurrent assignments for the various subnational tiers. In practice, China typically assigns the responsibilities based on economies of scale and the subsidiarity principle. For example, provinces operate universities and large hospitals, while lower-tier governments run primary and middle schools and small hospitals and health clinics.

This approach has led to two undesirable outcomes in China over the past decade. First, expenditure assignments are murky, with a good deal of uncertainty about which level of subnational government is responsible for what. With all subnational levels jointly responsible, no one is accountable. Second, this murkiness has worsened the fiscal status of the lowest tiers and adversely affected service delivery. This has been evident in rural provision of basic education: provinces, prefectures, and counties have done little or nothing to help rural townships that lack the resources to implement the national policy of providing nine years of free education.

Table 5.5 shows what happens in the absence of formal rules. For China as a whole, and for three of the four provinces in the sample, counties and townships together lost expenditure shares from 1994 to 1999, indicating that they had fewer resources to finance their responsibilities, which did not change. These trends confirm the complaint in many localities that each administrative level tries to capture more revenues by redefining how to share "local" taxes with the level below. Since the county and township levels together provide the bulk of basic services, including 70 percent of total public expenditures on education and 55 percent of expenditures on health, this trend could significantly undermine services, especially in rural areas. Provinces, in contrast, have gained significant expenditure shares even though they are not directly involved in providing services or redistributing income.

A third result of the lack of clear assignments occurs when central ministries and departments resist giving up their authority under decentralization. In Vietnam, the roles of sectoral ministries and provinces in prioritizing expenditures are unclear. Ministries establish unrealistic service norms that provinces largely ignore. This phenomenon is common in China and the Philippines as well. In fact, national standard setting on civil service wages and salaries, and even nationally mandated wage increases, are common in all EA5 countries to varying extents. This is extremely disruptive to local budgeting, given the large share of local expenditures absorbed by personnel costs (see chapter 7).

The realities of service delivery are often such that simplistic assignment of complex services to a single level of government is not practical. Most countries have overlapping assignments. However, clarifying responsibility for regulation, financing, implementation, provision, and maintenance of assets is still important, as is ensuring that these assignments are clear to all, including the public. Most of the EA5 countries have considerable scope for improvement in this regard.

Matching of Resources to Responsibilities. The literature on fiscal federalism implicitly assumes that local governments are largely financing their own services—hence the choice between high-tax, high-service packages and low-tax, low-service packages across localities. The reality is that there is no a priori reason why, under a well-designed intergovernmental system, the expenditure needs of subnational governments will match their ability to generate own-revenues to meet those needs. Thus, intergovernmental transfers play a crucial role, both vertically (in determining whether local governments have the resources to perform their assigned responsibilities) and horizontally (in keeping interregional disparities to acceptable levels).

All the EA5 countries face problems coordinating the decentralization of revenues and expenditures, albeit for different reasons. In Thailand, the transfer of revenues has outpaced the transfer of responsibilities. In principle, the laws provide local governments with minimum transfers, but the central bureaucracy has been slow to decentralize commensurate functions. As a result, in mid-2003, local revenues were about 22 percent of national revenues, while the country has decentralized only about 4 percent of expenditures.

In Indonesia, even though central authorities scrambled to decentralize expenditures to avoid huge deficits, they devolved more than enough revenues in 2001 to match expenditure responsibilities. In the Philippines, decentralization has also transferred more resources than responsibilities to the *barangays* (fourth tier), specifying that they can levy a tax of up to 1 percent of gross receipts on businesses and collect fees, but without specifying that they perform any significant duties(Azfar et al. 2000).

China reveals the opposite mismatch: subnational governments account for a much larger share of expenditures (70 percent) than revenues (45 percent). Central transfers—which finance about 45 percent of subnational expenditures on average—fill the vertical fiscal gap. However, the transfer system is not equalizing, often giving more to rich provinces than to poor ones (see chapter 4). Thus, resource gaps emerge in poor regions with inadequate self-financing, and at lower tiers of the administrative hierarchy such as counties and townships. Since fiscal capacities vary greatly across localities—reflecting the uneven distribution of economic activities—the result has been large and growing service disparities between urban and rural areas, and between regions.

As interregional disparities in spending have risen sharply since the mid-1990s, public services have gradually deteriorated in poor regions (World Bank 2002a). In Yunnan Province on China's southwestern border, 106 of 127 counties were reportedly unable to meet budgeted expenditures in 1995. In neighboring Guizhou, the poorest province in China, many counties could not meet payroll (Dai Xiaoming 1997). In the Liangshan Yi minority Prefecture in Sichuan Province, this led to the elimination of free medical care and epidemic prevention programs, among other services. Many clinics and health stations closed, and epidemic diseases thought to have been wiped out reappeared. In 1996, only 40 percent of Yi children attended school, a figure that dropped to 10 percent in poorer villages (Heberer 2001). With ambitious mandates for many public services, local governments must raise their own funds off-budget, relying heavily on user charges to finance primary education, and on the sale of medicines, supplies, and other assets to finance public health.

Fiscal pressures have also reduced the resources available to local governments in the Philippines. With revenues falling from 18.7 percent of gross

BOX 5.1 The Backdoor Route to Decentralization in China

While straining under diminishing fiscal resources but facing growing demands for services, local governments in China have turned to a plethora of fees and levies on local constituents to bridge the budget gap. These include education surcharges, traffic safety fees, family planning fees, and contributions to National Day celebrations and preparation for the Olympic Games. The central government sanctioned these efforts, and encouraged and even urged local governments to "find local solutions."

Today local governments depend on extrabudgetary resources to finance nearly half their expenditures, on average.[a] In 1998, for example, the budget financed an average of only 53 percent of China's expenditures in education; tuition, fees, social contributions, and profits from school-run enterprises provided the rest. In the health sector in 1999, budgetary appropriations provided only 11 percent of total operating revenues in public hospitals and clinics, while out-of-pocket payments by patients accounted for 59 percent.

A 1999 survey in China's Shanxi Province illustrated the dominance of fees over taxes in some sectors and localities. The survey found that annual fee payments averaged almost ¥ 11,000 in the nine cities surveyed, while taxes were less than ¥ 1,500. The ratio of fees to taxes ranged from a high of 13 to a low of 4, with the highest in smaller cities. These fees were almost entirely outside the purview of the budget, as different departments collected and used the fees until public expenditure management reforms implemented since 2002. Once authorized, the reporting requirements for fees were lax, and finance departments were often unable to track total collections and how they were used. Expenditure management reforms are attempting to bring these extrabudgetary revenues under tighter supervision, but resistance is reportedly widespread.

These extrabudgetary funds provide a backdoor route to decentralization in China, as they give local governments real autonomy on both the revenue and expenditure sides, which they lack under the formal budget. However, these funds are not transparent, and the user charges from which they are financed are often highly regressive.

a. Wong 1998; Fan 1998; and World Bank 2002a.

national product in 1997 to 14.6 percent in 2001 and continuing to fall through 2003, the resulting budget deficits and rising interest costs have squeezed social spending and the ability of local governments to fulfill their responsibilities. The decline is exacerbated by budgetary inflexibility at the sectoral level. For example, in education, the ratio of personnel costs to the total recurring budget rose to 92.4 percent in 2001, severely limiting room to maneuver (World Bank 2003e).

None of the EA5 except China has assigned local governments significant revenue bases, and China did so through the "backdoor"—that is, largely off-budget (see box 5.1).

Matching of Authority to Responsibilities. Another significant shortcoming in the institutional framework and incentive environment for subnational expenditure management has been frequent mismatch between authority and responsibility. Local governments and service providers often have functional responsibility without the authority to manage related public expenditures. This undercuts the promised benefits of both devolution and delegation strategies (see box 5.2).

One dimension of this problem is a lack of local authority regarding sectoral spending allocations. Directives by the central government often tie a significant proportion of revenues and resources transferred to local governments to specific sectors, functions, or services.

In Vietnam, for example, provincial finance departments must allocate their budgets in accordance with norms specified by central line ministries. However, budgets allocated to provinces have not enabled them to meet all the obligations imposed by the center. Provincial finance departments, in consultation with the People's Committee and People's Council, have therefore used their discretion in allocating funds between sectors and spending units. A new State Budget Law, which took effect in January 2004, consolidated this

BOX 5.2 China: Devolution by Default Rather Than by Design

During China's transition to a market economy, decentralization has occurred more by neglect than by design. Subnational expenditures have risen from about 45 percent of the total on the eve of transition to around 70 percent today. However, this increase reflected changes in the composition of expenditures and relative prices rather than a major change in expenditure assignments.

As in other Soviet-type economies, in China the central government was responsible for national defense, economic development (capital spending, research and development, industrial policy, and universities and research institutes), and national institutions such as the judicial system. The central government had delegated to local governments responsibility for day-to-day public administration and social services, such as education (except universities), public safety, health care, social security, housing, and other local and urban services. A large portion of central spending focused on making capital investments and financing state-owned enterprises. When the transition began, the transfer of financing for state-owned enterprises from the budget to the banking system reduced central spending, while wage increases pushed up the cost of labor-intensive services, which were mostly local. Safety net expenditures—also local responsibilities—rose rapidly with retrenchment in the state-owned enterprise sector, which entailed unemployment stipends, early retirements, and pension payouts. As a result, local expenditures grew relatively.

Behind these numbers, real decentralization had in fact occurred. While local governments are performing largely the same functions as before, under the planned economy they had acted as agents in fulfilling deconcentrated functions of the central government, which bore the costs through revenue-sharing arrangements. During the transition, however, incremental changes in revenue-sharing arrangements weakened and then severed the link between retained revenues and expenditure needs, and local governments became responsible for financing their assigned functions from own-revenues. This devolution had occurred without fanfare in the mid-1980s and was later codified in the Budget Law of 1994.

de facto discretion. Recognizing this reality in law will help clarify accountability and strengthen local transparency. But some constraints on provinces remain. They must spend 15 percent of their budgets on the national priority sector of education by 2000, 18 percent by 2005, and 20 percent by 2010. They must also spend 2 percent of their budgets on science and technology.

In China, a multiplicity of laws stipulating spending increases in certain sectors and regions constrain local governments. For example, the central government required education expenditures to rise to 4 percent of GDP by 2000, that agricultural spending must grow faster than revenues, and that spending on propaganda and culture should be no lower than overall revenue growth. The center also required that spending on science and environmental protection each rise to 1.5 percent of GDP by 2000, and that health care spending keep pace with revenue growth, with per capita spending rising from ¥ 2.6 to ¥ 4 by 2000.

Reconciling all these constraints and unfunded mandates is almost impossible for local governments. These constraints have contributed to China's backdoor decentralization, whereby local governments have moved more and more funds outside the purview of the budget and fiscal authorities.

In Indonesia, the central government continues to enforce regulations that determine spending on certain items, including the Education Law, which calls for providing nine years of education to all, with free primary schooling. Government regulations 109 and 110 of 2000 also regulate the ceiling for spending by the head of a region and the provincial representative assembly, but these regulations are widely ignored.

Another common problem is a lack of authority transferred from the central or local finance function to local service providers, which have little discretion in using resources. In Vietnam, provincial finance departments required spending units to agree to every detail in their budgets and obtain formal approval before reallocating spending. However, recent decrees have gradually delegated greater budgetary flexibility, within a fixed block

BOX 5.3 The Block Grant Experiment in Ho Chi Minh City

In 1999, the Vietnamese government authorized a pilot to introduce block grant budgeting in 10 administrative units (districts and departments) in Ho Chi Minh City. An early World Bank–sponsored assessment found that the pilots had made significant progress in meeting their objectives:

Restructuring departments and streamlining administrative procedures. In most pilot agencies, restructuring and streamlining had already begun. The pilot gave a further boost to this, although centrally prescribed functional obligations limited the scope for restructuring.

Reducing administrative costs. Reported gross financial savings in the first year of the pilot ranged from 13 percent to 29 percent, based on administrative economies as well as staff reductions. Because departments used the savings to supplement salaries, as planned, net savings were zero.

Reducing overstaffing. Most agencies cut their staff by around 15 percent compared with their quota, and some made bigger cuts. However, most staff were transferred rather than retired or retrenched.

Raising incomes of employees by reapplying savings. Departments used gross savings to raise incomes, with 70 percent going to salaries, 20 percent to a bonus fund, and 10 percent to a staff welfare fund.

Increasing transparency. Departments launched various initiatives to monitor service delivery standards and customer satisfaction. No evidence suggests that service quality declined in the pilot agencies.

Source: Bartholomew et al. 2005.

grant, to spending and service delivery units.[8] Units will have the freedom to shift resources between recurrent budget lines and—crucially—to use savings from staffing cuts or lower operational costs to finance salary supplements. Selected spending units in Ho Chi Minh City have piloted this approach over two years, and a recent World Bank–sponsored assessment concluded that the pilots may have resulted in significant staffing reductions and savings (Bartholomew et al. 2005). (See box 5.3 for further details on this experiment.)

Nominally decentralized expenditure management regimes involving high levels of central control are likely to be both inefficient and ineffective. Such regimes will tend to make the allocation of resources overly rigid and encourage compliance with rules and red tape rather than a focus on responsiveness and service outputs and outcomes. Such regimes also remove incentives among service providers to find savings, because officials cannot transfer savings within expenditure items or subitems to other categories but must forfeit them to the treasury. Above all, micromanagement and second-guessing blur the lines of accountability for results between the finance function and the spending unit.

Nevertheless, central governments need to manage the passing of budgetary authority to subnational governments carefully. Checks and balances need to be in place if the move away from line-item budgeting is not simply to replace one form of inefficiency with another. As they lift line-item budget constraints, central governments need to create alternative mechanisms such as stronger capacity and greater ex post accountability for the use of resources and service performance. Strong financial management systems are essential for preserving fiscal discipline. We turn next to issues of capacity, accountability, and reporting.

Local Capacity. Local capacity for managing fiscal resources varies greatly, not only across administrative tiers but also within each tier. As the Ho Chi Minh City block grant experiment suggests, the administrative capacities of large cities may sometimes be equal to those of the central government. That story also clearly reveals that mobilizing these capacities to improve resource allocation and service delivery depends critically on establishing appropriate incentives and constraints.

For the most part in the EA5, however, local governments typically have weaker capacity in expenditure management skills, such as planning, budgeting, execution, audit, and procurement. In China, local public expenditure management is extremely poor. Budgeting is passive and input oriented rather than results oriented. Budget formulation is almost totally inertia-driven, as it adds incrementally to past year's allocations without focusing on goals, outcomes, or performance. Accounting standards are lax, and waste of resources is common (World Bank 2002a). That these problems persist after more than two decades of economic decentralization suggests that their root cause lies elsewhere. The inefficiencies of local expenditures can be explained by the bifurcated Chinese fiscal system: local officials are often not interested in improving financial management of budgets over which they lack real control; they focus instead on developing extrabudgetary resources over which they exercise near-total control.

Another dimension of the problem is that countries have sometimes made "wrong assignments" by devolving responsibility for providing services to levels of government that do not have the resources and administrative capacity to respond. Again, China provides a good example. Throughout the history of the People's Republic, rural basic education has been the responsibility of township governments, which average 27,000 in population, and their antecedent, agricultural people's communes.[9] Under the collective economy, public funds of the collectives financed rural education, with teachers mostly paid in "work points," or shares in the collective's net income. Under that system, the level and quality of education varied among collectives, depending on their resources and allocative choices. Through the 1980s the government imposed rising standards on rural schools and teachers, and by the late 1980s directed that all rural teachers be upgraded to the status of public employees. This greatly raised the cost of providing rural education, as the average salary for teachers in state-run schools was several times that of teachers in rural "community" schools.

Expenditure pressures on townships rose further when the government introduced a Compulsory Education Law calling for nine years of Universal Compulsory Education (UCE) by 2000—a level that far surpassed provision in most rural areas. Townships—primarily agricultural units—have no significant tax base, except for the lucky ones in coastal provinces, where township and village enterprises thrive. For them, education is by far the largest budgetary outlay, which even in the early 1990s absorbed 40–60 percent of the total. Despite pressure from upper levels to comply with UCE, townships in poor regions have not met targets (Wong et al. 1995).[10] At the same time, the strain of trying to do so has led townships to impose escalating fees and involuntary contributions on rural residents, spawning a rising tide of collective protests through the 1990s.[11] Thus, decentralizing basic education to townships has hindered the priority national program of universal compulsory education while imposing high tax burdens on local populations.

Local Accountability. Institutions for managing expenditures focused on effective and responsive service delivery are likely to evolve only if institutions also hold local governments accountable for the way they use resources. As previous sections make clear, however, local governments cannot be held accountable for nonperformance if they have not been given clear assignments, if they do not have the resources and authority to respond, or if their assignments and capacities are poorly matched.

One of the key assumptions of decentralization is that local governments are more responsive because they are "closer to the people." The literature on fiscal decentralization tends to emphasize bottom-up mechanisms of "voice" (elections) and "exit" (mobility), both exercised by the electorate. In the nascent democracies of Indonesia and Thailand, these mechanisms may take time to develop. Even in the Philippines, where grassroots democracy began a decade earlier, a 1999 study found that a lack of information limited popular influence on local decision making—citizens generally knew less about local government than about national government. While citizens rely on the media for information on the national government, they rely largely on local officials and personal contacts for information on local government, as the media tend to focus only on "big news." In turn, local officials have little awareness of the preferences of local citizens, although municipal officials were more aware than provincial officials. In the Philippines, decentralization also does not seem to have improved civic discipline despite the democratic setup. Measured corruption remains high and has grown under decentralization (Azfar et al. 2000).

Analysts also often assert that local taxing authority enhances local accountability: when local citizens are paying directly for public services, they devote more attention to local politics and officeholders. However, this assertion lacks empirical justification anywhere in the world, is conceptually suspect to the extent that it elides citizens and taxpayers, and is particularly questionable in the EA5, where only a small proportion of citizens pay direct taxes.

The exit option is not an effective mechanism for holding local governments accountable in countries where government is the sole provider of many services. This is true in China and Vietnam, where private providers are just emerging in vital services such as education and health care, and where government monopolies and administrative restraints hinder the development of many services. In these countries, people's option of moving to another jurisdiction ("voting with the feet") is constrained. Political culture also hinders the responsiveness of local governments and service providers. Officials who are used to responding to rules and regulations will need time to become more client oriented.

National Accountability. The transition economies of China and Vietnam, and to some extent the other countries in the EA5, also have top-down mechanisms to hold local governments accountable. A study of transition economies in Eastern Europe and the former Soviet Union found that intermediate levels of government tended to respond to higher levels of government rather than to local people (Wetzel 2001).

In China and Vietnam, through the *nomenklatura* system of appointing the top officials, the Communist Party continues to wield control over senior civil servants. In China, the government relies on elaborate systems of evaluation and performance bonuses for top officials at all levels of government to induce compliance on priority goals such as growth, family planning, and prevention of social unrest. These mechanisms have been spectacularly successful in ensuring that local officials promote growth and invest in basic infrastructure. Judging from the remarkable record of high and sustained growth rates over the past two decades, China is arguably a successful case where the central government gets more of what it wants by giving incentives to local governments to fulfill the central agenda. This is the argument of the so-called "market-preserving fiscal federalism" school. That approach has been far less successful in meeting other targets, however, such as exerting aggregate fiscal discipline, ensuring the delivery of vital services to all citizens, and protecting vulnerable social groups.

Although Vietnam remains a one-party state, the National Assembly is growing in importance, reviewing government plans, budgets, and implementation and exercising its constitutional authority as the highest organ of the state. The bureaucracy sees the National Assembly as a significant source of authority and a potential arena for independent criticism of government performance. However, the People's Councils at provincial levels and below have yet to emerge in all but the major cities as significant checks on the executive. The memberships of the People's Councils (the legislature) and the People's Committees (the executive) often overlap, and their capacity is often limited.

Given the fragile nature of local democracy in EA5 countries, the central government plays an important role in managing decentralization. It must have strong capacity to monitor and evaluate decentralization, and it must set up mechanisms to hold local governments accountable in fulfilling their responsibilities. But central governments must balance these imperatives against the need to give local governments autonomy and incentives, and the need to guard against micromanagement and the reassertion of authority.

The availability and timeliness of information on subnational governments is weak for most countries in the world, and the EA5 is no exception. Improving local transparency and information flows is vital to building subnational accountability to both citizens and higher-level governments.

Conclusion

Building sound public expenditure management processes at the subnational level in the EA5 is a large and daunting program. The success of that program will depend on establishing appropriate institutions and incentives. In other parts of the world, expenditure management processes and the supporting institutions and incentives evolved over decades and even centuries. The East Asian experience is still unfolding. Nevertheless, a number of preliminary conclusions emerge from this review of the region's early experiences in decentralizing public expenditures.

First, expenditure management processes at the subnational level are generally weak. Planning processes are disconnected from fiscal planning and budgeting processes, and poorly coordinated with planning at other levels of government. Budget formulation suffers from major delays and is fragmented, with parallel budgets for investment projects and recurrent expenditures managed by separate institutions. Budget execution is slow, with long delays in effecting appropriations, significant divergences between approved appropriations and outputs, and corruption in procurement. Monitoring and accounting systems often produce data that are neither timely nor accurate. Auditing is typically weak and evaluation almost nonexistent.

Part of the explanation is that countries such as Indonesia, Thailand, and Vietnam are just beginning to decentralize expenditures. However, time does not automatically solve these problems: China and the Philippines are still struggling to build the needed institutions despite starting one and two decades ago. There is no regional panacea: every country will need to find its own way forward. Nevertheless, all the EA5 countries clearly need to prioritize strengthening core expenditure management processes at subnational levels as part of wider decentralization programs. In so doing, countries need to devote attention to budget formulation and execution, and focus on "getting the basics right" rather than attempting to jump to any perceived world "best practice."[12] Most EA5 countries should pay early attention to coordinating subnational planning and budgeting, integrating extrabudgetary resources into the budget process, and strengthening information on financial management.

Second, none of the EA5 countries score highly on the institutions and incentives needed to manage subnational expenditures effectively. Assignment of responsibilities is often fuzzy. Resources and the authority to manage those resources are often poorly matched with responsibilities. Local capacity and accountability to both local people and central government are often limited. Although EA5 countries can take immediate steps to strengthen expenditure management processes, governments cannot expect healthy local institutions to develop organically until they have addressed these structural issues. Over the longer term, central governments need to assign functions clearly and match resources and authority to responsibility. These efforts should go hand in hand with strengthening capacity and accountability institutions at both local and central levels.

Third, decentralizing expenditure appears to have yielded some benefits. In particular, given flexibility and the right incentives, local governments have shown significant capacity to innovate, both in responding to local demands and conditions and in achieving cost savings. Innovations in service delivery associated with flexibility given to frontline service providers by subnational governments in Vietnam and China are cases in point. Such innovation has occurred despite imperfect conditions for decentralization and its incomplete nature. However, major distortions have emerged as well. In particular, inequalities in service provision have often grown. EA5 governments need to pay greater attention to the impacts of decentralized management of public expenditures and service delivery on poverty reduction and equity. The process for learning through local innovations must be formalized. Both positive and negative experiences need to be analyzed, compared, and disseminated, and both local and central authorities must respond flexibly to facts on the ground. Central governments—as well as regional groups such as the Association of South East Asian Nations (ASEAN) and international organizations such as the World Bank—have an important role to play in capturing and disseminating such lessons.

Fourth, perhaps the defining challenge in EA5 countries is to balance the need for bottom-up local discretion with the need for top-down direction in subnational expenditure management. In country after country, central ministries continue to overplay their role by creating unfunded mandates and impinging on the necessary discretion of local governments. At the same time, central governments play an important role in guaranteeing minimum service standards, transparency, and accountability; in transferring resources between regions; in ensuring coordination between central and local initiatives as well as between local initiatives; and in creating incentives for developing local expenditure management capabilities. This is particularly the case given the weaknesses of local democracy in EA5 countries. Efforts to decentralize public expenditures need to focus on redefining the role of central ministries as well as developing new roles for local agencies.

Endnotes

1. Our study does not include Cambodia.
2. The study sample included countries for which subnational budgetary data were available from the International Monetary Fund, the World Bank, the Organisation for Economic Co-operation and Development, and other sources.
3. Bahl's regression results (2002) showed a "decentralization effort" of 2.6 for Vietnam, 1.4 for China, 1.0 for the Philippines, 0.9 for Indonesia, and 0.6 for Thailand. The author measured decentralization as the ratio of actual subnational expenditures to "predicted" expenditure share.
4. In the cases of China and Vietnam, we drew on our own interactions with central and subnational governments. We also benefited from conversations with colleagues in the World Bank's East Asia and Pacific Region.
5. The classic formulation of this can be found in Oates 1972.
6. Examples include the ministries of Land Management and Investment Approval (World Bank 2003a).
7. Russian-educated Vietnamese often refer to this nested hierarchy as the "Matrouchka" system.
8. Government of Vietnam, Decision 192/2001/QS-TTg: 17, Decision of the Prime Minister on the Expansion of the Pilot Block Grant Scheme, 2001; Government of Vietnam, Decree 10/2002/NS-CP, Decree Regarding Financial Regulation of Service Delivery Agencies Whose Operation Generate Revenue, 2002.
9. Townships were traditionally units of rural government. They were replaced by people's communes during the period of collective agriculture. When the communes were disbanded in 1983, townships were restored as units of government.
10. At year-end 2000, the deadline for reaching the targets, 500 of China's 2,100 counties had not yet achieved UCE, and another 600 counties needed help in shoring up their UCE status. In Gansu province in the northwest, 35 of 86 counties had not achieved UCE. Among them, 6 counties were not yet providing even six years of primary schooling (World Bank 2002a).
11. Responding to these protests, in 2001 the government introduced a major reform program to eliminate all rural fees, and is incrementally addressing excessive decentralization to rural townships of key functions such as basic education and health.
12. On the case for "getting the basics right" in public expenditure management, see Schick 1998.

Bibliography

Azfar, Omar, Tugrul Gurgur, Satu Kahkonene, Anthony Lanyi, and Patrick Meagher. 2000. "Decentralization and Governance: An Empirical Investigation of Public Service Delivery in the Philippines." Mimeo. College Park, MD: Center for Institutional Reform and the Informal Sector, University of Maryland, College Park, MD.

Bahl, Roy. 2000. "Intergovernmental Transfers in Developing and Transition Countries: Principles and Practice." Report No. 21097. Urban and Local Government, World Bank, Washington, DC.

———. 2002. Presentation at the World Bank and State Council Development Research Center workshop on rural public finance, Beijing.

Bartholomew, Ann, Stephen Lister, Ed Mountfield, and Nguyen Van Minh. 2005. "Crossing the River by Feeling the Stones: Vietnam's Experiment with Block Grant Budgeting." *International Journal of Public Administration*. 28 (3/4).

Bird, Richard. 2003. "Local and Regional Revenues: Realities and Prospects." Mimeo. University of Toronto, Toronto.

Bird, Richard, Jennie Litvack, and M. Govinda Rao. 1995. "Intergovernmental Fiscal Relations and Poverty Alleviation in Vietnam." Policy Research Working Paper No.1430. World Bank, Washington, DC.

Burki, Shahid Javed, Guilhermo E. Perry, and William R. Dillinger. 1999. "Beyond the Center: Decentralizing the State." Report No. 19616. Latin American and Caribbean Studies, World Bank, Washington, DC.

Dai Xiaoming. 1997. "Concerning Fiscal Autonomy in Minority Nationalities Autonomous Regions and the Legal Issues." *Nationalities Research (minzu yanjiu)* 6: 8–17.

Faguet, Jean-Paul. 1997. "Decentralization and Local Government Performance." Centre for Economic Performance and Development Studies, London School of Economics, London.

Fan, Gang. 1998. "Market-Oriented Economic Reform and the Growth of Off-Budget Local Public Finance." In *Taxation in Modern China*, ed. Donald Brean. New York: Routledge.

Heberer, Thomas. 2001. "Nationalities Conflict and Ethnicity in the People's Republic of China, with Special Reference to the Yi." In *Perspectives on the Yi of Southwest China*, ed. Stevan Harrell. Berkeley: University of California Press.

Kitchen, Harry, and Enid Slack. 2001. "Providing Public Services in Remote Areas." Paper prepared for *Fiscal Federalism in Russia*. World Bank Institute, Washington, DC.

Martinez-Vazquez, Jorge, and Charles E. McLure. 1998. "Intergovernmental Fiscal Relations in Vietnam." Andrew Young School of Policy Studies, International Studies Program, Georgia State University, Atlanta, GA.

Mountfield, Edward. 2001. "Public Financial Accountability in East Asia." *East Asia Update*. Washington, DC: World Bank.

Oates, Wallace E. 1972. *Fiscal Federalism*. New York: Harcourt Brace Jovanovich.

Prud'homme, Rémy. 1995. "The Dangers of Decentralization" *World Bank Research Observer* 10 (2): 201–20.

Schick, A. 1998. "A Contemporary Approach to Public Expenditure Management." World Bank, Washington, DC.

Weist, Dana. 2001. "Thailand's Decentralization: Progress and Prospects." Paper prepared for the King Prajadhipok's Institute (KPI) Third Annual Congress on Decentralization and Local Government in Thailand.

Wetzel, Deborah. 2001. "Decentralization in the Transition Economies: Challenges and the Road Ahead." Report No. 25132. Poverty Reduction and Economic Management Unit, Europe and Central Asia, World Bank, Washington, DC.

Wong, Christine P. W. 1998. "Fiscal Dualism." In *Taxation in Modern China*, ed. Stevan Harrell. New York: Routledge.

———. 2000. "Central-Local Relations Revisited: The 1994 Tax-Sharing Reform and Public Expenditure Management in China." *China Perspectives* 31: 52–65.

Wong, Christine P. W., C. Heady, and W. T. Woo. 1995. *Fiscal Management and Economic Reform in the People's Republic of China*. New York: Oxford University Press.

World Bank. 2000a. "Managing Public Expenditures for Better Results." Report No. 20342-CHA. World Bank, Washington, DC.

———. 2000b. "Thailand: Public Finance in Transition." World Bank, Washington, DC.

———. 2000c. "Vietnam: Managing Public Resources Better." Report No. 24469. World Bank, Washington, DC.

———. 2000d. *World Development Report: Entering the 21st Century.* Washington, DC: World Bank.

———. 2001. "Vietnam: Country Financial Accountability Assessment." World Bank, Washington, DC.

———. 2002a. "China: National Development and Subnational Finance: A Review of Provincial Expenditures." China Subnational Expenditure Review Report No. 22951. World Bank, Washington, DC.

———. 2002b. "Implementing Decentralization in Thailand: The Way Forward." Capacity-Building Project. World Bank, Washington, DC.

———. 2002c. "Vietnam: Delivering on Its Promise." Development Report No. 25050. World Bank, Washington, DC.

———. 2003a. "Decentralizing Indonesia." Report No. 26191. World Bank, Washington, DC.

———. 2003b. "Fiscal Decentralization in Thailand." Decentralization flagship background note. World Bank, Washington, DC.

World Bank. 2003c. "Philippines: Decentralization and Service Delivery—From Promise to Performance. Cross-Cutting Themes in Local Government Functioning." Report No. 22181. World Bank, Washington, DC.

———. 2003d. "Philippines: Decentralization and Service Delivery—Strengthening Local Government Financing and Resource Management in the Short Term. Cross-Cutting Themes in Local Government Functioning." Report No. 26104-PH. World Bank, Washington, DC.

———. 2003e. "Philippines: Improving Government Performance—Discipline, Efficiency, and Equity in Managing Public Resources." World Bank, Washington, DC.

———. 2003f. Regional public expenditure reviews. World Bank, Washington, DC.

———. 2004. *World Development Report: Making Services Work for Poor People.* Washington, DC: World Bank; and New York: Oxford University Press.

6

SUBNATIONAL OWN-SOURCE REVENUE: GETTING POLICY AND ADMINISTRATION RIGHT

Robert R. Taliercio

Once countries decide to decentralize—whether gradually, as in Thailand and Vietnam, or with an initial dramatic change, as in the Philippines and Indonesia—they must get the fiscal design right. Critical to effective fiscal design is the ability of local governments to adjust budgets and thus respond to community preferences regarding the quantity and quality of public services. Ideally, and according to theory, subnational governments provide services to their constituents up to the point at which the cost—in terms of taxes—equals the benefit, in terms of the value of the services. To satisfy this condition, local governments must have the authority to exercise own-source taxation, and be in a financial position to do so. This is the essence of accountability and efficiency under decentralization, and that is why decentralized revenue policy matters.

The design of a local revenue system includes three central dimensions: the assignment of revenue sources among types of government, the degree of autonomy with which subnational governments can exercise their assigned authority, and the efficiency of the revenue administration system. For a decentralized system to meet expectations, policymakers must ensure coordination between these dimensions.

This chapter follows this logic. It begins by analyzing the links between revenue assignment and autonomy by country and type of revenue, and then assesses the region's revenue performance. The ensuing two sections take up the question of revenue administration and address the politics of local taxation, highlighting issues of policy implementation. The last section offers final comments on the implications of these findings for both policy and administration.

The chapter's overarching conclusion is that East Asian countries reveal many inconsistencies and contradictions vis-à-vis commonly accepted criteria for a "good" intergovernmental revenue system. However, this newly decentralized region is also seeing rich experimentation and innovation, which bodes well for further reform.

The Setting and Normative Framework

Except in the Philippines and perhaps Indonesia, subnational governments in East Asia make little use of own-revenues to finance local services (see table 6.1). That is, the region is not characterized by significant fiscal decentralization. The implications

TABLE 6.1 Estimated Own-Source Revenue of Subnational Governments
(as percentage of total subnational government revenue)

Country	Percentage
Cambodia (2003)	< 5
China (2003)	< 5
Indonesia (2002)	15.4
Philippines (2002)	31.1
Thailand (2002)	10.9
Vietnam (2003)	< 5

Sources: Indonesia (Ministry of Finance), Philippines (Department of Finance), and Thailand (World Bank 2004c). World Bank staff estimates for Cambodia, China, and Vietnam.
Note: Most recent year available. Figures include only official, legal revenues.

of this are considerable. The fact that subnational governments have both limited powers to raise revenues and limited capacity to collect them poses profound questions about the actual benefits of decentralization. Can local governments respond to local preferences in taxation and thus service delivery, thereby achieving greater accountability and efficiency? Are fiscal tools and capacities sufficient to generate sustainable own-source revenues? Has a reliance on transfers, in their myriad forms, made subnational governments dependent on national governments and weakened subnational incentives to improve own-source collections?

The three dimensions of revenue policy provide a framework for addressing these questions:[1]

Which taxes should be authorized or assigned to central governments and which to subnational governments? The decision should be legal and transparent, occurring through both constitutional and legislative processes. However, as discussed below, governments sometimes assume "authority" illegally. That such illegality and informality are undesirable will become clear; nonetheless, in some countries, particularly China, these approaches are commonplace. Focusing on assignment of revenue sources among governments stresses the importance of understanding decentralization as an intergovernmental partnership.

Numerous public finance economists have provided guidance on how to think about assigning taxes between national and local governments, and many of the resulting perspectives place a high priority on economic efficiency. The first principle of revenue assignment—summed up by the "finance-follows-function" refrain—is that it should be based on assigned expenditures. A second principle, given the matching of revenues to expenditures, is that local taxation should avoid introducing economic distortions by inappropriately taxing the factors of production. The third general principle—subsidiarity—holds that revenue-raising powers should be assigned to the lowest-possible level of government, except where such assignment would produce economic distortions or negative externalities.[2]

These three principles provide a general framework for assessing revenue assignment, which—when fleshed out with more specific considerations—offers a set of practical guidelines. According to Norregaard, governments should not levy "local taxes" on very mobile factors lest they encourage taxpayer migration (though what constitutes "very mobile" is largely an empirical issue) (Norregaard 1997). Such taxes should not be unevenly distributed among jurisdictions (as in the case of natural resource taxation), should raise enough revenue to avoid large vertical fiscal imbalances, should not be exportable to nonresidents (which would weaken the accountability link), and should be based on the benefit principle. Taken one step further by Bird, these principles suggest a number of major tax sources usually prescribed for subnational governments, "more or less in order of preference—user charges, property taxes, excises, personal income taxes, payroll taxes, general sales taxes, and business taxes" (Bird 2003b, 4–5). The following sections address each of these options.

Autonomy and Policy

The decentralization literature can be surprisingly unclear about the fundamental question of what constitutes a subnational tax. However, if terminology is not clear as to what constitutes subnational own-source revenue, policymakers will not have the conceptual tools needed to design fiscal systems and appreciate their consequences. Such a situation will also obfuscate debate over the policy changes needed to allow a jurisdiction to realize the efficiency benefits promised by decentralization.

Subnational revenues may be divided into categories of decreasing local autonomy (see table 6.2).

TABLE 6.2 Classification of Subnational Taxes by Degree of Central vs. Local Control

Local autonomy in revenue policy	Subnational government (SNG) sets tax rate and base.	Greatest access to own-source revenues. These usually include fees and charges.
	SNG sets tax rate only.	Necessary and sufficient condition for "own-revenue." Piggybacking and tax base harmonization permitted.
	SNG determines the tax base.	Refers largely to local authority to grant exemptions that erode the local base.
Limited autonomy	SNG sets tax rate, but within centrally permissible ranges.	In this case the center typically specifies a high/low tax range or caps the top rate.
	Tax sharing, whereby central/local revenue split can change only with consent of SNG.	Can result when a local authority collects the tax and remits it to the center.
No local autonomy	Revenue sharing, with share determined unilaterally by central authority.	100% control by center; this is a source of misspecification of central vs. local revenue. (For example, the International Monetary Fund's Government Finance Statistics includes this category as a "local tax.")
	Central government sets rate and base of "SNG revenue."	May accompany political decentralization.

Sources: Adapted from OECD 2002; Ebel and Yilmaz 2002.

If subnational governments have total or significant control over a tax, fee, or charge, as shown by control over the tax rate (that is, if it is necessary and sufficient), it is a subnational tax. If, in contrast, subnational governments have no control over the base and rate of a tax, as, for example, when the central government determines how to split revenues ("tax sharing"), it is not a subnational source of own-revenue.

This taxonomy of taxation serves the very useful purpose of setting out the basic definition of what is and is not a source of own-revenue. Thus, for example, the taxonomy makes clear that although a shared tax adds to subnational budget receipts, such revenue is not "own" taxation. Tax sharing occurs when the base and rate of a tax are centrally set and then some percent is returned, typically on a derivation basis, to the "originating locality." To be an own-tax or revenue source, the subnational unit must, at the very least, legislate the rate.

More nuanced is the practice whereby a central government restricts the rate of an own-revenue source (such as the rate ceiling). This clearly limits subnational autonomy, and some would argue that once the cap is reached it fully eliminates local autonomy, as the subnational government loses its ability to raise taxes at the margin. Such rate regulation is particularly common in East Asia.

A typical argument for rate ceilings is that they prevent local governments from doing egregiously inappropriate things (though ceilings may simply be a nontransparent mechanism for central control). The practice, however, counters the accountability and efficiency arguments for decentralization. One might make a case for centrally imposed rate ceilings during the transitional period from centralization to decentralization, as they might allow local governments to develop policy and administrative capacity, but such limitations should be short-lived. Subnational governments build capacity by using their assigned powers.

Autonomy and Administration

The third dimension of revenue policy—that subnational governments must have some control over revenue administration—matters for two reasons. First, control over some aspects of revenue administration is instrumental for controlling revenues at the margin, as this allows for changes in the effective tax rate (a ratio of actual tax collected compared with the size of the legal tax base). Local governments can change the effective tax rate by boosting compliance through audits and enforcement, or by lowering compliance costs for taxpayers through better services (such as more

TABLE 6.3 Tax Assignment by Local Government in the Philippines

Revenue source	Provinces	Cities	Municipalities	Barangays
Real property tax	✓	✓	✓ 40% of provincial collections	✓ 25% of provincial or 30% of city collections
Transfer of real property tax	✓	✓		
Tax on sand, gravel, and other quarry resources	✓	✓	✓ 30% of provincial collections	✓ 40% of provincial collections
Amusement tax	✓	✓		✓ 50% of provincial collections
Business taxes		✓	✓	✓
Franchise tax	✓	✓		
Community tax		✓	✓	✓ 50% of collections

Source: Local Government Code (R.A. 7160), 1991.

user-friendly tax forms and payment processing, and access to information).

This dimension is relevant in all cases, especially in China and Vietnam, where subnational governments collect taxes whose rates and bases are determined centrally. Second, and conversely, this consideration suggests that subnational governments need not have full control over administration to call a tax or fee an own-source revenue. Devolved responsibility does not necessarily imply fully devolved administration, especially in the context of weak local capacity. National governments, for example, might take responsibility for certain administrative functions, such as assessing property, or assist local governments with core functions related to information and communications technology. This opens up a much-needed discussion of the appropriate division of labor between national and subnational jurisdictions, and of the options for assisting low-capacity subnational governments with revenue administration (see below).

Review of Current Practice and Initial Evaluation

Whereas several East Asian revenue systems rely on central controls, countries are also showing a willingness to review the twin features of assignment and autonomy. This represents an important policy crossroads: if, as shown, assignment and autonomy can be reinforcing, the opportunity to combine political with fiscal decentralization promises more efficient delivery of public services.

The Philippines has the region's longest-running record of an explicit decentralization policy and is also the most revenue decentralized of all the focus countries. Yet, as the Philippines example also attests, the decentralization sorting-out process takes time, and even the Philippines is a "young" decentralizing state. The country has clear opportunities for further reform.

In the Philippines, primary responsibility for subnational taxation rests with provinces, municipalities, and cities (see table 6.3). Cities are the most autonomous: they are authorized to impose the full set of local taxes, while provinces and municipalities can levy only subsets. In some cases the revenues collected by provinces and cities are allocated to municipalities and *barangays*. The latter are also responsible for collecting miscellaneous taxes and fees and charges.

But again, whereas this assignment suggests a well-designed system of revenue decentralization, the Local Government Code is not fully consistent with the autonomy criteria (see table 6.2). The central government sets tax rate ceilings, leaving local governments little control over one of the main levers for mobilizing revenue, including the property tax, which is a large revenue generator. The code also fixes maximum rates for most other taxes and nominal per unit amounts (as in the case of the professional tax). The code further specifies that local governments can adjust tax rates only once in five years, and not by more than 10 percent.[3]

In Indonesia, subnational governments have the authority within the framework of Law 34 of 2000 on regional revenue to levy a number of important but minor revenue sources. The central government controls the most potentially productive local revenues—those on real estate and personal income—and shares the receipt.[4] Less revenue-productive taxes are assigned to the provinces (motor vehicle registration, transfer and fuel taxes, and a water user fee, all of which are shared with cities and regencies), and cities and regencies (excise taxes on hotels, entertainment, advertisement, street lighting, mining of selected minerals, and parking).

The national government restricts this arrangement even further: subnational governments may not impose surcharges on national taxes, and Law 34 of 2000 sets maximum rates on those that are assigned.[5] Evidence suggests that most regions already charge the maximum rate, and that some would raise it further if allowed to do so. For example, the widely assessed hotel and restaurant rate is limited to 10 percent, yet a World Bank report concludes that some jurisdictions (such as Bali and Jakarta) could gain from rate increases (World Bank 2003a).

China overhauled its subnational revenue system under the 1994 Tax Sharing System reform. The tax structure now includes three tiers of taxes: those fully accruing to the national government, those shared between the national and subnational governments, and those fully accruing to subnational units. Allowable subnational own-source revenues include the urban land use tax, for which the local government can set the rate up to a ceiling; local option entertainment and slaughterhouse taxes; and a local option surtax on collective enterprises, for which the subnational government can influence the rate (Bahl 1999).

Revenues in Thailand are national, local, or shared. Shared taxes include the value-added tax and sales tax, the special business tax, the natural resource tax, excise taxes, and the vehicle tax, all of which accrue to local governments. Own-taxation is limited to the house and land tax, land development tax, signboard tax, petrol tax, tobacco tax, and hotel tax. Local governments may also collect user fees, charges, permits, license fees, and fines.

Cambodia is still at an early stage of decentralization: it has not yet assigned functions or revenues to communes. However, communes and *sangkats* (urban communes) may collect four types of own-revenue. These include administrative fees for civil registry functions, agency fees for functions performed on behalf of line ministries and others, contributions to development projects to meet the matching requirement imposed by transfers from the Commune *Sangkat* Fund, and user fees and charges to cover the recurrent costs of providing services (UNCDF 2004). Data on actual collections are not available, but the amounts are thought to be quite small. Provinces—deconcentrated levels of the national government—may also collect own-revenues, which accrue to governors' budgets (the *Salakhet*).[6] These revenues, which are not proper own-source revenues, accounted for 48 percent of the total *Salakhet*, of which the tax on motor vehicles (17.4 percent), the excise on public lighting (12.3 percent), the wealth transfer tax (7.0 percent), and the business tax (6.8 percent) are the most significant (World Bank 2003b).

Vietnam, as a transitional country, reveals some similarities with China. The Law on State Budget, which took effect in January 2004, establishes three types of revenue assignments. These include revenues assigned completely to the central level, those assigned completely to the local level, and those shared between the central and subnational governments. Shared revenues—which include the value-added tax, enterprise (corporate) income tax, personal income tax, special consumption taxes, and gasoline and oil fees, among others—constitute the bulk of revenues at all levels. Own-source revenues are virtually nonexistent in Vietnam. The only exception is user fees, such as road tolls and select fees for schools and hospitals, which are not generally significant sources of revenue (World Bank 2000).

Own-Source Revenue Practices and Options

Revenue assignment in East Asia is consistent with the framework's principles and guidelines in some ways and inconsistent in others. The next section further highlights specific regional practices for each revenue source. This discussion serves to stress that a well-designed subnational revenue system should rely on a mix of taxes, and also suggests further options for reform.

As table 6.4 reveals, there is no own-source revenue common to all six countries, though a number of countries make use of user fees and charge business taxes, excise taxes, and property taxes. As admirable as the user charge and property tax package is, international experience has shown that such taxes can be both difficult to implement and unlikely to provide an adequate fiscal base if subnational governments have major social spending responsibilities (Bird 2003b). Accordingly, several options are available to further mobilize own-source revenues.

Property Taxation

Given the role of property taxes as revenue generators in the developing world, the fact that the property tax is not an own-revenue source in many countries raises concerns about sustainable revenue flows, subnational autonomy, and thus the promised benefits of decentralization. In the 1990s, property taxes accounted for 40 percent of all subnational taxes in developing countries, but only 12 percent in transition countries (Bird and Slack 2002). Except for the Philippines and Indonesia, East Asian countries do not come close to the benchmarks of either developing or transition countries, suggesting that property taxes could yet serve as a greater source of revenue in the medium term, and an important source in the longer term.

Vietnam, Thailand, and Cambodia diverge the most from international practice. Vietnam has no property tax in the modern sense of the term. The country does have taxes on land and housing, land rent, and transfers of land use rights, but local governments have little or no control over these taxes. Thailand imposes land taxes, but they account for only about 5 percent of subnational resources, and subnational governments lack authority over their rates and bases. Cambodia's land taxes are insignificant in revenue terms.

China has multiple taxes on property, often on the same base, which do not rest on market or updated property assessments. Thus, these taxes do not deliver on their revenue potential. Yet unlike in Vietnam, local governments can set the tax rate on urban land use subject to legislated maximums and minimums (larger cities can set higher rates, for example). In fact, the tax on urban land use is one of only a small set of own-source revenues in China. The tax base is the physical land area, not the market value, as the country has no formal market for land transactions.

Indonesia provides another important example of limited local autonomy over the property tax. Subnational governments are not responsible for taxing property (or property transfers). While the central government shares about 80 percent of property tax revenues with the originating region, and distributes another 10 percent among all regions, policy and administration are firmly in central hands. This has led to two negative developments: a reliance on taxes that essentially substitute for property taxes, such as the street lighting tax; and the proliferation of nonbenefit taxes—user charges and service fees not linked to the provision of services.

The Philippines is the only country where a traditional property tax is a source of subnational own-revenue. The property tax accounts for nearly 37 percent of subnational own-revenues. However, the central government limits control over tax rates and bases. For example, the national government sets the real property tax rate (including the Special Education Fund levy) at 2 percent for provinces and 3 percent for cities and municipalities in metropolitan Manila. All provinces outside the capital region avail themselves of the maximum rate, while most cities are under the maximum.[7]

International experience suggests that subnational governments are likely to use discretion over property tax rates, so they vary widely. Bird and Slack report, for example, that the effective rate of property tax in the United States ranges from 0.4 percent to 2.9 percent for residential property and 0.7 percent to 6.0 percent for commercial property (Bird and Slack 2002).

Property tax reform can offer a source of revenue, perhaps modest in transition countries, and a source of autonomy and accountability across the region. Rationalizing land taxation in Vietnam—and moving toward a modern property tax with some local discretion over rates and introducing modest property taxes in Cambodia—would be first steps in those countries. Devolving authority over rates in China, Indonesia, the Philippines, and Thailand is also a reform option.

Business Taxation

Some analysts regard business taxes as a potentially inefficient means of raising revenue. Often levied at high rates, these taxes can distort firms' investment

TABLE 6.4 Own-Source Revenue Assignment

	Cambodia	China	Indonesia	Philippines	Thailand	Vietnam
User charges?	Yes, provinces and communes can collect for some basic services.	No, but "informal" or "illegal" local extrabudgetary fees have proliferated in health, education, and roads. Some are "nuisance" charges.	Yes; these are numerous, and some have high administrative and compliance costs. Some are "nuisance" charges.	Yes; these are numerous, and some have high administrative and compliance costs. Some are "nuisance" charges.	Yes, on transportation, public utilities, and markets.	Yes, on roads, education, and health.
Property taxes?	No, but minor provincial taxes on unused land.	Yes, to an extent, in that SNGs can set the rate for the urban land use tax up to a ceiling. There are also numerous other taxes on the same property and land base.	No; revenues shared with SNGs, but they have no control over rates and little control over administration.	Yes; rates set by SNGs subject to a maximum. Administered by SNGs with little central assistance.	No, for the land development tax and the house and land tax. The central government sets rates.	No; some taxes on land and housing, land rent, and transfer of land use rights. But SNGs have no control over rates and little control over administration. No modern property tax.
Excise taxes?	No, but taxes on motor vehicles at the provincial level.	No, but taxes on vehicle and vessel use.	Yes, on motor vehicles and fuel, though assigned to provinces. Also on minerals, raising equity issues.	No; SNGs are prohibited from levying excise taxes, including on motor vehicles.	No; central government controls motor vehicle and other excise taxes.	No.
Personal income taxes (PIT)?	No.	No; a PIT is assigned to SNGs, but they have no control over tax policy.	No; a PIT is shared with SNGs, but they have no control over tax policy.	Not exactly, though the community tax is in the form of a poll tax.	No.	No, but central government and SNGs share PIT.
Payroll taxes?	No.	No.	No.	No.	No, though base of national PIT includes payroll.	No.
General sales taxes?	No.	No, but central government and SNGs share value-added tax.	No.	No.	No, but central govenrment and SNGs share value-added and sales taxes.	No, but central government and SNGs share value-added tax.
Business taxes?	No, though business license charges and market taxes are assessed at the provincial level.	Yes; a business tax on gross receipts, an enterprise income tax, and other surcharges and surtaxes (e.g., urban maintenance and construction tax).	Yes, though officially limited to a few sectors. The number and type of "business taxes" are growing, raising concerns about "nuisance" taxation.	Yes; relatively large revenue source.	Yes, though limited to a small number of sector-specific business-type taxes.	No, but central government and SNGs share corporate income tax.

Source: World Bank staff.
Note: SNG = subnational governments. Own-source revenue defined as a legal tax or charge over whose rate an SNG has some control.

decisions (such as their debt-equity ratio). These taxes might also serve as barriers to new firms and the expansion of small ones. On the other hand, business taxes are potentially large revenue generators and more elastic than other traditional subnational taxes (such as the property tax), although they may also be more distortionary. Business taxes can be justified according to the benefit principle: firms are consuming benefits provided by subnational governments and thus should be charged for them.

This principle offers a rationale for differentiated business taxes at local and regional levels, such as user charges along with some form of business licensing tax, and perhaps a low-rate tax on gross receipts, either in place of or in addition to those options. At the regional level, the benefit case argues for a broad-based levy that remains neutral toward the factor mix, such as a value-added income tax or a business value tax (both options for taxing value-added income). One further option is to levy both a payroll tax and a tax on capital. Payroll taxes are easy to administer and productive at low rates. However, they can act as a barrier to employment in the formal sector—a concern that might outweigh their benefits in economies struggling to boost rates of formal employment.

Table 6.4 shows that China and the Philippines have formal business taxes, which are major subnational revenue generators. The business tax in China—levied on gross receipts not subject to the value-added tax—covers a wide range of sectors, including transportation, communications, and construction, and accounts for a large share of provincial tax revenues (22.6 percent, on average, in 2001). The business tax in the Philippines is similar, in that it is also levied on gross sales and accounts for a significant share of local revenues (29.8 percent, on average, in 2002, including business licenses). Giving subnational governments in China and the Philippines control over rate setting could be both revenue-productive and autonomy-enhancing.

Cambodia and Indonesia do not have local business taxes per se. Indonesia relies on taxes on specific sectors, including hotels, restaurants, and advertising. A growing number of subnational governments in Indonesia are also taxing specific sectors, mimicking business taxes. There is concern that the proliferation of these taxes will result in distortions and inefficiencies at the local level. This suggests the need to rationalize the taxes imposed on businesses to minimize distortions, such as by introducing a simple low-rate, broad-based "single business tax" to replace sectoral and "nuisance" levies and fees.[8] Cambodian provinces levy business licenses, though it might be more appropriate to transfer business licensing to the commune level and introduce a standard business tax at the provincial level.

Personal Income Taxation

No country in the region makes use of personal income taxes as a source of subnational own-revenue. China, Indonesia, and Vietnam use such taxes as shared revenues, however. Such taxes would thus appear to be a potential new source of revenue for Cambodia, the Philippines, and Thailand. Allowing regional (provincial) governments to piggyback taxes on national personal income taxes is an important option for boosting local revenues, and potentially for increasing autonomy. This assumes that subnational governments could set the rates, and that the central government would administer the tax to avoid burdening local administrative capacity.[9]

User Fees and Charges

Official use of charges and fees is widespread in the region.[10] In Thailand, subnational governments levy user charges on garbage collection, public utilities, mass transportation, and medical and childcare. The Philippines has more than 33 different types of user fees and charges, ranging from animal and civil registration to garbage collection fees. Total collections from each major source are relatively small, reflecting the dispersion of revenue sources (see table 6.5). Moreover, a large number of fees and user charges together generate less than 0.10 percent of the total operating and miscellaneous revenue of subnational governments. It is important to note, however, that the main economic rationale for levying user charges is to promote efficient use of public resources through the pricing mechanism, not necessarily to raise revenue. Still, eliminating these extremely low-yield fees would reduce the administrative and compliance costs arising from the complexity of the system.

In Indonesia, the most significant provincial collections from user fees come from charges for health services. Collections from charges for building licenses are second in importance. At the city and district level, 62 percent of fee revenue comes from public service fees, 23 percent from licensing fees,

TABLE 6.5 Highest-Yield Fees and Sources of Operating Revenues of Subnational Governments in the Philippines, 2000
(pesos)

	Pesos	% of total
Market receipts	1,568,806,000	15
Electrical light and power fees	738,108,000	7
Mayors' permit fees	659,004,000	6
Hospital fees	657,528,000	6
Rents	368,598,000	4
Building permit fees	361,172,000	4
Garbage fees	337,992,000	3
Total operating and miscellaneous revenue	10,218,000,000	100

Source: COA 2001.

TABLE 6.6 Most Significant Charges by Local and Provincial Governments in Indonesia, 2002
(million rupiah)

Local government	Revenue	Share of total (%)
Charges for health services	745,903	33.25
Charges for building permit	240,547	10.72
Charges for market services	194,134	8.66
Charges for printing resident's ID card and birth certificate	128,072	5.71
Charges for use of regional property	96,259	4.29
Garbage disposal/sanitation levies	92,160	4.11
Bus terminal levies	87,353	3.89
Disturbance permit levies	62,824	2.80
Public roadside parking levies	60,387	2.69
Motor vehicle inspection levies	46,347	2.07
Provincial government	**Revenue**	**Share of total (%)**
Charges for health services	311,133	45.42
Charges for building permit	134,071	19.57
Charges for use of regional property	46,384	6.77
Motor vehicle inspection levies	36,259	5.29
Regional production sale levies	20,451	2.99
Wholesale market and shopping complex levies	15,607	2.28
Public roadside parking levies	12,603	1.84
Recreation and sports ground levies	11,774	1.72
License allocation of land use	10,711	1.56
Garbage disposal/sanitation levies	8,741	1.28

Source: Ministry of Finance.

and 15 percent from business service fees. All other provincial and local charges together contribute a very small percentage of total revenue. In fact, provinces levy 14 charges that generate less than 1 percent of charge revenues, and local governments levy at least 30 such charges (with at least 93 different local charges throughout the country in 2002). Many of these low-yielding fees are levied on businesses, creating a heavy administrative burden and suggesting the need for rationalization (see table 6.6).

Bird and Tsiopoulos sum up the challenge of user charges as ensuring "that the *right* prices are charged for the *right* services" (1997, 33). They also argue that central governments need to provide guidance—perhaps in the form of an overarching legal framework—to subnational governments on creating and managing user charges. Elements of such a framework include clear and transparent parameters for setting prices and a process for consulting with local stakeholders. National governments in countries with a particular concern in this area, such as China, Indonesia, and Vietnam, might be warranted in intervening—at least in the near term—with lists of allowable or prohibited charges.

Excise Taxes

East Asian countries are split on excise taxes. The Philippines, Thailand, and Vietnam do not use major excises, which suggests another reform option for these countries.[11] Allowing local governments to impose excise taxes or fees on motor vehicle registration would give those governments an appropriate and potentially important source of revenue that would be relatively easy to administer.[12]

Significant Others: Fees, Other Taxes, Charges, and the Problem of Illegal Proliferation

Illegal Activities

Lack of control over tax policy has encouraged local governments to seek other tax and nontax sources of revenue. In a number of East Asian countries, local governments have the authority to enact new taxes and fees, though their authority is regulated by law, and in some countries is subject to review by the central government. Central control has encouraged local governments to become entrepreneurial, with both positive and negative results. In China, this situation has led to the proliferation of "illegal" extrabudgetary fees, some of which have distortionary effects. Indonesia has seen the proliferation of nuisance taxes, which collect very little in revenue yet impose high administrative costs on local governments and compliance costs on taxpayers. In the Philippines, local revenue codes yield a tax system of great complexity, with a resulting loss of transparency and ability to monitor the system. Some subnational governments are avoiding collecting legal taxes and others are collecting "illegal" taxes, undermining the integrity of local governance and thus public support.

The Chinese case is particularly acute given the large number of "unofficial" charges. Because of a lack of autonomy, local governments have resorted to introducing fees not permitted by law, and these represent a significant percentage of local budgets.[13] The fees include surcharges on household utility bills, hospitals and school charges, road maintenance, advertisement, vehicle purchases and others (World Bank 2002). While these fees may introduce distortions and raise compliance costs imposed on taxpayers, the World Bank has argued that "fears of run-away local governments arbitrarily creating a jungle of local fees and charges do not appear to be justified." Yet the growth of extrabudgetary financing among local governments has become a serious concern. The World Bank estimates that extrabudgetary funds and off-budget activities may represent 18 to 22 percent of gross domestic product (GDP) (World Bank 2002).

The Chinese government has had a policy of converting informal fees into official taxes, but it is implementing this policy unevenly. In Gansu province, for example, provincial officials reportedly approve all local fees at the prefecture, county, and township levels. But no one knows the extent to which local governments are staying ahead of provincial authorities by implementing new fees.

Similarly, Cambodia has had serious concerns about the proliferation of "informal" fees and charges at the commune/*sangkat* level. In fact, this proliferation seems to be impeding development of a system of own-source revenues for newly elected subnational governments. Evaluations of existing practices have been only exploratory, but there are reports of birth registration fees being "unofficially inflated" from US$0.10 to US$10 (UNCDF 2003).

In China, fees and charges undermine the tax system because they are not officially on the books. In the Philippines, a similar argument can be made—but with a variation. In the Philippines, numerous fees and charges on the books undermine the system because they are either not collected, or are not collected in accordance with the revenue code. In the city of Bacolod, for example, the mayor's business permit fee has more than 200 different rates, which vary by type of establishment. This complexity adds greatly to administrative costs. Thus, putting revenues on the books and legalizing them does not necessarily solve the problem or eliminate the need to develop the local capacity to manage user charges.

Overall, the proliferation of illegal, extrabudgetary revenues raises concerns about efficiency losses stemming from distortions and relatively high administrative (and possibly compliance) costs. At the same time, citizens of some localities may be willing to pay for off-budget services from local governments (in these cases, efficiency losses would presumably be lower). Some subnational governments collect these off-budget sources in response to limited autonomy, so the practice is somewhat understandable, if not justifiable. However, these levies can undermine public trust in the tax system, which cannot be good for long-term compliance. A policy of reviewing and converting illegal fees into official ones, as in China, is warranted.

Open Lists

One of the issues around the use and abuse of user charges is the authority to enact new levies. In both the Philippines and Indonesia, local governments have formal authority to introduce some new taxes and fees. In the Philippines, the Local Government Code provides a range of tax and fee options for local governments, though the country should consider more options. The code gives local governments the option to levy other taxes, fees, and charges, provided that the code does not specifically prohibit them and the National Internal Revenue code does not already include them.[14] That all makes sense within the framework established above. But what is problematic is if subnational governments abuse this "open list" approach by levying taxes and fees in a nontransparent, illegal manner. Monitoring and enforcement of tax law matter.

In Indonesia, besides formally assigned taxes, Law 34 of 2000 allows cities and regencies to levy additional taxes if they follow a number of general criteria.[15] To ensure that governments meet these criteria, the central government requires them to submit regional regulations to the Ministry of Home Affairs for review. If the ministry, in consultation with the Ministry of Finance, finds that a tax violates legal provisions, the ministry may cancel the regulation, in which case the local government must rescind the tax.[16]

As noted, the "open list" approach has its merits. However, countries might not want to seize on it as a major reform option for at least two reasons. First, the positive list of taxes provided in Indonesia (Law 34 of 2000) does not include any taxes that can generate significant revenue. This prompts many subnational governments to introduce taxes that do not necessarily generate much revenue either, as a way to assert their autonomy. As a result, nuisance taxes and charges abound. The Ministry of Finance found that more than 200 regulations submitted to the central government between August 2001 and January 2003 violated Law 34. Many are levied on agriculture, mining, and interregional trade. In Lombok, for instance, three local governments jointly impose a 5 percent tax on 174 products leaving the island (Ray 2003). Thus, the problem in Indonesia is not the open list itself but the fact that it does not include appropriate broad-based taxes.

Second, the review mechanism does not seem to work very well without adequate monitoring. For example, Lewis estimates that subnational governments send just 40 percent of all regional tax- and charge-related regulations to the Ministry of Home Affairs for review, so many potentially harmful taxes and charges remain in effect (Lewis 2003).

Revenue Assignment between Subnational Levels

Revenue assignment between local governments in East Asia often seems to create incentive problems. These occur between provinces and subprovincial levels in China and Vietnam; between provinces, cities and municipalities, and *barangays* in the Philippines; and between provinces, cities and regencies, and villages in Indonesia. In China and Vietnam, the lack of formal revenue assignment creates unpredictability and reduces accountability. In the Philippines and Indonesia, the transfer of significant shares of collections from province to subprovincial levels may reduce provincial incentives for collecting own-revenue.

In China, provincial governments may assign revenues to local governments within their jurisdiction (see box 6.1). Most, if not all, provinces seem to follow the traditional hierarchical approach, assigning revenue between the province and the first layer of local government (cities and prefectures), and leaving each layer to work out arrangements with the one below it. As mentioned, while the lack of

BOX 6.1 Revenue Assignment across Subnational Governments in China's Gansu Province

Gansu province is centralized, in that the provincial level retains a relatively large share of all local taxes and rebates. For example, the province retains the entire amount of the value-added tax shared with subnational governments (that is, 25 percent of total national collections). A number of important features characterize subprovincial revenue assignment:

- Revenues from the enterprise income tax and the value-added tax are allocated to the level of government that "owns" the enterprise.
- The city maintenance tax is shared 30 percent with the province and 70 percent with prefectures and cities.
- The resource tax is shared 70 percent with the province and 30 percent with prefectures and cities.
- The urban land tax is shared 40 percent with provinces and 60 percent with prefectures and cities.
- For all other local taxes, prefectures and cities have full discretion over sharing arrangements.
- For certain local taxes, counties have full discretion over sharing arrangements with towns and township governments. These taxes include the farmland occupation tax, the land appreciation tax, the housing property tax, the vehicle license tax, and animal husbandry charges.
- Given discretion at each level of government, a variety of other arrangements exist. For example, in some counties the prefecture government received a share of the county value-added tax despite the provincial rule that allocates the tax by ownership.

Source: World Bank 2002, pp. 57–58.

formal assignment may have some advantages for provinces, the disadvantage for subprovincial governments in terms of uncertainty would seem to outweigh the potential advantages.

Revenue Performance

Own-source revenues in Indonesia and the Philippines have risen in nominal (and real) terms, but have not fared as well as a percentage of GNP. In the Philippines, own-source revenues rose significantly right after decentralization, but have been stagnant as a percentage of GNP—at 0.91 in 2001—ever since. In Indonesia, own-source revenues rose from 1.1 percent of GNP in 1995 to 1.4 percent in 2002. In China, in contrast, local taxes, which are predominantly shared revenues as opposed to own-source revenues (in fact, official own-source revenues are minimal), grew significantly as a percentage of GNP since the Tax Sharing System reform, from 5.0 percent in 1994 to 7.0 percent in 1999. Moreover, estimates of buoyancy in the post-reform period—a measure of revenue productivity as a result of economic growth—show that it is quite high.[17] Overall, these results indicate that despite policy, administrative, and political challenges, own-source collection shows some positive signs, which augurs well for the future.

However, in most cases, own-source revenues compose a small percentage of total subnational revenue and their share has either not improved much or has actually declined. This means that subnational governments have not reduced their dependence on central government transfers. The next sections analyze that result for several countries.

Composition of Own-Source Revenues

From 1992 to 2002, own-source revenues in the Philippines composed 34 percent, on average, of total resources available to local governments. However, own-source revenues declined from 38 percent in 1992 to 31 percent in 2002. Thus, these revenues, although nominally growing, have not kept up with the growth in transfers from the central government (the Internal Revenue Allotment).

In the Philippines, as in numerous developing countries, property taxes account for the largest single component of local revenues. In 2002, the real property tax accounted for 36.5 percent of subnational own-source revenues, while business taxes and licenses accounted for nearly 30 percent, and operating and miscellaneous revenue accounted for 22 percent (see table 6.7).[18] These percentages have remained stable over time.

In Indonesia, own-source revenues accounted for about 39 percent of total revenue at the provincial level, but only 7 percent at the city and regency level (see table 6.8). Moreover, the percentage of own-source revenues to total revenue at the city and regency level declined from 12 percent to 9 percent from 1995 to 2000, and dropped further to 6 percent in 2001, after decentralization. Transfers rose in relative importance over the same period, from 84 percent to 87 percent of total revenues.

Trends in Own-Source Revenues

Both the Philippines and Indonesia show a clear trend: own-source revenues have risen slowly but steadily. In the Philippines, nominal and real

TABLE 6.7 Own-Source Revenue Composition by Type of Local Government in the Philippines, 2001
(percentage distribution)[a]

Sources	All SNGs	Provinces	Cities	Municipalities
Real property taxes	36.5	47.3	36.8	30.3
Business taxes and licenses	29.8	0.3	36.3	26.3
Other taxes	11.2	22.4	10.0	9.0
Operating and miscellaneous revenue	22.3	29.2	16.9	34.3
Capital revenue	0.1	0.7	0.0	0.1

Source: COA 2002.
Note: SNGs = subnational governments. Totals may not sum to 100 percent because of rounding.

TABLE 6.8 Composition of Regional Revenue in Indonesia, 2002
(millions of rupiah; percentage of total revenue)

	Provinces	Cities/regencies
Own-source revenues	14,207,830 *38.46%*	7,454,629 *7.19%*
Taxes and charges	12,500,929 *33.84%*	5,109,501 *4.93%*
Other	1,706,901 *4.62%*	2,345,128 *2.26%*
Grants	7,393,745 *20.02%*	64,100,112 *61.83%*
Revenue sharing	8,084,119 *21.89%*	17,310,428 *16.70%*
Carryover	6,307,652 *17.08%*	9,752,994 *9.41%*
Other	944,849 *2.56%*	5,052,425 *4.87%*
Total	36,938,196 *100.00%*	103,670,588 *100.00%*

Source: Ministry of Finance.
Note: Figures are projections based on data for 28 provinces (including Jakarta) and 324 cities and regencies.

TABLE 6.9 Annual Nominal Growth in Local Own-Source Revenue in Indonesia, 1996–2002
(percent)

Annual increase	1995/1996	1996/1997	1997/1998	1998/1999	1999/2000	2001	2002
Regional tax	31	22	20	48	26	21	23
Regional charges	18	14	11	−12	20	32	32
Profits—enterprises	18	33	−2	20	26	10	89
Other	40	0	15	75	−1	155	93
Total	24	16	14	20	20	40	42

Source: BPS and Ministry of Finance.

collections have grown steadily in all major categories: property taxes increased nearly fourfold from 1993 to 2000, while taxes on goods and services rose fivefold. Taxes on goods and services recorded the highest average annual increase, followed by the property tax. Growth rates for all categories slowed during the latter part of the period.

In Indonesia, decentralization spurred a 40 percent nominal rise in local own-source revenues between fiscal years 2000 and 2001.[19] While revenues from taxes and charges grew by 21 percent and 32 percent, respectively, the largest increase occurred in the category of "other," which rose by 155 percent (see table 6.9). In 2001, locally raised taxes contributed 43 percent of own-source revenues, while charges raised 33 percent and the share of "other" revenues grew to 21 percent.

Between 2000 and 2001, provincial tax revenue more than doubled in Indonesia. Several factors may explain this sudden jump. One factor seems to be that provinces received additional taxing powers under Law 34 of 2000 (even though the law abolished some nuisance taxes). Another factor is that tax collections, especially from the vehicle transfer tax, rose considerably. Third, changes in revenue-sharing arrangements may have created stronger incentives for provincial governments to increase collections.

Fuel and motor vehicle–related taxation dominate provincial own-source revenues in Indonesia. Provinces also appear to levy taxes that are formally assigned to local governments, such as the hotel and restaurant tax and the street lighting tax. Despite their insignificant expenditure responsibilities, provinces raise almost twice the own-source revenues as cities and regencies. In 2001, for example, revenues from local taxes and charges were less than half those from provincial taxes and charges.

Street lighting and hotel and restaurant taxes account for over two-thirds of own-source collections among cities and regencies. "Other" taxes—which most likely include a large number of nuisance taxes that local governments have introduced since Law 34 of 2000—represent only 6 percent of tax revenue, indicating that the new taxes do not generate significant additional revenue.

Own-Source Revenue Administration

Arrangements for tax administration vary throughout the region, ranging from highly decentralized in the Philippines to highly centralized in Vietnam, with Indonesia and China between these two poles. Yet in all cases the relative roles of local and national governments have not been well designed, resulting in both capacity and incentive challenges. The Philippines, for example, is highly decentralized with respect to tax administration. The Bureau of Internal Revenue (BIR) administers national taxes, while each local government administers its own-source revenues according to the Local Government Code and local revenue codes. Moreover, the law provides for little formal cooperation: the BIR operates independently of local tax administrations, and the national government provides little support to local governments.[20] Meanwhile, local tax administrations usually operate independently of one another.

At the other extreme is Vietnam. The General Taxation Department—operating under the Ministry of Finance, with offices at the provincial and district levels—is responsible for collecting all internal revenues. Local governments have no tax administrative responsibilities. However, tax administrators operate under a system of dual subordination, in that they are responsible to their ministerial management as well as to representatives of local governments.[21] Thus, the system is characterized by built-in tensions. Martínez-Vázquez notes that administrative centralization may reduce incentives for revenue collection, as central officials have fewer incentives to collect local revenues compared with local administrators, who would have greater incentives to collect local revenues. On the other hand, he notes, provincial authorities have been known to pay bonuses to tax administrators who improve their collection performance (Martínez-Vázquez 2003). In this sense, subnational governments have some administrative control at the margin.

In Indonesia and China, the central government administers all shared taxes, while local governments administer revenues assigned to them. In Indonesia, local revenue agencies administer the taxes for which they are responsible, with little support from the central government. As in the Philippines, the result is that administrative capacity and collection costs vary widely by locality. China's Tax Sharing System reforms of 1994 created two separate tax administrations—one at the national level to administer national and shared revenues, and a provincial tax administration tasked with all subnational revenues. According to the World Bank, "de facto dual subordination" of central tax administrators to local governments is still a problem, owing to old allegiances and the fact that local governments provide bonuses and assess penalties to stimulate collection, thus creating potential conflicts of interest (World Bank 2002).

Local Revenue Administration: Models and Options

Tax administration can also be assessed from the perspectives of autonomy and efficiency. Vehorn and Ahmad (1997) offer four models for tax administration in decentralized polities. These include central tax administration with revenue sharing, central tax administration with assignment of taxing powers to different levels of government, multilevel administration with revenue sharing, and self-administration by each level of government. Mikesell (2002) stresses another dimension: the extent to which national and subnational authorities cooperate or operate independently. Table 6.10 reveals a great deal of diversity in the region on the administrative side, with transition

TABLE 6.10 Tax Administration Models in East Asia

Models	Countries	Observations
Central administration with tax sharing	Vietnam Cambodia	Highly centralized, but dual subordination of tax administrators gives SNGs some control at the margin.
Multilevel administration with tax sharing	China	Formally separate administrations for national and provincial levels, though dual subordination in practice.
	Indonesia	Formally separate administration, though some cooperation between central and SNG tax agencies, including on property tax.
	Thailand	Formally separate administration at the national, municipal/city, and subdistrict levels.
Self-administration by each level of government	Philippines	Separate provincial, municipal/city, and *barangay* administrative levels; little cooperation between central and SNG tax agencies.

Source: World Bank staff.
Note: SNG = subnational government.

economies closer to the centralized pole and Indonesia, the Philippines, and Thailand closer to the decentralized pole.

Guidance from the literature on good practice in tax administration in decentralized contexts is less clear. No consensus has developed on the principles of devolved administration.

The efficiency criterion would argue for reducing total administrative and compliance costs by taking advantage of economies of scale and scope. The Philippines, for example, includes hundreds of small-scale tax administrations collecting revenues throughout the country. Their ability to attract and retain qualified personnel is limited, as is their access to information technology. This limited capacity has direct consequences for taxpayers in terms of higher compliance costs. Variations in local capacity also mean that taxpayers do not receive uniform treatment throughout the country.

The key question is whether it is possible to centralize some administrative functions to reduce costs while not curtailing local autonomy. That is, to what extent is local tax administration a sine qua non of autonomous local governance? One could argue that since some functions of tax administration effectively control marginal revenues, subnational governments must have control over these functions in order to have—by definition—own-source revenues. Looking at administration as a bundled set of functions rather than a homogeneous process allows one to think about differential treatment of administrative functions. For example, the level of enforcement activity will have a direct bearing on the level of tax arrears collections. Thus, a subnational government that controls enforcement activities would be able to increase revenues at the margin. The same holds for taxpayer registries, which can be managed more or less aggressively, and taxpayer services. The argument is less true for other functions. Take property valuation. If valuation relies on market methods, there is not much scope for differences in implementation. The point is that administrative as well as policy levers can affect marginal revenues (though some administrative effects might be quite small).

Local governments do not, in theory, need to control all tax functions directly if they control the administration of those functions. The law requires tax administrators, as bureaucrats, to do as their political principals say. One definition of a good tax administration is one that simply follows the tax code, leaving aside the question of whether the law is good policy. In the Philippines, bureaucrats are employees of the local government and therefore agents of local executives. But bureaucratic agents of higher-level governments could also be responsible to the local chief executive. The point is that tax administrators do not need to be local government employees to ensure accountability to local governments. Devolved responsibility does not necessarily imply devolved administration, especially in the context of weak local capacity.

A number of options would preserve local autonomy while improving efficiency. These options need not be universal for all subnational governments in a given country. Rather, subnational governments could consider the options on a case-by-case basis, which would imply asymmetrical treatment. Depending on local conditions, asymmetry might make sense, and would likely generate useful pilots for more comprehensive reforms.

A similar approach would encourage local governments with greater capacity to perform, for a fee, some functions for other local governments with less capacity. That occurs with Lima's Tax Administration Service, which collects property taxes for two other Peruvian municipalities (Ate and La Victoria) for a 5 percent commission. The critical issue is whether subnational governments would control administration at the margin.

Another option would be to establish a tax agency that would assist local governments—on a case-by-case basis, for a fee—with core administrative functions: registration, collection, and compliance. Such a subnational tax agency would allow economies of scale and scope, which could lower administrative and compliance costs. At present there are no known examples of this approach.

Yet another approach is for the national government to take responsibility for functions such as property assessment, or to help local governments with core functions. National governments assist with core functions in many countries. In Colombia, the central government maintains the property register and updates property valuations. In Cyprus, Estonia, Jamaica, Malawi, and Pakistan, the central government is responsible for assessing property and collecting taxes, even though property taxes are assigned to local governments (Vehorn and Ahmad 1997; McCluskey and Williams 1999, cited in

Mikesell 2002).[22] To add a dynamic element to this approach, one could envision local governments progressively taking over more functions as they develop capacity in these specialized areas. All local governments would not necessarily perform all tax administration functions, as some undoubtedly make more sense administered centrally.

Some East Asian countries have already taken advantage of economies of scale and scope. Responsibilities for administration vary among subnational levels of government, with larger jurisdictional levels having some responsibility for collections for smaller jurisdictions in many countries. For example, in Indonesia and the Philippines, provinces collect and transfer some revenues to lower levels. This option—provided that higher jurisdictions are given adequate incentives—is worth exploring as a way to rationalize administrative arrangements between national and subnational governments, and between subnational governments themselves.

Though there are some success stories in the region (see, for example, box 6.2), the administrative capacity of subnational governments is weak in many cases, and is the binding constraint on

BOX 6.2 Improving Tax Administration in Quezon City, Philippines

Quezon City—the largest city in metropolitan Manila in land area and population—faced a serious budget deficit in 2001. The administration of Mayor Feliciano Belmonte, Jr., who assumed office in July 2001, inherited outstanding obligations of ₱1.4 billion and bank debt of ₱1.2 billion. The city decided to improve its revenue collection.

The mayor's first step was to convene a search committee, headed by the dean of the College of Public Administration of the University of the Philippines, to recommend candidates for treasurer. The mayor settled on Dr. Victor Endriga, who quickly implemented reforms over the next 18 months designed to reverse the city's fiscal course. Treasurer Endriga adopted a "carrot-and-stick approach." The "sticks" include the following:

- Property auctions for delinquent property taxpayers. The city conducted three auctions in 2002—the first postcode auctions in Quezon City. (Although delinquent taxpayers have sued the city, they do not phase the treasurer: "it's part of the game.")
- Delinquency letters sent to recover the estimated ₱10.7 billion owed the city. (Each staff member must send out at least 20 letters daily, as staff had sent few before.)
- The use of presumptive minimum levels of gross sales for the business tax and for markets.
- A requirement that all business establishments with gross receipts over ₱500,000 submit their previous year's financial statement, as well as information on monthly tax payments from the Bureau of Internal Revenue.
- A requirement that all payments of real estate taxes include confirmation of payment of other taxes, including the business tax and mayor's permit fees.
- Direct withholding of taxes from city contractors and suppliers, which rose from 12 percent to 75 percent of gross collections.

The "carrots" include the following:

- An increase in the discount on early payment of property taxes, from 10 percent to 20 percent for annual payers, and from 5 percent to 10 percent for quarterly payers.
- Improved taxpayer facilities, including modern air-conditioned lounges with automatic queuing systems, free coffee and tea, free local telephone calls, and televisions.
- Plaques from the mayor presented in a public ceremony to the 10 most "outstanding" taxpayers.

The city also computerized its property and business tax registries and collection processes, hired an outside firm to input all paper records, instituted new security features, raised tax rates, and reassigned employees within the treasurer's office to avoid familiarization. The city now rewards (such as with overseas trips) and punishes revenue examiners based on actual collections, and conducts house visits of delinquent taxpayers.

This reform program has paid off. Own-source revenues rose from ₱2.3 billion in 2001 to ₱3.9 billion in 2002, and the city closed the year with a surplus of ₱0.5 billion.

Source: Endriga 2003.

improving revenue performance throughout the region (see box 6.3). As Bahl has argued regarding China, "Tax administration shortcomings plague Chinese fiscal policy" (1999, 66). The principal problems include the following:

- The prevalence of stop filers, nonfilers, and late filers, owing to low local capacity to register taxpayers. This results in delinquent payments and the accumulation of arrears, especially in the Philippines.
- Infrequent audit and enforcement (temporary closures and property auctions), resulting in low compliance. This seems to be a problem in both Indonesia and the Philippines.
- The limited availability of taxpayer services, although some local governments in Indonesia and the Philippines offer important examples of good practice.
- The low professional qualifications of staff in all three countries.
- Inadequate support from and coordination with the national government.

Overall, the East Asian experience suggests that the multilevel administration model (with tax sharing) may hold the most short-term promise. The advantage of this model is the possibility that different levels of administration could assume different functions, and it could also facilitate assistance to subnational governments. Assigning complex tasks with economies of scale (such as property valuation) to either a central government agency or an agency dedicated to subnational support would reduce administrative costs and likely improve service quality. East Asian countries could further explore the idea of a subnational tax support agency, funded by subnational governments and under their control. Other solutions, such as for subnational governments to contract out to other local governments or piggyback on national taxes, are also worth consideration.

The Politics of Local Taxation

While policy and administrative constraints on local taxation are critical, political constraints also affect performance. Several local governments in the Philippines, for example, reported that "political intervention" underlay their limited use of the power to auction or close businesses. Other governments reported that instead of confrontation, mayors used their "charisma" to persuade businesspeople to pay taxes. One government reported active opposition from the chamber of commerce to the General Revision of Assessment, and another reported intense lobbying from the private sector against increases in tax rates, which resulted in compromise. Other localities report that businesses have taken legal action against property auctions and tax increases. Taxpayers sued Quezon City, for example, over "confiscatory" tax rates.

While no one knows the precise impact of political constraints on local taxation, a number of hypotheses—focusing on incentives—may be posited. One possibility is that politicians simply weigh the net impact, or political tradeoff, of higher revenues against greater expenditures. Simply put, officials decide to increase taxes (either through higher rates or better administration) when the discounted benefits of greater expenditures are higher than the discounted costs of higher taxes. Many officials seem to decide that the political costs of higher taxation are greater than the expected benefits. There are several possible reasons. First, the expected marginal benefit is small compared with the political cost of unhappy constituents. Inefficiencies in delivering services (such as patronage or padded projects) might also outweigh the impact of greater revenues, "wasting" the tax increase.

Another possibility is that the incidence of benefits and costs—in terms of expenditures and revenues—might undercut local elites. Increases in property tax collections would most likely harm the wealthy from a distributive standpoint, while increases in service delivery would most likely favor lower-income groups. However, politicians may not weigh these impacts equally, and may be reluctant to use higher tax collections to fund pro-poor service delivery.

Other explanations focus on the timing of benefits and costs, the extent of executive control over spending, and the electoral strength of the incumbent. Term limits on local executives—which limit them to two terms of three years each in the Philippines, for example—might also make them reluctant to invest in tax improvement programs that would yield fruit over the long term.

Property tax collection by local governments in the Philippines may be particularly problematic. As in most former Iberian colonies, landholding in

BOX 6.3 Local Revenue Administration in Action in East Asia

Evidence from Indonesia:

- Revenues are administered according to a multilevel model:
  - The central government administers national taxes.
  - Local tax agencies, generally known as DIPENDAs, play a minor role in administering the property tax.
  - Vehicle and vehicle transfer taxes are jointly administered by the provincial DIPENDA, the national police (as the coordinator), and a state-owned insurance firm.
- Own-source revenues are administered directly by DIPENDAs of the cities, regencies, and provinces, except for street lighting and fuel taxes. However, by issuing permits and licenses, local departments actually collect the user charges coordinated by the DIPENDAs.
- The administrative performance of the DIPENDAs varies widely.
- DIPENDAs have few cooperative agreements or information exchanges with other agencies within the same government, except for property tax field offices of the Directorate General of Taxation.
- DIPENDAs may use a certain percentage of total tax revenues to pay allowances to staff, though these bonuses are not usually based on performance.
- The quality of tax administration varies. Most DIPENDAs receive taxes directly in their offices, while others use partially government-owned regional development banks.
- One of the highest priorities of most DIPENDAs is developing the ability to professionally audit taxpayers, considered the weakest link in the system. The approach to taxpayer auditing varies by local government. DIPENDAs tried to introduce information technology in the early 1990s, but few local governments are still operating the computer systems because of lack of training.

Evidence from the Philippines:

- Principal constraints on taxpayer registration include:
  - A lack of regular maintenance and validation of the property tax and business registers.
  - A lack of automated registers.
  - Low-quality record keeping.
- Business tax registers are known to be incomplete, given frequent changes in registered establishments, which results in low levels of control and compliance.
- Problems undermining property tax collections include:
  - Collection efficiency for property taxes is low, resulting in the hemorrhaging of the most important source of local revenues. Local governments seem to be in a weak position to collect the taxes. Improving the efficiency of collection can raise these revenues significantly.
  - Property assessments have not kept up with changes in market values. Most local governments have not performed the General Revision of Assessment since 1991, resulting in significant undercollection of property taxes.
  - Noncompliance with the requirement for regular assessment requires urgent attention. The country could revise the code to allow the national government to do the assessments for local governments that do not comply.
- The compliance function seems inadequate. Major constraints include:
  - Infrequent exercise of local audit authority.
  - Infrequent exercise of local enforcement authority, in the form of temporary closures of firms and auctions of property.
- The difficulties of local governments in enforcing compliance suggest the need for presumptive taxation in some cases, especially for the business tax and some fees and charges.
- The principal constraint on taxpayer services is their limited availability. The lack of even the most basic taxpayer services and written materials means high compliance costs are likely to be the norm across the country.
- One main cause of underperformance is weak administrative capacity, owing partly to the low professional qualifications of staff. Inadequate coordination with the Bureau of Internal Revenue, and low levels of support from the Bureau of Local Government Finance, which might establish information-sharing protocols, are also factors.

that country has been concentrated. This legacy pits powerful landowners—some of whom have diversified their wealth into other assets—against weak local governments, some of which have been run by local elites for generations. Not surprisingly, the ability of local governments to enforce compliance with local revenue codes is weak in the face of elite resistance.

Conclusions and Implications

This review of experiences in Cambodia, China, Indonesia, the Philippines, Thailand, and Vietnam finds that local governments have limited authority and ability to raise their own revenues at the margin. As a result, own-source revenues are low as a share of total subnational resources, and in some cases have been declining as a share of total resources. Limited revenue-raising power and capacity raise questions about the supposed benefits of decentralization in improving accountability and allocative efficiency. Reliance on transfers in their myriad forms creates dependence on the national government and may weaken subnational incentives to improve own-source revenue. Four key messages merit emphasis.

First, local governments have limited control over tax policy, including the ability to set rates and define the tax base. Decentralization is thus more political than fiscal. Lack of control over taxation at the margin breaks the tax-accountability link, undermining the expenditure efficiency promised by decentralization. While the general limit on own-source revenues is not the only constraint, policy autonomy is essential for significant improvement to occur over the medium term.

Second, the lack of authority over tax policy seems to have spurred local governments to seek unofficial tax and nontax sources of revenue, with deleterious consequences. In a number of countries, local governments have the authority to enact new taxes and fees and thus engage in entrepreneurial behavior, yielding both positive and negative results. The resort to informal and illegal fees is even more unfortunate considering that subnational governments in the region are unable to avail themselves of many taxing options open to governments in other regions.

Third, despite the lack of opportunity to raise revenues and the apparent interest in "unofficial" avenues, subnational governments do not appear to have exhausted all their options. In some countries and for some taxes, local governments appear to prefer a lax collection strategy (property taxation in the Philippines, for example). Moreover, to the extent that the quality of local tax administration reflects both capacity and interest (according to the "revealed-preference" line of thought), then many subnational governments "prefer" weak administration.

Incentives thus play a role in determining collection levels of own-source revenues. This chapter suggests that two kinds of incentives play a role. The first is the systemwide incentive. For example, inherent in the intergovernmental fiscal transfer system are incentives that affect own-source collections. In Indonesia, the fact that the principal intergovernmental grant is based on the difference between fiscal needs and revenue capacity, rather than actual revenues, gives subnational governments incentives to raise collections to close the gap. The opposite is the case in Vietnam, which bases transfers on the difference between expenditure needs and forecasted revenues, which are based on previous collections. This formula could provide negative incentives, since higher collections result in lower transfer amounts (World Bank 2004b). Second, rational politicians might not prefer to increase own-source collections under certain circumstances.

Fourth, improvements in local tax administration would greatly strengthen subnational finance systems. Tax administrations vary throughout the region, ranging from highly decentralized in the Philippines to highly centralized in Vietnam, with Indonesia and China between these two poles. Yet the relative roles of local and national governments have not been well designed, resulting in both capacity and incentive challenges. Local governments tend to underperform on own-source collection and administration, reducing the credibility of the local tax system and contributing to a culture of noncompliance by raising compliance costs for taxpayers. Local administrative capacity is thus quite weak in many cases, and the binding constraint on improving revenue performance.

This chapter points out that the lack of development of significant own-source revenues in many countries is limiting the extent to which subnational governments can finance decentralized service delivery and make decisions about taxation and service levels. However, it must be noted that local governments in some East Asian countries receive relatively large shares of national income. Thus any efforts to boost own-source revenues would need to occur in the broader context of matching total resources—including transfers and shared revenues—to expenditure responsibilities.

Challenges remain for improving local tax policy and administration. The lack of autonomy undermines the ability of local governments to realize the benefits of decentralization by tapping significant revenue sources to satisfy local preferences regarding the level and quality of services. Fiscal sustainability requires improvements in own-source revenue collection and administration more generally. Weak administration undermines local tax systems by contributing to high rates of noncompliance, high compliance costs for taxpayers, and high administrative costs for local governments. Getting the relationship between the national and local governments right—in both policy and administrative terms—is pivotal.

Endnotes

1. For further discussion, see Bird 2003b; and Martínez-Vázquez 2003.
2. For further discussion, see Mikesell 2002. Many of these papers and others are available at www.decentralization.org.
3. Local Government Code, Sec. 191.
4. The percentage split for the Land and Building Tax (excluding mining and plantations) is: center (9 percent), which is intended to cover administrative costs of the deconcentrated revenue offices; provinces (16 percent); originating local government (65 percent); 6.5 percent equally across regions; and 3.5 percent to regions that exceed their previous year's revenue target. A Land and Building Transfer tax is also shared: provinces (16 percent), originating local government (64 percent), and the remainder to all local governments. The personal income tax is 80 percent central, 8 percent provincial, and 12 percent originating local government. See Law 25/1999, GR 115/2000, GR 104/2000.
5. Reference to Indonesia's "regions" generally means provinces and regencies and cities, while the term "local governments" refers to regencies and cities.
6. The *Salakhet* refers to the portion of the provincial budget that is under the control of the provincial governor, not the budgets of the deconcentrated line ministries at the provincial level. Nationally, the *Salakhet* represents about 20 percent of the total provincial budget allocation.
7. Only 7 cities charge the maximum 3 percent rate, and only 21 cities charge rates greater than or equal to 2.5 percent (outside the National Capital Region). No cities or provinces in the NCR charge the maximum allowed.
8. For example, countries could impose the business tax on gross receipts or rely on a subtraction method value-added tax. Note that this will require interjurisdictional apportionment of the tax base. However, the process need not be complex as in Pakistan, where small towns (*tehsils*) adopted levies on gross receipts in 2002 (and contracted out collections).
9. It is noteworthy that the region has no cases of piggyback taxation with local rate setting.
10. User charges are defined here, following Bird and Tsiopoulos (1997, 39), as "charges levied on consumers of government goods and services in relation to their consumption," when consumption is voluntary (such as public water charges). Fees are defined, in contrast, as cost recovery for a mandated public service (such as automobile licensing).
11. In fact, provincial councils will set the rate for Thailand's vehicle tax as of 2005.
12. However, the Local Government Code in the Philippines prohibits local excise taxes (Sec. 133 (h)) as well as levies on motor vehicle registration and driving (Sec. 133 (l)).
13. Ahmad et al. (2000), report that extrabudgetary funds represented nearly 40 percent of all local revenues in 1999.
14. R.A. 7160, Sec. 186.
15. For any taxes not listed in Law 34, local governments can decide on appropriate tax bases and rates, as the central government establishes only general principles.
16. The regional parliament must pass these regulations to authorize the introduction of a new tax or charge.
17. The World Bank calculated the buoyancy coefficient of local taxes at 1.6 for the 1994–1999 period (2002, 55).
18. However, a significant share of property tax revenues is earmarked for education spending. On average, over the period 1992–2000, the Special Education Fund, which is earmarked for education, accounted for 44 percent of total property tax collections, which is quite high considering that property taxes are the main source of subnational own-revenue. Earmarking is another form of reduced subnational autonomy.
19. This is based on annualized data for fiscal year 2000 (which lasted nine months). In general, observers agree that the quality of fiscal year 2000 data is questionable, since—besides being shorter—this year was the transition to decentralization. Thus, it would not be appropriate to place much emphasis on comparisons involving fiscal year 2000 data.
20. The only notable exception, in some ways, to this rule is that subnational treasurers are employees of the Department of Finance.
21. Still, the General Taxation Department is responsible for appointing, promoting, and transferring departmental staff. To what extent local officials have input into these processes is unknown.
22. See also Mikesell 2002 on intergovernmental tax administration compacts in the United States.

Bibliography

Ahmad, Ehtisham, Li Keping, and Thomas Richardson. 2000. "Recentralization in China." Paper for IMF Fiscal Decentralization Conference, Washington, DC.

Aoki, Naomi. 2003. Internal draft document on China and Vietnam. World Bank, Washington, DC.

Bacolod City, Philippines. 1995. Ordinance no. 154. Revenue Code.

Bahl, Roy. 1999. "Fiscal Policy in China: Taxation and Intergovernmental Fiscal Relations." San Francisco, CA: The 1990 Institute.

Bird, Richard M. 2003a. "A New Look at Local Business Taxes." *Tax Notes International* (May): 695–711.

———. 2003b. "Local and Regional Revenues: Realities and Prospects." Internal draft document. World Bank, Washington, DC.

Bird, Richard M., Robert D. Ebel, and Christine I. Wallich. 1995. *Decentralization of the Socialist State: Intergovernmental Finance in Transition Economies*. Washington, DC: World Bank.

Bird, Richard M., and Enid Slack. 2002. "Land and Property Taxation: A Review." Internal draft document. World Bank, Washington, DC.

Bird, Richard M., and Thomas Tsiopoulos. 1997. "User Charges for Public Services: Potentials and Problems." *Canadian Tax Journal* 45 (1): 25–86.

Byrne, Peter. 1995. "Overview of Privatization in the Area of Tax and Customs Administration." *Bulletin for International Fiscal Documentation* 49: 1.

Cabanatuan City, Philippines. 1992. Ordinance no. 165-92. Revised Revenue Code.

Chakeri, Jasmin. 2003. "Regional Tax Policy and Administration in Indonesia." Internal draft document. World Bank, Washington, DC.

Commission on Audit. 2001. *Annual Audit Report on Local Government Units*. Quezon City: Republic of the Philippines.

———. 2002. *Annual Audit Report on Local Government Units*. Quezon City: Republic of the Philippines.

Devas, Nick, and Roy Kelly. 2001. "Regulation or Revenues? An Analysis of Local Business Licenses, with a Case Study of the Single Business Permit Reform in Kenya." *Public Administration and Development* 21: 381–391.

Ebel, Robert, and Serdar Yilmaz. 2002. "On the Measurement and Impact of Fiscal Decentralization, Part 2." In *Public Finance in Developing and Traditional Countries: Essays in Honor of Richard Bird*, eds. Jorge Martínez-Vázquez and James Alm. London: Edwin Elgar Press.

Endriga, Victor B., Treasurer, Quezon City, Philippines. 2003. Interview.

———. 2001. "Manila, Makati, Pasig, and Quezón City: Local Government Taxation." Manila: Quezon City.

———. 2003. "The Financial Recovery of Quezon City." Manila: Quezon City.

Guevara, Milwida. 2003. "Feeling the Pulse of the Public." Internal draft document. World Bank, Washington, DC.

———. 2003. "Taming the Deficit." Internal draft document. World Bank, Washington, DC.

La Union Province, Philippines. 1996. Provincial Tax Ordinance no. 001-96,

Lewis, Blane. 2003. "Tax and Charge Creation by Regional Governments under Fiscal Decentralization: Estimates and Explanations." *Bulletin of Indonesian Economic Studies* 39 (2): 177–192.

Makati Municipality, Philippines. 1993. Municipal Ordinance no. 92-072. Makati Revenue Code.

Martínez-Vázquez, Jorge. 2003. "Improving the Design of Fiscal Decentralization in Vietnam." Internal draft document. World Bank, Washington, DC.

McCluskey, William, and Brendan Williams. 1999. "Introduction: A Comparative Evaluation." In *Property Tax: An International Comparative Review*, ed. William McCluskey. Brookfield, VT: Ashgate Publishing.

McLure, Charles E., and Jorge Martínez-Vázquez. 2002. "The Assignment of Revenues and Expenditures in Intergovernmental Fiscal Relations." Internal draft document. World Bank, Washington, DC.

Mikesell, John L. 2002. "International Experience with Administration of Local Taxes: A Review of Practices and Issues." Internal draft document. World Bank, Washington, DC.

Musgrave, Richard. 1959. *The Theory of Public Finance: A Study of Public Economy*. New York: McGraw-Hill.

Norregaard, John. 1997. "Tax Assignment." In *Fiscal Federalism in Theory and Practice*, ed. Teresa Ter-Minassian. Washington, DC: International Monetary Fund.

OECD (Organisation of Economic Co-operation and Development). 2002. "Fiscal Design Surveys across Levels of Government." Tax Policy Studies no. 7. Paris: OECD.

Ortega, Mary Jane, Mayor, San Fernando City, Philippines. 2003. Interview.

Ortega, Victor, Governor, La Union Province, Philippines. 2003. Interview.

Philippines Center for Investigative Journalism. 2001. *Investigating Local Governments*. Manila: Philippines Center for Investigative Journalism.

Ray, D. 2003. Summary paper for conference on Decentralization, Regulatory Reform, and the Business Climate, Partnership for Economic Growth and U.S. Agency for International Development, Jakarta.

Republic of the Philippines. *Local Government Code, 1991*. Republic Act 7160. Manila.

San Fernando City, Philippines. 1998. Tax Ordinance no. 98-001.

San Fernando Municipality, Philippines. 1993. Tax Ordinance no. 92-002. Revenue Code.

Sugana, Rubi. 2003. "Local Own-Source Revenue Administration in Indonesia." Internal draft document. World Bank, Washington, DC.

Tabunda, Manuel S., and Mario M. Galang. 1992. *A Guide to the Local Government Code of 1991*. Manila: Mary Jo Publishing House.

Taliercio, Robert R. 2003. Internal draft document on the Philippines. World Bank, Washington, DC.

United Nations Capital Development Fund (UNCDF). 2003. "Supporting Cambodia Fiscal Decentralization Priorities: 2004 and Beyond." Phnom Penh.

———. 2004. "Draft Material for UNCDF Project Document for Support to the Cambodian Ministry of Economy and Finance on Fiscal Decentralization." Phnom Penh.

USAID (U.S. Agency for International Development). n.d. "Geographic Information Systems Applications in Local Governance: Selected GIS Outputs Produced by Philippine Local Government Units, 1999–2000." Washington, DC: USAID.

Vehorn, Charles L., and Ehtisham Ahmad. 1997. "Tax Administration." In *Fiscal Federalism in Theory and Practice*, ed. Teresa Ter-Minassian. Washington, DC: International Monetary Fund.

Vergara, Jay, Mayor, Cabanatuan City, Philippines. 2003. Interview.

World Bank. 2000. "Vietnam: Managing Public Resources Better." Joint report of the Donor Working Group on Public Expenditure Review. Hanoi: World Bank.

———. 2002. "China: National Development and Subnational Finance—A Review of Provincial Expenditures." Washington, DC: World Bank.

———. 2003a. "Decentralizing Indonesia: A Regional Public Expenditure Review—Overview Report." Washington, DC: World Bank.

———. 2003b. "Enhancing Service Delivery through Improved Resource Allocation and Institutional Reform." Washington, DC: World Bank.

———. 2004a. "Decentralization in East Asia: Country Review—The People's Republic of China." Background paper. Washington, DC: World Bank.

———. 2004b. "Decentralization in East Asia: Country Review—Vietnam." Washington, DC: World Bank.

———. 2004c. "Fiscal Decentralization in Thailand." Internal draft document. World Bank, Washington, DC.

7

MANAGING HUMAN RESOURCES IN A DECENTRALIZED CONTEXT

Amanda E. Green

A central rationale for decentralization is that, by moving government closer to the people, it brings public sector activities and decisions in line with popular preferences. Yet, in practice, the civil service—a critical component of government—rarely enters the decision calculus of decentralization design. The civil service is often recognized as an afterthought rather than seen as essential to successful decentralization. This is lamentable but not surprising, as decentralization is quintessentially a political process. In East Asia, whether it was the desire to quell the forces of regional disintegration in the Philippines and Indonesia, the urgent need to meet the demands of economic transition in China and Vietnam, or pressure to improve service delivery and citizen participation in Cambodia and Thailand, the primary motivation for decentralization has been political—notwithstanding varied proximate causes.

The common failure to address the details of civil service management as an integral part of the decentralization package has significant implications. Civil servants form a crucial link between the delivery of financial resources to the government and the delivery of essential public services to the people (World Bank 2003a). The relationship between decentralization and civil service management is a two-way process. The behavior of civil servants has important consequences for government performance in a decentralized setting. Conversely, decentralization alters both the incentives of and the demands on the civil service. Managing this behavior is critical to realizing the benefits of decentralization.

Accordingly, this chapter argues that civil service management—or more broadly human resource management—should be seen as an essential component in the design of decentralization rather than a separate, stand-alone process. The discussion marshals evidence from across East Asia and around the world. The following section presents a framework for exploring the interaction between administrative decentralization and civil service management—in terms of both the theoretical goals of decentralization and their realization in practice. The third section delves into the realities of administrative decentralization in East Asia through the experiences of six countries: Cambodia, China, Indonesia, the Philippines, Thailand, and Vietnam. The varied approaches and responses of these countries offer insights into the process of managing civil servants in a decentralized setting. The final section examines the central dilemmas that arise in designing administrative decentralization and draws lessons on how countries in East Asia and beyond can maximize the benefits and minimize the risks of decentralization.

The Interplay between Decentralization and Human Resource Management

Decentralization is a spectrum rather than a single state, ranging from deconcentration to delegation to devolution (see box 1.1). As table 7.1 shows, key features of the civil service vary with the degree of administrative decentralization. Overall, East Asian countries fall into the intermediate category, with local managers enjoying some freedom to recruit and allocate staff subject to central guidelines on pay levels and total employment. Indonesia and the Philippines took the biggest leaps along the decentralization continuum in both law and practice, but central governments retained considerable control over civil service wages at the local level. In Indonesia, recent revisions to the Law on Regional Administration have rolled back decentralization in hiring decisions. In the Philippines, the momentum behind implementing decentralization policy has slowed considerably. China and Vietnam have taken a more opportunistic approach, experimenting with different degrees of local autonomy. However, the central government and Communist Party continue to influence how decentralization plays out. In Thailand, a legal framework defines an intermediate form of administrative decentralization, but most of this framework has yet to materialize in practice. Finally, Cambodia can best be described as a deconcentrated system, with a high proportion of staff based in the field but working on behalf of the central government.

Movement along the spectrum of administrative decentralization depends partly on interplay with the political and fiscal aspects of decentralization. For example, a local government that has full authority over the size of its civil service can nonetheless face restrictions in the use of funds transferred from the center. Similarly, the strength of a country's accountability framework is influenced by whether political decentralization has created institutions for locally elected politicians to oversee the activities of local governments. The case studies illustrate the results of a mismatch in the dimensions of decentralization.

TABLE 7.1 Key Features of Administrative Decentralization

Administrative Decentralization →

Deconcentration (minimal change)	Delegation (intermediate change)	Devolution (substantial change)
• Provider staff working at local level are employees of and accountable to the center, usually through their respective ministries; central employees compensate for weak local capacity. • Accountability remains distant: the *short route* of accountability may be weak if provider monitoring is weak, and citizens may have to rely on a weak *long route* stretching to politicians at the center; a strong *compact* between policymakers and providers can compensate to some extent.	• Providers could be employees of central or local government, but the center typically defines pay and employment. • Local government has some authority over hiring and location of staff, but is less likely to have authority over firing. • Both *long* and *short routes* of accountability are potentially stronger; greater local knowledge can allow better matching of supply with local preferences and better monitoring, strengthening both the *compact* and *client power.*	• Providers are employees of local government. • Local government has full discretion over salary levels, allocation, and numbers of staff, as well as the authority to hire and fire. • An overarching civil service framework covering local governments may still establish standards and procedures for hiring and managing staff. • Potentially strongest *long* and *short routes* to accountability, but influenced by local social norms and vulnerable to local capacity constraints and politics.

Source: Adapted from World Bank 2003h, 189.

What Makes a Decentralized Civil Service Work?[1]

To better understand the opportunities and obstacles that a country may encounter on the road to administrative decentralization, it is first useful to consider the destination. A functioning system of decentralized civil service management—as distinct from a centrally directed model—has several key characteristics:

- Local government *functions are clearly defined* so staff know what is expected of them and managers can adapt the local civil service to reflect what needs to be done, without inefficient gaps or overlap with other levels of government.
- Local government can *allocate staff across functions as needed.* This requires that civil service managers have autonomy—or at least influence—in operating the local establishment as well as deploying staff across different departments and facilities.
- Local government is able to *attract and retain qualified individuals*, and to build a team with a diverse set of skills. This requires that local government have something to offer, through competitive pay, career opportunities, prestige, or other incentives.
- Local government has *flexibility in managing financial resources.* Managing civil servants requires managing their cost, either directly through pay levels or indirectly through staff numbers.
- Local government can *hold staff accountable for their performance.* This requires the capacity to supervise and monitor civil servants, the ability to reward good performance through pay increases, promotions, and other benefits, and the authority to punish deficient performance through disciplinary measures or dismissals.

Countries may not meet some or all of these criteria for numerous reasons. In some cases, the failure is one of design. For example, as mentioned, comparatively limited independence among local governments on fiscal and political matters may constrain their administrative autonomy.

In other cases, it is by design that the criteria are not met. First, keeping local civil services under the umbrella of central direction can ensure some standardization in working conditions across the country. Otherwise, local governments in poorer areas will find it difficult to compete against richer areas, and national coverage of public services may suffer. Second, central government involvement in staffing may expand civil servants' career paths by opening channels between local and central employment. Third, the center may wish to retain control over hiring and pay to shield subnational governments from local pressure to overspend on wages and salaries. Fourth, centralized rules can be important in sectors that need to enforce minimum professional qualifications, such as with teachers, doctors, and nurses. Fifth, where ethnic or other tensions threaten stability, the central government may use the civil service as a tool for national integration. Finally, the central government's reluctance to decentralize may stem simply from a desire to retain control.

The Implications of Decentralization

How a country resolves the tension between the motivations for decentralizing the civil service on the one hand, and the reasons for caution on the other, will shape the design of decentralization and, ultimately, how the process plays out. The implications of decentralizing civil service management can be examined along four critical dimensions: capacity, incentives, autonomy, and accountability. Each factor plays a significant role in the success of decentralization and is, in turn, heavily influenced by the decentralization process.

These four dimensions are closely linked and entail important tradeoffs. For example, civil service training programs are not likely to strengthen capacity in a sustainable way unless incentives motivate civil servants to use what they learn. Similarly, improvements in accountability at the local level require that civil servants have the capacity—through accounts and records—to render that accountability effectively. Finally, holding local civil service managers accountable for their decisions is difficult when they do not have autonomy in making those decisions.

Capacity. For civil servants to deliver the higher-quality local services envisioned under decentralization, they need to have the capacity to do so. This involves both individual and institutional elements. First, the success of decentralization depends on the ability of individual civil servants to take on new tasks, at both central and local levels. Second, smaller size and budgets can constrain the institutional capacity of local governments. The process of decentralization itself can have important implications for capacity needs at the local level. The devolution of public service responsibilities requires both a broader variety of skills and a greater depth of knowledge in specific areas, such as financial management and performance monitoring. Moreover, local leaders need to learn to supervise staff, mobilize more own-source revenues, interact with local constituents and elected officials, and develop local institutions. Formerly central civil servants who move to local levels can transfer some of these skills; local governments need to gain the rest through experience. At the same time, central employees need to shift from "doing" to facilitating and supervising.

Incentives. In some cases, what appears to be a lack of capacity to carry out the functions of decentralized government is instead a lack of motivation to act in the public interest. The structure and management of the civil service influence the outcome of decentralization reforms by affecting how local civil servants behave. The level of pay and benefits, options for career mobility, and degree to which merit is recognized or unsatisfactory performance penalized can determine the dedication with which a civil servant works, as well as the type of individuals who choose to become civil servants. Decentralizing functional and management responsibilities to the local level, in turn, modifies the incentive structures of local civil servants. The proximity of local government to the recipients of public services can tighten the link between efforts and results. However, some local civil services are too small to offer significant opportunities for career advancement, and poorer local governments may be unable to pay salaries high enough to attract talent. In remote areas, a combination of low pay and difficult conditions creates a vicious circle whereby an inability to attract high-quality staff leads to further deterioration in conditions.

Autonomy. The argument that decentralization boosts the responsiveness of civil servants assumes that local managers have the authority to respond to the demands of their constituents. Local autonomy in allocating human resources can improve efficiency by allowing managers to hire staff whose skills align with planned activities, to discipline or dismiss ineffective staff, and to trim numbers to keep costs down. Though less common at the local level, direct financial autonomy—such as the ability to set pay levels and charge user fees—can improve staff performance and thereby enhance the benefits of decentralization. However, to achieve these benefits, performance incentives and accountability frameworks must be robust enough to prevent inefficiency and mismanagement. By definition, administrative decentralization would seem to augment local autonomy, but this is not always the case. The center often retains a significant degree of control, particularly in financially sensitive areas such as the size and wage levels of the civil service, especially when local capacity and accountability are in question. Table 7.2 provides a stylized but useful comparison of East Asian countries in these areas.

Accountability. The potential for improving service delivery through decentralization depends, among other factors, on accountability relationships—the degree to which civil servants are held to account for their performance and integrity, and to whom they are accountable. Without a strong system of local accountability, devolving authority and financial resources to local governments can lead to waste or misuse of public funds, and the potential for political capture at the local level can distort the benefits of decentralization. On the other hand, where corruption is systemic at the central level, devolution may enhance service delivery. Where political decentralization allows for oversight by locally elected bodies, the need for reelection offers strong incentives for better performance. If civil society monitoring mechanisms are strong, the downward accountability of local staff will tend to encourage a closer connection between public services and citizen demands. If accountability is only to the center, however, decentralization may not deliver the potential benefits of bringing government closer to the people.

Decentralization can, in turn, affect local accountability. In shifting responsibility for monitoring civil servants to local managers, decentralization can make it more difficult for civil servants to get away with laziness and corruption. The closer proximity of local citizens to government decision makers can enhance their ability to hold those decision makers accountable. However, if critical checks and balances to protect the neutrality and independence of civil servants are not in

TABLE 7.2 Central Authority over the Subnational Civil Service

	Cambodia	China	Indonesia	Philippines	Thailand	Vietnam
Legislation and regulations:						
Designation	1	2	1	2–3	2	1
Recruitment	1	4	2	3	2	2–3
Structure and career management:						
Establishment control	1	3	2	2–3	2	1
Appointment and mobility	2	3	3	4	2	3
Employment framework	1	1	1	3	1	1
Performance management:						
Standard setting and rewards	2	2	2	3	2	2
Training and development	2	3	3	4	3	3
Accountability	2	4	3	4	2	2

Sources: World Bank 2003d, 16; staff estimates.
Note: 1= total central authority; 2 = central dominance; 3 = central guidance; 4 = central leadership; 5 = autonomous.

place, decentralization can lead to nepotism, with local managers rewarding family members and supporters with coveted positions, and can facilitate political capture by bringing civil servants within reach of local power bases.

Taken together, the capacity, incentives, autonomy, and accountability of civil service management provide both a lens through which to evaluate the design of decentralization and a picture of how administrative decentralization has played out in practice. The following section shows how these four dimensions have influenced decentralization in East Asian countries, and how policy makers can leverage those dimensions to get the most out of decentralization.

Civil Service Management on the Ground in East Asia

The structure of government and, by extension, the civil service varies greatly across East Asia. Some countries have focused decentralization efforts on the lowest levels of government, while others have emphasized deconcentration to an intermediate level, such as provinces. Countries also differ in whom they consider civil servants. Some countries treat teachers, health workers, and police as part of the civil service, while others consider them separate categories. The distinction between ministry staff on the one hand, and employees of public service agencies and state-owned enterprises on the other, may also blur the definition of a civil servant. Finally, the determination of which civil servants are subnational employees can reflect either their physical location or the level of government that pays them.

Even in the absence of agreed standards and definitions, broadly characterizing civil service decentralization in the region is worthwhile. Figure 7.1 shows the wide variation in civil service structures across the region. The share of employees at the subnational level ranges from around 19 percent in Thailand to just over 90 percent in China. The share of personnel expenditures in total subnational spending also reflects the extent of administrative decentralization. As figure 7.2 shows, average subnational spending on personnel ranges from roughly 41 percent of total spending in Thailand to around 60 percent in China. It is important to note, however, that these figures do not necessarily point to China as the region's most

FIGURE 7.1 Subnational Employees as a Share of Total Government Employment

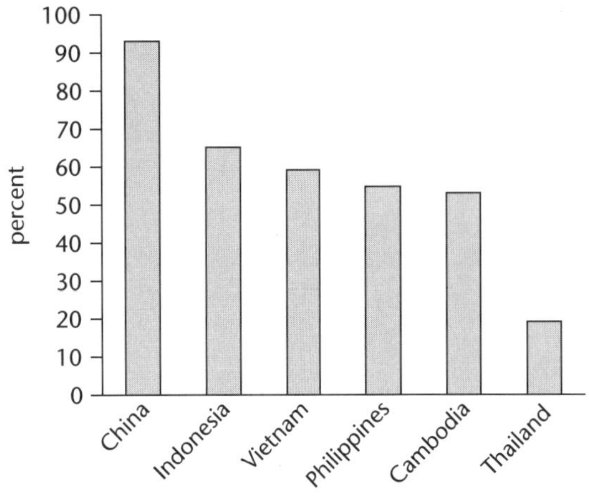

Sources: Cambodia—World Bank 2003a (includes political appointees and nonpermanent staff); China—World Bank 2002a, annex 2 (includes Public Service Units outside health and education); Indonesia—World Bank 2003d; Philippines—World Bank 2003f; Thailand—Kingdom of Thailand, Office of the Civil Service Commission; Vietnam—Government of Vietnam, General Statistical Office, 2003.
Note: Data are for the most recent available year, ranging from 2000–3, and exclude staff in the education, health, military, and police sectors, unless otherwise noted.

FIGURE 7.2 Personnel Spending as a Share of Total Subnational Government Expenditures

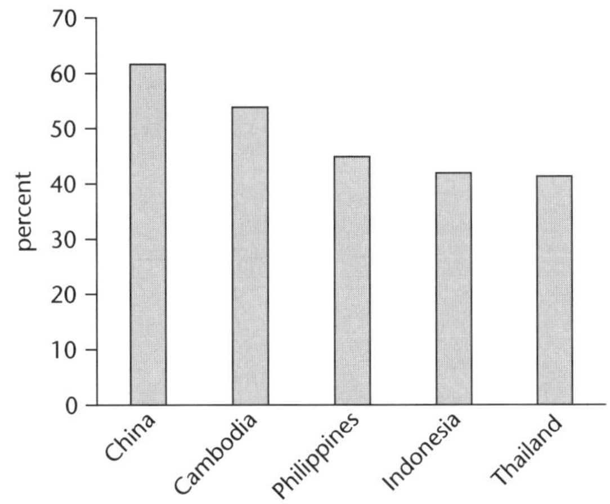

Sources: Cambodia—World Bank 2003a; China—World Bank 2003b; Indonesia—World Bank 2003d; Philippines—World Bank 2003f; Thailand—Weist 2003.
Note: Data are for the most recent available year, ranging from 2000–3.

decentralized country. The degree of authority exercised by subnational civil service managers in determining the amount, structure, and allocation of resources plays an important role. Though different countries have focused their decentralization policies on different levels of government, table 7.3 provides a general picture of how civil service management practices have taken shape in East Asia.

The remainder of this section outlines the experiences of East Asian countries in dealing with the human resource implications of decentralization. In Indonesia and the Philippines, extensive decentralization of the administrative apparatus has brought to light both the opportunities and the risks of devolving authority to local managers. In China and Vietnam, where decentralization has proceeded in stages, the roles of state and party offer additional insights into the relationship between decentralization and civil service management. Finally, in Cambodia and Thailand, the focus on building capacity before rather than through decentralization has meant limited implementation of decentralization policies, and this experience offers an opportunity to consider how best to balance caution and progress. Together these six case studies explore the realities of human resource management in a decentralized setting. In addressing both pitfalls and innovative responses, the cases attempt to glean important lessons about the interplay between capacity, incentives, autonomy, and accountability in decentralized civil service management.

The Big Bang and Beyond: The Philippines and Indonesia

In both the Philippines and Indonesia, decentralization was an integral part of a political opening following the overthrow of an authoritarian regime. In these sprawling archipelagos, rising social tensions added a note of urgency to the decision to decentralize, and local autonomy came to be seen as the key to quelling threats to national unity. Neither government felt it had the luxury of perfecting the design of intergovernmental fiscal and administrative arrangements before decentralizing. Following the logic that a chasm cannot be crossed in two leaps has worked well in many ways.[2] Neither country experienced major service disruptions during the transition, and the relatively open-ended design of decentralization has encouraged innovative local responses to new responsibilities. However, once the dust settled, momentum slowed, and important challenges remain in correcting some of the imperfections

TABLE 7.3 Staffing Authority among Subnational Governments

Enabling mechanisms	Cambodia	China	Indonesia	Philippines	Thailand	Vietnam
Budget control						
• Determine the wage envelope	○	○	○	◑	○	◑
• Dismiss surplus staff	○	◑	◑	●	○	○
Establishment control						
• Control overall staffing numbers	○	◑	○	◑	○	◑
• Control staffing numbers in individual offices and facilities	○	◑	◑	●	○	◑
Recruitment						
• Formal employer	●	●	○	●	◑	●
• Have authority to hire	◑	●	◑	●	○	●
• Have independent merit-based recruitment mechanism (local civil service commission)	○	◑	◑	○	○	○
Career management						
• Promotion is available	○	●	◑	●	○	○
• Transfers within local government are possible	○	●	●	●	○	◑
• Horizontal mobility within local civil service cadre	○	○	○	○	○	○
Performance management						
• Direct and supervise activities and tasks	●	●	◑	●	●	●
• Conduct evaluations	○	●	◑	●	○	○
• Offer financial rewards	○	○	◑	◑	○	○
• Discipline and fire underperforming staff	○	○	◑	◑	○	◑
Pay policy						
• Set overall wage rates	○	○	○	○	○	○
• Set local incentives/ salary top-ups	◑	●	◑	●	○	◑

Source: Author's estimates.
Note: ● = yes; ◑ = partial; ○ = no. Data are for most recent available year, ranging from 2000 to 2003. Ratings refer to the subnational level prioritized by the country's decentralization policy and to de facto practices as well as de jure authority.

brought to light by the decentralization process. As East Asia's two most rapid decentralizers, the Philippines and Indonesia provide a useful starting point for addressing administrative decentralization in the region.

Central Rules and Local Responses in the Philippines. The 1991 Local Government Code (LGC) provided the major impetus for "genuine and meaningful local autonomy" in the Philippines, devolving substantial government functions, and attendant financial and human resources, from the national to the local level.[3] Over 70,000 staff were transferred to local governments.

In each tier of government, the local chief executive—governor, mayor, or *barangay* captain—can hire, fire, and promote staff, subject to guidelines from the central Civil Service Commission (CSC).[4] Civil servants are bound to a code of conduct and required to declare their net worth and financial and business interests. Government employees are also supposed to disclose a list of close relatives in the public service, but this does not in practice seem to limit family connections in the civil service. Indeed, despite the constitutional requirement that "appointments in the civil service shall be made according to merit and fitness," several mechanisms cause merit and fitness to lose out to patronage and nepotism at the local level.[5] For example, although candidates on the shortlists for civil service appointments generally meet the minimum qualifications set out by the CSC, the local chief executive is not bound to choose the top-ranked applicant.

Moreover, recruitment for confidential, highly technical, and noncareer staff positions is exempt from the prescribed appointment process. Perhaps because these workers are relatively easy to hire, noncareer employees composed over one-third (38.6 percent) of total local government staff in 2001—significantly more than in national government agencies (4.67 percent) (World Bank 2003e). Furthermore, local governments can retain emergency and casual staff for up to six months without CSC approval. Local officials often use this provision to circumvent central controls and delays and avoid contributing to the national employee benefit scheme. Repeated extensions of temporary contracts lead to de facto permanent employment, and not all local governments advertise nonpermanent positions. This lack of transparency undermines merit-based hiring, as temporary positions are often handed out as patronage for loyal supporters.

Central regulations on local establishment size and expenditure allocations constrain the chief executive's flexibility in appointing staff. A uniform system of job classification imposes rigidities on small local civil services. The central government limits local personal services expenditures to 45 to 55 percent of the previous year's income, depending on the income class of the local government.[6] The center also determines salary scales and benefit entitlements. Base wages tend to be low, but are supplemented by a complex system of both monetary and in-kind allowances and benefits. From 1992 to 2001, aggregate local spending on personal services averaged 56.8 percent of the previous year's total regular income, exceeding the nationally mandated cap on the wage bill. In municipalities, the average was 64.4 percent (World Bank 2003f).[7]

The 1989 Compensation and Position Classification Act set salaries in all but first-class local governments lower than those at the center.[8] However, because the salaries of national staff transferred to local governments remained the same, this created a wage gap between local and devolved staff. In fact, some civil servants who transferred to lower-income municipalities earned more than the mayor. This influx of better-paid staff imposed a budget crunch on local governments. The 1993 Salary Standardization Law, which called for unifying pay regimes across all levels of government, exacerbated this problem by raising salaries at lower levels. The law has also affected the incentives of civil servants by compressing salaries and thus lowering the increases that employees can expect as they move up the ranks. The compact organizational structure of local governments also restricts the career mobility of civil servants.

Local governments have responded in different ways to these central directives. Some cash-strapped governments are forced to simply ignore the mandated salary scales and pay their employees less. Some local chief executives have elected not to fill mandatory positions to leave room for other staff or salary supplements. Others have attempted to lay off workers, though this is rare owing to the political sensitivity of retrenchments. Local governments with greater access to own-source revenues supplement staff incomes even for positions covered by the national government, such as police. Local governments have also responded to rising personnel costs by charging some expenditures, such as payments for contract workers, to other budget lines. This crowds out nonpersonnel expenditures while masking the true extent of staff costs. As the central government does not have the capacity to enforce its regulations, local governments have much more flexibility than the legal framework implies.

Balancing National Unity and Local Autonomy in Indonesia. Indonesia's Big Bang decentralization—ambitious and swift as it was—risked disrupting public services, inciting local unrest, and leaving civil servants unpaid. In actuality, the transition went quite smoothly. Delivery of services continued for the most part unscathed, and expected upheavals among reassigned civil servants failed to materialize. Over 2.1 million staff—nearly 60 percent of central employees—were transferred to provincial and (primarily) district civil services with relatively little difficulty, although few people had to physically move because the previous system had been highly deconcentrated. The central government greatly aided the process by continuing to pay devolved civil servants from national coffers for five months.

In the wake of the Big Bang, several legal discrepancies came to light. Considerable confusion ensued in applying various laws and regulations, leading to overlapping authority and eroding efficiency. According to the original administrative framework (Law 22 of 1999 on Regional Administration), the head of region had the right to hire, fire, promote, transfer, and discipline staff. The Civil Service Law, however, maintained that authority for civil service appointments rested first and foremost with the central government, which could delegate that authority to heads of region. Government Regulation 97 of 2000 allowed the head of the regional administration to determine the size of the regional establishment. However, central regulations requiring nationwide advertising for some posts—although perhaps intended to spark interregional mobility—limited the flexibility of regional managers.

Recent changes to the framework laws have moderated the initial thrust toward devolution and introduced even more uncertainty about the roles of different levels of government in managing the civil service. The revised Law on Regional Administration (Law 32 of 2004) has rolled back local authority to manage human resources, stipulating that the central government will supervise regional civil servants within a national framework, and that regional heads can hire, fire, and relocate only lower-level staff at the same level of government.[9] Regional managers no longer have explicit authority to manage their civil services.

The central government also determines pay levels and increases regardless of their affordability at the local level, limiting the autonomy of regional managers.[10] Local governments must further pay the pensions of civil servants transferred from the center, which can create an unsustainable burden, particularly as the cost of pensions rises along with salaries. In 2001, the *dana alokasi umum* (DAU)—or general allocation grant—was supplemented by a "contingency fund" to cover the 14–30 percent pay increase mandated by the center. Though the central government introduced this transitional mechanism with good intentions, it created incentives for overstaffing at the local level, as regional governments began to assume that excess personnel costs would continue to be covered by supplementary funding.

The structure of the DAU itself discourages prudent local management. Currently, the DAU is divided into three parts: a "lump sum" distributed in equal amounts to every region, a "formula" amount determined by the extent to which a region's financial need outstrips its fiscal capacity, and a "balancing factor" based largely on the region's wage bill as a share of total subnational wage expenditures in the previous year. The balancing factor deters local managers from cutting costs because lowering the wage bill lowers next year's DAU allocation. This disincentive will become stronger with the implementation of the revised Law on Fiscal Balance (Law 33 of 2004). The equalizing lump sum component will be eliminated in 2006, and the "hold harmless" clause that keeps regional DAU allocations from decreasing over time applies only until 2008. Moreover, in the interest of national unity, the central government has resolved to fully fund regional salaries through the DAU, which will create strong incentives for subnational managers to increase staffing.

Until recently, a zero-growth policy prevented formal recruitment to the Indonesian civil service. New staff appointments in November 2004 were the first of their kind since decentralization was implemented. At the same time, Government Regulation 8 of 2003 on Local Government Structure and Organization defines the maximum number of staff in the regions, though it is not clear how strictly this regulation is enforced. Both the central and regional governments have taken to hiring contract workers to circumvent these formal restrictions. At the local level, this strategy has allowed managers to hire and fire temporary staff and consultants as desired, without interference from the center. Contract workers, who now account for about 10 percent of government employees, are also attractive because their employment is not subject to qualification standards or pension obligations.

In theory, the government must base hiring and promotion decisions on merit, but anecdotal evidence reveals that this needs strengthening in practice, especially in promoting staff. The head of region has the right to discipline and dismiss lower-level staff who are underperforming, subject to due process and approval from the provincial governor. Dismissals are rare in practice, however, and staff reassignment seems to be the preferred penalty.

The civil service agency, BKN, has begun to define job classifications and qualifications for the civil service as a whole, including regional governments. The Indonesian government has also been developing minimum standards for service delivery, including broad directives on supervising minimum wage levels as well as highly specific technical guidelines. Heads of region have generally been enthusiastic about this initiative, both because they prefer to be held accountable against established criteria rather than arbitrary standards set by local parliaments, and because they expect to receive more funding in exchange for taking on greater responsibilities (World Bank 2003d). In principle, minimum service standards can improve civil service management by offering some basis for unity among public servants, ensuring a minimum level of performance across the country, and enhancing local accountability through improved understanding of what is expected of local civil servants. In Indonesia, however, most line ministries are issuing standards without giving enough thought to their feasibility and affordability at the local level. To be effective, minimum standards must be designed carefully, so they are specific enough to provide clear direction on what is expected of the local civil service but not so detailed as to hamstring regional leaders.

The design of decentralization in Indonesia constricts the interregional mobility of civil servants, and therefore their career paths. No streamlined system exists for relocating subnational civil servants to other areas. Discriminatory hiring practices at the regional level seem to further limit mobility. Despite regulations designed to prevent this, some heads of region are reportedly engaging in preferential treatment of "sons of the soil," or discriminating based on ethnicity, religion, or other special interests. Many regions have resisted taking on staff transferred from the center, owing largely to ethnic tensions (central civil servants are primarily Javanese) and the association of staff in Jakarta with the authoritarian rule of Soeharto (World Bank n.d.). Curbing this tendency before it becomes deeply entrenched will be important, as interregional mobility of civil servants can help ensure national unity and acceptable levels of service delivery in more remote regions. Possible measures to address this issue include joint training across regions and a secondment system, in which fixed-term placements in local areas improve the career prospects of central civil servants.

Ironing Out the Wrinkles. Both the Philippines and Indonesia considered decentralization necessary to keep the nation together and regain the trust of disaffected local governments. There was a strong sense that decentralization plans could not await the relatively long process of institutional development and capacity building, and thus that human and institutional capabilities should be expanded during the decentralization process. This approach succeeded in focusing the policy agenda on the actual transfer of functions and management authority to the local level, but left in its wake some unfinished business that has slowed the momentum behind decentralization. In Indonesia, concern over the loose ends has prompted the central government to roll back devolved authority.

Capacity. Decentralization policies in the Philippines and Indonesia have focused on the lowest tier of local government, but implementation of devolved functions is running up against the limited capacity of staff in these administrations, particularly in planning, budgeting, and financial management. In response, the Indonesian government has adopted a National Framework for Capacity Building, but will now have to work to finance and implement this plan. It is also unclear whether the top-down application of this framework will adequately address the capacity-building needs of local governments. In the Philippines, the continuing mismatch between required and available skills at the local level points to a need for better coordination in training local civil servants. Most activities are now provided in isolation, either by individual central agencies or by local governments themselves.

Incentives. The decentralization process has also affected incentive structures at the local level. Both the Philippines and Indonesia have encountered difficulties in designing intergovernmental financing mechanisms. The Internal Revenue Allotment in the Philippines has not followed the assignment of functions as closely as it should have, flooding some localities with excess resources while saddling others with unfunded mandates. The former situation skews incentives toward overspending and overstaffing, while the latter discourages long-term planning and spending on maintenance. In Indonesia, the central government's historical use of the DAU to cover local salary shortfalls and, now, to fully fund subnational wages creates a perverse incentive for overstaffing regional governments. In both countries, performance incentives for civil servants are dampened by compressed salary structures, ineffective monitoring of performance, and weak links between performance and pay. These effects have been compounded by a lack of mobility within the civil service—vertically in the case of the Philippines, and horizontally in Indonesia.

Autonomy. In its initial thrust, decentralization in the Philippines and Indonesia significantly boosted the autonomy of local managers. Indonesia, however, has recently repealed local staffing authority. In both countries the central government has retained control in defining pay levels for local civil servants. Subnational governments are subject to national wage scales that impose significant fiscal burdens, especially in poorer localities. Centrally imposed salary increases have further strained local budgets. In Indonesia, the DAU covered these, but in the Philippines, the Salary Standardization Law is not yet fully implemented because many local governments find it simply unaffordable. Another unfunded mandate that impinges on the autonomy of local civil service managers in the Philippines is the 1993 Magna Carta of Public Health Workers Act. The central government extended this generous package of wage and benefit guarantees to health employees as an inducement to accept devolution. This has widened an already noticeable gap in the remuneration of local versus devolved staff, and has imposed significant costs on local governments while reducing the ability of local managers to allocate resources according to need. In both Indonesia and the Philippines, limits on local authority have led managers to bypass established regulations by hiring staff on a temporary basis and topping up salaries with nontransparent allowances.

Accountability. The tendency to circumvent the rules may reflect an adaptive response by local managers to do what needs to be done, but the resulting lack of clarity and transparency poses a considerable risk in reduced accountability and vulnerability to corruption. In the Philippines, weak controls on staff appointments open the door to patronage and nepotism in local government. In Indonesia, though the speed of decentralization probably prevented vested interests from influencing decentralization policies, there is evidence that local positions are bought and sold in return for the promised rewards of graft in the public service (World Bank 2003c). The accountability of local civil servants is further threatened by a lack of clarity—in Indonesia because of imprecise roles, and in the Philippines owing to the "double subordination" of local staff to the local executive and the relevant central agency. Internal accountability mechanisms remain weak in both countries, though external accountability institutions—such as ombudsman institutions, complaint bureaus, and citizen monitoring—are growing in importance.

Overall, the experience of East Asia's rapid decentralizers shows that, although establishing the right rules is important to administrative decentralization, good design on paper is not enough. Countries must pay attention to the realities of implementation, particularly to creating incentives for local governments to work within the rules and to maintaining the momentum to make needed policy adjustments.

Decentralization in Transition: China and Vietnam

Administrative decentralization in China and Vietnam was born of the transition to a market economy. During the economic opening, central governments relinquished control over some of their activities and offered greater administrative and, to a lesser extent, political independence to subnational entities in return for greater central authority over revenue assignments. This system has confused the roles of subnational civil servants and limited the autonomy of local leaders in managing their activities.

On the other hand, in "crossing the river by feeling the rocks,"[11] decentralization in China and Vietnam has encouraged governments to experiment with local autonomy and address problems before moving on to the next stage of decentralization. And local governments in both countries have formulated innovative responses along the way. The decentralization experiences of these two countries—different in size yet emerging from similar bureaucratic traditions—provide insights into the impacts of administrative decentralization on civil service management and local service delivery in transition countries.

The Ebb and Flow of China's Decentralization. In a country as large and varied as China, some form of administrative decentralization is a necessity, yet the statutory basis for decentralized human resource management is fairly limited. The 1993 Provisional Regulations on Civil Servants address the nationally unified core civil service, which includes only white-collar workers such as managers and professional staff. Teachers, doctors, support staff, research institute employees, and members of the military are not considered part of the core service, but of separate Public Service Units (see below). Political appointees are considered civil servants, however, as no distinction is drawn between political and bureaucratic personnel. Though the Chinese Communist Party (CCP) is formally separate from the government, it does influence staffing and other aspects of public management. Central and subnational civil servants alike are subject to national guidelines; although local jurisdictions prepare their own regulations, these usually conform to the national rules (Wong 2003).

The People's Congress usually makes the decision to hire or fire a local civil servant at the corresponding level; however, the CCP controls the appointments of senior staff through the nomenklatura system of bureaucratic patronage common in many communist countries. Since 1984, high-level officials in each administrative tier have been appointed by the party committee at the next-highest level.[12] Recruitment is supposed to be determined by open, competitive examinations, and the selection and promotion of employees based on merit and performance. It is important to note, however, that these criteria are generally defined to include "political integrity," or commitment to party policies. Local staff are accountable to the central government rather than to local administrations. Civil servants must follow codes of conduct set out in both the Provisional Regulations and party writings. Temporary workers, such as substitute teachers, are exempt from the national guidelines.

The number of posts authorized for local jurisdictions is determined by local branches of the State Commission for Post and Establishment, a joint government-party organization, at the next-highest level of government. The commission uses a weighted formula to calculate each jurisdiction's overall staff complement, including a quota for the number of support staff.[13] Staffing numbers are not necessarily efficient, however, and inefficiencies can be preserved over time because responsibilities for budget preparation and staffing policy are separate—a holdover from the days of central planning.

Civil servants are paid according to a national salary scale, which is benchmarked to the wages of staff with similar responsibilities in state-owned enterprises. This restriction pegs salaries closer to those of staff in larger, urban localities. Bonuses and benefits are determined locally and often compose a hefty proportion of overall remuneration. Well-off localities use these perks liberally to supplement the pay of civil service cadres. Poorer areas have difficulty meeting nationally mandated wage increases, and some have been forced to ignore these instructions or supplement personnel budgets with funds originally allotted to capital expenditures. The central pay scale does not, therefore, ensure nationally consistent pay. The fact that local governments must cover civil service pensions, unemployment benefits, and other safety net expenditures intensifies the fiscal pressures caused by central control over wage levels. When the national government raises pay, these salary-based expenditures rise as well, tightening local budgets beyond the control of local managers.

Relatively high salary scales further burden less prosperous local governments, where the civil service may be one of few sources of wage employment. Indeed, the tendency for local administrations to serve as the employer of last resort is exacerbated by higher-level insistence that they absorb streams of recent graduates (Wong 2003). These forces together inflate staffing levels, especially at the county level, which accounts for over half of the excess staff (World Bank 2002a). Despite several attempts to downsize the civil service and streamline the structure of government, redundant agencies remain and have tended to staff up again over time.

Wage levels appear to be high enough to allow governments to recruit and retain qualified employees. The number of higher-level staff with university degrees has risen from about 20 percent in 1981 to more than 80 percent in 1994. Though pay increases and bonuses are designed to reflect performance evaluations, this does not seem to motivate staff to perform well. The majority receive positive appraisals, and managers generally hand out bonus payments across the board rather than to reward exceptional work. Overall pay levels are highly compressed. The ratio of highest to lowest salary is 5.6 to 1 for base wages, but flattens to something on the order of 3 to 1 when subsidies and bonuses are included (World Bank 2002a).[14] The relatively small increments between pay categories substantially reduce the payoff gained by an employee who ascends to the next rung of the bureaucratic ladder. There are no explicit restrictions on the transfer of local civil servants from one locality to another, or up to the central level, but the structure of the Chinese labor market—in which the *hukou* system of household registration assigns workers to a designated area—limits mobility. Some movements occur among higher-ranked staff, but rarely in the lower echelons. In the late 1990s, the central government initiated a program to relocate mid-career officials to local jurisdictions for six months to one year as part of a career path to senior public service.

The core civil service, as defined by the Provisional Regulations, does not encompass a substantial proportion of government-financed workers employed by Public Service Units (PSU), such as schools, hospitals, and research institutes. PSUs figure prominently in the public employment landscape, accounting for 96 percent of the civilian non-state-enterprise workforce at the central level, and 73 percent at the subnational level. Human resource management is slightly more flexible in PSUs than in core government entities. Local PSUs can be run at the central or local level or managed jointly. As in the core service, the next-highest branch of the State Commission for Post and Establishment determines the size of PSU staff. These restrictions do not seem to be heeded in practice, however, as local PSU employment averaged 110 percent of the authorized staff size in 1999. And PSU employment is growing, particularly at the subnational level. In provinces, prefectures, and counties, PSU staff complements expanded by 21, 21, and 75 percent, respectively, between 1991 and 1999 (World Bank 2002a).

PSUs are subject to the authority of and accountable to the central government. The boundaries between these two forms of public employment often blur. Throughout various attempts to downsize the civil service in the late 1980s and 1990s, PSUs often absorbed retrenched employees, limiting cost savings. There is an expectation that staff can move freely between PSUs and core government positions. In essence, PSUs are a reservoir of extrabudgetary human resources upon which the government can draw (World Bank 2002a).[15] Moreover, the functions of core agencies and PSUs often overlap, creating inefficiencies in administering and delivering public services.

Traditional and Innovative Approaches to Decentralization in Vietnam. Along with the transition to market-oriented economic principles, a major outgrowth of the *doi moi* reforms begun in 1986 has been a shift in the balance of state power, first from the Communist Party of Vietnam (CPV) to the government, and then from central to subnational levels. The impetus for administrative decentralization is growing with the Master Program on Public Administration Reform, which strongly advocates realigning the management of human and financial resources to address the fact that "administrative machinery at local levels is not really responsive to people" (Government of Vietnam, 2001, 2).

Most civil servants in Vietnam are hired and fired by the People's Committee at the next-highest level of government. In the provinces, the Provincial People's Committee makes these decisions, though high-level appointments require the approval of the prime minister. Openings must be advertised within the locality, usually by way of a public posting outside the Office of the People's Committee. While job classifications have been defined centrally, they are not accompanied by precise job descriptions, and thus offer local governments significant discretion in determining their staffing profile.

All civil service appointments and promotions are to be based on merit, as determined by examinations conducted by provincial-level political schools. There are indications that, in practice, seniority is accorded more weight than performance in promotion decisions. Selection to higher-level positions also requires ranking membership in the CPV. No performance management system links high-quality work to high return on a civil servant's career path. Two 1998 regulations—the Ordinance on Complaints and Denunciations and the Ordinance on Procedures for Resolving Administrative Disputes—offer mechanisms for disciplining staff, but managers do not exercise either of these very often. This is due in the former case to a lack of specificity in the provisions, and in the latter case to the limited effectiveness of Administrative Courts. No formal procedures are in place to allow dismissed civil servants to address grievances or appeal personnel actions.

Though officially no geographical constraints hinder the recruitment and transfer of staff, incentives for interregional mobility are generally inadequate, as local residents fill most local positions. Furthermore, remote areas tend to have difficulty attracting high-quality employees. There is also room to boost recruitment of regional minorities, particularly above the commune level. In theory, local civil servants are not barred from moving into the central civil service, but in practice, only People's Committee chairs move up to service in Hanoi.

Instead, central civil servants seem to be spending more time away from the capital. In 2003, the government launched a new program of staff rotations aimed at deepening the hands-on experience of top central bureaucrats. The intent is that time spent at the grassroots level will serve as a critical step on the path to high-level government posts (Cohen 2003). Whether this promising initiative will bear fruit, however, remains to be seen. There is concern that the rotation scheme has been used not as a tool for instilling an improved public service ethos but instead to banish political opponents.

The central Ministry of Home Affairs manages the personnel establishment through staff quotas at each level of government. Until 2004, these staff quotas also determined the budget allocations for personnel expenditures at the local level, but the one-to-one relationship between a larger staff size and a larger budget allocation created incentives for overstaffing and penalized leaner, more efficient administrations. Budgets now reflect a province's population rather than its staffing levels.

Salaries and allowances are specified centrally and apply uniformly to all levels of government. Wage levels have traditionally been considered low compared with alternative sources of employment, though new analysis casts doubt on the validity of these comparisons. Bales and Rama argue that, while professional and technical employees may be underpaid compared with the private sector, the alternative employer for most civil servants—particularly those based in rural areas—is most likely the informal sector, where salaries tend to be lower (Bales and Rama 2002). In poorer regions, in fact, the comparatively high wages fixed by the center—along with recent salary increases—are tightening budgets. This pressure will only build with the planned pay reform program, which promises to raise salaries by 30 percent, on average. Because staff pay represents a considerable share of spending in service sectors, wage costs can freeze out other important spending. Though the crowding out of operations and maintenance expenditures is not a major problem overall in Vietnam, it is an important issue in poorer areas.

Turning Transition into Forward Momentum. Decentralization in China and Vietnam has been incremental, with the central government reacting to the effects of each policy before taking the next step. While this approach allows experimentation to address unexpected results before they become entrenched, the lack of a predefined plan can create inconsistencies in decentralized governance. For example, sufficient fiscal resources have not accompanied administrative mandates—indeed, in China, the recent trend has been toward recentralization of finances. In Vietnam, the PAR Master Program, which sees the capacity and accountability of civil servants as critical to improving the effectiveness and efficiency of public service, is an important step toward redressing imbalances in fiscal and human resources.

Capacity. The PAR Master Program calls for developing a capacity-building plan to provide better training opportunities at local as well as central levels, refresh the curriculum and methods, and align content more closely with needed on-the-job skills. Enhancing the reach of educational opportunities will be important in addressing the low capacity of many local governments in Vietnam, particularly in remote areas. China has also made training civil servants a priority: local governments must upgrade the skills of civil servants in line with the needs of the market economy. In both countries, the central government provides resources for locally organized training programs. In China, local governments are taking advantage of these resources to send their employees to Chinese universities as well as training programs outside the country. However, local administrations in both China and Vietnam continue to lack expertise in accounting and financial management. In Vietnam, a recent audit found an absence of record keeping in the communes, which keeps local managers from effectively overseeing the civil service and prevents the center from tracking the use of funds.

Incentives. Improving the ability of local governments to manage financial resources addresses only part of the problem when the incentives of civil service managers are skewed away from prudent supervision of local budgets. Until recently, Vietnam's system for allocating administrative budgets—calculated per staff member per year—encouraged local managers to inflate staffing levels to obtain more resources from the center. In China, local officials have little motivation to reduce personnel costs, as they are budgeted separately from other expenditures. Indeed, managers who save on wages lose part of their budget allocation. In poor regions, adding staff is often seen as the only way to increase the local budget allocation. Coupled with the government's position as employer of last resort, this system has encouraged overstaffing in local governments.

The ability of decentralization to improve service delivery also depends on the incentives of civil servants themselves. In both China and Vietnam, despite official rules defining merit as the basis for promotion, the career paths of local staff appear to be more limited than those of their central government counterparts. Seniority and party loyalty receive as much or more consideration than performance, and salary compression limits the benefits gained from hard work. China's attempt to enhance incentives for high-quality work through performance-based pay has not succeeded because managers have applied bonuses across the board. Staff rotation schemes in both countries focus on developing the careers of central civil servants through time spent in regions, rather than on rotating local staff to other areas to facilitate sharing of experiences and information (see box 7.1). The Vietnamese government has had significant success in improving incentives for prudent management of administrative expenditures through an innovative pilot program for block-grant budgeting in Ho Chi Minh City (see box 5.3).

Autonomy. Controlling administrative expenditures has indeed proved difficult for local managers in these countries because of their restricted autonomy in setting wage and staffing levels and, in China, associated safety net expenditures. The high percentage of local budgets preempted by personnel costs, in turn, limits local discretion regarding other expenditures. In the meantime, local leaders have focused on a few areas of personnel management in which they do have autonomy. In China, local governments determine bonus pay, and have used it to supplement civil service wages. In both countries, local governments have the right to supplement their budgets by collecting user fees for certain services. While this has eased the strain on some local budgets, many of these fees fall disproportionately on the poor. Moreover, because these resources are external to the budget, governments often spend them in nontransparent ways that do not reflect budget priorities and undermine accountability.

Accountability. The accountability of local civil servants in China and Vietnam is blurred by a lack of clarity on the roles and responsibilities of each level of government, though Vietnam's new Budget Law has helped to address this problem. In Vietnam, and at the township level in China, the lack of clarity is intensified by dual subordination, in which local staff are beholden to both the directives of the central government and the demands of local elected assemblies. Audits of local expenditures in both countries have found that accountability mechanisms are weak. In China, the internal audit function is strong, focusing mainly on ensuring compliance and preventing fraud. External ex post audits are less effective, as local audit bureaus report to the central government and thus lack needed independence. The effectiveness of audits in Vietnam is constrained by a lack of capacity and low pay. In both countries, efforts are under way to improve accounting and financial management at central as well as local levels. These measures will help the central government improve and monitor local service delivery. The presence of the Communist Party in China and Vietnam holds

BOX 7.1 Personnel Exchange in India and Japan: Whose Capacity Is Being Strengthened?

In many civil services around the world, systems enable staff to transfer across levels of government. The motivations behind these personnel transfers are varied. In some cases, the intent is to groom central civil servants for high-level postings by using hands-on work at the local level to ground and broaden their policy skills. In other cases, central government staff are transferred to subnational jurisdictions to fill gaps in local capacity to implement national programs. Where civil servants are transferred across subnational governments, the aim may be to keep them at a safe distance from local vested interests.

A comparison of civil servant rotation schemes in India and Japan demonstrates how the design of these human resource management tools can shape their impact in a decentralized setting. In India, the principal focus is on preparing members of the elite Indian Administrative Service (IAS) for senior positions in central and state governments. Those who make the cut in the highly competitive recruitment process and rigorous training program are dispatched to state governments, where they spend several years working in field and secretariat assignments in different sectors. After reaching senior positions in the field, IAS officers typically rotate between central and state governments, as repeated exposure to field conditions is key to keeping abreast of changing on-the-ground realities. The IAS system also fosters active collaboration between the center and subnational governments.

In Japan, on the other hand, the impetus for personnel exchange arose from the need to boost technical capacity in newly established local governments. Many local postings have since become "hereditary," in the sense that staff members returning to central government are typically replaced by other central staff from the same ministry. Though it could be argued that this practice has prevented qualified local staff from gaining access to senior positions in subnational governments, the fact that autonomous local administrations continue to pay for relocated central staff implies that the transfer of information and knowledge from the center still plays a useful role. Moreover, the Japanese system of personnel exchanges is much broader than that in India. Staff not only transfer from the center to prefectural governments, but from prefectural governments to municipalities, from local governments to central postings, and across prefectures as well. While in both countries placing centrally recruited officials in local administrations can strengthen the capacity of local staff as well as transferred officials, the design of the Japanese system is more conducive to developing the skills of local staff.

Sources: Schiavo-Campo et al. 1997; Inoki 2001; Iqbal 2001.

important consequences for the accountability of civil servants in a decentralized setting. The party exerts considerable influence over staff appointments and promotions, particularly at senior levels. As such, civil servants most likely feel more accountable to the party than to the local population. While the party can be seen as a source of discipline in an otherwise weak system, its traditional control over the flow of information can reduce transparency and undercut efforts to hold civil servants accountable (Wong 2003).

Government transparency is beginning to improve in China and Vietnam, both within the civil service and with respect to the public. The state-run media and citizens are paying increasing attention to corruption issues. In Vietnam, after peasant protests in Thai Binh and Dong Nai provinces brought to light the extent of corruption in the local civil service, the central government introduced a Grassroots Democracy Decree to enhance local consultation with residents on decisions that affect them. While this could in principle provide a strong check on abuse of power and strengthen accountability by increasing the demand for good governance, implementation has been weak because of limited management responsibility at the commune level, insufficient training of civil servants in sharing information with local citizens, and inadequate mechanisms for tackling corruption in social assistance funds.

The Cautious Decentralizers: Cambodia and Thailand

The implementation of decentralization has been relatively limited in Thailand and Cambodia. In response to growing demand for improved service delivery at the local level, both countries have recognized the importance of devolving some management responsibilities—and the rights that accompany them—to local governments. Yet concerns about the limited capacity of subnational governments have engendered a cautious approach that has concentrated on developing the legislative framework and building local capacity to manage and monitor public services. In Thailand, a weakening political imperative to decentralize has also stalled implementation of outlined policies.

In low-capacity countries, a gradual transfer of responsibility can be a pragmatic way to ensure continuity in service provision and limit the potential for political capture of inexperienced local civil servants. However, gradualism also has its disadvantages. Piecemeal approaches may lack an overall strategic focus, leading to a mismatch between responsibilities and resources, and between authority and accountability. Moreover, caution can serve as an excuse for inaction on the part of central officials who are reluctant to relinquish their authority. Thailand and Cambodia have faced some understandable reasons for delay. Yet in taking such a long time to establish the building blocks of decentralization, these countries have deferred potential improvements in service delivery. In the meantime, the success of several small-scale experiments with local autonomy indicates that, with careful design, decentralization can work in these countries. The following discussion of guarded decentralization in Thailand and Cambodia explores how countries may resolve the tension between exercising caution and achieving tangible results.

Building the Foundations for Decentralizing Personnel Management in Thailand. Thailand's 1997 Constitution represents a significant step in bringing government closer to the people in a traditionally centralized country. Building on this solid foundation, efforts have shifted to creating the institutions and developing the legal basis for devolving responsibilities to subnational administrations.

So far, few civil servants have been transferred to local administrations. Only about 4,000 staff (less than 1 percent of the 1.2 million national civil servants) in five departments—principally the Department of Public Works and the Ministry of Interior's Accelerated Rural Development Department—have moved to local service. The transfer of staff has thus not followed the transfer of functions, as stipulated in the decentralization legislation.[16] The strategy of the Office of the Civil Service Commission for transferring remaining staff prioritizes voluntary transfers, though mandatory transfers and compensated retrenchment are still options. The commission has set up a Public Sector Personnel Development and Deployment Center as a hub for training and deploying central staff to positions in local government. Provincial personnel transfer centers are evaluating the staffing implications of devolved authority for local governments.

Still, the low number of relocations thus far points to a lack of motivation on the part of both central agencies and public employees. Ministries in Bangkok are understandably unenthusiastic about letting their staff go. Poorer local governments, especially the small *tambons,* may be reluctant to accept more staff because of the burden they may pose to tight budgets. Employees hesitate to move owing to a lack of clarity about comparable pay, benefits (including pension fund provisions), recruitment and dismissal procedures, career mobility, and local quality of life. Some staff worry that relocation to smaller local communities will leave them—and their jobs—at the mercy of local politics (Wegelin 2002). Civil servants who transfer to the regions are entitled to the same pay as in the center, but the system for classifying local positions does not offer the same range of job levels (and accompanying pay grades).[17] The central government has offered a financial incentive to public servants who volunteer to serve in local governments for a three-year term, but this does not address the longer-term issue of permanent personnel transfers.[18]

The central government exercises general authority over personnel decisions at each level of subnational government through the Civil Service Commission. Local administrations may hire low-level staff and contract workers but are not authorized to recruit higher-skilled or career employees. Vacancies are not formally advertised. Recruitment is based on competitive examinations administered by the commission, although it can waive the exam requirement in certain circumstances. All civil servants are subject to a code of professional ethics, which requires those in higher-level positions to publicly declare their assets. Disciplinary procedures are rigorous and provide for appeal.

The center rigidly prescribes the number and grade level of authorized staff positions at each level of local government. Fifth-class *tambons* may employ no more than 3 staff members, and first-class *tambons* no more than 21. Limiting staff so strictly may undercut remote rural areas that need the most intensive work on service delivery and public outreach. Yet keeping staff lean can help localities manage the fiscal burden of civil service salaries. Local governments must adhere to a central pay scale and a 40 percent cap on personnel expenditures as a proportion of local spending. This is a Catch-22 for poorer *tambons,* where a sheer lack of staff constrains the capacity to perform local functions, while paying more people would leave little money for anything else (Wegelin 2002). To address local personnel issues and redress disincentives to staff transfers, the Local Civil Service Administration Working Group has proposed creating a Local Government Civil Service Commission—as distinct from the provincial and municipal commissions that already exist. The Ministry of Interior is also looking into a personnel management system to track the pay, benefits, and career streams of subnational civil servants. Finally, the Thai government's recent acceleration of broader civil service reforms may reinvigorate the decentralization process.

Top-Down and Bottom-Up Approaches to Decentralization in Cambodia. According to its *National Poverty Reduction Strategy for 2003–2005,* Cambodia is pursuing a two-pronged approach to the devolution of power, tackling both political decentralization to the communes and functional deconcentration to provincial-level outposts of the central government. The government has recently initiated a process to develop an integrated policy framework.

Cambodia has established the legal framework for devolution, but its impact on staffing has been limited. While recognizing that communes should have their own financial resources, the Law on Administrative Management is much less ambitious about decentralizing personnel and human resource management. The law requires only two technical staff positions at the commune level: a commune clerk appointed and paid by the Ministry of Interior to assist the commune council, and an accountant from the provincial treasury. These individuals wield central influence over the otherwise relatively autonomous commune councils, although the commune chief can request the appointment of a new clerk based on the council's decision. If needed, councils may directly employ other staff, whom the law deems outside the "State framework." These employees are retained on a temporary basis for the duration of the council's mandate, but the next council can extend their terms.

At the commune level, general administration expenditures are restricted to 30 percent or less of the allocation from the center. This limit reduces the temptation for nepotism and overstaffing while giving communes considerable discretion in how funds are spent within the threshold. There is concern that the centrally determined allowances paid to commune councilors are high relative to civil servant salaries, especially as the former are only part-time functionaries. This can foster resentment among local staff and further restrict administrative expenditures.

The legal framework for deconcentration is less well defined, but the number of staff affected is high. As of 2003, some 78 percent of staff were based in provinces, including health and education employees. The relevant central ministry determines staffing needs and positions at the provincial level, but provincial administrations have discretion in whom they hire (World Bank 2002b). Though recruitment is supposed to be based on competitive examinations administered by the State Secretariat for Civil Service, anecdotal evidence indicates that provinces do not strictly follow this requirement (World Bank 2003a). Similarly, promotions within each grading category are to be based on merit, but seniority appears to play a stronger role in practice. Performance evaluations should be conducted annually, but this is not common. Disciplinary procedures exist but are rarely used. Incentives are therefore not structured to encourage civil servants to perform well and improve over time.

Incentives are further dampened by extremely low and highly compressed pay. Wages are so low that many civil servants are forced to seek additional employment in the private and informal sectors, and the resulting absenteeism undermines public sector performance. While ministries are responsible for monitoring attendance, punishment for absenteeism is rare (World Bank 2002b). Low pay also affects how civil servants spend their time when they are at work. For example, the payment of per diems for field visits encourages staff to focus on activities that require travel, regardless of whether this is the most efficient use of their time or is indeed necessary.

The central government determines salaries, allowances, and social benefits, which local governments must pay on a priority basis. This limits the flexibility of provincial budget managers and may crowd out other important activities. At the provincial level, personnel expenditures averaged 48 percent of total expenditures in fiscal year 2002, though this figure ranged from 18.6 percent in Mondul Kiri to 57.4 percent in Kandal (World Bank 2002b). This share is much higher than the 33 percent that the central government spends on its wage bill (World Bank 2003a).[19] Throughout the Cambodian civil service, a lack of systematic establishment control has allowed the proliferation of contract workers and high levels of overtime pay, and these problems are likely even more noticeable at the local level.

The combination of low pay, low staff motivation, and low mobility has left line ministries desperate to skew incentives back toward improved service delivery, and several ad hoc responses have evolved. The Ministry of Health has allowed health centers to collect user fees and to apply 49 percent of receipts to supplement staff salaries.[20] This approach has shown tangible benefits, as the use of health centers has risen by up to 60 percent. Clients are evidently willing to pay extra for better service. As Turner notes, "The salary supplements mean that staff are likely to devote more time to their official duties. When salaries might be only US$15 per month, an extra US$10 makes a considerable difference" (2002, 357). However, these supplements may lead to pay inequalities across regions. The Ministry of Education, Youth, and Sports has tried to improve the efficiency of education services through financial incentives, including pay supplements for work in remote areas, double shifts or multigrade teaching, and performance incentives to heads of provincial and district education offices.

Balancing Caution and Action. The measured approaches to decentralization in Thailand and Cambodia reflect expressed concerns on the part of both governments that local administrations and their staff do not yet have the capacity to take responsibility for service delivery. In Cambodia these concerns have some basis in reality; in Thailand, however, they may reflect a weakened political drive toward decentralization. In both cases, policy makers have sought to avoid the potential dangers of decentralization by putting capacity building first.

Capacity. Low capacity is certainly an issue in Cambodia, where decades of civil war and the atrocities of the Khmer Rouge regime took a devastating toll on the country's pool of human resources. Even in Thailand, a middle-income country with a bustling capital city, most local governments lack the technical skills and institutional resources to deliver even basic services. Both countries have created decentralized structures without devolving significant authority or responsibility.

Developing the skills of local staff is seen as the bridge between these initial steps and more significant decentralization. In Thailand, municipal staff are regularly rotated to enhance the sharing of knowledge and experience among subnational civil servants. Various training institutions offer a wide array of courses, but these have not yet been incorporated into a focused strategy for developing local capacity in a sustainable manner. Training and technical assistance for decentralization are also growing rapidly in Cambodia, building on the success of the donor-supported Seila Program. A critical challenge for Cambodia is to leverage this positive experience to design coherent and sustainable capacity-building initiatives that extend to all local staff. Thailand and Cambodia have also turned to deconcentration as on-the-job training for civil servants—in Thailand, through Local Education Authorities and Area Health Boards, and in Cambodia, through Health Center Management Committees, which have the authority to supplement staff salaries with proceeds from user fees.

Capacity is not just about technical and bureaucratic skills, however. The institutional and financial capacity of local governments is also crucial. In both Cambodia and Thailand, many local governments are simply too small—in geographical size, population, staff numbers, and budgets—to execute their functions. Most of Thailand's *tambons* employ only a handful of staff and cannot be considered viable units of government, as many are unable to support even a primary school let alone more technical services such as infrastructure. In Cambodia, a maximum of 11 people sit on the commune councils, supported by two centrally appointed civil servants.

Incentives. The small size of local governments has influenced the incentives of civil servants to take local employment, which has, in turn, affected service delivery. Few local civil service positions are available, and those that are sit at lower grade levels with low salaries and limited career paths. Attracting highly skilled professionals is difficult, as local governments do not have enough work to sustain full-time technical experts. As a result, central officials in Thailand have strongly resisted transfer to local service. The Thai government has attempted to address this by offering financial incentives to those who volunteer, but unclear rules and benefits have prevented this program from having any significant effect. In Cambodia, where over three-quarters of staff are based in the field, local staff are reportedly migrating to provincial centers in search of opportunities to supplement very low public sector wages. Local public servants are in effect being paid full time to work for part of the day. This is a particular problem in health clinics, which despite a 24-hour mandate often remain closed for most of the day. The government may want to consider explicitly allowing part-time work in public health facilities so they can ensure continuous availability of care.[21]

Autonomy. In both Thailand and Cambodia, limits on personnel expenditures have prevented local governments from hiring enough staff to get the job done—and even from filling all the positions to which they are entitled. In Cambodia's Kampong Cham province, however, low use of health services means that even the small numbers of local staff employed in provincial and district offices are excessive compared with the workload (WHO 2003). This hinders the efficiency and effectiveness of service delivery. Though local managers in these two countries do enjoy discretion in whom they hire, rural communities do not have access to the highly skilled staff available in the center. In Cambodia, a lack of predictable financing further constrains the autonomy of local leaders. Unsure of when and in what quantity resources will arrive, field-based managers are reluctant to make long-term investments, including in human resources. The government has taken some steps to alleviate this problem by piloting mechanisms for streamlined execution of budgets in priority sectors. One example is the Priority Action Program, which allows local education authorities to supplement the low pay of their staff. Still, in these traditionally hierarchical societies, local managerial autonomy remains limited.

Accountability. The limited autonomy of subnational governments in Cambodia and Thailand poses important challenges for the accountability of local staff. In both countries, local governments at the lowest tier are officially accountable to popularly elected assemblies. Yet, so far, they are responsible only for a limited set of tasks, and most decisions are handed down from higher levels. As a result, it is difficult for local citizens to hold civil servants responsible for the quality and timeliness of their services. Community monitoring is also limited by incomplete dissemination of information on decentralization plans and transferred responsibilities. The flow of information on public preferences is interrupted by the "missing middle" of decentralized politics, as provincial authorities in Cambodia and Thailand are not elected and thus report only to the central government. Despite the time taken by both governments to lay a solid foundation for decentralization, many local officials are still not fully aware of their own responsibilities—and thus the outcomes for which they are accountable. Local standards and benchmarks are not yet in place to help the Thai and Cambodian central governments evaluate local performance. In both countries, vote buying, corruption, and elite capture may be significant at local levels, posing an important risk to decentralization plans.

Successfully Managing the Civil Service: The Way Forward

East Asia's experience with administrative decentralization highlights both the opportunities and the challenges associated with devolving authority for managing the civil service to lower levels of government. As the case studies show, decentralizing the management of human resources can improve the responsiveness and resourcefulness of local governments. Yet, without careful design, devolution can also bring fiscal imbalances, negative incentives, and confused accountability at the local level. There is no single formula for successful civil service management in a decentralized context.

Success can be found in various forms, and tactics that work in one context may produce the opposite result in a different environment. The diverse approaches of the six cases offer lessons for countries considering decentralizing civil service management. The relatively smooth start to Big Bang decentralization in Indonesia shows the importance of carefully managing administrative elements of the transition, as when the central government continued to pay the salaries of transferred civil servants on an interim basis. The limited implementation of decentralization policies in Thailand shows that having the approach right on paper does not necessarily lead to getting it right in practice. Nonetheless, the latter is important, as evidenced by the legal ambiguities and reversals arising in the wake of Indonesia's rapid decentralization.

The experience of East Asian countries in managing the capacity, incentives, autonomy, and accountability of the subnational civil service can provide valuable lessons for other countries. The relatively stable transitions to decentralization in the Philippines and Indonesia show that countries can strengthen local capacity on-the-job. Cambodia's positive experience with improving the use and quality of health services validates the role of positive incentives—such as salary supplements from user fees—in motivating civil servants to perform better. Vietnam's experiment with block-grant budgeting in Ho Chi Minh City has reduced administrative costs and overstaffing, showing that more local autonomy can improve civil service efficiency.[22] Finally, Vietnam's recent passage of a Budget Law that clarifies the responsibilities of various levels of government, as well as the experience of the Philippines in improving performance through community report cards, shows how efforts both within and outside the government can improve the accountability of civil servants.

The experiences of East Asian countries also highlight several critical dilemmas that governments must address in designing policies and institutions for administrative decentralization:

Centralized Control vs. Decentralized Management

Implicit in the notion of decentralization is the devolution of some responsibility and authority to local levels, which brings decisions on public service delivery closer to clients while freeing central government of the day-to-day details of local administration. On the other hand, retaining some control at the central level can yield substantial benefits, including national minimum standards for service delivery and wider mobility within the civil service.

It is critical for decentralization policy to achieve a rational equilibrium between these opposing but valid considerations. Decentralization policies should not aim to devolve all authority to the local level, but rather to redefine the responsibilities of the center and local governments. Central authorities must recast themselves as guides, providing local administrations with a comprehensive, feasible national policy framework and enhancing their ability to evaluate local performance. At the same time, policies must align the responsibilities and autonomy of local managers. The roles of local governments and their civil servants must be clearly specified and accompanied by the resources and flexibility to tailor activities to the needs of residents, as well as by mechanisms to ensure accountability and prevent proximity from opening the door to elite capture. Clear, locally feasible standards for minimum performance can mitigate the risks of devolving autonomy to subnational governments, as can better monitoring of performance through the collection, maintenance, and transmission of information on performance across levels of government.

Uniformity vs. Unification of the Civil Service

The degree to which countries devolve authority for civil service management has implications for uniformity across the civil service. If the center totally circumscribes the conditions of local public employment, administrative decentralization will remain a myth, and its potential benefits unrealized. On the other hand, if local managers are entirely free to adjust salary and staffing levels, the

BOX 7.2 Lessons from Uganda's District Service Commissions

Uganda's decentralization experience is generally considered a success story in terms of its extent and impact. As in Indonesia and the Philippines, decentralization in Uganda took on the characteristics of a Big Bang following an era of political opening. Along with the launch of regular local elections and the transfer of broad service responsibilities and attendant fiscal resources to local governments, the country took steps to decentralize the administrative apparatus. Staff posted to districts formally transferred to local governments, and separate District Service Commissions (DSCs) were set up to manage human resources in district and local administrations.

The right of the DSCs to hire, fire, and oversee subnational staff was enshrined in the new Constitution and further detailed in the Local Government Act. DSCs were meant to provide institutional protection for the relative autonomy of district governments in managing subnational civil servants. However, the system has encountered several obstacles. Recruitment procedures are slow, performance evaluations rarely occur, and the authority of DSCs to enforce disciplinary decisions is limited. Moreover, because the central Public Service Commission defines the size of local governments and institutions, vets DSC membership, and approves recruiting standards, the central government retains influence over subnational personnel decisions. Finally, the existence of a separate DSC in each district—and the associated rise in fiscal transfers and local employment—has created political pressure to add new districts. This can lead to the proliferation of smaller and smaller local administrations and eventually to a loss of scale economies and operating efficiency.

As East Asian countries grapple with how best to manage civil servants under decentralization, the Ugandan experience with DSCs—both positive and negative—may provide a useful guide. If designed well, subnational public service commissions can promote the qualifications and professionalism of local civil services throughout the country.

Sources: Ndegwa and Levy 2003; Evans and Manning 2003.

size and composition of local governments—and their paychecks—are likely to vary considerably and may lead to interregional inequalities in employment conditions.

In its ideal form, a country's civil service will be uniform but not unified. Public servants will share a distinct national identity without necessarily being subject to identical rules on pay and employment. Countries can foster servicewide identity through joint training of civil servants working in different localities, or by creating subnational associations such as the League of Mayors in the Philippines or professional groups that bring together civil servants who confront similar issues across the country. At the same time, some degree of local variation is important. Solutions to inequitable salary differentials include allowing local governments to top up centrally defined base wages through user fees and other own-source revenues, as in Cambodia, China, and Vietnam, or having the center set a salary range but allowing local managers to establish exact salaries. If working conditions vary across subnational governments, public service commissions could manage the careers and interregional mobility of subnational civil servants. These commissions must have the authority to recruit, transfer, and properly oversee staff, however (see box 7.2).

Economies of Scale vs. Client Responsiveness

Administrative decentralization also raises questions about the appropriate level of government to which responsibilities should be devolved. If the goal is to bring government closer to the people, then countries should hand off public service provision to the lowest tier of government, where civil servants are best placed to understand and respond to the needs of local residents. However, improving the responsiveness of local governments through proximity can disrupt the potential for economies of scale. Running a government, no matter how big or small, requires a minimum number of staff—accountants, managers, and secretaries, for example—and thus a minimum of human and financial resources.

In devolving responsibilities to the local level, central governments must consider the capacity of small civil services to undertake complex technical and managerial tasks, and avoid the proliferation of unviable local administrations. Small local governments generally have difficulty paying the salaries of highly skilled staff, and those staff are unlikely to have enough technical work to keep them busy full time. Diseconomies of scale in providing public services are a particular issue in Cambodia and Thailand, where local budgets and staffs are too small to viably provide such services. In these countries, ongoing boundary reviews may boost local technical capacity by consolidating local units, but they have not led to any decisions thus far. Alternatively, local governments could consider joining forces to provide public services that require more sophisticated technical equipment and skills, or that create spillover benefits for other jurisdictions. In China and Indonesia, on the other hand, the larger scale of subnational governments limits their ability to effectively reach local populations.

In addition to striking a balance in decentralization design, countries also face important decisions in sequencing reforms. Administrative decentralization entails two main temporal tradeoffs:

Capacity First or Capacity through Decentralization? How best to sequence decentralization reforms and capacity-building initiatives is a subject of considerable debate. On the one hand, analysts see devolution of responsibility for management and public services as a necessary step in building individual and institutional capacity. Skills development, performance incentives, and innovation are encouraged through "learning by doing," which is generally a more sustainable and individualized approach than occasional courses developed without close attention to the specific tasks performed by civil servants. On the other hand, Prud'homme and others warn of the "dangers of decentralization": the low capacity and inexperience of local civil servants can mean a sharp deterioration in the quality and efficiency of public services (Prud'homme 1995).

The critical challenge is to maintain forward momentum while balancing capacity considerations. Asymmetric approaches to decentralization can allow gradual devolution of responsibilities to local governments that have demonstrated the capacity to take on new tasks. Thailand, for example, has seen some success with ad hoc forms that devolve autonomy to social sector agencies based on "readiness" criteria. However, it is important not to allow overly targeted approaches to delay the realization of decentralization's potential benefits. The experience of East Asia's rapid decentralizers—Indonesia and the Philippines—shows that countries can build capacity *through* decentralization. In this scenario, careful planning for coordinated training within a national framework that is sensitive to local considerations is essential.

Civil Service Reform before or after Decentralization? Though a full discussion is outside the scope of this chapter, the nexus between decentralization and civil service reform is worth mentioning. In principle, it makes more sense to decentralize the structure and management of the civil service after ensuring that it is efficient and effective at the national level. Yet given the political drive for decentralization and the difficulty of civil service reform, many countries cannot wait for these to occur before decentralizing. On the other hand, the decision to delay civil service reform until after decentralization can allow the central government to transfer the political burden of difficult policy measures. Countries should explicitly consider the links between these two key reforms to avoid replicating national flaws—such as duplication of effort or overstaffing—at the local level.

Endnotes

1. This section draws on Evans and Manning 2003.
2. Vaclav Havel, former president of the Czech Republic, used this phrase to describe the Czech reform experience.
3. The Local Government Code of the Philippines, Section 2, Sections 76 to 97, address human resource management and development at the local level.
4. The exception to this general rule is the local treasurer, who is appointed by the Department of Finance but paid by the local government. Manasan n.d., 12.
5. Philippine Constitution, Article IX, Section 2 (2).
6. The 45 percent cap applies in first-class through third-class local governments, and the 55 percent cap in fourth-class through sixth-class local governments.
7. Owing to the penchant among local governments to use alternative sources to supplement wages, these official figures likely underestimate the degree to which local governments have exceeded restrictions on personnel expenditures.
8. Pay scales were set at a fixed percentage of national levels, ranging from 75 percent in sixth-class local governments to 95 percent in second-class local governments.

9. Under this revised law, provincial governors will have authority to hire, fire, and relocate provincial staff only at echelon 2 and below. Similarly, heads of districts and cities will be able to hire, fire, and relocate staff only at echelon 2 and below, and only after consulting with the provincial governor.
10. Some local governments, though, have begun to informally supplement salaries. Also, several regional allowances are offered that are imperfectly recorded.
11. At the 11th Party Congress in 1978, Deng Xiaoping used this analogy to urge Chinese policy makers to take a gradual approach to economic reform.
12. Before 1984, these appointments were made by party committees two levels up in the territorial hierarchy. Burns n.d., 8.
13. At all levels, the criteria used are population, land area, and value of industrial and agricultural production; at the city level, additional factors include the number of component administrative units, local budget income, and the amount of developed land.
14. Including rank-based benefits, such as housing and car allowances, does widen the gap.
15. In Hebei province, for example, the director of budget preparation had kept his post as director of the Budget Department in the Hebei finance bureau.
16. Webster (2002) argues that functional devolution does not require the transfer of all corresponding civil servants. He argues that if decentralization is meant to improve the efficiency of public services by transferring authority to units closest to the beneficiaries, then fewer people should be able to perform the same task just as well as or better than at the center.
17. Teacher pay, for example, could be much lower after employees transfer to the local level. See Wegelin 2002, 23.
18. The amount of this incentive is B 6,000 per month, or roughly US$150.
19. The national wage bill includes defense and security expenditures.
20. The other 51 percent is to be spent on operational expenses. See Turner 2002, 357.
21. Conversation with Pamela Messervy, World Health Organization, Phnom Penh, Cambodia, October 2003.
22. See box 5.3. Most surplus staff were transferred to other localities rather than retired or retrenched.

Bibliography

Asia Foundation. 2002. *First Indonesia Rapid Decentralization Appraisal (IRDA) Synopsis of Findings.* College Park, MD: University of Maryland, IRIS Center.

Asian Development Bank. 1999. "Governance in Thailand: Challenges, Issues, and Prospects." Manila: Asian Development Bank.

Azfar, Omar, Tugrul Gurgur, Satu Kähkönen, Anthony Lanyi, and Patrick Meagher. 2000. "Decentralization and Governance: An Empirical Investigation of Public Service Delivery in the Philippines." College Park, MD: University of Maryland, IRIS Center; and Washington, DC: World Bank.

Baleo, Sarah, and Martin Rama. 2002. "Are Public Sector Workers Underpaid? Appropriate Comparators in a Developing Country." World Bank. http://econ.worldbank.org/files/3358_wps2747.pdf.

Burns, John. "Country Reform Summaries: China." www1.worldbank.org/publicsector/civilservice/rsChina.pdf.

Cohen, Margot. 2003. "Cadres Get a Field Lesson." *Far Eastern Economic Review* 166 (45): 24.

Evans, Anne, with Nick Manning. 2003. "Decentralization: A Review of Staffing Practices in Eight Countries." Internal draft document. World Bank, Washington, DC.

Fritzen, Scott. 2002. "The 'Foundation of Public Administration'? Decentralization and Its Discontents in Transitional Vietnam." Paper presented at the Asia Conference on Governance in Asia: Culture, Ethics, Institutional Reform, and Policy Change, City University of Hong Kong.

Government of Vietnam. 2001. "Master Programme on Public Administration Reform for the Period 2001–2010." Attachment to the Prime Minister's Approval Decision No. 136/2001/QD-TTg, September 17.

Government of Vietnam, General Statistical Office. 2003. *Statistical Yearbook 2002.* Hanoi: Government of Vietnam.

Government of Vietnam, Ministry of Finance. 2000. "Vietnam: Improving the Budget-Norm System for Recurrent Expenditures." VIE/96/208, Public Expenditure Review Phase II. www.undp.org.vn/projects/vie96028/norms.pdf.

Inoki, Takenori. 2001. "Personnel Exchange among Central and Local Governments in Japan." Working Paper. Washington, DC: World Bank Institute.

Iqbal, Farrukh. 2001. "Evolution and Salient Characteristics of the Japanese Local Government System." Working Paper. Washington, DC: World Bank Institute.

Kingdom of Thailand. 1997. Constitution of the Kingdom of Thailand. www.oefre.unibe.ch/law/icl/th00t___.html.

Litvack, Jennie, Junaid Ahmad, and Richard Bird. 1998. "Rethinking Decentralization in Developing Countries." Sector Studies Series. Washington, DC: World Bank.

Litvack, Jennie, and Jessica Seddon. 1999. "Decentralization Briefing Notes." Working Paper. Washington, DC: World Bank Institute.

Manasan, Rosario G. "Fiscal Decentralization: The Case of the Philippines." World Bank. http://www.worldbank.org/wbi/publicfinance/documents/ASEM/manasan.pdf.

Ndegwa, Stephen, and Brian Levy. 2003. "The Politics of Decentralization in Africa: A Comparative Analysis." Paper presented at the Regional Workshop on Governance and Public Management, Johannesburg.

OECD (Organisation for Economic Co-operation and Development). 1997. "Managing across Levels of Government." Paris: OECD.

People's Republic of China. 1982. Constitution of the People's Republic of China. http://english.peopledaily.com.cn/constitution/constitution.html.

Prud'homme, Rémy. 1995. "The Dangers of Decentralization." *World Bank Research Observer* 10 (2): 201–20.

Republic of the Philippines. 1987. 1987 Constitution of the Philippines. www.chanrobles.com/philsupremelaw1.htm.

———. 1991. The Local Government Code of the Philippines (Republic Act No. 7160). www.chanrobles.com/localgov.htm.

Royal Government of Cambodia. 2002. *National Poverty Reduction Strategy, 2003–2005.* Phnom Penh: Royal Government of Cambodia.

Schiavo-Campo, Salvatore, Giulio de Tommaso, and Amitabha Mukherjee. 1997. "Government Employment and Pay: A Global and Regional Perspective." Policy Research Working Paper No. 1771. Washington, DC: World Bank.

Steedman, David W., and Lloyd R. Kenward. 2005. "Civil Service Reforms at the Regional Level: Opportunities and Constraints." Internal draft document. World Bank, Washington, DC.

Turner, Mark. 2002. "Whatever Happened to Deconcentration? Recent Initiatives in Cambodia." *Public Administration and Development* 22: 353–64.

Webster, Douglas. 2002. "Implementing Decentralization in Thailand: The Road Forward." Internal draft document. World Bank. http://www.worldbank.org/wbi/publicfinance/documents/East%20Asian%20Decentralization%20Dialogues%20II/Douglas.pdf.

Wegelin, Emiel. 2002. "Thailand: Decentralization Capacity Assessment, Findings, and Recommendations." Internal draft document. World Bank. http://www1.worldbank.org/wbiep/decentralization/eaplib/wegelin.pdf.

Weist, Dana. 2003. "Thailand's Decentralization: Progress and Prospects." Paper prepared for the Asian Development Conference on Decentralization in Asia, Kita-kyushu, Japan.

Wong, Christine. 2003. "Country Review: The People's Republic of China." Internal draft document. World Bank, Washington, DC.

World Bank. 2000. "Vietnam: Managing Public Resources Better." Public Expenditure Review. Washington, DC: World Bank.

———. 2001. "Indonesia: Priorities for Civil Service Reform." Internal draft document. World Bank, Washington, DC.

———. 2002a. "China: National Development and Subnational Finance—A Review of Provincial Expenditures." Washington, DC: World Bank.

———. 2002b. "Decentralization and Deconcentration in Cambodia." Internal draft document for the Cambodia Public Expenditure Review. World Bank, Washington, DC.

———. 2002c. "Vietnam: Delivering on Its Promise." Vietnam Development Report. Washington, DC: World Bank.

———. 2003a. "Cambodia: Enhancing Service Delivery through Improved Resource Allocation and Institutional Reform." Integrated Fiduciary Assessment and Public Expenditure Review. Washington, DC: World Bank.

———. 2003b. "China Country Economic Memorandum: Promoting Growth with Equity." Washington, DC: World Bank.

———. 2003c. "Combating Corruption in Indonesia: Enhancing Accountability for Development." Washington, DC: World Bank.

———. 2003d. "Decentralizing Indonesia. A Regional Public Expenditure Review Overview Report." Washington, DC: World Bank.

———. 2003e. "Human Resource Management." Internal draft document for Philippines Decentralization and Service Delivery Study. World Bank, Washington, DC.

———. 2003f. "Philippines Decentralization and Service Delivery Study." Internal draft document. World Bank, Washington, DC.

———. 2003g. "Thailand Country Development Partnership: Governance and Public Sector Reform," Phase I Monitoring Workshop. Washington, DC: World Bank.

———. 2003h. *World Development Report 2004: Making Services Work for Poor People*. Washington, DC: World Bank; and New York: Oxford University Press.

———. n.d. "Subnational Government." www1.worldbank.org/publicsector/civilservice/subnational.htm.

WHO (World Health Organization). 2003. "Functional Analysis for Human Resources: Kampong Cham Province." Geneva: World Health Organization.

8

DECENTRALIZING HEALTH: LESSONS FROM INDONESIA, THE PHILIPPINES, AND VIETNAM

Samuel S. Lieberman, Joseph J. Capuno, and Hoang Van Minh

This chapter examines the decentralization experience of three East Asian countries from the perspective of how well they have addressed the special features and requirements of the health sector. These features include the substantial role of externalities, the high degree of specialization, the critical role of quality and timeliness, and the high level of knowledge required to participate in the health care system at all levels. These characteristics have important implications for the design of health policy in general, and especially for a decentralized system of service delivery and sector management. This chapter outlines the decentralization health policies and programs of Indonesia, the Philippines, and Vietnam, focusing on the period 1985–2003, spanning the years before and after significant decentralization began in these countries. The chapter also points to areas where reforms may facilitate more effective health care delivery.

The Health Care Context of Decentralization

Experience with decentralizing health in developing economies is limited, and the literature reveals no widely accepted, best-practice health policy framework. This is partly because decentralization in many low-income countries is a recent development, while affluent countries historically moved in a centralizing direction as constituent states came together to form federal unions.

Another constraining factor has been the top-down, centrist bias in the influential Health for All (HFA) paradigm, used to build dominating but difficult-to-manage and ineffective health ministries in many countries. HFA's main sponsor, the World Health Organization (WHO), has been traditionally uncomfortable with decentralization. The literature on government roles in health systems is relevant to the extent that privatization is a form of decentralization, but this literature misses the critical decentralization issue: the allocation of roles among levels of government. The literature also lacks a connection between options for decentralization and health financing. Meanwhile, most approaches that focus on health challenges—including the Millennium Development Goals of the United Nations and the World Bank–sponsored Poverty Reduction Strategy Papers in developing countries—assume a strong central role for ministries of health.

Nevertheless, a debate has developed around decentralization design issues, with contributors dividing into two camps. Proponents see decentralization, if handled well, leading to systematic citizen involvement in setting the goals, design, and financing for health policy, and in monitoring service provision and other functions. In this view, decentralization can also spur providers to obtain the skills, material support, and authority they need to offer high-quality services. Decentralization can further enable clients to secure information, financing, and bargaining power, and offer health ministries a chance to jettison impractical obligations and carve out a new role and image.

Detractors warn, however, that (badly designed) decentralization heightens vulnerability to near-term crises and longer-term risks. Typical start-up problems include staff opposition, leading to breakdown of deployment and other personnel mechanisms; mismatches between health care funding and spending requirements; ambiguity in responsibilities and premature delegation of functions, leading to deteriorating service quality; and disruptions in reporting, accountability, and quality control. Medium-term concerns include rising system costs. Specifically, downsizing administrative units may yield designs for key health functions that are neither technically efficient nor cost-effective because of diseconomies of scale. Such "transitional" problems may be difficult to correct.

Because of these risks, public health commentators have called for careful introduction and management of decentralization. Most analysts support WHO's recommendation that countries phase in devolution under central guidance, subject to stringent criteria, with health ministries continuing to take responsibility for specialized services, medical supplies, basic education and training, and other key functions (WHO 1995). This advice illustrates two recurring themes: that the overriding rationale for health decentralization is improved effectiveness and efficiency, and that the timing of the process is subject to ex ante design.

Such premises are usually not valid, since the impetus for decentralization is generally political. Improved health is only a second-order objective, with imperatives such as preserving national unity usually driving the process and shaping the decision to devolve to particular levels of government.

That was arguably the case in the Philippines, Vietnam, and Indonesia, which decentralized their health services starting in 1992, 1996, and 2001, respectively.[1] Evidence suggests that health ministries in these countries initially were not prepared to articulate and assume a new specialized role of system manager rather than main provider. Inconsistent policies further indicated that expediency rather than strategy guided official responses to transition problems.

At the same time, the faltering performance of the health systems in these countries before decentralization signaled a need for significant changes in health policy. In the Philippines, improvements in infant survival rates and other health status indicators in the 1980s were beginning to plateau, indicating decreasing returns from health expenditures that were higher than in other developing countries in terms of gross domestic product (GDP) (Solon et al. 1992).

In Vietnam, the collapse of the agricultural financing system and economic reform in the 1980s undermined funding for primary health care services and produced shortages of drugs and skills, deteriorating quality of care, and a decline by a half or more in use of government facilities. Funding gaps also led to higher user fees, which became a financial barrier and reduced access to care by the poor.

In Indonesia, the 1997 financial crisis brought funding cuts that confirmed the susceptibility of the government network to drug shortages and other breakdowns. But performance problems had existed earlier. The country did not sustain favorable trends in survival and nutrition rates from the 1980s in the 1990s, despite large-scale intervention. Use of public services also faltered. After rising to nearly a third, the share of people who sought outpatient care from public providers fell below 30 percent by 1995, and below 20 percent by 1998. Meanwhile, households in the top expenditure quintile were far more likely than the poor to use public facilities as inpatients, and nearly as likely as to use such facilities as outpatients.

Objectives of the Chapter

This chapter examines decentralization experiences in Indonesia, the Philippines, and Vietnam with an eye toward three sets of questions. First, how can developing countries design decentralization to provide an appropriate framework for a public health system, and what policies and instruments promise to be effective in improving the efficiency and equity of a decentralized health system? Second, how should countries handle transition problems and other risks? Third, what lessons do the experiences of these three countries reveal?

In addressing these questions, the chapter examines the emerging role of central health ministries. Critical functions include monitoring and controlling communicable diseases, setting standards and assuring quality for devolved health services and pharmaceuticals, ensuring access of the poor to health services, and sustaining health financing.

The three countries have broad features that facilitate comparison. All have tropical or semitropical climates, and all are highly populated developing countries composed mostly of rural-based agricultural households, with significant numbers of poor. Each country also has a colonial history in which the struggle for independence led to a unitary form of government with a strong center. Communicable diseases are the main cause of morbidity and mortality in all these countries, although each is now experiencing an epidemiological transition that brings growth of noncommunicable, lifestyle-related diseases. Yet each country also possesses unique features that provide interesting contrasts to the other two. Unlike the Philippines and Indonesia, for example, Vietnam has adopted a market-oriented economic policy only recently while retaining socialist features in its government structure. Unlike Vietnam, Indonesia and the Philippines are archipelagos that are insulated to a degree from disease transmission across land borders.

The available data limit comparison between these countries. Official statistics on health, demographics, government finances, and other socioeconomic indicators vary in scope, detail, and quality. The same applies to secondary sources of information. Data constraints also add to the methodological challenges of tracing the impact of decentralization on health amid other socioeconomic factors, external conditions, and policy interventions. Thus, the analysis draws only broad conclusions and policy guidelines.

The analysis suggests that decentralization dividends so far have proved modest and concentrate in some areas of each country. Decentralization may have helped sustain overall improvements in health status and spurred local initiatives in health planning, service delivery, and financing. However, decentralized arrangements have not worked as well as hoped, especially regarding access to high-quality health services for the poor.

The Origins of Decentralization

The fact that these countries have experienced only modest health gains from decentralization reflects circumstances outside the control of policy makers. In particular, these countries introduced decentralization in less than favorable economic and political environments. For example, the 1997 Asian financial crisis underscored the direct link between macroeconomic performance and health expenditures. Before 1998, the Philippine economy—much like that of Indonesia and Vietnam—was growing steadily. Per capita income in the Philippines rose from US$2,310 in 1985 to US$3,870 in 1997. Following the outbreak of the crisis in late 1997, per capita income fell to US$3,730. The impact of the crisis in Indonesia was graver. Its per capita income declined from US$3,030 in 1997 to US$2,580 in 1998; by 2001 per capita income was US$2,900, still lower than before the crisis. Vietnam was less affected by the crisis, although per capita government health spending leveled off and may have fallen after the crisis.

In the Philippines, the crisis prompted the national government to invoke "an unmanageable public sector deficit"—a provision under the Local Government Code of 1991 that allows a 10 percent cut in the Internal Revenue Allotment (IRA) distributed to lower levels of government.[2] Because most local governments depended heavily on the IRA, the reduction further reduced local health spending, especially among provinces and municipalities, which had absorbed the bulk of devolved health functions.

Uneven regional growth aggravated the situation. In the Philippines, provinces in the Eastern Visayas and Northern Mindanao continued to lag behind other provinces, especially those in Metropolitan Manila and surrounding provinces. In Vietnam, the cities of Hanoi and Ho Chi Minh were developing faster than other areas, and similar unevenness existed in Indonesia. Utilization rates and other indicators of health access therefore varied widely across regions in all three countries.

Indonesia and the Philippines also implemented decentralization amid considerable uncertainty following political crises. After the fall of the Marcos regime, the Philippines ratified a new Constitution in 1987 and further articulated strong decentralist provisions in the Local Government Code of 1991. In Indonesia, the overthrow of the Soeharto regime in 1998, and then de facto secession of the erstwhile province of East Timor in 2000, contributed to the clamor for decentralization. The Philippines experienced several military uprisings after 1986, the most recent in late 2003, and has had four presidents and nine secretaries of the Ministry of Health under the present Constitution. These frequent musical chairs in the health ministry have disrupted policy priorities and the ministry's momentum in adapting to a decentralized setting. Persistent rural insurgencies and kidnappings in areas such as Southern Mindanao have made it difficult for both the private sector to pursue investments and the public sector to reach out to the poor.

Weak governance in the Philippines, including corruption in key branches of government, has also led to loss of revenues and waste of limited resources. Mechanisms like Health Boards and other local consultative bodies have seldom been convened for counsel or feedback, contrary to the intent of the Local Government Code (World Bank 2000a). However, the proliferation of nongovernmental organizations (NGOs) and other civil society groups has been a major positive development. Many such organizations now work side by side with key national agencies in agrarian reform, health advocacy, local capacity building, livelihood projects, community mobilization, and governance reform.

A second set of reasons for the modest gains from decentralization in these three countries relates to weaknesses in policy itself. While external factors limited the potential benefits, better management by the central ministry of health, especially in critical health functions, would have helped. Experiences in the three countries suggest how to define and pursue an effective role for the central health ministry.

The next section analyzes the features and implementation of each country's decentralization policy. The following section examines the impact of decentralized health services on health status, service coverage, overall efficiency, and equity in these three countries. Ensuing sections examine intergovernmental fiscal challenges, personnel management, and service delivery under the decentralized health care systems in these three countries. The final section summarizes findings and draws lessons regarding the role of the central health ministry in managing the health sector.

Health Policy under Decentralization

Consistent with their respective constitutions, the three countries passed legislation that enabled, if not mandated, the decentralization of health services. Besides added administrative powers and responsibilities, local governments attained greater fiscal autonomy through higher shares of national government revenues and expanded taxation powers.

In Indonesia, the principal enabling legislative acts were Law 22 and Law 25 of 1999, while Regulation 25 of 1999 facilitated implementation. The Philippines promulgated decentralization through the Local Government Code of 1991, implemented the following year.

In Vietnam, the *doi moi* economic reforms that began in 1986 and the Public Administration Reform of 1995 shaped health decentralization, with implementation based largely on the 1996 and 2002 State Budget laws. The latter two measures brought fundamental changes in the preparation, approval, and execution of budgets for all government agencies, from the central to local levels. Since 2004, province-level People's Councils have had more authority to prioritize expenditures and determine sectoral allocations and transfers to lower tiers, and stronger means of mobilizing resources. Transfers from the center for stable periods of three years will promote local planning, while provinces must produce forward-looking expenditure plans in return.

Decree 10, another element in Vietnam's legal underpinning for decentralization, took effect in July 2002. When fully implemented, this decree will give managers of facilities much greater control over their budgets, and more (though still limited) discretion regarding pay and employment, user charges for nonbasic services, and domestic borrowing.

In each country, later laws further articulated, directly supported, or affected the decentralization of health services. In the Philippines, for example, these laws included the Magna Carta for Public Health Workers of 1992, the *Barangay* Health

Workers' Benefit and Incentives Act of 1995, and the National Health Insurance Act of 1995. In Vietnam, the Seventh Communist Party Congress passed a resolution to broaden the "scope of responsibilities and power of the sectors and localities," and passed the Grassroots Democracy Decree in 1999 (Communist Party of Vietnam 1993; Government of Vietnam 1999).

Main Design Features and Implementation

At first glance, the division of responsibility for critical health functions between the national and local governments in these countries broadly reflects efficiency principles. That is, local governments have assumed responsibility for health functions that are simple to administer or confer localized benefits. The central government or higher local governments have assumed responsibility for health functions with significant economies of scale or interjurisdictional spillovers. For example, basic, primary health care services are assigned to communes in Vietnam, including the network of village health workers, to villages in Indonesia, and to *barangays* (villages) in the Philippines. Primary-level health facilities are assigned to cities and municipalities in the Philippines and to districts in Vietnam. Secondary-level hospitals are assigned to provinces in the Philippines and Vietnam. Tertiary-level and specialty hospitals, on the other hand, are mainly the responsibility of the central government—that is, the central heath ministry—in all three countries.

Central governments continue to provide certain public goods such as health research and development, and merit goods such as maternal, child care, and family planning services. Local governments are often involved in and sometimes cofinance these programs. However, overall, the devolution of health functions and corrective measures reveal flaws.

Decentralization occurred gradually in Vietnam and not without setbacks. Local mobilization was seen as a key element in the country's impressive achievements by the mid-1980s in delivering primary health care. As mentioned, the combined province and commune share of government health outlays was already significant in the early 1990s. Thus, local officers had experience with decentralization when the 1996 State Budget Law assigned additional health tasks to provinces and districts (Fritzen 1999). The law established financial links underpinning a unitary system in which national authority is delegated to lower levels. At each level, budget preparation and implementation are the responsibility of the People's Council.

In contrast, implementation in the Philippines and Indonesia occurred in Big Bang fashion. The former completed the transfer of 45,896 health personnel, along with hospitals, clinics, and other facilities, in 1993, two years after passing the Local Government Code. Indonesia completed a similar transfer in 2001, less than two years after enacting Laws 22 and 25.

The Big Bang approach has its merits, but experiences in Indonesia and the Philippines reveal its disadvantages. In Indonesia, decentralization laws and rules and regulations do not provide enough detail on functional and operational responsibilities, resulting in confusion and divergence between provinces and districts. For instance, provinces are supposed to handle cross-district tasks, but no definitive finding tells them how to apply that rule. The laws and regulations governing decentralization are also often inconsistent with other laws, especially civil service rules. This inconsistency has limited the ability of local governments to right-size inherited health bureaucracies and anticipate personnel matters.

Moreover, administrative preparation was inadequate. For example, many local officials in the Philippines were unaware of the precise nature and extent of their new expenditure responsibilities and powers, and the central Department of Health (DOH) was slow to transform itself structurally and operationally.[3] Lack of personnel severely hampered the Local Government Assistance and Monitoring Service, created to troubleshoot transition problems, and the service lacked clout, as different DOH divisions managed public health programs as before. With DOH looking uncertain, many local governments seemed to adopt a wait-and-see strategy, apparently hoping that the agency would be blamed for the breakdown in the public health system and be forced to recentralize health functions.

In different degrees, these three countries also introduced local governance mechanisms to promote transparency, accountability, and participation as they devolved health services. This, of course, complicated the transition, as local governments initially had to adopt these mechanisms on their own without much guidance or experience, leading to delays, perfunctory compliance, or failure to convene the mandated consultative bodies.

Health Dividends under Decentralization

On the whole, each country sustained favorable trends in overall health status after decentralization (see table 8.1). In the Philippines, gaps in health status across regions continued to close during the 1990s. Measured as the difference in infant mortality rates (IMR) between the poorest region (Eastern Visayas) and the richest region (Metropolitan Manila), the gap narrowed from 15 in 1980 to 9.8 in 1985. By 1990 the gap was almost zero, with the IMRs of Metropolitan Manila and Eastern Visayas 27.4 and 27.1, respectively. In 1995, the gap remained near zero, although the IMRs of Metropolitan Manila and Eastern Visayas improved to 21.3 and 21.6, respectively. Following the 1997 Asian financial crisis, however, the disparity widened. By 2000 the IMR of Metropolitan Manila was 19.4—worse than the 10.7 of Eastern Visayas.[4]

Each study country also experienced an epidemiological transition in the 1990s, in which the incidence of chronic, lifestyle-related diseases like cancer and heart diseases began to match—if not overtake—that of communicable diseases such as tuberculosis and malaria (Solon et al. 1999).

In Vietnam, disparities in survival rates between regions appear to have widened in the late 1990s, captured in the rising ratio of highest to lowest regional IMRs by region. After growing from 1.7 in 1989 to 2.3 in 1994, this ratio rose to 3.6 in 2002. This is not to imply that rates and underlying conditions were static. On the contrary, IMRs themselves fell by at least half in every region between roughly the early 1990s and 2003. However, the decline in these changes was extraordinary, dropping to a third or less of the early 1990s figure in the Mekong, Central Highlands, Southeast, and Central Coast regions.

Some Progress in Health Outputs and Access

The favorable trend in overall health status was arguably due partly to progress in health outputs and service coverage. In the Philippines, for example, the proportion of births attended by trained health workers, and of the population with access to clean water source and sanitation services, rose in the 1985–2000 period.

Similar developments in health status, outputs, and access indicators occurred in Indonesia over the same period. The 2002 Demographic Survey

TABLE 8.1 Selected Health Status Indicators

	Year						
Indicators	1980	1985	1990	1995	2000	2001	2002
Infant mortality rate (per 1,000 live births)							
Indonesia	79	70	60	46	35	33	1.9
Philippines	65	55	45	36	30	29	1.9
Vietnam	50	43	36	32/30	28/18	30/18	1.9
Under-5 mortality rate (per 1,000 live births)							
Indonesia	125	108	91	66	48	45	1.9
Philippines	81	74	66	51	40	38	1.9
Vietnam	70	60	50	43	34	38	1.9
Life expectancy at birth							
Indonesia	55	59	62	64	66	66.3	66.7
Philippines	61	63	66	68	69	69.5	69.8
Vietnam	60	63	65	67	69	69.4	69.7

Sources: World Bank 2002; WHO 2002.

and Health Survey pointed to a continuation or even an acceleration of favorable trends in fertility, contraceptive use, malnutrition, and trained maternal care. Some indicators worsened: immunization rates fell between 1997 and 2002–3 for children under age two, for example, while the prevalence of childhood illness remained the same as in 1997. In Vietnam, on the other hand, output and access measures all pointed in a positive direction between the mid-1990s and 2002. For example, the country reported a significant increase in childhood vaccination coverage, and in the proportions of women receiving prenatal care and giving birth attended by skilled health personnel (Committee for Population, Family, and Children 2003).

Health Expenditures

Decentralization may have more than sustained momentum in improving health status and even reversed worsening trends. Unfortunately, available data do not allow us to verify these two suppositions, nor do input measures such as health expenditures enable definitive conclusions.

According to the *World Development Report 2004*, annual health expenditures remained more or less a constant proportion of GDP throughout 1997–2001 in the three countries. The average annual proportion was 2.5 percent in Indonesia, 3.5 percent in the Philippines, and 4.9 percent in Vietnam. In per capita terms, however, total health spending fell in Indonesia from US$26 in 1997 to US$16 in 2001, and in the Philippines from US$41 in 1997 to US$30 in 2001 (World Bank 2004).[5] Asia's financial crisis led to a steep decline in 1998 in health spending in these two countries: 50 percent in Indonesia and 24 percent in the Philippines. Seemingly immune to the financial crisis, Vietnam's per capita health spending rose from US$16 in 1997 to US$21 in 2001.[6] In general, health expenditures as a percentage of GDP in these three countries were similar to those of most of their neighbors. For example, the average percentage share of health expenditures in GDP in Thailand and Malaysia was 3.7 and 3.2, respectively.

Meanwhile, the public sector share of total health expenditures in each of the three countries did not change much between 1997 and 2001. Indonesia's public sector accounted for roughly a fourth of total health expenditures. In Vietnam, the public sector share fell slightly from 31.5 percent in 1997 to 28.5 percent in 2001. In the Philippines, the public share rose from 43 percent in 1997 to 45 percent in 2001.

A closer look at public sector outlays reveals a shift in the financing burden from the central to local governments. Most local governments devoted health spending to hospital and personal care services, much like the pattern before devolution. This is understandable, as local governments absorbed many hospitals under decentralization. However, this orientation may be inappropriate given the high prevalence of communicable diseases and high relative cost of hospital-based interventions.

The Philippines certainly saw such a shift in financial burden. The annual share of local governments in public health expenditures climbed up from less than 5 percent before 1992 to 12.5 percent in 1993. By 2001, the local share reached 20.9 percent, exceeding the 16.6 percent share of the national government. Moreover, personal care services constitute the bulk of public expenditures for health in the Philippines, and, ominously, a growing portion of the health outlays of local governments as well (Solon et al. 1992).

In Indonesia, regional governments now account for most routine spending, while development spending at the regional level grew fourfold. However, central development outlays rose almost threefold, and nearly half of development expenditures still come from the central budget. Understandably, local governments continue to regard the Ministry of Health as a key supplier of financial resources as well as personnel, equipment, drugs, and vaccines.[7]

In Vietnam in the early 1990s, subnational governments, including those at the commune level, were already spending more on health than the central government (Knowles et al. 2003). Provincial spending accounted for 68 percent of government health expenditures in 1991 (not including revenues from user fees and donor support), while central spending accounted for 13 percent. However, five years later, after the country passed the Law on State Budget, provinces accounted for 53 percent and central units 26 percent of all government outlays. By 2000 the latter figure had fallen to 17 percent, while the province-level share (narrowly construed) had dropped to 44 percent.

However, the thrust of the 1996 legislation would seem to suggest including revenue from health insurance and user fees in the provincial total. In that case, provincially "controlled" outlays accounted for 76 percent of total government health spending, up from 70 percent in 1996. (Donor outlays are treated as a separate category influenced by particular agendas and criteria.)

In light of these financing and spending patterns, it is doubtful that decentralization has widened access by the poor to quality health care. A national client survey confirmed that Filipinos in general were more satisfied with private hospitals and clinics than with government health facilities. Filipinos also tended to rate traditional healers as more satisfactory than any public providers (World Bank 2001a). The low regard for public health services prevailed even among the poor, an indication that the public health system does not serve its target clients well.

A World Bank study of socioeconomic differences in health, nutrition, and population in selected developing countries corroborated these observations (see table 8.2). In the Philippines, children born in 1998 to the poorest families were twice as likely to die within a year as children born to the richest families. The infant mortality rate for the poorest families (48.8) was 1.7 times that of the richest families (28.8). The life chances of these unfortunate Filipinos did not seem to improve with age: under-five mortality rates were 79.8 and 29.2 for the poorest and richest families, respectively.

Vietnam also had disparities in health status across economic groups, resembling those in Indonesia before decentralization. Like their counterparts in the Philippines, the poorest families had infant and under-five mortality rates several times higher than those of the richest families. Discrepancies in health status between the poorest and richest households appeared to be worse in Indonesia than in Bangladesh, India, the Philippines, and Vietnam.

Perhaps because of the inferior quality of public health services, the poor—like well-off fellow Filipinos—continue to self-finance their access to private health services. Private sources, including direct out-of-pocket payments, accounted for an annual average share of 57 percent of total health expenditures in the Philippines from 1991–2001.

Local Initiatives in Health Services and Financing

Decentralization has given local authorities and other stakeholders greater leeway to adapt or even replace once-standard methods for delivering and financing health services. And these greater discretionary powers have led to numerous local innovations in health planning, service delivery, and financing. Most notably in the Philippines, there are the provincial health insurance programs of Bukidnon and Guimaras, as well as other "textbook" cases, such as the health card system of Paranaque City, the City in the Pink of Health program of Marikina City, and the Community Primary Hospital Program of Negros Oriental (Pineda 1998; Bautista et al. 1999; Quimpo 1996; and Legaspi 2001). Several of these programs have received formal recognition from government

TABLE 8.2 Health Status of the Poorest and Richest Population Groups in Selected East Asian Countries[a]

Country (year)	Infant mortality rate (per 1,000 live births)			Under-5 mortality rate (per 1,000 births)		
	Poorest	Richest	Poorest/ richest	Poorest	Richest	Poorest/ richest
Bangladesh (1996–7)	96.3	56.6	1.701	141.1	76.0	1.857
India (1992–3)	109.2	44.0	2.482	154.7	54.3	2.849
Indonesia (1997)	78.1	23.3	3.352	109.0	29.2	3.733
Nepal (1996)	96.3	63.9	1.507	156.3	82.7	1.890
Philippines (1998)	48.8	20.9	2.335	79.8	29.2	2.733
Vietnam (1997)	42.8	16.9	2.533	63.3	23.0	2.752

Source: www.worldbank.org/hnp.
a. Economic groups are based on asset (wealth) quintiles.

BOX 8.1 Local Innovations in Health Service Delivery in the Philippines

Charging User Fees for Health Services in Malalag, Davao del Sur

In December 1993, the local *Sangguniang Bayan* (municipal council) of Malalag, in the province of Davao del Sur, enacted the Malalag Revenue Code. This code established a socialized fee schedule for health services, among other provisions. The graduated payment scheme reflects users' annual family income: those earning ₱15,000, from ₱15,000 to ₱50,000, and more than ₱50,000 pay 25 percent, 50 percent, and 100 percent, respectively, of fixed service charges. The code also gave low-income families priority in receiving health services. Public consultations, hearings, and an information and education campaign overcame initial resistance to the scheme. Partly as a result, the local government earned about ₱1 million worth of fees on an outlay of ₱688,888. This enabled the government to provide additional health services, including surgical, medical, and dental services. With these improvements, the local clientele have become more demanding of the quality of health services and the performance of health personnel.

Transforming a Rural Health Center into a Community Clinic in Sebaste, Antique

Under Mayor Juanita de la Cruz, Sebaste in Antique—a remote sixth-class municipality—became a prime example of how to transform a basic rural health center into a full-service community clinic despite limited resources. With only ₱800,000 in IRA funds from the center, the government tapped foreign donors, local people, and former residents living abroad for support for its health goals while also appealing to the sense of mission of health personnel. After creating a trust fund, the government infused ₱3.085 million into the project from 1994 to 1998. By 1997, the community clinic employed 16 people, including two physicians, and remained open 24 hours a day, providing primary health care, laboratory and pharmacy services, and minor surgery. The clinic has reduced the cost of these services to the local clientele while also serving the medical needs of residents of neighboring municipalities.

Source: Galing 2001.

agencies and private bodies such as the Galing Pook Foundation (see box 8.1) and the Philippine Human Development Network.[8]

Vietnam has seen numerous instances of sponsored and spontaneous innovation at the province level. An example of the former was the health ministry's effort to encourage local responses to childhood diseases, including community-determined indicators (Fritzen 1999). Reactions to HIV/AIDS illustrate the spontaneous case. As in several other provinces, the epidemic spurred the Thanh Hoa government to pursue preventive activities such as harm reduction and 100 percent condom use. These initiatives resulted from strong commitment by the People's Committee. Besides ensuring the participation of the police (Department of Public Security), the committee allocated an annual budget to fight HIV/AIDS. The committee also organized a provincial Steering Committee on HIV/AIDS headed by the Department of Health, under an umbrella Steering Committee on HIV/AIDS, Drugs, and Prostitution Control chaired by the vice-chair of the People's Committee. District and communes adopted the same structures.

In Indonesia, Yogyakarta province showed how to use the country's still immature decentralized framework to introduce health sector reforms and elements of a health insurance system. The province used donor funds to secure technical assistance and conduct assessments, trials, benchmarking, workshops, training, and coordination meetings with districts, as well as advocacy events. The province established a board of trustees and new fund-holder institutions, as well as a benefit package and an insurance premium.

The province has created a plan for a quality council to accredit facilities and license practitioners based on local standards. Meanwhile, the province increased user fees under local control to reflect the actual unit costs of providing services. Task forces developed strategies for improving service quality based on consumer surveys; purchasing equipment; developing accountability mechanisms based on focus groups and the complaint resolution system established during the financial crisis; and improving health workforce management, and submitted a tighter organization structure to the provincial government for consideration.

The province launched the new system in 2003 by paying the premium to enable the poor to use public facilities. The program became available to the nonpoor in 2004, competing with private providers in providing a benefit package. The approach in Yogyakarta gives districts a key role, as specified in Law 22, but also responds to the loss of economies of scale that may make health services ineffective and inefficient. The province encourages cross-district collaboration, especially in upgrading technical support, sharing medical and technical specialists and trainers, and organizing communicable disease control, quality assurance, and health education and advocacy. The Joint Health Council facilitates such activities, with task forces making recommendations. But the provincially staffed Technical Review Team plays the largest role by reviewing district proposals and providing feedback and guidance.

A number of other provinces are closely watching and applying this approach. Central agencies have not been deeply involved, although Yogyakarta sought their guidance on establishing standards for its regulatory framework.

Overall, the health impacts of decentralization are not easy to estimate. Few data indicate significant windfalls in health benefits linked to decentralization. The early phases were not incompatible with sustaining impressive overall improvements in health status, and decentralized governance opened the way to promising local initiatives in health planning, service delivery, and financing. However, much better results would seem to be within reach through policy adjustments.

Identifying appropriate policies—though not easy—is critical. In the Philippines, central agencies, often in partnership with NGOs, have documented, disseminated, and advocated best practices in local public services through the media, educational trips for local officials, and various training programs. Despite these initiatives, however, the speed of innovative practices has been limited, and the overall level and quality of local health services have barely improved. A lack of incentives rather than missing models—including political dividends and other signals—appears to be holding back needed policy interventions by local decision makers.

Health Care and Intergovernmental Fiscal Challenges

A country's intergovernmental fiscal system should meet the complex goals of its health system, as with other public services. The key to an effective fiscal system is "finance follows function." The intergovernmental fiscal system must also usually address horizontal as well as vertical equity, key relationships between levels of government and jurisdictions, and incentives for collaboration. Weaknesses in the design of each country's fiscal system have had important consequences for the delivery of health services.

In Vietnam, the budgeting and financing system formalized in the 1996 Budget Law revealed such challenges:

- Norms emerged during the 1990s to determine almost every kind of input into the system. For example, gaps between provinces in per capita health spending reflect a complex fund allocation based on population norms and allocations to and within sectors. These take into account differing geographical conditions between provinces but do not offset revenue and cost disadvantages and variations in need. The Ministry of Finance may also rely on other criteria during the budget negotiating process.
- Provinces have substantial discretion in allocating resources to districts and communes, and the methods they use vary considerably. Districts have little autonomy, and interdistrict variations are significantly greater than at the province level.
- The norm-based system relies on flows of accurate data. For example, user fees and insurance reimbursement rates reflect costs and expenditures in different settings. Besides the high cost of regularly updating such information, these figures are unlikely to capture variations linked to scale and quality as well as discretionary elements. What's more, because the steps to create fee schedules are cumbersome, time consuming, and costly, the schedules remain in effect for years; that in use today dates from 1995.

- Despite formal autonomy at lower levels of government, the norm-based system constrains flexibility. Civil service salaries have first call on funds and absorb most expenditures. Provinces with fewer local revenues have less flexibility.
- The norm-based process limits sectoral interventions. The Ministry of Health did not fully participate in budget discussions and lacked detailed information on expenditures by provinces and lower levels of government. The ministry also could not assess whether actual spending by lower levels was consistent with sectoral policies.
- Limited investment in local facilities, such as upgrades to community health centers, also affected quality of care, and more patients bypassed such facilities as a result.
- The Ministry of Health focused on allocating funds to national programs aiming at combating high-priority diseases such as tuberculosis. Some of these programs were particularly important to disadvantaged groups and implemented mainly through local governments. However, no mechanisms ensure that once national goals are met, those programs are discontinued.
- Reliance on norms has also discouraged creation of medium-term planning frameworks that facilitate recognition of tradeoffs and set priorities between and within sectors.

The December 2002 budget law, which took effect in January 2004, gives more discretion to subnational governments. Province-level People's Councils have more power and a greater obligation to prioritize health spending, determine allocations and transfers to lower tiers, implement policy, and mobilize resources. The fact that the central government establishes three-year transfers once it reaches agreement with provinces on expenditure plans may allow the Ministry of Health to influence allocations across functions and service levels.

In the Philippines, the primary fiscal vehicle supporting decentralization is the Internal Revenue Allotment (IRA), which transfers funds to local governments. As noted, most local governments depend heavily on this source, as do devolved health services. The central Department of Health (DOH) also created the Local Government Assistance and Monitoring Service to manage transition problems, and to provide financial assistance to local governments unable to maintain health services or meet their Magna Carta obligations because of inadequate resources. DOH also implemented a conditional matching grant program, the Comprehensive Health Care Agreements, intended to secure local funding for devolved functions and core public health programs. This reflected an important part of the country's strategy of using incentives and disincentives to achieve national objectives in a decentralized system.

However, the relationship between service delivery and financing arrangements entailed significant weaknesses. For example, devolution of public facilities led to fragmentation of the hospital referral system. Under the new regime, each hospital or clinic primarily serves the constituency of a local government. Several provinces therefore reduced budget appropriations to urban hospitals and channeled resources to less-well-off municipalities, in the process raising the average cost of urban services. Instead of cofinancing these facilities with the provinces, many cities opted to refurbish their own clinics or build enclave hospitals. Further, weak monitoring of local compliance with Comprehensive Health Care Agreements did not help ensure financing of the devolved services.

Ensuring Equity

In Vietnam, two factors have undermined the distribution of heath services to the poor. First, the central government has not targeted resource flows to poorer provinces, concentrating instead on the supply side by improving multitiered service delivery. The government has taken demand for services largely for granted and has not weighed it heavily in policy making, at least until recently.

Second, longstanding funding shortfalls continued through the decentralization process. Starting in 1989, hospitals in Vietnam were allowed to collect user fees and mark up drug prices, and the resulting revenues became, and still are, a sizable source of health financing. However, user fees were a disincentive to enhanced utilization by the poor. And with user fees only partially offsetting funding gaps, lower quality followed. All this led to reduced use of health services from the late 1980s, with demand often shifting to "private" providers ranging from retired government doctors to informal drug vendors. These developments likely exacerbated variations in health indicators by region and income group, with poorer areas such as the northern uplands recently falling further behind.

Some cities and provinces reportedly reduced user fees charged to the poor and other groups. Recent findings show that distribution of central and local budget funding, official development assistance (ODA), and health insurance reimbursements among provinces benefit the poor disproportionately more than do other sources of province-level funding. However, only the ODA is strongly propoor. Neither central and local budget funding nor ODA relates significantly to province-level measures of health needs, household poverty rates, or the percentage of minorities. The distribution of public health expenditures among provinces is weakly propoor, thanks largely to the state budget and ODA (Knowles et al. 2003).

Decision 139, issued in October 2002, further requires each province to set up a Health Care Fund for the Poor to finance free health care for disadvantaged groups, with budgetary support from the central government. Decision 139 entails a major increase in health spending in Vietnam amounting to D 700 billion (some US$0.5 billion) per year. This program is starting slowly to allow the country to overcome difficulties in identifying the poor and channeling funds to poorer provinces. The program may improve health access in remote areas as it does not cover the indirect costs of care. Along with Decree 10, which gives hospital managers much greater control over their pay and employment, user charges, and use of surplus funds, Decision 139 represents a shift in that the Ministry of Health is moving from direct service provider to sectoral steward, directing central resources to the poor and other vulnerable groups based on clear definitions of eligibility. The directives also imply differentiation of government roles, with provincial health departments organizing delivery of care and Vietnam's insurance agency responsible for collecting contributions and purchasing services.

This change is important because while the main clients of devolved health services in all these countries are the rural poor, their access to quality health services is highly uneven owing to wide variation in local revenues and the flawed design of fiscal transfer programs. In the Philippines, for example, economic growth remains uneven across regions, and only cities have generally robust economies. Most provinces and municipalities rely heavily on fiscal transfers, principally the IRA. However, the IRA formula favors highly populated local governments and those with large land areas, and so does not ensure an overall propoor bias in health services. Studies have also shown that other fiscal transfers, including those administered by the central Department of Health, correlate only weakly with poverty, with poor regions appearing to have received lower DOH budget allocations in 1994 and 1997. On the other hand, one of the richest regions in the country receives a disproportionate amount of the DOH budget (Mercado 1999; Capuno 2002).

As in Vietnam, government hospitals in the Philippines may collect user fees and impose up to a 30 percent markup on drugs. However, cost-recovery rates remain low because of the inordinate volume of charity and subsidized patients. In the case of provinces, for instance, the combined share of hospital fees never reached 13 percent of total hospital outlays from 1992 to 2000. Municipalities fared better, with the share of fees in total hospital outlays rising from 9 percent in 1992 to 29 percent in 2000 (Capuno 2002). But because most hospitals were devolved to provinces, the unintended result of low cost-recovery rates is that many hospitals are poorly maintained, understaffed, and ill-equipped.

Vietnam and the Philippines instituted health insurance schemes in 1993 and 1995 that target the poor. Health insurance in Vietnam has become a significant financing source, more important than in the Philippines (Knowles et al. 2003). Nevertheless, in Vietnam coverage is still low and mainly includes civil servants and others employed in the formal sector. Decision 139 represents a potentially significant scaling up of the number of people with insurance.

Records from the Philippine Health Insurance Corporation (PHIC) show that among those enrolled in the national health insurance program, the number of paying members, from both the public and private sectors but excluding the insured indigent families, grew from about 5.57 million in 1999 to 7.62 million in 2001. This suggests that nearly four in eight Filipinos have social insurance coverage, but that the program is still far from achieving its target of universal coverage. However, since 2000, the PHIC has been aggressive in enrolling indigent families under its Medicare para sa Masa (indigent program). As a consequence, the total number of indigent families enrolled has grown from 2,904 in 1997 to 1,762,116 in 2003. By June 2004, the total ballooned to 6,175,651 indigent families. Whereas in 2001 about 37.8 percent of these indigent members were concentrated in the richest regions, by 2003 the same regions accounted for only about 19.91 percent of the total membership. The fact that other regions have gained significance suggests that a wider set of poor households now enjoys coverage. However, this trend is likely to slow as more local governments must copay with the national government the insurance premium of poor constituents. Most local governments see this contribution as another unfunded mandate.

Health Care Personnel and Civil Service Management

Many local governments find it difficult to hire physicians, nurses, and medical technicians, who are in great demand in foreign markets. In the Philippines, for example, local governments in many areas where tuberculosis is epidemic have found it difficult to hire medical technologists and rural physicians. Indeed, staff anxiety and opposition were major problems during the transition to decentralization in Indonesia and the Philippines. Though usually temporary, staff discontent can affect the quality and quantity of personnel available under decentralization.

In the Philippines, health workers were perhaps the largest group opposing decentralization. Many initially feared loss of job security, "politicization" of their functions and positions, limited career prospects, and lower pay.[9]

To appease devolved workers, the central Department of Health pushed for the Magna Carta for Health Workers in 1992. Among other features, this law provides for higher compensation and extra benefits and allowances to all health workers, including those devolved to local governments, and requires the latter to pay the additional compensation. This unfunded mandate would have demoralized other staff and made some rural physicians the highest-paid local public employees, earning more than mayors, which they considered unacceptable.

As a stopgap measure, the Department of Health instituted the Doctor to the Barrios Program, which supplied temporary, contractual, and better-paid doctors to remote areas. In May 1993 the program began to deploy physicians to 271 municipalities lacking doctors, and by December 2003, 198 of these municipalities had received doctors. They receive an attractive package of salary and benefits for serving two years, and some also receive honoraria and material support, such as free board and lodging, from local governments. However, only about a third remain after their two-year tour of duty, discouraged by the lower pay and fewer privileges that accompany local employment. The number of applicants to the program is dwindling owing to a surge in foreign demand, and conflict areas remain underserved because of a lack of incentives.

To supplement the local health force, the *Barangay* Health Workers' Benefit and Incentives Act of 1995 provided for training volunteer workers and providing minimal incentives to convince them to join *barangay* health stations. These volunteers assist in clerical tasks and minor health procedures, such as weighing and measuring patients. However, these workers do not effectively cater to the health needs of the population.

In Indonesia, the central government established the contract doctor (PTT) scheme in the early 1990s to ensure a flow of doctors to remote locations. Doctors hired after completing their initial medical degree received substantial monetary incentives for practicing in more remote areas for three years, as a condition of advancement. Specialists also had to complete compulsory assignments for one to four years or two to three years as PTT staff.

Discontent grew over the obligatory nature of assignments, relatively low salaries, and poor administration of program benefits. In 1999, regulations were eased to permit alternatives such as teaching in a medical school, working as a PNS (civil servant) in designated areas, or working in private practice as a clinic employee in remote areas. Service requirements for very remote areas were reduced to two years, and new graduates could postpone mandatory service if they wanted to start specialist training. These changes did not satisfy the PTT lobby, and doctors continued to press to scrap the regulations.

PTT issues remained unresolved as decision makers launched decentralization. The Ministry of

Health has been exploring new ideas such as allowing medical personnel to serve in the military and the police. Districts, meanwhile, have stayed with the residual national system despite its flaws, as without central funds and guidance they might not have been able to integrate the numerous centrally assigned, locally based staff transferred overnight via Law 22. Moreover, few districts can turn down central offers to recruit and assign PTT doctors using central funds. Still, district officials are concerned that staffing policies that reflect local priorities and conditions have not been established, including options to "right-size" staffs within each district. This issue arises especially in districts obligated to handle staff oversupply left behind by flawed centralized-era policies.

Strong political and administrative leaders in some provinces have created master plans to reshape the bureaucracy to fit local conditions. These include using downsizing mechanisms such as redeployment of staff, early retirement, voluntary resignation with severance payments, and retraining to encourage entrepreneurship. However, implementation of these plans awaits full political commitment, facilitating legal steps, and an injection of cash. The inability to proceed highlights concerns voiced by district and province decision makers about dependence on central government for salary payments and methods for "right-sizing."

Vietnam confronted personnel issues under decentralization as well, as the distribution of health personnel did not occur exactly as planned. Enough doctors and other higher-level staff are generally available in cities, but numbers are inadequate in rural areas. Provinces with medical schools have about the right number of staff, but poorer provinces do not, especially newer ones with no secondary medical schools. One study showed only 1.7 doctors per commune in the North Highlands and the North Central Coast, while a commune in the Southeast Region averages 6.8 doctors (World Bank 2001b).

The number of health workers at the provincial level is generally adequate (in relation to Ministry of Health guidelines), although some provinces do not have enough specialists. But districts generally lack enough doctors who specialize in priority areas, such as obstetrics and gynecology and emergency surgery. Communes do not have enough doctors (nearly all at commune health centers are upgraded former assistant doctors), and often lack enough staff with other training as well, except in densely populated delta areas and near cities. For example, in 1997, 26 percent of communes lacked an obstetric-pediatric assistant doctor or a midwife. The Ministry of Health requires all communes to retain such an employee, reflecting the high priority accorded to local maternal and child care.

Average monthly salaries of health staff have remained essentially unchanged in real terms since 1994. In 1998, the average monthly salary of a government health worker was merely US$29, even though user fees supplement salaries somewhat. This low pay, compared with the education sector, has induced many health staff to seek additional sources of income, reducing the time, attention, and dedication they devote to their work (Dung et al. 2001).

Service Delivery Mechanisms

Health programs are prime examples of the need to design institutional arrangements carefully to ensure that parties in the service delivery process have the understanding, ability, and incentives to fulfill their roles. Coordination is invariably a crucial requirement of system effectiveness. While a country's central health ministry should take key responsibility for controlling communicable diseases, it cannot do this efficiently and effectively without the cooperation of local governments, as the latter are at the forefront of service delivery.

In the Philippines, programs to combat communicable disease depend on devolved health personnel and local counterpart funds, which are in short supply. Local governments see their participation as another unfunded mandate, and program coordination has suffered as a result. To elicit local support, the central Department of Health under the Comprehensive Health Care Agreements (CHCAs) matches each peso that a local government commits with a higher amount. However, the local government must first commit a minimum amount for its devolved health functions. This requirement has proved stringent, as many local governments initially lacked the resources to finance these functions, much less meet their contractual obligations for vertical programs. DOH also did not develop a monitoring and enforcement mechanism to track compliance. Worse, many local officials believed that strict compliance with the program was not necessary, as DOH would always take the blame for public health failures (Esguerra 1997; Medalla 1996). Hence, only after two rounds of implementation, CHCAs were discontinued in 1997.

In the three study countries, integration between programs within provinces as well as across provinces remains poor. Subnational governments implement national programs separately, leading to overlap and overload of grassroots health facilities.

Vietnam partly solved this problem by giving provinces a greater role in setting goals, developing plans, and using funds for national targeted programs. This is appropriate given variations in disease profiles across regions, and is said to have raised immunization rates and lowered fatality rates.

Low Quality and Unsteady Supply of Drugs at the Local Level

The supply and quality of drugs at the local level have become a concern owing to limited funds, deficient drug management systems, and loopholes in procurement rules. In Indonesia, provinces have not been aware of or prone to intervene in drug supply, stocks, and use at the district level under decentralization. Districts have been able to plan for and purchase their own drugs based on standard procurement practice. However, compliance with quality assurance procedures has been poor, partly because responsibilities have not been clear and districts do not have the technical capacity to handle the task.

In the Philippines, each local government similarly manages its own system of drug procurement, inventory, dispensing, and financing. The quality of locally procured drugs is generally poor, the purchase price is often higher than in private pharmacies, stock shortages are frequent, and irrational drug use occurs. A principal reason is that local therapeutic committees are not constituted, not functioning, or not well trained in modern drug management. Local drug procurement is also corrupt in many places: bids are rigged, qualified bidders are "preidentified," and bidders connive. Moreover, the supply chain extends only to urban centers; poor outlying municipalities rely on itinerant drug peddlers who arrive infrequently.

To ensure drug quality in all public health facilities, the central health ministry in all three countries has adopted drug formularies and drawn up an essential drug list. In Indonesia and the Philippines, the central ministry even advocates and promotes generic drugs. However, these regulatory measures have not ensured the overall quality of drugs, owing to weak information campaigns and enforcement mechanisms. In the Philippines, for example, many local governments, with support even from their own health officials, routinely buy branded drugs because of their supposed proven efficacy. Further, the Bureau of Food and Drugs, which lacks laboratory and regulatory capacity, has not convinced doctors of the supposed equivalence of generic drugs (Lim and Pascual 2003). In Indonesia, hospitals buy drugs and unbranded products outside the essential drug list.

Unlike in the Philippines, in Vietnam and Indonesia state-owned enterprises dominate the drug supply, as they can assure quality more easily than a private drug market. In Vietnam, the state-owned VINAPHARM, which includes central and provincial trading and manufacturing enterprises, is responsible for supplying drugs countrywide. The Drug Administration Department within the Ministry of Health is responsible for overall drug management, supported by the Drug Quality Control Institute and the Drug Inspectorate. In each province a Drug Quality Control Department falls under the Provincial Health Bureau, while a Drug Testing Center and Inspection Department monitor drug quality in the local market.

In Indonesia, four state-owned enterprises produce generic drugs and vaccines. Regulatory functions, including enforcement, are the responsibility of the Directorate General of Food and Drug Control, a unit of the Ministry of Health. Quality assurance efforts include establishing the essential drug list; enforcing standards in the development, testing, registration, manufacture, and distribution of drugs; and overseeing health professionals. Working through 26 province-level branches, the directorate monitors drug quality and safety through follow-up visits and testing programs. The directorate bases inspection of manufacturers on criteria for good practice adopted in 1971.

State-owned enterprises impose their own inefficiencies on the market. In Indonesia, these units are protected by tariffs and limits on final-product imports, constraints on foreign investment, and restrictions on registering new drugs, opening new pharmacies, and the nonpharmaceutical activities of retailers. Reforms adopted in the 1990s relaxed some restrictions on foreign drug companies, encouraged generic drug prescriptions in public health centers, and enforced good manufacturing practice. Hospitals could also keep drug revenues to secure supplies at the facility level.

However, inconsistencies and missteps weakened or negated these pre-2001 reforms, and the outcomes were unsatisfactory. Moreover, districts inherited a flawed and incomplete reform agenda, with impacts on government stewardship obligations. Since Law 22 has taken effect, deviation from established standards, patterns, and procedures has grown. For example, complaints about the physical appearance or expiration date of drugs are widespread, suggesting that longstanding quality assurance procedures are not being observed. Reporting of drug quality problems is not formalized, and procedures for addressing quality concerns are unclear and complicated by multiple sources of drugs and funding. Limited skills surely play a role as well, as many service units and district warehouses depend on unqualified staff. Nor can provinces step in, as they lack the authority to monitor, yet alone supervise, district drug procurement.

More generally, laws and regulations provide little detail on operating responsibilities and have brought confusion and divergence between provinces and districts. For instance, some procurement procedures have spurred small purchases from 15 or more suppliers. Districts usually reject pooled procurement despite possible cost savings.

Nor is there a definitive view on which drugs belong in categories defined by the Ministry of Health in pre-2001 preparations. Central involvement appears to be limited, and provinces reveal no common pattern of procurement. Some are not supplying any drugs, and plan to reduce future drug supply. Some still buy drugs to cover emergencies and temporary district shortfalls. Districts are using their own funds to buy drugs from all three classes of the essential drug list. Meanwhile, the drug supply and regulatory system in hospitals is different from that at the primary care level. Hospitals, which have long been allowed to procure and dispense drugs outside the essential drug list, are buying mainly branded drugs, funded through self-financing revolving funds and using spot buying methods. The change from central to district procurement may have also increased drug prices because of lower procurement volumes. This would likely widen variations in drug prices, reducing equity and lowering the availability of orphan drugs.

Vietnam represents an interesting comparator. As in Indonesia, deregulation of pharmaceutical production and distribution brought heightened activity among informal drug vendors and pharmacy shops and greater availability of drugs throughout the country. Consumer purchases of drugs, especially for self-medication, grew as well, from 2.1 annual contacts per capita with drug vendors and pharmacy shops in 1993 to 6.8 by 1998. However, the two countries differ in their experiences with drug prices. In Vietnam, deregulation brought a 30 percent fall in the real price of medicines in the 1993–98 period, while in Indonesia price reductions do not seem to have followed policy reforms.

Moreover, the risks facing Indonesia are comparable to those of Vietnam, where drug vendors account for roughly two-thirds of health service contacts, and antibiotic resistance has reached epidemic levels thanks to excessive and otherwise inappropriate use.[10] The resistance problem is compounded by the limited training of pharmacists and the low average education level of drug vendors and the public. Even when doctors prescribe drugs, compliance with appropriate treatment guidelines is low. Oversight of health providers is weak as well. Enforcement of the many regulations and decrees governing minimum quality standards and the protocols expected of health providers through regular inspections of health facilities is less than satisfactory.

In the Philippines, on the other hand, a few drug manufacturers and importers, which are mostly multinationals, dominate the upstream segment, while a single drugstore chain effectively controls the retail segment of the domestic drug industry. A parallel drug importation policy has not helped bring down the overall price of drugs because the government chose to maintain an import monopoly with capital of just ₱50 million—not enough to affect the multibillion-peso domestic drug trade.

Health Information Systems

Decentralization in Indonesia, the Philippines, and Vietnam has fragmented the health information system and undermined coordination among various sectors, and thus effective and efficient control of communicable diseases. Subnational governments are unaware of their roles, and, more critically, lack the incentives and technical capacity to assume those roles. Subnational governments need support for activities from collecting health information to providing further inputs to performing overall health planning to actually implementing programs.

From 1992 to 1995, the Philippine Department of Health implemented the German-funded Health and Management Information System, whose main objective was to institutionalize a "need-responsive and cost-effective health information system" at the national and local levels. The initiative introduced software modules and processes to fortify the production and use of information. Besides developing district-level health indicators, the system supported innovations in community health care financing and service delivery. However, the initiative stopped short of a nationally integrated but locally operated health information system and was not sustained.

In Indonesia and the Philippines, the central health ministry relies on local governments to report information voluntarily. This has resulted in erratic or delayed submission and poor-quality data. The devolved staff members who were responsible for such data under the old regime now supply information on health expenditures and input indicators to provincial and lower-level elected officials, who are less concerned with outputs and outcome indicators.

In Indonesia, only 36 percent of health centers reported infectious disease surveillance data in 2002.[11] Those that do report do so irregularly or late. Thus, the limited data that flow through the system may not be reliable enough for use in planning, policy analysis, or evaluation.

In these countries, the central health ministry, lacking information, is less able to monitor the quality of laboratory services, hospitals, and other devolved services. This is worrisome as, for example, local health centers in the Philippines are responsible for both finding cases of tuberculosis, which requires sputum examination, and monitoring cases. Indonesia discontinued some programs such as those tracking leprosy because districts did not monitor the number of cases. Quality assurance systems for provincial hospitals in both the Philippines and Indonesia continue to rely heavily on input indicators such as the number of beds, floor area, and medical instruments, with only infrequent verification of such information by local governments.

In the Philippines, although the Department of Health deploys its own representative to provinces, cities, and municipalities to help monitor disease outbreaks and coordinate vertical programs, the flow of health information remains slow. DOH representatives must often double-up as service providers, as many local governments lack the needed personnel.

Performance Standards and Incentives

In the Philippines, efforts to improve the quality of health services have relied on both incentives, including awards and accreditation measures, and disincentives. One example of an approach that encourages local governments to upgrade their health services is the Sentrong Sigla accreditation. Aside from providing a mark of quality, this accreditation originally conveyed a ₱1 million grant to local health centers. Based mostly on input indicators of a health facility's "readiness to provide services," the program had certified some 48 percent of health centers, 14 percent of district and provincial hospitals, and 3 percent of *barangay* health stations by October 2003. Though these numbers are encouraging, they represent only a minority of the country's facilities. Moreover, most of the cash awardees are better-off municipalities that do not need the funds as urgently as localities that do not qualify (Lamberte 2003).

In the Philippines, the Department of Health issued Administrative Order no.100 in 2003, which established new guidelines to improve the Sentrong Sigla program. Instead of cash awards, the new guidelines specify a matching grant for new qualifiers, and also make certification a prerequisite for other DOH grants and the Capitation Fund program, recently introduced by the Philippine Health Insurance Corp. Under the latter program, an accredited local government can claim reimbursement for services extended to PHIC-insured indigent families in their localities. However, these accreditation schemes are voluntary.

Vietnam and Indonesia, in contrast, have adopted norm setting as their approach. Vietnam's Ministry of Health sets province-level norms, but quality remains uneven because province and district health officials introduce norms and guidelines as well. The Ministry of Health has used decrees and circulars to define the quality of human resources and equipment and performance standards. The ministry also has issued more than 100 treatment guidelines, though a survey conducted in 20 district hospitals in 2000 on acute respiratory infections showed that compliance was 25 to 40 percent, probably reflecting weak support and supervision at the local level. Meanwhile, overuse and overprescription of injection drugs were common, with representatives of drug companies influencing physicians' prescriptions (Dung et al. 2001).

Indonesia established minimum health service standards by ministerial decree in 2003. Districts must deliver services according to local needs in 32 areas, including immunization, nutrition services, prevention of communicable diseases, and curative care. Such standards will help define the service levels that districts are accountable for delivering. Whether these standards will be requirements or targets needs further consideration, along with measures for dealing with districts that do not meet the standards.

Toward a New Role for Ministries of Health

Decentralization in Indonesia, the Philippines, and Vietnam may help sustain overall improvements in health that have occurred during the last two decades. Decentralization has appeared to spur local initiative in planning, delivering, and financing services. Users are now participating in planning in many regions, leading to more appropriate and better-targeted health services. Volunteers supplement limited local financial and technical resources. More important, perhaps, citizenship and trust in local government have deepened. The resulting efficiency gains and social capital support the decentralization of health services.

Still, experience in these three countries reveals that decentralization dividends have been modest for two reasons. First, these countries decentralized health services in less than favorable environments. Inequitable economic growth, population pressures that brought epidemiological changes, and political uncertainties have limited the potential gains from decentralization. Improvements in health status are therefore greater in well-off provinces, and service innovations have failed to spread beyond areas where the local economy is robust and the political situation relatively stable. In these provinces, local governments have had the resources to meet growing demand for health services.

Weakness in decentralization policy also contributed to lower-than-expected health payoffs. These include ambiguities in goals, lack of detailed design, inconsistency with other policies, and poorly thought-out implementation strategy. These follow from the fact that health was not the main—much less the sole—driver of decentralization. The Philippines, for example, included health services in its decentralization strategy only when resistance from the education lobby forced legislators to look at other national expenditures.

Inconsistent priorities have translated into inconsistencies in policies and poor design of policy instruments, especially the intergovernmental fiscal transfer system. Local governments are also typically unaware of the types and timing of national interventions—information that is crucial to their own budget and investment planning. With prior knowledge of available grants, technical assistance, and other support from national agencies, local governments can use information on local needs, and proximity and direct accountability to beneficiaries, more effectively.

In Indonesia, the slow and arduous emergence of a consensus on a health decentralization framework partly reflects a governmentwide determination to avoid service interruptions. But this focus has also allowed the central government to postpone difficult decisions over the role and scale of key central ministries.

The Indonesian Ministry of Health also tends to view the public as passive service recipients rather than discriminating customers, owners, and potential allies, and to present itself as a policing and standards-upholding authority rather than a technical agency. What's more, the government has not yet developed a clear concept of the role of provinces in the health system. Decision makers know that districts are typically too small to support cost-effective programs, but they have not designed institutional solutions to encourage joint service areas, or to make provinces agents of public health and related programs.

Policy weaknesses also stem from laws and regulations, introduced in Big Bang fashion, that lacked detail on functional and operational responsibilities and brought confusion and divergence between provinces and other local governments. The Ministry of Health also failed to coordinate with local governments and other actors in performing critical health functions.

In these countries, reactive responses to transition problems did not necessarily resolve fundamental design issues. For instance, in the Philippines, the Magna Carta for Public Health Workers—which provided supplemental funds to only a few local governments—temporarily appeased disgruntled health workers but upset local governments by imposing unfunded mandates. Similarly, the country "resolved" the mismatch between the distribution of the IRA and devolved expenditures after 1992 by providing grants to cities for hospitals they were already financing before 1991. Thus, compensating cities for their supposed "losses" due to the adjustments in the IRA was a politically necessary but costly way of ensuring adequate funding for the health functions devolved to provinces and municipalities (Capuno 2001).

However, efforts to correct these weaknesses could expand the gains from decentralizing health, even within a less-than-favorable environment. Toward that end, central health ministries must focus on specific tasks such as setting up quality assurance mechanisms for drug supplies, safeguarding access to medicines by the poor, and dismantling state monopolies on drugs. Responsibilities for communicable diseases include monitoring national and regional trends, supporting laboratory capacity and quality control and assurance, alerting provinces to outbreaks elsewhere, and advocating for emergency financing.

With the Stewardship of the Ministry of Health

These examples illustrate the contributions needed from central government during decentralization of health services. Above all, central agencies should concentrate on activities that go beyond the direct provision of preventive and curative services, focusing on core public health functions, responding to overall imperatives, and preventing potential failures.[12] These efforts include not only tasks related to pharmaceuticals and communicable diseases but also workforce training, recruitment, pay and benefits, and supervision.

Other core public health functions include ensuring that the poor have access to affordable care, overcoming micronutrient shortfalls, creating sustainable funding arrangements, acting as a source of ideas and best practices from the provinces, and providing technical assistance on a selective basis. As the steward, a Ministry of Health would build consensus on national health objectives and standards, and coordinate rather than require local governments and civil society groups to meet these goals. Instead of relying on sometimes heavy-handed regulation, the ministry should align incentives to elicit the cooperation and participation of all sectors. Rather than impose high standards, the ministry should perhaps promote them through advocacy and by strengthening local governance mechanisms.

The stewardship role also entails pushing for greater consistency among goals, programs, and policies of different national agencies to support local governments. Finally, stewardship includes more than content: it clearly entails leadership and a flexible, opportunistic mode of building partnerships and exploiting opportunities.

Central interventions are warranted partly because these functions may not convey the urgency or tangible appeal of disease-specific programs, and thus districts may neglect them. Subnational governments have little incentive to pursue core public health functions because they cannot fully capture the returns, and because some functions are difficult to perform well because of limited resources or lack of scale economies. The impacts of core public health functions are also hard to measure: gauging the effects of a strong disease surveillance and reporting system is difficult, while the direct distribution and use of drugs by infected patients has obvious benefits.

Has the Philippines Turned the Corner?

The central health ministries in all three countries have taken steps to fulfill this new role, but no definitive transformation into stewardship has yet occurred. Furthest along is the Philippines, whose Department of Health has examined whether decentralization has paid off as a health reform vehicle.

In 1999, under the Estrada administration, DOH formulated a comprehensive decentralization strategy called the Health Sector Reform Agenda (HSRA). The HSRA noted a slight resurgence of certain diseases and persistent inequities in service access. To counter these problems, DOH positioned itself as a health leader, enabler, and capacity builder, administering only certain services (Department of Health of the Philippines 1999b). As a leader, it would primarily be responsible for setting national health policy and regulations and strengthening regulatory agencies. As an enabler and a capacity builder, it would seek to promote innovations and standards in health services, especially at the local level. And as an administrator, it would confine itself to pushing hospitals toward fiscal autonomy, securing funds for priority public health programs, and promoting universal coverage under the National Health Insurance Program.

The novel aspects of this strategy are DOH reengineering and the convergence of all DOH interventions in each province under the HSRA framework. DOH reengineering meant streamlining operations, finances, and bureaucracy, and deploying 1,638 personnel from the central office to regional health offices, retained hospitals, and other DOH agencies. Under the convergence strategy, some provincial officials have drawn up health development plans and interlocal health zones, with the DOH providing technical input and other assistance. These zones bring together contiguous local governments around a district hospital to find ways of improving the hospital referral system, exploiting economies of scale, and containing spillovers.

In December 2004, for example, Capiz province devised a five-year development plan for enrolling indigent families in the National Health Insurance Program, upgrading selected hospitals, and adopting revolving drug funds and new drug management systems, with specific targets and activities at provincial and zone levels. With initial DOH support of ₱10 million, the Capiz plan is expected to yield gains from economies of scale in hospital operations, pooled procurement of drugs, and control of epidemics. Similar arrangements are expected in 2005 in other sites such as Pangasinan, Agusan del Sur, and Misamis Occidental.

As a dynamic process, decentralization in the Philippines will continue to require adjustment guided by HSRA. For example, the country can do more to prepare the intended beneficiaries, such as local governments and health care users, and diffuse political resistance. At the same time, the central Department of Health needs to extend its partnership with health NGOs and civil society organizations with whom it is already working. Local health finances must rest on a firmer footing, including through greater reliance on local funds. Carefully designed user charges would not only make service delivery more efficient but also make local health programs sustainable and help subsidize the health needs of the poor. But to justify higher user fees, local governments must improve service quality and require up-front financing for facility improvements, personnel training and hiring, and drugs and medical equipment. DOH matching grants could support enhanced services if local governments introduced new fee schedules. Grants would also make local public employment more attractive to health workers.

Waiting for Indonesia...

Indonesia has not clarified the health roles and responsibilities of central and lower governments after three years of decentralization. Nor has the country moved to emphasize core public health functions, or seen marked improvements in specific areas such as infectious disease control, pharmaceuticals, and human resources. Sectors besides health also have indeterminate policies, prompting advice to clarify assignments across levels of government and sectors (World Bank 2003a).

Two strands of thinking on decentralization are evident within the Ministry of Health. The first is distilled in a 2003 decree that lists 29 strategic issues related to core public health functions and adds key steps to address them, such as minimum service standards (MSS), partnerships with NGOs, and services for the poor. The decree points to accountability mechanisms and traditional command-and-control instruments to limit the risks of service disruption. The former include the use of MSS to elicit district commitment, including assistance in funding core public health functions. The Ministry of Health has been relatively assertive in exerting its authority in responding to infectious disease outbreaks such as severe acute respiratory system (SARS), and overseeing surveillance of and programs to combat diseases of national importance and involving international obligations, such as tuberculosis and HIV. The Ministry of Health depends on central and donor funding to achieve these ends, though each is unreliable, and has looked for district support, seeing MSS as targets for district spending.[13] The decree assigns key responsibility to district chief executives, and states that efforts to attain MSS should rely entirely on district budgets, with central and provincial governments providing technical help, supervision, and oversight.

This approach is risky. Detailed, extensive MSS could undermine decentralization, and poorer districts could reject them because of limited fiscal capacity. Most MSS have been set at high levels, imposed on rather than owned by local governments, with the means of enforcement and penalties for noncompliance undisclosed. MSS would be better seen as medium-term goals rather than performance requirements that trigger funding and require enforcement. The Ministry of Health needs to develop ways of boosting district ownership of efforts to prevent and control infectious diseases.

The second strand of thinking within the Indonesian Ministry of Health takes a more benign and constructive view of decentralization. This approach is embodied in initiatives under way in Yogyakarta and three other provinces (Lampung, North Sumatera, and West Java), with twenty-one other provinces due to come on stream later. Ministry officials who support this approach are trying to use the momentum of decentralization as a catalyst for sector reform, with provinces playing an important mid-level role. However, the above-cited decree limits provinces to backstopping central and district-level initiatives.

The province-based approach remains new and under trial. It has already survived early bureaucratic and other challenges, but the Ministry of Health needs to carefully assess experiences, implications, and lessons emerging from the province-based framework and disseminate them to key stakeholders. The ministry can also help implement new and existing provincial programs, including interventions that widen and deepen the decentralized approach. The ministry can also support pilot work and research aimed at helping provinces respond to the diverse challenges of managing and developing the health workforce, such as by helping provinces rationalize staffing numbers. The ministry could also sponsor trials of approaches to attract doctors, especially specialists, to remote and undesirable locations. The ministry also needs to develop standards that provinces and districts can use to license service providers; work with professional associations to strengthen quality improvement efforts and establish partnerships for professional development; consult with consumer groups and hospitals on workforce quality; focus on trends in medical education; and fund and deploy special-purpose health teams.

Opportunities, imperatives, and stakeholder pressures could support the Ministry of Health's impetus toward devolution and health reform. Budget constraints may force the ministry to look to districts and provinces as sources of funds and jobs for the health workforce. Demands for better service quality and other public pressures have begun to register with local political leaders and within the national ministry. A medium-term scenario resembles that in the Philippines: contested decentralization followed by a faster pace and major adjustments, leading to consolidation and mid-course correction. The Filipino experience most relevant for Indonesia is arguably the change in outlook within the Department of Health regarding its role in a decentralized system.

Stewardship by Vietnam's Ministry of Health

The tempo of change in Vietnam is quickening, with several distinct drivers governing the pace. The first is the reappearance of deadly public health threats at the top of the policy agenda. Vietnam is clearly vulnerable to new and more virulent strains of diseases such as SARS, HIV/AIDS, and influenza, and reemerging diseases such as tuberculosis and dengue fever. Malaria remains a major public health problem in mountainous and ethnic minority areas.

Successive crises have spawned rapid-reaction structures and shown the importance of timely and well-targeted responses guided by updated disease surveillance data. The Ministry of Health appears to be developing expertise in explaining disease challenges and engaging the public and political leaders while soliciting various sorts of assistance. The ministry has also gained credibility and built stronger ties to decision makers at the provincial level and in key central ministries, including the Ministry of Finance, the Ministry of Public Information, and the Ministry of Labor, Invalids and Social Affairs. These drivers of change could intersect if, as seems likely, the revised agenda on communicable diseases leads to requirements for more spending. This effort should involve a review of arrangements for funding disease control and the possibility of consolidating such outlays. A related issue is the need to avoid substituting for local expenditures; the ministry could make a case for requiring matching contributions from local governments.

The 2002 law requires some acceleration in efforts to adjust government roles. These efforts will entail significant shifts, and the experience and credibility accumulated in fighting SARS and other diseases could prove helpful.

In particular, the advent of provincially managed service delivery suggests the need for formal recognition backed by real authority and resources, with the Ministry of Health focusing on key stewardship functions. Implementation of the 2002 law will thus enable the ministry to get out from under second- and third-best aspects of the de facto health decentralization system that took hold in the 1990s:

- Provinces are supposed to provide updates on how they are allocating their recurrent budget. However, this requirement appears to be largely a formality. The Ministry of Health has little information on health budgets, and it is not clear to what extent, if at all, it can influence provincial spending of budgets already approved.
- The ministry lacks a clear role in formulating and assessing policy and determining central allocations to health; the ministries of Finance and Public Information are the key agencies in this process. Central recurrent health spending reflects projected revenue growth and recurrent expenditures.
- Such incremental budgeting is not sensitive to the goals and priorities set by the Ministry of Health.

The ministry can respond to the 2002 law partly by strengthening budgeting procedures as well as improving allocation. These efforts may include replacing allocation norms and hospital payment mechanisms with instruments based on the price of health care services. The ministry would like to prepare expenditure norms to support management, monitoring, supervision, and control functions, and explore the use of norms that reflect population needs and improve equity in service access and use.

The Ministry of Health also recognizes that it needs other policies with significant near-term impacts to address disparities in health outcomes and per capita health expenditures across provinces. Per capita spending in the richest seven provinces is over three times that in the poorest seven provinces. Central and donor transfers do not provide a counterweight, as the richest provinces receive the largest per capita amount, and because the resources involved are relatively small.

Endnotes

1. No consensus has developed on the starting point for health decentralization in Vietnam. This chapter treats the 1996 Law on State Budget as a path-breaking measure.
2. On December 27, 1997, then-President Ramos issued Administrative Order 372, which effected the withholding of the "amount equivalent to 10 percent of the IRA." Local governments challenged this order before the Supreme Court and won in June 2000.
3. This is a common observation by local officials interviewed for the *Rapid Field Appraisal of Decentralization* (Associates in Rural Development 1993a, 1993b, 1994).
4. The standard deviation in regional IMR also fell from 8.51 in 1980 to 4.84 in 1990, and then to 3.34 in 2000.
5. Figures from the Philippine National Health Accounts also show that total per capita health spending rose from US$20.82 in 1991 to US$29.79 in 2001. In real terms, however, the country recorded a per capita decline from US$12.15 in 1991 to US$8.84 in 2001.
6. Vietnam also achieved a hefty threefold nominal rise in total health expenditures over a five-year period, from US$0.68 billion in 1993 to US$2.17 billion in 1998 (Knowles et al. 2003).
7. This occurs through the JPS-BK (the health component of the social safety net); the fuel subsidy; and the DAK (a special-purpose grant) channels.
8. The Galing Pook Foundation presents awards to local governments for the best innovations in public service delivery. The Philippine Human Development Network uses the Human Development Index to identify and honor provinces that made the greatest strides in promoting health, wealth, and education.
9. Moreover, the Department of Health itself did not anticipate these issues, as the initial plan was to decentralize education first. Opposition from that sector led the government to consider decentralizing health instead (Diokno 2003).
10. Data from the 1998 Vietnam Living Standards Survey indicate that 93 percent of all drug vendor contacts entailed efforts to obtain medicines without a prescription, with little variation across economic groups.

11. A survey conducted by the National Family Planning Coordination Board in 2002 found that less than 10 percent of health centers followed the manual on preventing infections that may result from the use of contraceptives. The survey also discovered that counseling in the family planning program was poor, and that 20 percent of public facilities had never been supervised.
12. The Pan American Health Organization established 11 essential public health functions through international consensus. These have been field-tested and implemented in 43 countries of Latin America, the Caribbean, and Europe.
13. Central spending is limited and subject to strong competition from outside and inside the Ministry of Health. For example, during 2001 and 2002, the central budget was highly constrained, and the ministry's main funding initiative aimed not to control disease per se but to hire doctors to fill vacancies. The ministry allocated some funds for combating tuberculosis and HIV and a few other programs, leaving insufficient central resources for tackling other diseases.

Bibliography

Associates in Rural Development. 1993a. *Synopsis of Findings: Second Rapid Field Appraisal of Decentralization*. Reports submitted to the USAID-Governance and Local Democracy Project. Manila: Associates in Rural Development.

———. 1993b. *Synopsis of Findings: Third Rapid Field Appraisal of Decentralization*. Reports submitted to the USAID-Governance and Local Democracy Project. Manila: Associates in Rural Development.

———. 1994. *Synopsis of Findings: Fourth Rapid Field Appraisal of Decentralization*. Reports submitted to the USAID-Governance and Local Democracy Project. Manila: Associates in Rural Development.

———. 1995. *Synopsis of Findings: Fifth Rapid Field Appraisal of Decentralization*. Reports submitted to the USAID-Governance and Local Democracy Project. Manila: Associates in Rural Development.

———. 1996. *Synopsis of Findings: Sixth Rapid Field Appraisal of Decentralization*. Reports submitted to the USAID-Governance and Local Democracy Project. Manila: Associates in Rural Development.

———. 1998. *Synopsis of Findings: Eighth Rapid Field Appraisal of Decentralization*. Reports submitted to the USAID-Governance and Local Democracy Project. Manila: Associates in Rural Development.

Bautista, M. C. G., M. E. C. Yap, and E. S. Soriano. 1999. "Local Government's Health Financing Initiatives: Evaluation, Synthesis, and Prospects for the National Health Program in the Philippines." Bethesda, MD: Abt Associates.

Brinkerhoff, D., and C. Leighton. 2002. "Insights for Implementers: Decentralization and Health System Reform." Partners for Health Reform, No. 1. Bethesda, MD: Abt Associates.

Capuno, J. J. 2001. "Policy Reform under Decentralization: Financing of Health Services in the Philippines." *Regional Development Studies* 7: 109–28.

———. 2002. "An Analysis of Health Care Financing and Service Delivery in the Philippines under Decentralization." Paper prepared for the Philippine Public Expenditure, Procurement, and Financial Management Review. Manila: World Bank.

Chen, Lincoln, and Linda Hiebert. 1994. "From Socialism to Private Markets: Vietnam's Health in Rapid Transition." Working Paper No. 94.11. Cambridge, MA: Harvard University, Center for Population and Development Studies.

Committee for Population, Family, and Children. 2003. "Demographic and Health Survey 2002." Hanoi: Population and Family Health Project.

Communist Party of Vietnam. 1993. 7th Congress's Resolution of Vietnam's Communist Party. Hanoi: Communist Party of Vietnam.

Department of Health of the Philippines. 1997. "An Assessment of the Devolved Health System in the Philippines, 1996." Manila: Department of Health, Local Government Assistance and Monitoring Service.

———. 1999a. *National Objectives for Health, 1999–2004*. HSRA Monograph Series No. 1. Manila: Department of Health.

———. 1999b. *Health Sector Reform Agenda, 1999–2004*. HSRA Monograph Series No. 2. Manila: Department of Health.

———. 2000. *Department of Health Strategic Plan 2000–2010*. Manila: Department of Health.

Diokno, B. E. 2003. "Decentralization in the Philippines after Ten Years: What Have We Learned? What Have I Learned?" Discussion Paper No. 0308. Quezon City: University of the Philippines, School of Economics.

Dollar, D., P. Glewwe, and J. Litvack, eds. 1998. *Household Welfare and Vietnam's Transition*. Washington, DC: World Bank.

Dung, P. H., et al. 2001. "Improving Physicians' Prescription at Outpatient Department of District Hospitals." Hanoi: Health Strategy and Policy Institute.

Esguerra, E. F. 1997. "Pursuing a National Health Strategy in a Decentralized Fiscal Regime." *Philippine Review of Economics and Business* 24 (2).

Fritzen, S. 1999. "Decentralization, Disparities, and Innovation in Vietnam's Health Sector."

———. 2002. "The 'Foundation of Public Administration'? Decentralization and Its Discontents in Transitional Vietnam." Paper presented at the Asia Conference on Governance in Asia: Culture, Ethics, Institutional Reform, and Policy Change, City University of Hong Kong.

Galing, Kaban. 2001. *The Philippine Case Bank on Innovation and Exemplary Practices in Local Governance*. Galing Pook Foundation.

Government of Socialist Republic of Vietnam. 1999. Decree 29/CP.

Gwatkin, D., et al. 2000. *Socioeconomic Differences in Health, Nutrition, and Population in the Philippines*. Washington, DC: World Bank.

Knowles, J. C., N. T. Hong Hoa, D. B. Huong, N. Khang, T. T. Mai Oanh, N. K. Phuong, and V. Ngoc Uyen. 2003. *Making Health Care More Affordable for the Poor: Health Financing in Vietnam*. Hanoi: Vietnam Ministry of Health and Asian Development Bank.

Lamberte, E. E. 2003. *Sentrong Sigla: The Challenge Ahead and Way Forward—Formative Assessment and Implementation Review Study*. Manila: Philippines Department of Health, Bureau of Local Health Development.

Legaspi, P. E. 2001. *The Changing Role of the Local Governments under a Decentralized State: Some Cases in Philippine Local Governance*. Quezon City: University of the Philippines, National College of Public Administration and Governance.

Lieberman, S. 2001. "Decentralization and Health in the Philippines and Indonesia: An Interim Report." www.worldbank.org/eap/eap.nsf.

Lieberman, S., and P. Marzoeki. 2000. *Indonesia Health Strategy in a Post-Crisis: Decentralizing Indonesia*. Washington, DC: World Bank.

Lim, J., and C. Pascual. 2003. *Toward a Pro-Poor Drug Policy in the Philippines.* Manila: World Bank.

Litvack, J., and D. Rondinelli, eds. 1999. "Fiscal Decentralization, Disparities, and Innovation in Viet Nam's Health Sector." In *Market Reform in Vietnam: Building Institutions for Development.* Westport, CT: Quorum Books.

Manasan, R. G. 1997. "Local Government Financing of Social Service Sectors in a Decentralized Regime: Special Focus on Provincial Governments in 1993 and 1994." Discussion Paper No. 97-04. Makati City: Philippine Institute for Development Studies.

Medalla, F. 1996. "Co-Financing of Devolved Health Services: Lessons from the CHCA Experience." Paper submitted to the Health Policy Development Project. Quezon City: University of the Philippines, School of Economics.

Mercado, R. G. 1999. "Regional Budget Allocation: A Policy Revisit." Discussion Paper No. 99-29. Makati City: Philippine Institute for Development Studies.

Ministry of Health of Vietnam. 1999. *Health Statistic Year Book 1999.* Hanoi: Ministry of Health.

———. 2002. *Annual Activity Report.* Hanoi: Ministry of Health.

Pham Tat Dong, Pham Trong Thanh, Dam Viet Cuong, Duong Huy Lieu, and Nguyen Hoang Long. 2002. "Impact of User Fees and Health Insurance on Equity in Financing, Access to, and Utilization of Health Services." Hanoi: Ministry of Health.

Philippine Health Insurance Corp. 1998. *Annual Report 1998.* Quezon City: Philippine Health Insurance Corp.

Pineda, V. S. 1998. "Health Management: Strategies from Selected Cities." Discussion Paper No. 98-36. Makati City: Philippine Institute for Development Studies.

Quimpo, B. A. 1996. "Devolution Matters. A Documentation of Post-Devolution Experiences in the Delivery of Health Services." Manila: Philippines Department of Health, Local Government Assistance and Monitoring Service.

Rood, S. 1998. "An Assessment of the State of Knowledge Concerning Decentralized Governance under the Philippines' 1991 Local Government Code." *Philippine Journal of Public Administration* 42 (1, 2): 58–82.

Smithson, P. 1993. "Health Financing and Sustainability in Vietnam." Hanoi: Save the Children.

Solon, O., R. M. Gamboa, Brad Schwartz, and A. N. Herrin. 1992. "Health Sector Financing in the Philippines." Health Finance Development Project, Monograph No. 2. Quezon City: University of Philippines School of Economics.

Solon, O., A. N. Herrin, R. H. Racelis, M. G. Manalo, V. N. Ganac, and G. V. Amoranto. 1999. "Health Care Expenditure Patterns in the Philippines: Analysis of National Health Accounts, 1991–1997." Discussion Paper No. 9908. Quezon City: University of Philippines, School of Economics.

Ter-Minassian, T., ed. 1997. *Fiscal Federalism in Theory and Practice.* Washington, DC: International Monetary Fund.

Tuan Tran. 1995. "Historical Development of Primary Health Care in Vietnam: Lessons for the Future." Takemi Program in International Health, Research Paper No. 100. Cambridge, MA: Harvard University, School of Public Health.

WHO (World Health Organization). 1995. *Decentralization and Health System Change: A Framework for Analysis.* Geneva: WHO, Division of Strengthening of Health Services, National Health System and Policies Unit.

———. 2002. *World Health Report: Reducing Risks, Promoting Healthy Life.* Geneva: WHO.

World Bank. 1992. "Vietnam: Population, Health, and Nutrition Sector Review." Washington, DC: World Bank.

———. 1995. "Vietnam: Poverty Assessment and Strategy." Washington, DC: World Bank.

———. 2000a. "Combating Corruption in the Philippines." Washington, DC: World Bank.

———. 2000b. "Vietnam: Public Expenditure Review." Washington, DC: World Bank.

———. 2001. "Vietnam Growing Healthy: A Review of Vietnam's Health Sector." Hanoi: World Bank.

———. 2001a. "Philippines Filipino Report Card on Pro-Poor Services." Washington, DC: World Bank.

———. 2002. "Philippines: Public Expenditure, Procurement, and Financial Management Review." Washington, DC: World Bank.

———. 2003a. "Decentralizing Indonesia: A Regional Public Expenditure Review Overview Report." Washington, DC: World Bank.

———. 2003b. "Poverty." Vietnam Development Report 2004. Joint Donor Report to the Vietnam Consultative Group Meeting, Hanoi.

———. 2004. *World Development Report 2004.* Washington, DC: World Bank.

9

EDUCATION REFORMS IN EAST ASIA: POLICY, PROCESS, AND IMPACT

Elizabeth M. King and Susana Cordeiro Guerra

In most developing countries, responsibility for providing primary and secondary education has resided with the central government. However, a growing number of countries throughout the world, including those in East Asia, are transferring this responsibility away from the center, typically as part of a broader reform to decentralize government functions. This transfer has taken various forms, including devolving fiscal responsibility and management to lower levels of government, making public schools autonomous, requiring the participation of communities in operating schools, expanding community financing, allowing families to choose their schools, and stimulating private provision of education. The impetus for decentralization has often been political or financial rather than educational, yet supporters of decentralization would argue that it can address difficult problems confronting education systems, especially those relating to performance and accountability. Education systems are extremely demanding of the managerial, technical, and financial capacity of governments, so the potential returns to making such systems more efficient and effective are great.

The promise of decentralization lies in giving more voice and power to local leaders and school personnel, who presumably know more about local educational problems than national officials, and who have an incentive to lobby for more resources and to innovate. Indeed, as the broader decentralization literature suggests, the benefits of decentralization lie in reinforcing accountability among those responsible for delivering services—between the central government and local governments, between governments and school personnel, and between school personnel and the communities they serve (Ahmad et al. 1998).[1] In countries as large and diverse as China and Indonesia, generating local solutions to educational problems and mobilizing local energies and resources can yield dividends for all.

Despite its promises, however, decentralization is not a policy panacea. As this chapter shows, choosing an appropriate design for transforming an education system is difficult. What's more, the reform process is never smooth. It is likely to be punctuated by bursts of progress and frequent setbacks, which may lead to rising frustration and growing mistrust among stakeholders who see themselves as losers under the reform process.

This chapter reviews the experiences of East Asian countries in decentralizing their education systems, with the goal of understanding the challenges of designing reforms, distilling lessons on implementation, and examining the impact on educational development. Decentralization laws typically stipulate dramatic reallocations of authority and responsibility among levels of government and also transfers of resources. However, the experience in East Asia—and, indeed, in nearly all countries that have decentralized—suggests a lack of congruence between design and implementation, or between de jure and de facto decentralization.

Several factors have given rise to this incongruence: incomplete design and implementation lags, which may be due to weak technical and administrative capacity, and lack of broad political support for reform. For example, central agencies are not shy about transferring responsibilities for financing and delivering education services to local governments but are not as eager to share corresponding authority and resources, and so find ways of reasserting control. Local governments that are supposed to yield some decision-making authority to schools may also hold back from doing so. Indeed, two common challenges are to align functions, powers, and resources among levels of governments, and to define an appropriate role for the central authority within a decentralized system. Achieving a better alignment of functions, powers, and resources is primarily a matter of improving design in some countries, and of improving implementation in others.

The next section examines the rationale for decentralization in East Asian countries. The principal motives rarely relate to expanding or improving public services, so the allocation of functions and resources often does not provide a coordinated framework for managing services more effectively. The third section reviews the nature and design of education reforms in these countries, as well as their implementation. This section focuses on the overall legislative framework: how decentralization has changed governance and management; which responsibilities and functions countries have devolved; whether resources are adequate to act on these; whether the structure of the system is aligned with the changes; and what functions the central agency has retained. East Asian countries reveal common design features but also important differences, emerging partly from differences in motivation for reform, initial conditions, and the political milieu.

The fourth section reviews evidence on the impact of decentralization and the factors that have influenced its effectiveness. Because educational development is rarely the rationale for decentralization, there is no guarantee that the reform will, in fact, improve education outcomes. With the exception of China, East Asia's experience with decentralizing education is fairly recent and research on its impact nascent, so the review focuses on shifts in education expenditures and on inequality, and then relies on lessons from around the world to evaluate the impact of decentralization on learning. The final section summarizes key findings and lessons about decentralization given experiences in the East Asian countries.

The Impetus for Decentralizing Education

Educational achievement in parts of East Asia is much admired. Japan, Korea, Singapore, Taiwan, and Hong Kong have achieved high enrollment rates and high-quality education, with their students consistently topping international tests (see table 9.1) (Martin et al. 2004a and 2004b). Other East Asian countries have not done as well, but they, too, have achieved high enrollment rates (see figure 9.1). These countries face other educational challenges: The emerging economies of China, Indonesia, Malaysia, the Philippines, and Thailand must better manage their education systems to reduce disparities between wealthier and poorer regions, and to improve the overall quality of education. The poorer countries—Laos, Cambodia, and Papua New Guinea—must expand the number of children who enter school, cut the number who drop out at the primary level, ensure that the system produces enough talent to support economic growth and development, and address difficult problems in financing and managing their education systems.

These challenges, however, have not been the primary rationale and main driving force behind efforts to decentralize the education systems in these countries. Rather, political factors and fiscal concerns have been the impetus.[2] Key design aspects of reform—including central-local transfers, local tax authority, and civil service rules—may therefore ignore legal, financial, and administrative issues that are critical for achieving national education goals, and may establish structures and incentives that imperil those goals.

TABLE 9.1 Student Performance on Mathematics and Science Tests
(ranking among 38 countries)

Country	Mathematics score and rank		Science score and rank	
	1999	2003	1999	2003
Singapore	604 (1)	605 (1)	568 (2)	578 (1)
Korea	587 (2)	589 (2)	549 (5)	558 (3)
Taiwan	585 (3)	—	569 (1)	—
Hong Kong	582 (4)	586 (3)	530 (15)	556 (4)
Japan	579 (5)	570 (5)	550 (4)	552 (6)
Malaysia	519 (16)	508 (13)	492 (22)	510 (21)
Thailand	467 (27)	—	482 (24)	—
Indonesia	403 (34)	411(35)	435 (32)	420 (27)
Philippines	348 (36)	378 (42)	345 (36)	377 (43)

Sources: Trends in International Mathematics and Science Study 1999 and Martin et al. 2004a and 2004b.
Note: — = not available. Scores reported are for eighth grade. Ranking is among 38 countries (1999) and 46 countries (2003).

FIGURE 9.1 Net Enrollment Rates in East Asia, 2000

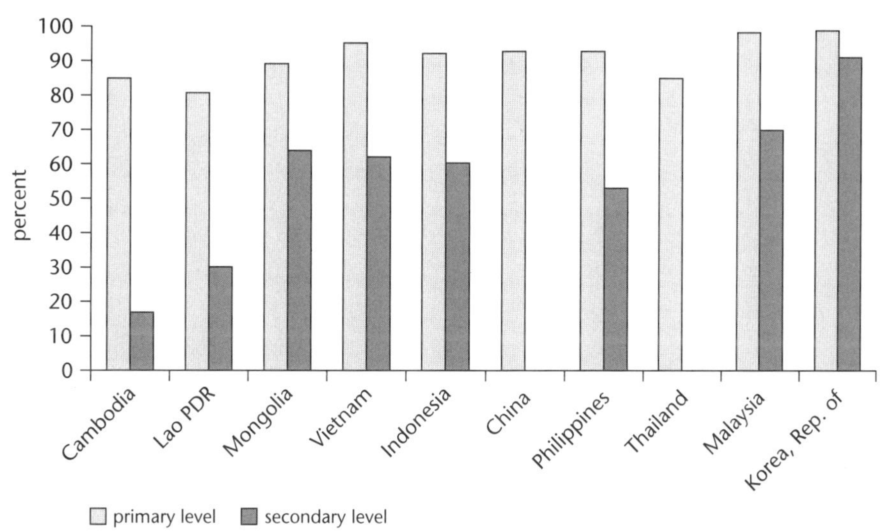

Note: Countries are listed according to their gross domestic product per capita for 2002—from Cambodia to Republic of Korea. Data on Thailand's and China's net enrollment rates at the secondary level are not available.
Sources: UNESCO 2002/2003; World Bank 2003b.

In China, decentralization of education can be traced to the decollectivization and economic liberalization reforms of the 1970s, which laid the groundwork for transferring responsibility for social services to local governments. Fiscal constraints on the central government were also seen as a primary motive for that transfer (Hawkins 2000; Bray 1999; Cheng 1997). In Indonesia, political factors—a national call for democracy, the end of the Soeharto regime, the failures of the highly centralistic government, intensified by the financial crisis of 1997—drove the decision to decentralize all but a few sectors in 1999 (World Bank 2003a). In the Philippines, the 1987 Constitution mandated decentralization, and the 1991 Local Government Code provided legal guidelines for transferring responsibility for providing services to subnational governments. Except for the transfer of construction and maintenance of school buildings to local governments, however, the Philippines has not formally decentralized governance of elementary education. Political considerations underlie this exception. One often-cited reason is that public schoolteachers have traditionally counted votes during elections, so decentralization would make them vulnerable to local politics, possibly compromising election results (Loehr and Manasan 1999).[3]

In Thailand, decentralization is said to result from the groundswell of support for greater democracy, shared powers and resources between the central government and local levels, and greater accountability, culminating in the 1997 Constitution (Mutebi 2003; Weist 2001). The motivation for decentralization in Cambodia was also predominantly political: building democratic governance in a country ruled by centralized power for most of its modern history. Because the regime that emerged from a long civil war was marked by rigid organization, inefficiency, leakage of funds, budget allocation difficulties, and little community participation, civil society and the development community pushed to deconcentrate government functions to improve service delivery, especially for the poor (Royal Kingdom of Cambodia 2001).

The Design and Practice of Education Decentralization

The design of decentralized education across East Asian countries reflects common features. One is that devolved education systems rest on multilayered governance and management structures, with the result that forging a coherent national policy requires a much larger effort. Central and intermediate (provincial, state, municipality, and district) levels of government generally continue to govern post-basic education, but the lowest level of government, and even schools themselves, govern basic education.

China's policy stipulates multiple layers of educational supervision involving the National Educational Supervision Agency as well as corresponding agencies in local governments (Hawkins 2000; Wang 2004). The provincial level takes responsibility for developing specific local policies and regulations in line with national education objectives. The local government—the township level in rural areas (the lowest level of the bureaucracy without education offices), and the district level in urban settings (with education offices)—has responsibility for ensuring that all children receive nine years of compulsory education. Earlier implementation revealed inadequate capacity of township governments to manage schools, so local responsibility for financing and managing basic education in rural areas was transferred from township to the county level in 2001.[4] In 2002, the People's Congress passed the Private Education Promotion Law, which defined the legal status as well as the rights and responsibilities of the private sector, further opening the door for diversified provision and multiple sources of funding for education (Wang 2004).

In Indonesia, Laws 22 and 25 of 1999 transferred governance and management of primary and junior secondary education to district governments, and the upper secondary level to provincial governments, while the central government retains control of the tertiary level. The Education Law 20 of 2003 takes decentralization a step further, moving control of basic levels of education from districts to schools (World Bank 2004a). In Cambodia, recent laws have transferred functions and powers—including the provision of public services—to communes, and the country plans to boost accountability further by increasing the "operational autonomy" of schools and postsecondary institutions (Royal Kingdom of Cambodia 2001).[5]

A second common feature of decentralized education across East Asia is that, at the deepest level, the vehicles for governance and management are typically community councils and school committees involving local officials, civic leaders, and parents. In Thailand, each school is supposed to have a board composed of representatives of parents, teachers, community organizations, alumni, and students. Parents' organizations with jurisdiction over schools are to establish a quality assurance system, and communities are urged to "participate in educational provision by contributing their experience, knowledge, expertise and local wisdom for educational benefits" (Kingdom of Thailand 1999). In Indonesia, each school is supposed to have a School Committee—declared an independent body by the 2003 Education Law—to provide advice, direction, and support for managing schools (Government of Indonesia 2003). In China, school principals are charged with greater responsibility than in the past but also enjoy more autonomy. They are expected to generate additional resources for the school and ensure teaching quality, because they can choose teachers without much intervention from the district or county, as well as determine incentives for teachers (Wang 2004).

Such deep decentralization is common outside the region, too, a means not only of mobilizing local resources but also of fostering greater accountability and better performance. In Brazil, reform in several states has entailed establishing school councils, allowing the direct transfer of resources to schools, and giving communities the power to elect the local principal. El Salvador's Community-Managed Schools Program—better known as EDUCO *(Educación con Participación de la Comunidad)*—transferred management of each preprimary and primary school to an elected Community Education Association composed mostly of parents and other community members (Jimenez and Sawada 1999). These councils are legally responsible for running the schools, raising funds, and hiring and firing teachers, with the goal of improving accountability, attendance, and achievement. Nicaragua's school autonomy reform gave school councils—composed of principals, parents, teachers, and students—the authority to hire and fire teachers, veto power over principals' decisions, and discretion over the sanctions of the Ministry of Education and the obligations of teachers and students (King and Ozler 1998). In Australia, under site-based management reform, school councils develop a school charter, which is a contract between the school and the government, while parents play a supervisory role through the council (Pascoe and Pascoe 1998). Overall, international experience suggests that deep decentralization with empowered, accountable schools presents the best opportunity for improving schools.

One important difference between experience in Latin America and East Asia, however, is that school councils in Latin America elect their members from the community, whereas this is not yet the practice in East Asian countries. Elected council members can truly represent the interests of the community and provide built-in accountability. In East Asia, the duties and legal powers of school committees—in general and relative to school principals, who tend to sit on the committees—are often unclear.

The Locus of Decision Making

Countries do not devolve responsibility and power to lower levels of government and schools wholesale. While a central government may transfer governance and overall management of basic education to lower levels, it may retain control of pedagogical matters, personnel management, and financing and resource allocation, or it may decentralize those functions to school councils. How each country assigns these specific decision areas is, in many respects, a more accurate measure of its degree of decentralization.

In 1998, the World Education Indicators survey, conducted under the auspices of the Organisation of Economic Co-operation and Development (OECD), collected information on the locus of decision making in lower secondary education in a small sample of developing countries, including a few East Asian countries (OECD 1998). The survey examined 38 decisions pertaining to instructional content, personnel management, and resources and financing. To update the resulting data for this chapter, we undertook a similar, though more modest, information-gathering effort in East Asian countries. (See the chapter annex for details on the method we used and a list of functions comparing the two sets of data.)

Both databases reveal de facto rather than de jure decentralization in East Asia.[6] However, these assessments of decision-making authority are subjective for at least two reasons: First, practice can vary widely within each country, so country-level information is impressionistic rather than a "weighted average" of practice across areas. Second, periodic assessments are likely to reflect variation in implementation of legislation, a change in legislation, or both. These factors affect these two data sets. We present the results briefly, nonetheless, as a rough indication of the change in the degree of decentralization of each country relative to other countries.

In 1998, the proportion of decisions related to secondary education made by the central government varied widely in East Asia—from one-fifth in China to three-fifths in Indonesia, indicating that China's education system was then much more highly decentralized than Indonesia's (see table 9.2). At that time, China's provincial and local governments were making one-third of such decisions and schools about one-half, while Indonesia's provinces made less than one-tenth of such decisions and schools about one-third. By 2003, the allocation of decision making in Indonesia and China had shifted considerably. China seems to have retracted powers from schools but widened

TABLE 9.2 Percentage of Decisions Related to Lower Secondary Education at Each Level of Government, 1998 and 2003

Country	Central government		State/provincial/ local government		School	
	1998	2003	1998	2003	1998	2003
Cambodia	—	75	—	11	—	14
China	21	3	33	77	46	20
Indonesia	63	36	7	28	30	35
Philippines	37	62	24	20	39	18
Thailand	55	75	0	6	45	20

Sources: OECD 1998; World Bank survey for this study, 2003.
Note: — = not available. Percentages may not add up to 100 because of rounding.

provincial and local power (among counties and townships)—not uncommon in the country's decentralization history. In Indonesia, the 1999 decentralization reform assigned powers and responsibilities to district governments, quadrupling the proportion of education-related decisions by these governments.

The numbers from 1998 and 2003 for the Philippines and Thailand are puzzling: they imply that these countries have recentralized rather than decentralized during this period. The 1998 data suggest that the central government was making only about one-third of decisions in secondary education in the Philippines, and about one-half of the decisions in Thailand. These countries seem to have pushed back decentralization in 2003, with three-fifths and three-fourths of decision making lying with the central government and the role of schools greatly reduced. Historical background, however, suggests that decentralization to the degree suggested by the 1998 numbers did not exist, and that the 2003 assessment more accurately reflects reality. In Thailand, following the 1997 Constitution and the Decentralization Act of 1999, a Decentralization Master Plan approved in 2000 stipulated details for transferring responsibilities. However, implementation has been slow. In the Philippines, the legal framework for decentralization has not transferred overall management of secondary education to local government, although strong local governments nevertheless use their substantial autonomy under the Local Government Code to supplement their administrative authority.

In sum, despite the transfer of governance of lower secondary education to lower levels of government in these countries, decision making on specific functions actually occurs at different levels of government and in schools.The next section asks whether these countries reveal a pattern in allocating specific decision areas, and whether such allocation is likely to improve the way the education systems operate and thus promote better outcomes.

Who Makes Which Decisions?

With different levels of government involved in multiple areas of decision making, the goal is to ensure delineation and alignment of responsibilities, coordination, and information sharing. Although these challenges may have existed before decentralization, pressure to address them has intensified. Decentralization is not likely to improve the education system if local governments have the authority to hire and fire teachers but not to influence their promotion, compensation, and development, or if schools have the authority to choose teaching methods but not textbooks.

Patterns emerge in the locus and mode of 22 of 38 decisions related to secondary education in the East Asian countries (see table 9.3). Setting curriculum content, instruction time, and teachers' salaries, and allocating resources to schools, remain the domain of the national or state and provincial governments. In contrast, all five countries leave the choice of teaching methods and support activities for students (such as remedial classes) entirely to schools; four of five countries also assign decision making on teachers' careers to local entities. Cambodia is the most centralistic with respect to the 22 decisions:

TABLE 9.3 Locus and Mode of Key Decisions in Lower Secondary Education, 1998 and 2003

	Cambodia		China		Indonesia		Philippines		Thailand	
	1998	2003	1998	2003	1998	2003	1998	2003	1998	2003
Instructional matters										
Instruction time	—	■	■	■	■	■	□	■	■	■
Designing programs of study	—	■	■	■	■	■	□	■	■	■
Defining course content	—	■	■	■	○	■	□	■	■	■
Choosing textbooks	—	■	○	△	■	◊	◊	■	◊	◊
Teaching methods	—	♦	♦	△	■	◊	◊	●	♦	○
Mode of grouping students	—	◊	♦	♦	♦	◊	♦	♦	♦	♦
Support activities for students	—	■	♦	♦	♦	♦	♦	♦	♦	♦
Creation/closure of schools	—	●	△	△	○	△	□	■	■	■
Creation/abolition of grades	—	■	■	■	♦	♦	○	■	■	■
Setting qualifying exams	—	■	■	△	■	■	□	■	◊	♦
Credentialing	—	■	△	♦	■	◊	□	♦	◊	—
Methods for assessing students' regular work	—	■	◊	△	♦	△	♦	■	♦	◊
Personnel management										
Hiring teachers	—	■	♦	△	■	△	○	●	■	■
Hiring principals	—	■	△	△	■	△	○	●	■	■
Fixing teacher salaries	—	■	◊	△	■	■	□	■	■	■
Fixing principal salaries	—	■	◊	△	■	■	■	■	■	■
Career of teachers	—	■	♦	◊	♦	△	◊	●	♦	○
Career of principals	—	■	△	△	♦	△	○	●	■	■
Resources										
Allocation to school for teaching staff	—	■	△		■	■	○	■	■	■
Allocation to school for nonsalary current expenditure	—	■	♦	△	■	△	○	■	■	■
Allocation to school for capital expenditure	—	■	▲	△	■	△	■	△	■	■
Use in school for capital expenditure	—	■	▲	△	■	◊	◊	■	■	■

Sources: OECD 1998; World Bank survey for this study, 2003.
Note: — = missing data. Symbols indicate locus and mode of decision according to this legend: Decision made in full autonomy: ■, Central government; ●, Intermediate government; ▲, Local government; ♦, School. Decision made in consultation or within framework: □, Central government; ○, Intermediate government; △, Local government; ◊, School.

Instructional matters. All these countries are reluctant to delegate standard setting and decisions on core curricula to local governments and schools, reflecting the widely held belief that the education system helps promote a national identity as well as shared values and culture. The management and quality assurance functions of local education councils and school committees remain fairly limited, bounded by a national framework. China's central government continues to keep a close watch on curriculum, selection of textbooks, school-leaving qualifications, and teacher education, and also retains control over core subject areas such as moral-political education (Bray 1999; Shen 1994; Hawkins 2000). A national curriculum framework—developed primarily by the central government with some consultation with local governments and adopted in 1992—specifies compulsory courses. Local autonomy in education content appears to be limited to art, music, and sports. Continuing to take control over the national core curriculum, in 1999 the central government developed new curriculum standards for 18 subject areas for the nine-year compulsory education level. These standards emphasized the need for the curriculum to respond to rapid changes in technology and China's economy (Wang 2004). The new core curriculum also allows for local and school curricula, however.

According to Indonesia's Education Law 20, the central government still determines the curriculum framework and structure for basic and secondary education (Article 38). The central government is also establishing minimum service standards for education. However, district governments, given constrained financial and technical resources, may have trouble meeting these standards. Likewise, in Thailand, the Commission of Basic Education—a pillar of the central education agency—is responsible for proposing standards and the core curricula for basic education in line with the National Scheme of Education, Religion, Art, and Culture. Parents' groups will provide internal oversight of each school, while a central agency will develop criteria and methods for assessing student performance and school quality. In the Philippines, the central government also retains responsibility for policy, curriculum, personnel, and operations.

Decisions on creating or closing a school are made at the national level in the Philippines and Thailand but at the local level in Cambodia, China, and Indonesia. These countries usually decentralize decisions on textbooks and teaching and assessment methods to provincial and local governments. All countries except Cambodia allow schools to make autonomous decisions regarding grouping students and providing extracurricular activities.

Countries outside East Asia show a similar reluctance to surrender control over the substance and quality of education to subnational governments and schools. For example, in Chile, the central ministry maintains curriculum-setting, regulatory, and quality assurance functions (Delannoy 2000). In Australia, the Curriculum Standard Framework defines eight key learning areas, incorporating both content and process standards (Pascoe and Pascoe 1998). Likewise, the British school reform established a national curriculum with learning objectives for core subjects each year and at each key stage (Rodríguez and Hovde 2002). In Spain, which is less centralized, the decentralization law established that the Ministry of Education defines 65 percent of the instructional material taught in all schools, while autonomous communities may define 35–45 percent of domains that reflect regional interests (Hanson 2000). But in other OECD countries, schools choose teaching methods, textbooks, and techniques for assessing students day-to-day, although usually within a framework established by a higher level of government (OECD 1998). This is similar to the approach among some states in Brazil, such as Paraná, Pernambuco, and Rio de Janeiro, where most schools are responsible for elaborating pedagogical proposals and integrating them into the core curriculum process (Machado 2002).[7]

Teacher management. Different levels of government make decisions regarding teachers, often leading to confusion and inefficiencies. These decisions range from teacher training to recruitment, deployment, performance evaluation, human resources databases, payroll, and redeployment. Some countries decentralize some functions, such as hiring and firing of teachers, while keeping others effectively centralized, such as setting compensation levels.

Indonesia illustrates a mixed—and confusing—policy regarding teacher management. The 2003 Education Law stipulates that the central and district governments share responsibility for "getting educators and education personnel to ensure the implementation of good quality education programs" (Article 41), and that these governments will "supervise and develop educational personnel in education units" (Article 44). However, many aspects of teacher management remain centralized, including managing the personnel database, registering personnel actions, and transmitting this information to the payroll system. While districts manage personnel and payroll, the recording of such actions—necessary to trigger the payroll—is still centralized, and, according to civil service law, the central government retains much authority over teacher wages, position allowances, family and rice allowances, and even honoraria. In focus-group discussions, teachers reported that while they support decentralization, they prefer central management of their employment (World Bank 2004a). According to teachers, given that processes such as promotion still require the center's approval, decentralization has slowed action on personnel matters because it has added a bureaucratic layer. Teachers also claim that management processes are neither more transparent nor better monitored, even though they occur at the district level. Without authority or significant influence over teacher-related matters, local governments and schools lack the single most important tool to influence the quality of education.

In countries outside East Asia, the approach to managing teachers is also mixed and reveals a willingness to experiment. In Chile and Mexico, control over contracts is centralized, and a national salary scale standardizes teachers' pay. Other countries have encouraged greater local participation. In El Salvador, community education associations are legally responsible for hiring and firing teachers. In the United Kingdom, while the national level sets a minimum pay scale and qualifications for educators, public schools are responsible for hiring and paying their own teachers. In Brazil, communities across an increasing number of municipalities rely on direct elections to select school directors (Namo de Mello 2005).

Financing and resource allocation. This decision area is the most decentralized, as countries have sought to mobilize local funds for schools—but not without second thoughts. Initial enthusiasm for granting revenue-raising authority to local governments has been dampened by inequalities, followed by attempts to rein in the tendency of local governments to impose many new taxes. Nonetheless, declines in subsidies from the central government and emerging fiscal gaps have forced communities and schools to seek supplementary funding, often by raising user charges.

Fiscal decentralization was a key feature of China's reform, with the central government reducing its subsidies to local schools, and local governments intensifying their efforts to find alternative funding for basic education through taxes, community contributions, and income from enterprises (Hawkins 2000; Tsang 2002). As the central government cut school subsidies, the share of nongovernmental sources rose from 19 percent in 1993 to 24 percent in 2000 (Hawkins 2000). Reform documents suggested six sources of funding: urban and rural surcharges levied by local governments, contributions from industry and social organizations, donations by individuals and community organizations, tuition fees, income from school-run enterprises, and central authorities. In 1994, however, the central government reversed itself and removed certain tax authority from local governments, and has continued to fund teachers' salaries and certain capital expenditures, citing growing disparities across regions (Tsang 2002; West and Wong 1995). The practice of charging fees is prohibited by the central government but encouraged by local governments, which use some of these additional resources to fund a compensatory mechanism. The local government defines the fee scale and collects a certain percentage from fee revenues. For example, district governments receive 25–50 percent of fee revenues collected by schools. The revenues remitted to local governments are then used to help other schools repair their school buildings and improve their facilities (Wang 2004).

Financing for education in Indonesia is also meant to be a "shared responsibility" of the central government, district governments, and communities (Article 46), but legislation has sent mixed messages about how autonomous local governments actually are in raising funds (Government of Indonesia 2003; World Bank 2004a). On the one hand, laws have expanded the revenue-raising ability of district governments and allowed them to determine their own financial management, accounting, and procurement systems within broad guidelines. On the other hand, three design features of the reform limit local autonomy. First, a supposedly temporary hold-harmless component assigns part of the block grant to districts to cover the salaries of existing teachers. Second, the reform earmarks at least 20 percent of the national budget and a similar percentage of the regional budget (net of salaries) for education (Article 49 of the Education

Law). Third, the funding mechanism for education is still too diverse and fragmented. Given these features, some regional education officials have expressed frustration at not knowing the total level of resources actually available to them (World Bank 2004a). Without information or transparency, they find it difficult to plan ahead, to develop coherent and effective educational programs, and to monitor and assess the flow of funds through the system.

In the Philippines, education financing is more centralized because public education is not formally decentralized, but local governments spend their own resources for education nonetheless.[8] The sources of local government financing are the Internal Revenue Allotment (IRA), which the central government sends to each municipality and city, and the Special Education Fund (SEF), which is a 1 percent tax on assessed values of real properties owned by a municipality or city. One-half of the SEF is spent at the municipality or city level and the other half is remitted to provinces for education projects. The provincial Local School Board determines the allocation of this fund among municipalities.[9] Because the Local Government Code devolved construction and maintenance of elementary and secondary school buildings to municipalities and cities, the SEF also sometimes finances such construction and repair, as well as equipment, educational research, books and periodicals, and sports development. Many local governments have also shown initiative in using the fund to establish new secondary schools and hire more teachers, or to top off the salaries of the centrally hired public teachers (Azfar et al. 2001; Manasan 2002).[10] User charges have also boosted local funding: the share of school fees in education spending by households rose to 17 percent in 1997 (Manasan 2002).[11] Fearing that fees might reverse gains in enrollments, in 2001 the central Department of Education prohibited elementary schools from collecting user charges.

If the central government adopts a strong compensatory policy in distributing funds across regions, then local financing and modest user charges can boost performance by allowing parents and the community to exert greater control over school operations. In the Philippines, schools that rely more heavily on local sources—including contributions from the local school board, municipal government, and parent-teacher associations—are more efficient. A 1 percent increase in the share of financing from local sources can lead to a 0.14 percent decline in total costs (Jimenez and Sawada 1996). In Indonesia, local government spending and parental contributions boost school efficiency: cost per student falls as the local share of funding rises, though at a diminishing rate (James et al. 1996). In sum, if used with an eye toward equity concerns, local funding can improve efficiency without worsening inequality.

The role of the central education agency. Under decentralization, the central education authority needs to redefine its role and reform its structures and processes so it can fulfill its new core functions. Lower levels of governments simply have no incentive to carry out some policies and programs because they cannot fully capture the returns, they are unable to perform them well because of a lack of economies of scale, or they do not have enough resources. These policies and programs include setting goals and standards for service provision, experimenting when needed, rewarding innovation from other parts of the system, disseminating information widely and regularly, establishing and enforcing a transparent regulatory framework, and ensuring more equitable education spending.

East Asian countries recognize these roles. The 1985 decision by the Central Committee of China's Communist Party on reforming the education system retains a guiding and monitoring role for the central government on major policies, principles, and the general plan. In 1993, the State Council issued the Program for China's Educational Reform and Development to address weaknesses in the education system and to emphasize the link between the country's economic development and education. This policy guideline provided for local governments to assume more responsibility for managing and financing basic education, and encouraged the gradual establishment of community-sponsored schools, while retaining the central government's role as the arbiter of rules and regulations (Hawkins 2000). This mandate of local responsibility and differentiated levels of management was reinforced by the State Education Commission in 1995 through the Education Law of the People's Republic of China (Wang 2004).

Thailand's National Education Act of 1999 assigned administration and management functions related to academic matters, budget, and personnel to "educational service areas, educational institutions, and local administration organizations" (Section 9) (Kingdom of Thailand 1999). However, this legislation maintains a large role for the central authority in designating standards and defining procedures while supporting local governance through boards and committees.

International experience illustrates the role of the central government in reducing education inequalities within a decentralized setting. In both Spain and Chile, the central government used revenue-sharing and transfer mechanisms to implement this goal. Besides a block grant budget transfer, Spain created the Inter-Territorial Compensation Fund (FCI). As a result, in 1996 Andalucia received 38 percent of state redistributed income and 39 percent of the FCI, while Madrid received less than 1 percent of state redistributed income (Hanson 2000). In Chile, the P-900 program designed pedagogic support initiatives for rural students and the least-advantaged 10 percent of the primary school population. Chile used several measures to improve equity in the 1990s: a capitation grant to rural schools; scholarships for indigenous, low-income, and distinguished students; school feeding programs; and an expansion of preschool education (Delannoy 2000). In 1998, the Mexican government adopted a formula-driven system for allocating transfers to states. Under the new formula, states receive at least the same amount as the previous year, as well as budgetary increments based on the number of needed schools and teachers (Lopez-Acevedo et al. 2003). In Brazil in the mid-1990s, the *Lei de Diretrizes e Bases da Educação Nacional* assigned the federal government the role of narrowing inequalities in access and finance, and launched the Fund for the Maintenance and Development of Basic Education and Teacher Appreciation (FUNDEF) to equalize financing for basic education. This fund guarantees a minimum per pupil expenditure in primary schools throughout the country and partially equalizes per pupil funding within states.

The Impact of Decentralization: Educational Dividends

East Asia's experience with decentralization has been relatively brief, so it is too early to assess the real impact of decentralization reforms on many measures of educational development. This section presents two measures of such impact: the level of spending on education, and geographical disparities in enrollment and literacy rates. The section focuses on three of the five countries—China, the Philippines, and Indonesia, which have had slightly longer experience with decentralization. The evidence is suggestive rather than conclusive, because it reflects not only the effects of decentralization but also those of other reforms and developments. Even if we could capture the direct impact of decentralization, the results would reflect its design, procedural and implementation capacity, and political maturity more than its inherent flaws and benefits. This section also presents the impact of decentralization on student performance, but focuses on lessons from international experience because of lack of data on East Asia.

Greater but More Unequal Education Spending

Has total spending on education grown as a result of decentralization? Are funding levels appropriate? Answers to these questions need to consider whether a country has created an appropriate balance between assigned expenditure responsibilities at various levels and allocated revenues ("vertical equalization"). In other words, local governments should control resources commensurate with their assigned responsibilities, and transfers from the national government should supplement what they lack. Has the spending share of local governments expanded relative to the share of the central government? Has the type of government spending for education changed? Have central governments tended to spend more on, say, capital investments than recurrent items such as salaries and operational expenditures?

China. This country's share of education expenditures in total fiscal spending more than doubled—from 6.7 to 18 percent—from 1978 to 2001. The central government devoted 16.3 percent of its budget to education in 2001 (People's Republic of China 2002). From 1986 to 1992, the budget allocation and out-of-budget funds grew annually by 3.5 percent and 19.7 percent in real terms, respectively, while per-student budgeted spending rose by 9.6 percent at the primary level and 5.1 percent at the secondary level. Yet because China's economy grew rapidly, the share of education spending in gross domestic product (GDP) fell from 2.9 percent

TABLE 9.4 China: Education as a Share of Total Fiscal Expenditures

	1997	1998	1999
Hezheng County	17.3	14.3	13.3
Jinshishan County	19.0	18.4	18.3
Linxia Prefecture	16.0	17.2	16.1
Gansu Province	14.9	15.5	16.0
CHINA	16.7	16.0	

Source: World Bank 2000.

in 1991 to 2.5 percent in 1997, and to 2.2 percent in 1999 (Tsang 2002). Even as a share of total government spending, education expenditures fell somewhat from 16.7 percent in 1997 to 16.0 in 1999, such as other fiscal expenditures rose faster (see table 9.4). Trends varied across counties, however. In some, as Hezheng and Jinshishan, education's share of total spending declined. In Gansu province, which began the period with a lower share for education, that share rose.

Interprovincial disparities in per-student spending have also widened. The highest-spending provinces spend many times more for primary and lower secondary education than the lowest-spending provinces, and these gaps have grown, especially for primary education (see table 9.5). Observers conclude that the lack of a clear equalization scheme is a fundamental weakness of the system's financing (Hawkins 2000; Tsang 2002; West and Wong 1997). While the central and provincial governments provide a financial subsidy to poor areas, the subsidy is small and an ad hoc instrument rather than a regular part of financing for compulsory education. The result is that teachers are not paid on time, many schools are in poor physical condition, and the goals of the Universal Compulsory Education program have been delayed. Despite the program's efforts to raise the minimum provision of education in poor regions, they provide less education in terms of quantity and quality and pass more costs along to families. And, contrary to the law, some county governments are borrowing from the private sector to finance their schools (Tsang 2002). In addition, although tuition fees in compulsory education are forbidden by law, fees in public schools are often collected in the form of a "joint construction fee" or as voluntary donations (Wang 2004).

Philippines. In this country, total public spending on education as a percent of GDP rose at an average annual rate of 6 percent from 1987 to 2001 (see figure 9.2). During this 15-year period, spending declined only during times of fiscal adjustment (1990–94) and financial crisis (1998–99), mainly because of dips in central government spending. GDP grew by 4.1 percent in real terms, so this larger share of education meant a substantial rise in real spending for education. As a share of total spending by local governments, education spending rose from 3.8 percent in 1990–91 to 7.8 percent in 1998–2000, with the Special Education Fund (SEF) fueling a growing part of this local spending, rising

TABLE 9.5 China: Per Student Educational Expenditure, 1989, 1997, and 2000

	Primary level			Lower secondary level		
	1989	1997	2000	1989	1997	2000
Highest-spending provinces	393	2,351	2,756	788	3,425	2,788
Lowest-spending provinces	75	255	261	174	491	420
Ratio of highest-to-lowest-spending provinces	5.2	9.2	10.6	4.5	7.0	6.6
Mean	166	593	492	353	1,096	680

Source: Tsang 2002.
Note: Data for 1989 and 1997 pertain to total education expenditures by provinces; 2000 data pertain only to recurrent expenditures. In 1997, for which both total and recurrent expenditure data are available, the ratios of recurrent spending by the highest- and lowest-spending provinces are similar (9.4 and 7.1, respectively).

FIGURE 9.2 Central and Local Government Education Spending in the Philippines

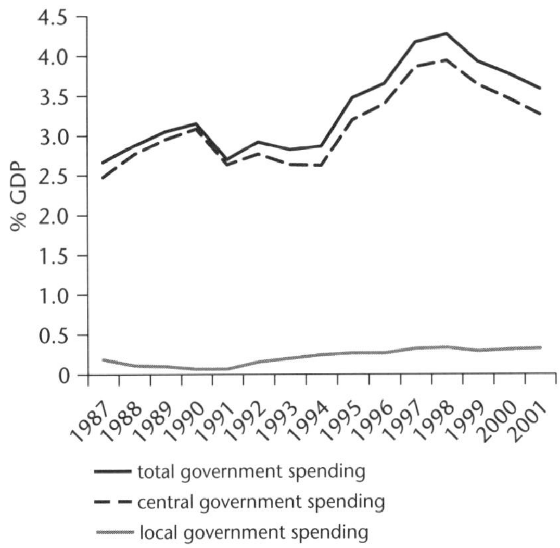

Source: Manasan 2002.

TABLE 9.6 Philippines: Median Values of SEF Resources per Pupil

Income classification	Median	40th percentile
City class 1	590	450
City class 2	382	270
City class 3	341	190
City class 4[a]		140
City class 5[a]		120
Class 1	132	101
Class 2	65.7	51
Class 3	50.2	40
Class 4	46.7	37
Class 5	32.5	26
Class 6	17.6	11

Source: Manasan and Atkins 2004.
Note: The classes pertain to income classifications: 1 to 5 for cities and 1 to 6 for other municipalities.
a. These numbers represent few observations.

from 57 percent in 1992 to 79 percent in 1999. The result has been a shift in the shares of central and local governments in education spending. In 1991, the local government share was only 2.5 percent, rising to 7.4 percent in 2001. Meanwhile, the shares of the central government in both capital expenditures and operating expenditures for education have declined.[12]

Data on average SEF spending per pupil indicate wide variation across income classes of municipalities and cities (see table 9.6). The poorest municipalities spend only 13 percent of the SEF per pupil resources of the richest municipalities, and only 3 percent of the SEF resources of the richest cities. These numbers plainly show that transferring responsibility for funding basic education to local governments leads to wide regional disparities in school inputs.

Indonesia. It is still too early to tell whether decentralization will raise overall public spending on education in Indonesia, but early signs have been positive. Before decentralization, Indonesia was spending the smallest share of GDP on education among East Asian countries: only 1.4 percent. This share rose to more than 4 percent in 2002—a significant expansion in resources for the sector. In 2001, district governments accounted for about two-thirds of total education spending, whereas the share of provincial governments was only 4 percent.

On average, district governments in Indonesia do have more resources at their disposal than in the past, and the allocation formula stipulates that poorer districts should receive larger transfers. However, the central government expects districts to mobilize more of their own resources to supplement the transfers. Herein lies the risk that inequalities among districts will grow, as in China and the Philippines.[13] Decentralization laws have given taxing authority to district governments if the central government authorizes the taxes and districts abide by principles in Law 34 of 2000.[14] The reality, however, is large inequalities in local revenue bases. Many district governments have limited capacity to raise taxes from land, buildings, and natural resources, which constitute only about 5 percent of their revenues. Provincial governments have a larger own-resource base but must share these revenues with district governments. For example, the per capita GDP (excluding oil and gas) of the richest province, Jakarta, is almost nine times larger than that of the poorest province, East Nusa Tenggara (Akita and Alisjahbana 2002). Partly as a result, per student allocations for recurrent and capital expenditures vary widely, with districts at the lower end of the range surely not meeting any kind of education standard (see table 9.7).

Summary. The trends in education spending in China, the Philippines, and Indonesia show that total

TABLE 9.7 Indonesia: Per Capita Education Spending, 2001–2
(in rupiah)

	2001 (actual)	2002 (planned)
Total	134,000 (1,586/463,753)	175,058 (1,193/540,479)
Recurrent	126,118 (998/450,789)	159,460 (1,013/539,287)
Capital	16,185 (177/205,044)	21,692 (402/415,463)

Source: Sistem Informasi Keuangan Daerah (SIKD), Ministry of Finance.
Note: Numbers in parentheses indicate minimum and maximum values.

resources for education have grown under decentralization; yet whether these increases are larger than they would have been without reform is difficult to say. It is also clear that the share of education spending by local governments has grown, partly because the central government has devolved resources and responsibilities for spending those resources to local governments, and partly because local governments are expected to generate their own resources to meet those expenditures. However, local governments are far from equal in their ability to mobilize their own resources, and thus the gap in education expenditures per student between wealthier and poorer areas can only widen. Central governments clearly need to establish a mechanism for equalizing education resources across municipalities and cities.

The block grant system—which gives local decision makers latitude to act on local goals with generally unrestricted funds—does not guarantee that officials will spend enough resources on education. On the one hand, local decision makers may choose to finance budget items that promise a quicker and more stimulating effect on the local economy. On the other hand, they may respond to the desire of local voters for more and better schools, or to the fact that schools provide local employment and can be a source of prestige for the community and its leaders. Greater local funding is expected to create public pressure to spend resources more wisely and thus make the sector more efficient, given an appropriate system of accountability.

Reducing Educational Disparities within Countries

As mentioned, developing countries in East Asia have generally made important progress in basic education. Enrollment rates at the primary level are high, and rates are rising even for post-basic education. These numbers hide large inequalities within each country, however. These inequalities predate decentralization reforms, but those reforms could exacerbate them. Large inequalities in the distribution of resources among geographical regions can produce large disparities in education outcomes. Transferring fiscal responsibilities to local areas and relying on local resources and expertise is likely to widen educational gaps between areas with a strong revenue base and those that are less prosperous while weakening the central government's ability to close these gaps.

China. So how large are within-country differences in education outcomes, and have they increased or decreased since decentralization? China's overall enrollment rates in basic education are high, but provinces differ widely in literacy rates and in enrollment rates at the secondary level. Literacy rates (for those aged 10 and above) rose significantly from 1982 to 1999—in a few provinces by as much as 25 percentage points—and inequality fell (see figure 9.3). The coefficient of variation for literacy rates declined from 0.19 in 1982 to 0.13 in 1999. With the sole exception of Tibet, where literacy was only 35 percent in 1999, literacy rates across China exceeded 70 percent. Despite this progress toward equalization, undoubtedly the result of the national policy of universal basic education, provinces such as Qinghai, Gansu, Guizhou, and Yunnan lag by nearly 20 percentage points behind the most literate provinces of Liaoning, Jilin, and Tianjin. Tibet's literacy rate also improved, but its gain was one of the smallest.

FIGURE 9.3 Literacy and Enrollment Rates in China, by Province

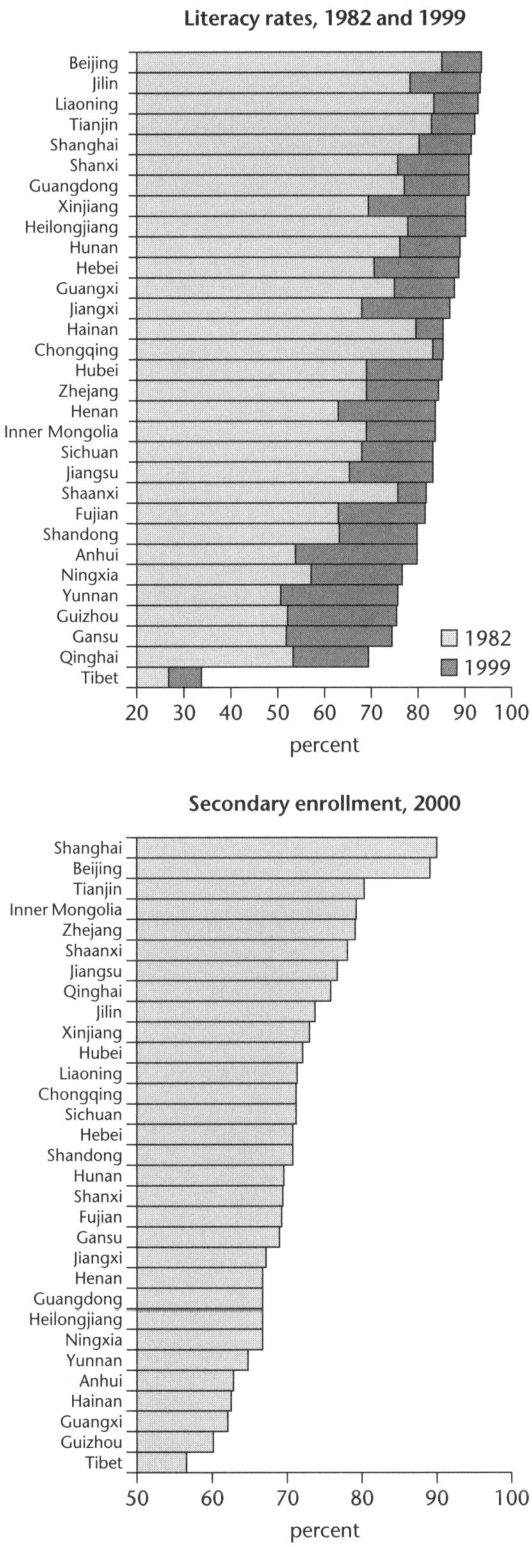

Source: People's Republic of China 2001.

Note: Provinces are arranged in descending order according to values in the more recent year.

Education of minority ethnic groups in poorer, interior rural regions has been a concern. Enrollment rates are 15 and 10 percentage points lower for minority girls and boys than for Han girls and boys, respectively (Hannum 2002). Secondary enrollment rates are also unequal among provinces. In 2000, Shanghai and Beijing had enrollment rates close to 90 percent, while Tibet, Guizhou, Guangxi, and Hainan had enrollment rates one-third lower. But while the coefficient of variation of enrollment rates is smaller (at 0.10) than that for literacy rates, the tendency is for provinces that had higher literacy rates in 1982 to have higher secondary enrollment rates in 2000, suggesting that lagging provinces will continue to fall behind.

Philippines. Similarly, in the Philippines, literacy rates and enrollment rates vary widely across provinces. Literacy rates (for the population age 10 years and above) increased substantially over the five-year period from 1989 to 1994—by as much as nearly 20 percentage points in Western Mindanao, and by almost 15 percentage points in three other regions (see figure 9.4). With these gains, the literacy gap narrowed among the regions, but by 1994 literacy rates still ranged from 61 percent in the Autonomous Region of Muslim Mindanao (ARMM) to 92 percent in the national capital region (metropolitan Manila).[15] These trends do not indicate that decentralization has helped reduce education gaps.

Enrollment rates at the secondary level have also shown significant gains since decentralization, with increases fairly equal across regions.[16] The notable exceptions are the regions in Mindanao: Northern Mindanao is the only region in which secondary enrollment rates declined, and the increases in the other Mindanao regions are smaller than in any other region. In 2002, enrollment rates varied from just 32 percent in ARMM to 94 percent in the Ilocos Region.

The experience of ARMM is noteworthy because it is the region with the fullest autonomy, including in managing its education system.[17] Legislation passed in 2001 contains detailed provisions that the region's schools will adopt the basic core courses, minimum curriculum, and textbooks required by the national government, but will have the preroga- tive and responsibility to add other courses and instructional materials that reflect Islamic values. With respect to the two indicators considered above,

FIGURE 9.4 Literacy and Enrollment Rates in the Philippines, by Region

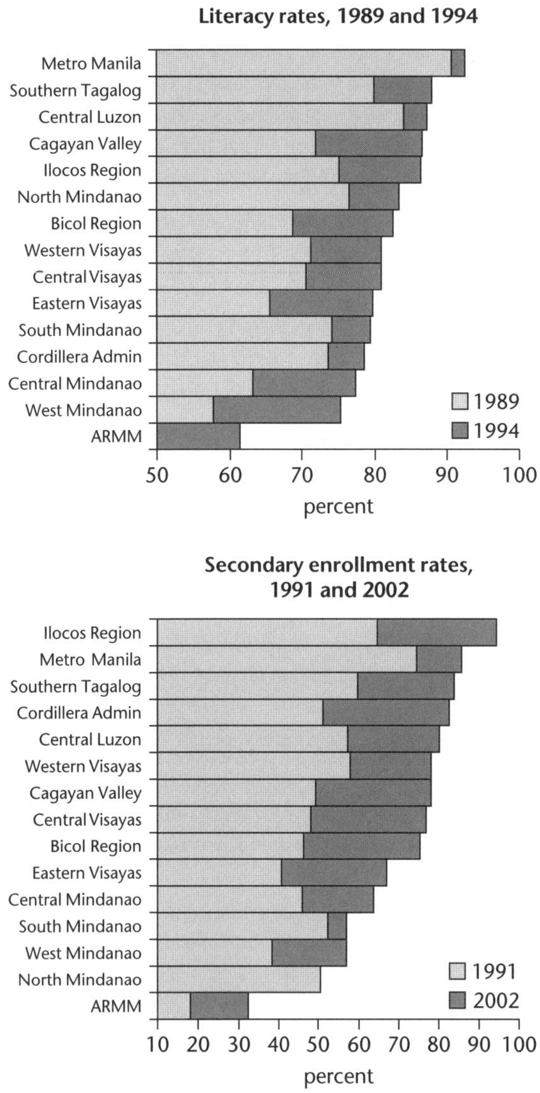

Source: Department of Education Statistical Yearbook, several years; National Statistical Coordination Board.

Note: Provinces are arranged in descending order according to values in the more recent year.

however, ARMM ranked dead last, with changes not large enough to allow it to catch up with other regions. Although the enrollment gap in primary education between ARMM and the rest of the country has narrowed since the 1990s, it remains substantial: nearly 20 percentage points separate school-age children in the poorest quintile in ARMM and those in other regions (World Bank 2003b). ARMM children begin school later and are only about half as likely to continue through the elementary grades, and the transition to high school is particularly difficult. As a result, fewer than 2 of 10 children who enter grade one complete high school. In sum, while at least two other factors might explain the region's poor education indicators—high poverty and protracted armed conflict—it is reasonable to conclude that greater autonomy has not produced better outcomes.

Indonesia. Indonesia's enrollment rates, especially at the primary level, compare favorably with those of East Asian countries with higher per capita income. With decentralization relatively nascent in Indonesia, these overall gains cannot be attributed to the reform. But differences among regions reveal the equity challenge for decentralization. In 2002, the enrollment rate of youths aged 13 to 15 (roughly the junior secondary level) ranged from 68 percent in South Sulawesi to 94 percent in Yogjakarta (see figure 9.5).[18] Increases since 1998 have been modest.

FIGURE 9.5 Enrollment Rates in Indonesia, by Province

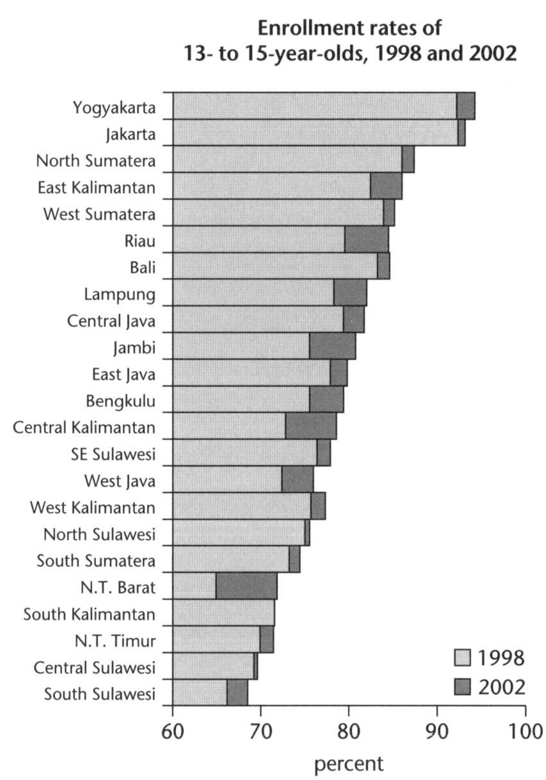

Sources: Susenas 1998 and 2002.

Note: Figure reflects provincial divisions in 1998; the provinces of Aceh, Irian Jaya, Maluku, and North Maluku have been excluded because their sample sizes in 2002 were much smaller and limited than in 1998. Provinces are arranged in descending order according to values in the more recent year.

Disparities within provinces are even larger than variation between provinces. Only about one-fourth to one-third of inequality in enrollment rates in primary and secondary education is due to differences among provinces—the rest reflects differences among districts within a province. This means that equalization among districts within each province is a greater challenge than equalization among provinces.

Overall, these changes in the levels and inter-provincial distribution of education expenditures, and in basic indicators, in China, the Philippines, and Indonesia point to both positive and negative effects of reform. However, the analysis is still at an aggregate level. Ultimately, the test of decentralization's effectiveness is whether schools are better and students are learning better. Decentralization laws encourage greater local and community participation in providing and financing education, but this feature exposes inequalities between prosperous and poor areas, and the inability of poor areas to mobilize adequate resources. Central transfer mechanisms need to equalize resources across areas. Indeed, the push for greater local mobilization of resources in decentralizing countries risks widening disparities between regions with a strong revenue base and those that are less prosperous. But implementing an equalization scheme is a considerable political challenge. On the one hand is the issue of how much inequality in educational outcomes the political system can tolerate; on the other hand is the question of to what extent the system can redistribute from richer areas to poorer areas, and from urban areas to rural areas.

Improving the Quality of Education

Good education is not only about quantitative targets, such as boosting the supply of classrooms, textbooks, and teachers, but also about incentives that lead to better instruction and learning. The level and use of public spending for education is only part of the educational story in East Asia.[19] East Asian countries do not yet have a record of the impact of decentralization on student outcomes, especially on learning. There are several reasons for this: Decentralization is a wide-ranging reform, encompassing and influencing school functions in different ways, so isolating its impact from other changes in the education system and the economy at large is difficult. Student-level data on national exam results are usually not available even to researchers. Summary test results do not allow study of whether differences in test scores result from changes in students' economic conditions or from aspects of the decentralization reform. Lastly, most East Asian countries have relatively brief experience with decentralization. However, evaluations of the experiences of countries outside East Asia provide lessons on the potential impact of decentralization on student performance.

In the United States, two examples are illustrative. The 1995 Chicago School Reform Amendatory Act modified a 1988 autonomy reform by establishing stronger central support functions and requiring external accountability mechanisms.[20] Although attributing causality to either the 1988 or the 1995 reform is difficult because of their complementary nature, student scores in elementary reading and math have improved consistently since 1995. The percentage of students scoring at or above the mean in elementary reading tests rose from 26.5 percent in 1995 to 36.1 percent in 1999.[21] In 1995, Memphis introduced a similar set of reforms that differed in one important feature: city schools received a menu of eight different restructuring models from which to choose. Before 1995, the schools that later became autonomous had lower student achievement; two years later, their scores were substantially higher than those in a control group (Ross et al. 1998).

In Chile, two phases of reform appear to have produced significantly different results. One evaluation concluded that the first phase had either a negative effect on student performance or no effect. A confounding factor was that education expenditures declined during the same period. A later evaluation concluded that the reform did not improve the quality of public schools, and that test scores for the majority of students declined. Another evaluation found that test scores were higher in private schools, but concluded that this was largely because those schools chose better students. Yet another study found that teacher autonomy exerts greater positive effects on student performance when decision-making authority is also decentralized (Winkler and Gershberg 2000; Prawda 1992; McEwan and Carnoy 1999; Hsieh and Urquiola 2001; Vegas 2002). Evaluations of the second phase show more positive results, with an 18 percent rise in language and math test scores on standardized tests. But again, isolating the effects of decentralization from other influences, such as the substantial rise in education expenditures throughout the decade, is difficult.

An evaluation of Nicaragua's 1991 school autonomy reform shows that schools took some time to exercise the new functions and powers given to school councils. Controlling for de jure and de facto autonomy, the results indicate that school autonomy—especially in decisions related to staffing and monitoring of teacher activities—improves student performance (King and Ozler 1998). Moreover, math and language scores were significantly higher in schools where teachers felt more empowered and influential in decision making.

Brazil's reform remains to be evaluated at the student level, but researchers have already used state-level measures of educational performance to assess progress. While school councils and the direct transfer of resources are not significantly related to better student performance, the election of school directors is positively associated with higher test scores.[22] Rather than testing the reform as a whole, the researchers decided to break it down into three components and analyze the impact of each innovation on educational performance.[23] Among reform-minded Brazilian states, the most prominent is Minas Gerais, whose reform included school autonomy and dramatically changed schools' internal structure of accountability (Guedes et al. 1997).[24] As in Nicaragua, however, qualitative studies have shown that while de jure autonomy rarely exerts any influence in most schools, de facto autonomy appears to boost teacher motivation, and thus the potential for improving student learning and participation in the classroom (Cordeiro Guerra 2003).

An evaluation of El Salvador's EDUCO reform found that parents in EDUCO schools participate more actively in school affairs, feel they have more influence over decision making in the school, and have a more direct relationship with teachers than parents in traditional public schools. This greater local participation has had a positive effect on education outcomes. Controlling for school and student characteristics, a study found that students in EDUCO schools do not perform worse on achievement tests despite the fact that they come from poorer families, and that student absences owing to teacher absences are significantly lower in EDUCO schools (Jimenez and Sawada 1999).

In sum, international experience yields mixed evidence on the impact of decentralization on student performance. U.S. experience provides positive evidence, but the experience in Latin America yields ambiguous results. Reform-oriented schools in the cities of Chicago and Memphis have substantially higher test scores than schools in the control group. In Latin America, whereas decentralization appears to have improved student performance in Nicaragua and Brazil, and to have reduced teacher and student absenteeism in El Salvador, evaluations of Chile's long-running reform are inconclusive concerning the impact of greater local participation and school choice on student performance.

Lessons about Decentralizing Education

Experiences in the five East Asian countries are beginning to provide lessons for implementing decentralization—the factors that have affected their experiences, the sources of resistance or support they have encountered, and the risks and challenges that have emerged. Actual practice often deviates from formal rules on decentralization, and it is important to understand why. As mentioned, China has had the longest experience with decentralization and thus offers valuable lessons. While Indonesia and Thailand previously tried to decentralize some functions, their formal decentralization reforms are recent. Cambodia's reform is more accurately characterized as deconcentration, while reform in the Philippines is largely a side effect of a broader decentralization that has formally bypassed education. Indonesia has chosen the rapid Big Bang approach, while Cambodia and Thailand are proceeding at a much more measured pace.

Lessons from these experiences include:

Strive to clarify the assignment of functions, simplify new processes and structures, and provide mechanisms to coordinate and foster a shared understanding of reform at different levels of government, as well as to adjudicate disagreements.

Decentralizing education systems requires harmonizing a complex set of functions at each level and type of education, and is a difficult reform to design and implement. Central governments tend to devolve management of education to different levels of government, but devolution does not happen wholesale. The central government may retain individual decision areas that may or may not cut across levels of education, or may devolve them even more deeply. This complexity leads to confusion, redundant bureaucracies, and weak implementation. Mixed signals from legislation and policies make it difficult for subnational governments and schools to fulfill their functions efficiently and effectively.

Despite two decades of implementing decentralization in China, for example, the division of responsibilities between county and townships is still unclear. The 1994 Guidelines for the Reform and Development of Education state that both county and township governments are responsible for delivering compulsory education, although the former manages education revenues and the latter safeguards the right to compulsory education for school-age children and adolescents. The legislation is unclear on how these responsibilities differ, and also seems to conflict with the Budget Law, which clearly states that each level of government should budget separately for its own jurisdiction (Hawkins 2000).

In Thailand, implementation difficulties stem from vague compromises on the overall decentralization plan and time frame. Local governments are poorly informed about their roles and responsibilities as well as the decentralization plan and time frame. Legislation is itself unclear about the decentralization process. For example, the 1999 National Education Act transfers authority from the central government's provincial and district offices to 175 school districts or local education areas (LEAs), each with its own committee and office. This aspect of the reform, if implemented, would require staffing cuts and redeployment totaling half of all education administrators in various provinces (Mutebi 2003).[25] In response, implementers of the National Decentralization Act argue that they have the authority to transfer power to local governments only after they fulfill a set of readiness criteria. The latter piece of legislation would seem to retrieve some of the autonomy delegated by the National Education Act. Parties have reached a compromise to merge both acts, which entails administrative deconcentration of central power to LEAs in the short to medium term, and gradual decentralization of responsibilities from LEAs to local governments in the long term (World Bank 2003d).[26] Ironically, even this compromise suffers from vagueness on a time frame.

In Cambodia, the initial framework for deconcentrating and decentralizing education is clear about delegating authority to provincial and district authorities, but is much less clear about the roles of the school cluster system and commune councils. The Cluster School Policy, created in 1996, encourages decentralized management of resources, but is ambiguous about what functions school clusters need to perform. Similarly, commune councils, though endowed with new financing mechanisms, lack clearly defined roles and responsibilities. This lack of clarity weakens the institutional structures that are closest to the community, ultimately weakening accountability as well.

The central government plays important but different roles in a decentralized context, and needs to transform both its structure and skills.

Though stripped of some traditional functions under decentralization, the central authority needs to step into its new roles quickly to facilitate successful reform. These roles include setting standards and performance measures for use throughout the education system; ensuring that decentralized units can meet the standards through systems development, training, and funding; and brokering links between local governments to capture economies of scale. The central government also needs to perform overall system planning and forecasting and prioritize investment, including of teacher supply and demand; design and implement an equalization scheme, fostering support from wealthier regions; and stimulate experiments and spread lessons learned.

The central government clearly has a critical role to play in designing and implementing equalization schemes. Decentralization laws encourage greater local and community participation in providing and financing education, but this feature exposes inequalities between prosperous and poor areas and the inability of poor areas to mobilize adequate resources for education, and risks widening those disparities. Appropriate transfer mechanisms can equalize resources across regions. However, equalization efforts are not only about infusing more money into local systems but also—and more importantly—about changing incentives. Implementing an equalization scheme can be a considerable political challenge, as efforts to redistribute from richer areas to poorer areas, and from urban areas to rural areas, may meet resistance.

Furthermore, the relative importance of the roles of the central government is likely to change as decentralization matures, requiring the central government to boost its involvement in certain functions at certain times. For example, it makes more sense for the central government to help build capacity in countries like Cambodia than in those like China, which have a larger national supply of experts. Ultimately, redefining the central government's roles means distinguishing between functions requiring critical involvement throughout the process, those requiring periodic involvement at different stages, and those requiring one-time initiatives with frequent follow-ups.

Decentralization puts the complex architecture needed to operate an education system—personnel, finances, procurement, student assessment, and information management systems—under pressure. This system needs to be reorganized to reflect the new intergovernmental relationships and decentralized functions, and capacity needs to be strengthened.

In decentralized education systems, replacing inappropriate structures and building the capacity to work within new arrangements are key challenges. A principal bottleneck is a lack of adequate technical and managerial experience among responsible parties. A lack of viable and coordinated management systems linking central agencies to local governments and schools exacerbates problems resulting from weak local capacity.

Countries may be tempted to slow the pace of decentralization because of fears that district and provincial governments do not have enough capacity to fulfill their newly assigned responsibilities effectively. Indeed, the traditional approach has been to build local capacity before transferring responsibility and authority because of concerns about irresponsible spending, local corruption, regional inequities, and service collapse. However, although capacity building is important, local governments may have more capacity than most central policy makers assume. As decentralization proceeds, local talents and capacities are likely to emerge and to improve with practice, as is becoming clear in Cambodia, Indonesia, and the Philippines. Furthermore, in China, the capacity of local governments to manage compulsory education seems to have improved substantially, in areas such as training personnel, collecting and using information, expanding the use of technology, and incorporating research findings and consulting experts in the decision-making process (World Bank 2004c; Kerr 1999; Tsang 2002).

For decentralization to exert a positive impact on student performance, information and evaluation systems—as accountability mechanisms—must not only be in place but must also function iteratively through participation.

Information problems become much more acute in a decentralized context. Dramatic shifts in responsibilities and powers often lead to the breakdown of information and evaluation systems, which typically depend on the central government to extract information from lower levels of government and schools. In Spain, decentralizing administrative functions to regions greatly undermined the country's capacity to collect and disseminate national statistics. Newly autonomous regions began to produce their own statistics using incompatible methods, and although the Spanish government took a strong stance on cooperation, it still met resistance. The Education Law in 1985 tried to overcome the lack of coordination across regions through a Conference of Counselors which included the Minister of Education and autonomous community counselors.

Information on performance at all levels is key to accountability. Countries can use sample testing, national surveys, and the census to assess the impact of programs, allocate resources, and identify geographic areas requiring special attention (Asian Development Bank 1999). Local governments, communities, and schools also need information and diagnostic tools to evaluate performance in specific subject areas, define learning challenges in different communities, and compare different pedagogical approaches and teacher training mechanisms. School-level data can also communicate results to parents and the larger community. At the deepest level, information is instrumental for greater accountability and control. Citizens rely mostly on frequent reports, magazines, and participatory workshops to gain information on student performance. However, linking teacher promotion to predetermined inputs and outputs

BOX 9.1 School Report Cards in Paraná: A New Incentive System

In the state of Paraná in Brazil, a new system of incentives at the school level entails producing school report cards. These report cards—known as *Boletim da Escola*—include three main sets of information. These are results from the Statewide Student Learning Testing (covering Portuguese, math, and science), school census data (on student promotion, retention, dropout rates, enrollment, teacher-pupil ratios, and teacher profiles), and surveys of school life (from students, parents, and school managers). The report cards therefore focus on individual school performance while allowing for cross-school comparisons in the state and region. This wealth of information enhances competition across schools, thus strengthening incentives and overall accountability at the state level. If applied consistently across time, this system will also help schools assess the impact of their policies on student performance. One lesson from these experiences is that such systems are not sustainable if they lack local ownership, and if schools do not have the technical capacity to maintain and use them.

Source: Vasconcelos-Saliba 2004.

could create perverse incentives for transmitting information. Some analysts, including the Education Commission in the Philippines, argue that the government should use incentives to make teachers and school heads directly accountable for student outcomes (see box 9.1 for an account of the information system of the Brazilian state of Paraná).

One area that deserves monitoring and evaluation is the flow of funds through the system. In Cambodia, the Department of Finance designed an improved system for monitoring financial performance in 2001. Supported by training and technical assistance, new budget management forms for schools, districts, provinces, and central departments, along with provincial and program reports, will feed into a computerized system. A fund tracking system will monitor inputs and outputs and relate them to strategic outcomes, and will include incentives for transmitting information. School inspection reports will now focus more on school performance indicators, such as development planning, financial management, community partnerships, teaching and learning processes, the learning and school environment, and promotion rates.

Accurate and timely information on enrollments, teachers, and school inputs is essential, especially for assessing the needs of remote areas and underserved populations. Widely conflicting statistics on these variables are still too common to support robust planning and policy making. Most problematic of all are student testing systems: the challenge is to make national tests comparable over time to allow policy evaluation, and to ensure that they reflect existing or desired curriculum content.[27]

To advance education outcomes, school stakeholders must have greater voice and exercise some control over school operations.

Decentralization is not just about increasing local management and technical skills, but also about strengthening the voice of the community in the delivery of public services. In many centralistic systems, local communities are not used to governing themselves, electing politicians who represent their interests, and using their right to vote to make their will known. Breaking out of this mold immediately is difficult. Despite commune councils in China, lack of popular representation persists at the local level. In Cambodia, the central government still appoints provincial governors and district heads. And in Indonesia, although the majority of schools now have school committees, they hardly meet and do not yet fulfill their designated functions (World Bank 2004a).

Beyond strengthening voice, experiences in countries outside East Asia suggest that giving parents, teachers, and other stakeholders decision-making authority in key areas such as curriculum, training, and pedagogical approaches leads to better student performance. This occurs through greater commitment from teachers, more focus on learning, stronger school leadership, and a sense of responsibility for results (King and Ozler 1998; Winkler and Gershberg 2000).

Top-down decentralization has largely precluded the involvement of teachers and teachers' unions in designing education reform.[28] Such limited agency reflects not only the impetus for decentralization but also political and unions' inability to mobilize. Unions have been less politically active (China) and have had fewer opportunities to play a significant role (Cambodia and Philippines) than in Latin American countries, where teachers' unions have wielded more political power and played critical roles in shaping education reform.[29] The Latin American experience shows that these responses can be diverse, including resistance (Mexico), negotiation (Bolivia and Chile in the 1990s), cooperation (Brazil), and inaction (Chile in the 1980s). Decentralization inevitably draws many stakeholders—namely, local authorities and associations—into the decision-making process in government and schools. Fearing a loss of negotiating power on critical issues such as salaries and the hiring and firing of personnel, unions have strongly opposed efforts to decentralize (Gaynor 1998). These experiences foreshadow the extent to which unions' political influence might affect both the pace and depth of decentralization in East Asia.

A review of 83 studies of school-based management in North America and among members of the OECD revealed greater teacher commitment, more collaboration and information sharing, and a change in classroom instruction. In India, student dropout rates declined and teacher attendance improved—from 33 percent to 78–86 percent—after village education committees began participating in schools and teacher monitoring (Leithwood and Menzies 1998; Pandey 2000). In the Philippines, about 2,000 schools adopted school-based management on a trial basis in connection with a World Bank–supported education project. Preliminary results show that greater involvement among teachers in planning and managing schools has greatly improved their motivation and enthusiasm, while principals' efforts to fully involve teachers in identifying problems and needs, and to improve communication, have helped yield solutions.

Countries vary in the extent to which they have decentralized functions directly affecting teachers, such as recruitment, deployment, promotion, and salary scales. Nonetheless, underlying these arrangements are incentives that influence the behavior of teachers and ultimately affect the quality of teaching and student learning. Research on teacher incentives has shown that teachers are not only sensitive to incentives but also responsive. Designing targeted incentives that translate into improved classroom performance and student learning is extremely difficult because teacher effort is both difficult and costly to measure (Murnane et al. 1991; Hanushek 1986; Waterreus 2003). Several countries in Latin America, in parallel with decentralization, have implemented policy reforms affecting teacher incentives, such as Mexico's *Carrera Magisterial*, Chile's *Sistema Nacional de Evaluación del Desempeño*, and Brazil's FUNDEF.

Annex: Research and Data Collection Methods

The 2003 World Bank study on which this chapter is based followed a method similar to that used in the 1998 World Education Indicators survey by OECD-INES (Indicators of Education Systems). Yet the Bank study also differs in significant ways. What follows is a description and comparison of our methodology and research approach, including the conceptual framework of the questionnaire, data collection procedure, and calculation of indicators. This annex also outlines the methods we used to make the two studies comparable.

Conceptual Framework of the Questionnaire

Decentralization focuses on the distribution of power between levels of government. The OECD-INES survey examined two dimensions of decentralization: the locus of decision making—that is, the level of government with authority—and the mode of decision making, or the degrees to which levels of government are autonomous or share authority. The World Bank study examined the former: the locus of decision making.

While the OECD-INES survey distinguished six levels of government (central, state, provincial/regional, subregional/intermunicipal, local, and school), the World Bank study focused on three main levels of government:

> *National/central:* The central government consists of all bodies at the national level that make decisions or participate in different aspects of decision making, including both administrative (government bureaucracy) and legislative bodies.

State/provincial/local: The state is the first territorial unit below the nation in federal countries, or in countries with similar types of governmental structures. The province or region is the first territorial unit below the national level in countries that do not have a federal or similar type of government structure, and the second territorial unit below the national level in countries with a federal or similar types of governmental structures. The municipality or community is the smallest territorial unit with governmental authority; the local authority may be the education department within a general-purpose local government, or a special-purpose government whose sole area of authority is education.

School: This level applies to individual schools and includes school administrators and teachers or a school board or committee established exclusively for that individual school. The decision-making body or bodies for this school may be an external school board, which includes residents from the larger community; an internal school board, which could include headmasters, teachers, other school staff, parents, and students; and both an external and an internal school board. The study considered parents and teachers as an element of the school level.

In practice, however, the decision-making process is not that simple. In determining at what level decisions are made, numerous unclear situations arise. In some cases, a higher level of government may have formal or legal responsibility for decision making, but in practice that level delegates its authority to a lower level of government. In describing the actual decision-making process, we identified the lower level of government as the decision maker. Similarly, a higher level of government may provide a lower level of government with choices in a particular area, such as the selection of textbooks, even though the higher level establishes the framework for the decision. In that case, too, we designated the lower level of government as the actual decision maker. Finally, one level of government may have responsibility for an individual decision, but inaction results in a decision by a lower level. If a decision is left to the discretion of a lower level through lack of determination at higher levels, then we chose the level that actually makes the decision.

Although the OECD-INES survey included fewer indicators (35) than the World Bank study (53), both studies organized those indicators into four broad categories. The main items within those categories included:

Organization of instruction: Decisions regarding which school students will attend, school careers, instruction time, choice of textbooks, grouping of pupils, assistance to pupils, teaching methods, and methods for assessing pupils' regular work.

Personnel management: Decisions regarding the hiring and firing of the principal and teaching and nonteaching staff, their duties and conditions of service, their salary scales, and their careers.

Planning and structures: Decisions on creating and abolishing schools and grade levels, selecting and designing programs of study and subjects taught at a particular school, defining course content, setting qualifying exams for certificates or diplomas, and credentializing students.

Resource allocation and use: Decisions on allocating resources to a school for teaching staff, nonteaching staff, capital expenditures, and operating expenditures, and on using resources for staff, capital expenditures, and operating expenditures.

Data Collection Procedure

The OECD-INES approach to collecting data was similar to that of the World Bank, although the two studies differed fundamentally in the composition of expert panels formed to assess decision making at different levels. In the OECD-INES approach, researchers created a panel for each level of education, composed of one member from each of the three decision-making levels. These groups completed the questionnaire and arrived at a consensus on all questions. The researchers also composed a second panel for each level of education, again composed of one member from each of the three decision-making levels, and repeated the process. The INES Network C representative or national coordinator for the World Education Indicators survey then compared the results of the two surveys. Where the responses differed, the INES Network C representative used source documents and consulted the national coordinator to reconcile disagreements.

We conducted the World Bank study in two phases, relying on intermittent consultation between two different panels of experts. The first panel was composed of World Bank education experts with knowledge and work experience within each of the countries. This group completed the questionnaire and arrived at a consensus on all questions. A second expert panel included World Bank education experts located in the field in the respective countries. This group reviewed the results from the first round of surveys. Where the responses differed, this panel reconciled differences with the first panel.

Calculating the Indicators

The OECD-INES study gave equal importance to the indicators within each of the four domains. Each domain contributes 25 percent to the results. Because each domain includes a different number of items, each item is weighted by the inverse of the number of items in its domain. The World Bank study followed the same approach.

TABLE 9A.1 Cross-Study Comparison of Functions

World Bank Study (2003)	OECD-INES (1998)
Pedagogical	**Organization of instruction**
Admissions criteria to enter school	Decision on what school a child should attend
Mode of grouping pupils/class size	Mode of grouping pupils
No. of periods of instruction/classroom hours	Number of periods of instruction
Selection of textbooks/teaching material	Choice of textbooks
Design of programs	
Design of program subjects	
Choice of subject matters	
Definition of curriculum	
Teaching methods	Teaching methods
Provision for extra help	Assistance to pupils
Extracurricular activities	
Evaluation methods	Methods of assessing pupils' regular work
Student promotion	Decisions affecting pupils, streaming
Setting of equivalencies	
Setting of goals/targets for the school	
Administrative	**Planning and structure**
Opening/closure of school	Creation and closure of a school
School calendar	
Creation/abolition of grade(s)	Creation and abolition of grades
Distribution of textbooks/teaching material	
Setting of qualifying examinations	Setting of qualifying examinations
Collection of student data (enrollment/exams)	
Community outreach	
Awarding of credentials	Awarding of credentials
Accreditation of new schools	Design of programs for a specific school type
	Definition of course content
Personnel management	**Personnel management**
Hiring and firing of staff	*Hiring and firing of staff*
Head of school	Principals
Teaching staff	Teachers
General staff	Nonteaching posts
Terms of service and duties	*Duties and conditions of service of staff*
Head of school	Principals
Teaching staff	Teachers
	Nonteaching posts
Fixing of salary levels/benefits/incentives	*Fixing of salary scales for staff*
Head of school	Principals
Teaching staff	Teachers
	Nonteaching posts

World Bank Study (2003)	OECD-INES (1998)
Evaluation methods/supervision	
Head of school	
Teaching staff	
Promotion	*Influence over staff careers*
Head of school	Principals
Teaching staff	Teachers
	Nonteaching posts
Training	
Head of school	
Teaching staff	
Certifying staff	
Head of school	
Teaching staff	
Allocation and use of resources	**Allocation and use of resources**
Allocation of resources to the school	*Allocation of resources to the school*
Salaries and benefits	Teaching staff; nonteaching staff
Administrative/operating costs	Operating expenditures
Capital expenditure (infrastructure/maintenance)	Capital expenditures
Scholarship/awards	
School projects/activities	
Budget/finances	
User charges/monthly fees/voluntary fees	
Fundraising activities	
Allocation from state/subsidies	
Procurement and disbursement	*Use of resources in the school*
Salaries and benefits	Staff
Administrative/operating costs	Operating expenditures
Capital expenditures (infrastructure)	Capital expenditures
Scholarship/awards	
School projects/activities	
Relationship with unions	

Sources: OECD 1998; World Bank study 2003.

If a single item produced multiple answers, although the instructions for the questionnaire did not specifically allow this, each answer received half of the original weight of that item.

The following table compares the indicators used in the two studies:

Endnotes

1. Accountability means more than "answerability" or "enforceability." It implies a precise set of relationships between principals and agents encompassing five main features: delegation, finance, performance, information about performance, and enforceability (World Bank 2004c).
2. This, however, is not different from what had occurred in other countries that had decentralized earlier, such as Spain and Chile (political reasons) and the United Kingdom and Australia (concerns about state finances). After Franco died in 1975, a new Spanish Constitution promoting a transition to democracy devolved central functions to regional governments (Hanson 2000). Through an opposite political transition in Chile—from a democratic to a military government—newly empowered neoliberal economists and social planners also pushed for more decentralization. In contrast, Australia's fiscal situation provided the principal motives for public service reform. The Victorian Commission of Audit assessed public expenditures in key sectors as too high and pushed for incremental change (Pascoe and Pascoe 1998).
3. One impediment to further devolution of education functions is increased politicization of elections at the local level. In the Philippines, teachers serve on the Board of Election Inspectors and thus play an important role in counting ballots (Manasan 2002).

4. This was undertaken with the 2001 Decision on the Reform and Development of Basic Education by the State Council (Wang 2004).
5. Cambodia's policy goals for education reform are contained in the Education Strategic Plan (ESP) for 2001–5 and implemented through the Education Sector Support Program and the Priority Action Program rather than through a single piece of legislation. The ESP reiterates the central government's vision: "The Ministry's vision of an inclusive education system also includes broad-based participation al all levels of Government and civil society in taking responsibility for planning and implementation of education services . . . An associated goal would be to incrementally delegate greater decision-making and spending authority to districts, possibly communes, and schools. In this way, all national stakeholders would also have to assume responsibility for frank and open evaluation of how the system is performing and in taking steps to put things right" (Royal Kingdom of Cambodia 2001, p. 1).
6. The OECD-INES method clearly distinguishes between de jure and de facto decision-making power: "The descriptions of 'at what level' and 'how' educational decisions are made reflect the actual decision-making process. In some cases, a higher level of government may have formal or legal responsibility for decision-making, but in practice, that level of government delegates its decision-making authority to a lower level of government. In describing the actual decision-making process, the lower level of government is identified as the decision-maker. Similarly, a higher level of government may provide a lower level of government with choices in a particular area of decision-making (e.g., the selection of textbooks for particular course). In that case too, the lower level of government is the actual decision-maker, but within a framework established by a higher level of government. Finally, there are cases in which one level of government may have the responsibility for an individual decision, but inaction by the higher level results in a decision being made by a lower level within the educational system" (OECD 1998, p. 407).
7. Although references are frequently made to state-level decentralization in Brazil, the process has progressed at such a rapid pace with FUNDEF's implementation that, as municipalities and mayorships are given responsibility for the first four years of basic education, discussing decentralization at the state level does not fully reflect the national context.
8. Local government expenditures on education rose nearly 14-fold, from ₱ 0.8 billion in 1991 to ₱ 11.6 billion, in 2001 (Manasan 2002).
9. The Local School Board is cochaired by the local chief executive and the division superintendent. Other members include the chair of the education committee of the local legislature, the local treasurer, a representative of the federation of local youth councils, the president of the local federation of teacher-parent associations, a representative of the local teachers' organization, and a representative of the nonacademic personnel of the local public schools (Manasan 2002).
10. Because of a shortage of teachers at the local level, many local governments hire and pay supplementary teachers despite the fact that this function is one of the primary responsibilities of the central Department of Education.
11. This high percentage may be due to the unclear distinction between fees and voluntary contributions.
12. The share of central government spending in capital expenditures fell from 10.5 percent in 1990–91 to 4.6 percent in 1996–2000, and the central share of maintenance and operating expenditures fell from 18.7 percent in 1990–91 to 10.4 percent in 1996–2000 (Manasan 2002).
13. With the transfer of authority and management to regional governments in Indonesia, "It is hoped that the local governments are capable of obtaining more funds in their regions and in managing them more efficiently and effectively. It is expected that the local governments are able to use or exploit the sources of funds in the regions, such as the private sector and other education stakeholders, in funding education" (Government of Indonesia 2001).
14. Until recently, the national government retained 10 percent of total tax revenues for its own use and provided 9 percent to local tax offices to assist with collections, 16 percent to provincial governments, and 65 percent to local governments (Lewis 2002).
15. The coefficient of variation in literacy rates declined from 0.11 in 1989 to 0.08 in 1994.
16. There was no change in the coefficient of variation of enrollment rates across the regions.
17. The creation of ARMM was a direct result of the 1996 peace treaty between the national government and the Moro National Liberation Front. Republic Act No. 9054—the law creating ARMM—contains detailed provisions that pertain to the governance, regulation, and funding of human development sectors in the region. However, the 1991 Local Government Code had already mandated devolution of many functions and responsibilities related to human development—notably health and social welfare services—to provinces, cities, municipalities, and *barangays* (World Bank 2003b).
18. These comparisons exclude a few provinces where the samples tended to be in urban areas. According to the SUSENAS Work Manual (Government of Indonesia 2002), "Because of the unfavorable security situation, in the following provinces/regencies SUSENAS 2002 is only conducted in Banda Aceh (Aceh), Ambon (Maluku), Ternate (North Maluku), Sorong (West Irian Jaya), Timica (Central Irian Jaya), and Jayapura (East Irian Jaya)." Because the samples were not representative, enrollment rates in these provinces appear to be surprisingly higher than in other provinces.
19. Education systems suffer from ineffective and substandard schools, persistent shortages of good textbooks, and unprepared and absent teachers. The nondelivery of publicly supplied textbooks and chairs at the beginning of each school year in several of these countries deprives millions of children of the chance to do better in school. In the Philippines, this problem was estimated at 30–60 percent of total contracts with the education central agency (Chua 1999).

    The proportion of teachers who are absent from the classroom is too high, according to a recent survey of teachers in several countries. For example, in Indonesia, 17 percent of teachers in primary schools were not on the school premises during school hours. And too many teachers do not know their subject matter better than their students, as indicated by the performance of teachers on tests conducted for a recent study of the quality of primary schools in Vietnam (World Bank 2004b). These problems are also found in a much wider set of countries for which policy and program evaluations do not point conclusively to gains from higher per pupil spending or from investments in specific school inputs (Glewwe 2002).

20. The newly established Academic Accountability Council, along with the Office of Accountability, was jointly responsible for overseeing a system of review and analysis of school performance, while local school councils lost some of their independence.
21. See the Chicago Public Schools website: www.cps.k12.il.us/.
22. Paes de Barros and Silva Pinto de Mendonça (1998) conducted a broad evaluation of decentralization across most Brazilian states. Their research base includes all geographical units in the country except the Federal District, northern states, and the state of Alagoas. The study examined data between 1981 and 1993 and included 220 observations.
23. The measures of educational performance used included the repetition rate (school census); the proportion of children outside school and two measures of grade-level lag (National Household Survey Sample, or *Pesquisa Nacional por Amostra de Domicílios*); and student achievement (National Basic Education Evaluation System, or *Sistema de Avaliação do Ensino Básico*).
24. The 10-year-old Basic Education Quality Improvement Project (*Próqualidade*) aimed to strengthen school autonomy by providing managers in central and regional offices with tools designed for information-based decision making; and help school directors assume their new roles as both leaders and managers in a more decentralized state education system. The project also aimed to increase teachers' access to training opportunities; deliver packages of instructional materials to public schools; and upgrade facility management to ensure equitable access of pupils to classroom time as well as rational use of school space.
25. The LEAs were created according to population distribution and density, number of institutions, geographic characteristics, sociocultural considerations, and the extent to which planned areas overlapped with existing district boundaries.
26. This act was supported by the National Decentralization Committee and part of the Decentralization Action Plan passed by Parliament in early 2002.
27. In China, the monitoring and evaluation system is quite comprehensive. Throughout compulsory education, students must take exams and tests following each semester and school year to graduate. In primary schools, students must pass tests in Chinese and mathematics, while tests in the remaining subjects are usually used as checkup. In secondary schools, exam subjects reflect the general subjects taught to a given graduating class, while exams in the remaining subjects are again used for checkup (China Education and Research Network 2003). Junior secondary school graduates seeking promotion to senior secondary schools must pass locally organized entrance exams prior to full admission.

    In Indonesia, final exams are set at both the national and school levels. While the national portion is based on multiple choice, the school portion is based on laboratory work, written portfolios, or demonstration of a given set of skills. Students are tested on core knowledge in three main subject areas: mathematics, Indonesian, and English. At the central level, test results play a strong role in resource allocation. At the school level, they provide comparable information on the relative strengths and weaknesses of individual schools. At the client level, parents and the community can use exam results to hold providers accountable. However, the new exam system does not include primary school, and does not provide information about the performance of children below the ninth grade. Confronted with this, provinces and districts can create their own complementary testing system using guidance available from the National Evaluation Center.
28. Some have argued, however, that even when reforms involve quality issues, unions still oppose them, given that such reforms require more effort and political sacrifices (Corrales 1999). Similar debates stem from the joint function of unions as both professional organizations aiming to promote efficacy and public knowledge and agents of collective bargaining (World Bank 2004c).
29. In Mexico, given strong leadership by the teachers' union, the government quickly realized that it could neither confront nor ignore it, and so openly included it in the process of negotiation on greater decentralization. Unions in Chile are also politically powerful and "have systematically stood in the way of true curriculum reform and teacher accountability, and the political class has been unwilling to confront them" (Edwards 2003). Less contentious than in Mexico and Chile, reform in Bolivia has shown progress in negotiating with teachers. Nonetheless, teachers' unions are also extremely powerful and reform has stalled at several points. In contrast, unions in Brazil did not stall reform; union representatives were active stakeholders in reform negotiations, and decentralization progressed to the school level. And, finally, in El Salvador, teachers' unions took a strong stance against the EDUCO model, but government dissuaded them with evidence of innovation in teaching practices (Marques and Bannon 2003; Stavenhagen 1999).

Bibliography

Ahmad, Junaid, Richard Bird, and Jennie Litvack. 1998. "Rethinking Decentralization in Developing Countries." PREM Sector Studies Series. Washington, DC: World Bank.

Akita, Takahiro, and Armida S. Alisjahbana. 2002."Regional Income Inequality in Indonesia and the Initial Impact of the Economic Crisis." *Bulletin for Indonesian Economic Studies* 38 (2): 201–22.

Asian Development Bank. 1999. *Philippine Education for the 21st Century.* 1998 Philippines Education Sector Study. Manila: Asian Development Bank.

Azfar, Omar, Satu Kahkonen, and Patrick Meagher. 2001. "Conditions for Effective Decentralization Governance: A Synthesis of Research Findings." College Park, MD: University of Maryland, IRIS Center.

Bray, Mark. 1999. "The Private Costs of Public Schooling: Household and Community Financing in Primary Education in Cambodia." Paris and Buenos Aires: International Institute for Educational Planning.

Cheng, Kai-ming. 1997. "The Meaning of Decentralization: Looking at the Case of China." In *International Handbook of Education and Development: Preparing Schools, Students, and Nations for the Twenty-First Century,* eds. William Cummings and Noel F. McGinn. New York: Pergamon Press.

China Education and Research Network. 2003. www.edu.cn/HomePage/english/index.shtml.

Chicago Public School System. n.d. "Chicago Public Schools: Every Child, Every School." www.cps.k12.il.us/.

Chua, Yvonne T. 1999. *Robbed: An Investigation on Corruption in Philippine Education.* Manila: Philippine Center for Investigative Journalism.

Cordeiro Guerra, Susana. 2003. "A Proposal for Teacher Empowerment in Minas Gerais." Cambridge, MA: Harvard University.

Corrales, Javier. 1999. "The Politics of Education Reform: Bolstering the Supply and Demand—Overcoming Institutional Blocks." *Education Reform and Management Series* 2 (1). Washington, DC: World Bank.

Delannoy, Françoise. 2000. "Education Reforms in Chile, 1980–98: A Lesson in Pragmatism." *Education Reform and Management Series* 1 (1). Washington, DC: World Bank.

Edwards, Sebastian. 2003. "How Chile Can Make the Most of Its U.S. Trade Deal." *Wall Street Journal*, January 3.

Gaynor, Cathy. 1998. *Decentralization of Education: Teacher Management.* Directions in Development Series. Washington, DC: World Bank.

Glewwe, Paul. 2002."Schools and Skills in Developing Countries: Education Policies and Socioeconomic Outcomes." *Journal of Economic Literature* 40 (2): 436–82.

Government of Indonesia. 1998 and 2002."Survei Sosial Ekonomi Nasional" [SUSENAS]. Jakarta: Bureau of Central Statistics.

———. 2000. *Statistik Indonesia [Statistical Yearbook of Indonesia].* Jakarta: Badan Pusat Statistik.

———. 2001. "Decentralization of Education." National Committee for Education, Subcommittee III, draft report. Translated into English. Jakarta: Government of Indonesia.

———. 2003. Act of the Republic of Indonesia Number 20, Year 2003, on National Education System. Jakarta: National Gazette.

Guedes, Andrea, Thereza Lobo, Robert Walker, and Ana Lúcia Amaral. 1997. *Gestión Descentralizada de la Educación en el Estado de Minas Gerais, Brasil.* Grupo de Desarrollo Humano América Latina y La Región del Caribe, informe no. 11. Washington, DC: World Bank.

Hannum, Emily. 2002."Educational Stratification by Ethnicity in China." *Demography* 39 (1): 91–117.

Hanson, Mark E. 2000. *Democratization and Educational Decentralization in Spain.* Education Reform and Management Series. Washington, DC: World Bank.

Hanushek, Erik A. 1986. "Production and Efficiency in Public Schools." *Journal of Economic Literature* 24 (3): 1141–77.

Hawkins, John N. 2000. "Centralization, Decentralization, Recentralization: Educational Reform in China." *Journal of Educational Administration* 38 (5): 442–55.

Hsieh, Chang-Tai, and Miguel Urquiola. 2001. "When Schools Compete, How Do They Compete? An Assessment of Chile's Nationwide School Voucher Program." elsa.berkeley. edu/~chsieh/c10.pdf.

James, Estelle, Elizabeth King, and Ace Suryadi. 1996. "Finance, Management, and Costs of Public and Private Schools in Indonesia." *Economics of Education Review* 15 (4): 387–98.

Jimenez, Emmanuel, and Vicente Paqueo. 1996. "Public for Private: The Relationship between Public and Private School Enrollment in the Philippines." *Economics of Education Review* 15 (4): 389–99.

Jimenez, Emmanuel, and Yasuyuki Sawada. 1999. "Do Community-Managed Schools Work? An Evaluation of El Salvador's EDUCO Program." *World Bank Economic Review* 13 (3): 415–42.

Kerr, Graham. 1999."Local Technical and Managerial Capacity." In *Decentralization Briefing Notes*, eds. Jennie Litvack and Jennica Seddon. Washington, DC: World Bank Institute.

King, Elizabeth, and Berk Ozler. 1998. "What's Decentralization Got to Do with Learning? The Case of Nicaragua's School Autonomy Reform." Washington, DC: World Bank, Development Research Group.

Kingdom of Thailand. 1999. National Education Act, B.E. 2542. Bangkok: Office of the National Education Commission.

Leithwood, Kenneth A., and Teresa Menzies. 1998. "Forms and Effects of School-Based Management: A Review." *Educational Policy* 12 (3): 325–46.

Lewis, Blane D. 2002. "Revenue-Sharing and Grant-Making in Indonesia: The First Two Years of Fiscal Decentralization." In *Intergovernmental Transfers in Asia*, ed. Paul Smoke. Manila: Asian Development Bank.

Loehr, W., and Rosario Manasan. 1999. "Fiscal Decentralization and Economic Efficiency: Measurement and Evaluation." IMCC Consulting Assistance for Economic Reform II. Cambridge, MA: Harvard Institute for International Development and U.S. Agency for International Development.

Lopez-Acevedo, Gladys, Vicente Paqueo, and Suhas Parandekar. 2003. "On the Use of Transparent Formulae to Allocate Federal Education Transfers." Washington, DC: World Bank, Latin America and the Caribbean Region.

Machado, Maria Aglaê de Medeiros. 2002. "School Autonomy in Brazil: General Overview and Selected States." Brasília: World Bank.

Manasan, Rosario. 2002. "Education Financing and Service Delivery: Selected Issues." Background Paper for *Philippines Public Expenditure: Procurement & Financial Management Review 3* (annex VI).

Manasan, Rosario, and John M. Atkins. 2004. "Normative Financing in Basic Education." Manila: Philippine Institute of Development Studies.

Marques, José, and Ian Bannon. 2003. "Central America: Education Reform in a Post-Conflict Setting—Opportunities and Challenges." Conflict Prevention and Reconstruction Working Paper. Washington, DC: World Bank, Social Development Department.

Martin, Michael O., Ina V. S. Mullis, Eugenio J. Gonzalez, Steven J. Chrostowski. 2004a. *TIMSS 2003 International Mathematics Report: Findings from IEA's Trends in Mathematics and Science Study at the Fourth and Eighth Grades.* Boston: International Association for the Evaluation of Education Achievement (IEA).

———. 2004b. *TIMSS 2003 International Science Report: Findings from IEA's Trends in Mathematics and Science Study at the Fourth and Eighth Grades.* Boston: International Association for the Evaluation of Education Achievement (IEA).

McEwan, Patrick J., and Martin Carnoy. 1999. *The Effectiveness and Efficiency of Private Schools in Chile's Voucher System.* Stanford, CA: Stanford University Press.

McMahon, W., with N. Suwaryani, Boediono, and E. Appiah. 2001. *Improving Education Finance in Indonesia.* Jakarta: Ministry of National Education, Institute for Research and Development, Policy Research Center; UNICEF; and UNESCO.

Murnane, Richard, Judith Singer, John Willett, James Kemple, and Randall Olsen. 1991. *Who Will Teach? Policies That Matter.* Cambridge, MA: Harvard University Press.

Mutebi, Alex M. 2003. "Thailand's Decentralization Experiment: Evolution: Dimensions and Challenges." Singapore: National University of Singapore, Lee Kuan Yew School of Public Policy.

Namo de Mello, Guiomar. Forthcoming. "Introdução: Breve Histórico." Background paper for Lemann Foundation. http://www.fundacaolemann.org.br.

National Statistical Coordination Board. 2003. *Philippine Statistical Yearbook*. Manila: National Economic and Development Authority.

OECD (Organisation for Economic Co-operation and Development). 1998. *Education at a Glance: OECD Indicators*. Paris: OECD, Centre for Educational Research and Innovation.

Paes de Barros, Ricardo, and Rosane Silva Pinto de Mendonça. 1998. "The Impact of Three Institutional Innovations in Brazilian Education." In *Organization Matters: Agency Problems in Health and Education in Latin America*, ed. William D. Savedoff. Baltimore, MD: Johns Hopkins University Press.

Pandey, Raghaw. 2000. "Going to Scale with Education Reform: India's District Primary Education Program, 1995–99." *Education Reform and Management Publication Series* 1 (4). Washington, DC: World Bank.

Pascoe, Susan, and Robert Pascoe. 1998. "Education Reform in Australia, 1992–97." *Education Reform and Management Publication Series* 1 (2). Washington, DC: World Bank.

People's Republic of China. 2001. *Essential Statistics of Education in China*, Vol.1. Beijing: Ministry of Education, Department of Development and Planning.

———. 2002. *China Statistical Yearbook*, Vol. 21. Beijing: National Bureau of Statistics, China Statistics Press.

Prawda, Juan. 1992. "Educational Decentralization in Latin America: Lessons Learned." Washington, DC: World Bank, Latin America and the Caribbean Region, Human Resources Division.

Rodríguez, Alberto, and Kate Hovde. 2002. "The Challenge of School Autonomy: Supporting Principals." Washington, DC: World Bank, Latin America and the Caribbean Region, Department of Human Development.

Ross, Steven M., William L. Sanders, S. Paul Wright, and Sam Stringfield. 1998. "The Memphis Restructuring Initiative: Achievement Results for Years 1 and 2 on the Tennessee Value-Added Assessment System (TVAAS)." Memphis, TN: University of Memphis, Center for Research in Educational Policy.

Royal Kingdom of Cambodia. 2001. *Education Sector Plan*, section I (1). Phnom Penh: Ministry of Education, Youth, and Sport.

Shen, A. 1994. "Teacher Education and National Development in China." *Journal of Education* 176 (2): 57–71.

Stavenhagen, Rodolfo. 1999. "Latin America's Challenge for the 21st Century." Cambridge, MA: Harvard University, David Rockefeller Center for Latin American Studies.

Trends in International Mathematics and Science Study. 1999. http://isc.bc.edu/timss1999.html.

Tsang, Mun C. 2002. "Intergovernmental Grants and the Financing of Compulsory Education in China." New York: Columbia University, Teachers College.

Turner, Mark. 2002. "Whatever Happened to Deconcentration? Recent Initiatives in Cambodia." *Public Administration and Development* 22 (4): 353–64.

UNESCO (U.N. Education, Scientific, and Cultural Organization). 2002/2003. "Education Statistics." Paris: UNESCO, Institute for Statistics.

Vasconcelos-Saliba, Alcyone. 2004. "Governance and Accountability Tools for Accountability: School Report Cards—The Case of Paraná (Brazil)." Presentation at the International Conference on Governance Accountability in Social Sector Decentralization. Washington, DC: World Bank.

Vegas, Emiliana. 2002. "School Choice, Student Performance, and Teacher and School Characteristics: The Chilean Case." Washington, DC: World Bank.

Wang, Yidan. 2004. "Governance of Basic Education: Service Provision and Quality Assurance in China." Washington, DC: World Bank.

Waterreus Ib. 2003. "Lessons in Teacher Pay: Studies on Incentives and the Labor Market for Teachers." Dissertation. Amsterdam: University of Amsterdam.

Weist, Dana. 2001. "Thailand's Decentralization: Progress and Prospects." Paper presented at the KPI Annual Congress IIII on Decentralization and Local Government in Thailand, November.

West, Loraine A., and Christine P. W. Wong. 1995. "Fiscal Decentralization and Growing Regional Disparities in Rural China: Some Evidence in the Provision of Social Services." *Oxford Review of Economic Policy* 11 (4): 70–84.

———. 1997. "Equalization Issues." In *Financing Local Government in the People's Republic of China*, ed. Christine P. W. Wong. Hong Kong: Oxford University Press, pp. 283–311.

Winkler, Donald, and Alec Gershberg. 2000. "Education Decentralization in Latin America: The Effects on the Quality of Schooling." In *Decentralization and Accountability of the Public Sector*, eds. Shahid Javed Burki et al. Proceedings of the 1999 Annual World Bank Conference on Development in Latin America. Washington, DC: World Bank.

World Bank. 2000. "China National Development and Subnational Finance: A Review of Provincial Expenditures." Washington, DC: World Bank, East Asia and Pacific Region, Poverty Reduction and Economic Management Unit.

———. 2003a. "Decentralizing Indonesia." Regional Public Expenditure Review overview report. Washington, DC: World Bank, East Asia and Pacific Region, Poverty Reduction and Economic Management Unit.

———. 2003b. "From Cyclical Recovery to Long-Run Growth: Regional Overview." Washington, DC: World Bank, East Asia and Pacific Region, Poverty Reduction and Economic Management Unit, East Asia Update.

———. 2003c. "Human Development for Peace and Prosperity in the Autonomous Region in Muslim Mindanao." Washington, DC: World Bank, East Asia and Pacific Region, Human Development Sector Unit.

———. 2003d. Thailand Country Development Partnership: Governance and Public Sector Reform. Phase I monitoring workshop.

———. 2003e. "Philippines: Decentralization and Service Delivery—From Promise to Performance. Cross-Cutting Themes in Local Government Functioning." Washington, DC: World Bank, East Asia and Pacific Region, Poverty Reduction and Economic Management Unit.

———. 2003f. "Vietnam: Delivering on Its Promise." Development Report. Washington, DC: World Bank, East Asia and Pacific Region, Poverty Reduction and Economic Management Unit.

———. 2004a. "Education in Indonesia: Managing the Transition to Decentralization." Indonesia Education Sector Review. Prepared in partnership with the Government of Indonesia, Ministry of National Education; and the Indonesia Education Donor Partnership. Jakarta: World Bank.

——— . 2004b. "The Quality of Education at the End of Primary School: Achievement in Grade 5—Baseline Data for the Nation and Each Province," Vol. 2. Washington, DC, and Hanoi: World Bank.

———. 2004c. *World Development Report: Making Services Work for Poor People*. Washington, DC: World Bank; and New York: Oxford University Press.

Zhang, Tiedao, Zhao Minxia, Zhao Xueqin, Zhang Xi, and Wang Yan. 2003. "Universalizing Nine-Year Compulsory Education for Poverty Reduction in Rural China." Case study on scaling up poverty reduction for Shanghai Poverty Conference.

10

DECENTRALIZING BASIC INFRASTRUCTURE SERVICES

George E. Peterson and Elisa Muzzini

Basic infrastructure services are those that households and businesses tend to use every day. The primary components are roads and transportation services, water supply and distribution, and sanitation—wastewater collection and removal, and solid waste collection and removal. These services are often bundled together under the heading of "urban services." However, parallel infrastructure systems are found in rural areas, where roads, irrigation networks, and latrines are critical to life. Irrigation systems, in particular, are sometimes underestimated as infrastructure networks. In the Philippines, irrigation systems account for 80 percent of national water consumption.

Efforts to decentralize infrastructure services raise distinctive issues regarding policy design and implementation. Because of their capital intensiveness, these systems require decision making at several different stages:

- Preparing capital investment plans and setting priorities for individual capital projects.
- Operating a network system to provide services and maintaining facilities to sustain the physical capital.
- Financing the system by both mobilizing capital to pay for the initial investment and generating revenues to cover operations and maintenance—that is, ensuring financial sustainability.

Each of these decision-making points presents an opportunity for decentralization, and different countries have responded by decentralizing different stages of the decision-making process. The issue is further complicated because infrastructure projects are subject to spillover effects and economies of scale. When this is the case, there are often substantial benefits to be achieved by coordinating projects across subnational governments. Accounting for economies of scale and externalities is especially important when decentralizing decision making and responsibility to low levels, and when infrastructure projects cover multiple jurisdictions, such as in managing water resources across large watersheds or trunk roads that connect regions. Promoting equity, harmonizing standards, and ensuring efficient revenue collection may also argue for limiting decentralization.

Infrastructure services are distinctive in another important respect. Because they are used so widely and often, citizens are familiar with their benefits and typically have strong opinions as to which types of projects and service improvements should have highest priority in their area. Choices among priorities for infrastructure investment often provide local citizens with their first opportunity to participate in public decision making. Participatory choice at the local level comes more naturally with small investment projects—which often quickly yield local benefits—than with school curricula and health services, which often require professional expertise and longer waiting times to produce benefits. Thus, decentralization strategies often include participatory choice in (small-scale) infrastructure investments, not simply to better respond to local service needs but as a deliberate seedbed for democratic participation in governance, with the intention of strengthening civic commitment to the entire decentralization program. The payoff is judged only partly by whether infrastructure services improve; equally important is whether mechanisms for public participation in decision making strengthen citizen involvement in governance.

This chapter views decentralization in the infrastructure sector as a work in progress. The transfer of service and investment responsibilities to the local level evokes an immediate response based on the capacities and institutional practices of local governments relative to those of the central government. More important, however, this first round of adjustment will reveal shortcomings in the new arrangements and stimulate responses by national agencies, local officials, local citizens, and international organizations supporting the decentralization process. The fact that East Asian countries have experience with both different strategies and implementation periods for decentralizing infrastructure enhances the opportunity to learn from comparative results.

A final introductory observation is appropriate. Decentralization tends to be seen as a transfer of responsibilities and revenues from higher-level to lower-level governments. Many decisions about infrastructure services, however, occur in a broader context that consists of unbundling the vast powers of previously centralized agencies responsible for investment and service provision. Some of this unbundling entails transferring authority to lower levels of government. Other elements may include transferring investment or responsibility for service delivery to the private sector or to public-private partnerships, including partnerships with nongovernmental organizations (NGOs); and restructuring the public enterprises traditionally responsible for larger-scale infrastructure services, such as urban water supply and wastewater removal. Decentralization typically entails restructuring public enterprises by making them accountable to local governments rather than central line ministries.

This chapter has two purposes. The first is to review the status of efforts to decentralize infrastructure services in East Asia, with a focus on countries that are more advanced in the process, namely, China, Indonesia, and the Philippines. The second purpose is to highlight the efficiency gains in providing infrastructure services achieved in decentralized settings, and to underline the main challenges to realizing the full benefits of decentralization.

The next section examines the key features of strategies for decentralizing infrastructure adopted by China, Indonesia, and the Philippines, and outlines the impact of decentralization on the level of infrastructure investment. The third section analyzes the available evidence from East Asia on the efficiency gains from more decentralized forms of providing infrastructure services. The fourth section reviews East Asian experience in enhancing community-level participation in managing infrastructure projects, and investigates the scope for scaling up the benefits of community participation within a decentralized government structure. The fifth section compares the approach to financing infrastructure adopted by China, Indonesia, and the Philippines, given their different strategies for decentralizing infrastructure. The sixth section discusses the critical role of higher tiers of government in decentralized infrastructure, drawing on the experiences of China and of Indonesia and the Philippines, with the drawbacks of a "missing middle" in the architecture of decentralization being particularly manifest in the latter two countries. The last section highlights key policy issues that have emerged from the analysis of decentralization in the region.

Decentralization Strategies in the Infrastructure Sector

East Asian countries have followed two broad strategies in decentralizing the infrastructure sector. China exemplifies a principal-agent approach. The central government as principal has retained and even strengthened its role in setting investment priorities across and within sectors, and has reinforced this role by setting highly specific targets and timetables for infrastructure coverage in different classes of cities. These targets and timetables have extended beyond physical investments to include, for certain services, mandatory adoption by all urban governments of specific guidelines for service charges, and, for all services, mandatory separation of asset ownership from service delivery. In this respect, the infrastructure sector remains highly centralized. At the same time, as agents for implementing centrally established policies, local governments have full responsibility for actually executing investments and providing services. They also have significant latitude in deciding how to mobilize funds to pay for capital investment, which they now must finance entirely without central grant support. Local governments further have significant latitude in framing development plans, including where they will site major capital projects and how they will sequence investments to meet nationally imposed standards most cost effectively.

Indonesia and the Philippines represent an alternative approach. As part of the Big Bang initiatives launched in those countries, the central governments assigned virtually complete responsibility for urban and rural infrastructure services to local governments almost overnight. At the heart of this transfer was local choice in investment priorities. Decentralization laws emphasize the importance of civic participation in making investment choices, and specify elaborate procedures designed to ensure that citizens, as well as collective groups like NGOs and civil society organizations, are represented in the priority-setting process for capital projects. In fact, decentralization is clearly intended to serve a dual purpose: to make investment choices in the infrastructure sector more responsive to locally perceived needs and thus more efficient; and to become a vehicle for introducing ordinary citizens to participation in governance.

Cambodia and Vietnam are in incipient stages of decentralization, with broader policy driven largely by the design of infrastructure programs. Cambodia's Seila Program, introduced in 1996, has created commune development committees in more than 1,000 villages and 100 communes, with the program expected to reach three-fourths of all communes by the end of 2004 and the rest shortly thereafter (Royal Government of Cambodia 2003b). The program provides government and donor funds for small infrastructure projects selected by citizens at the most grassroots level, with mechanisms for transmitting their priorities for slightly larger projects up to the commune level. Seila is expressly seen as a way of engaging the citizenry in participatory governance. In a country as poor and rural as Cambodia, Seila now accounts for the bulk of local infrastructure investment. Vietnam has passed legislation on grassroots participation as part of its public administration reform. However, the national level continues to set investment priorities for most infrastructure services and certainly for urban services, with provincial and local authorities viewed primarily as agents implementing national choices.

Investment Levels and National Standards

How has infrastructure investment fared during decentralization, and what is the role of national standards and investment targets in sustaining investments? Both China and Vietnam, which have employed the principal-agent model, have experienced extremely high—almost unprecedented—infrastructure expansion within the areas given top priority. During the latter half of the 1990s, China assigned top infrastructure priority to road building, implemented primarily by provincial governments for national and provincial highway networks, and by local governments for urban networks (see tables 10.1 and 10.2). Both levels attracted some private investment under the direction of provincial and local authorities. Almost 85 percent of China's road and highway investment over the two decades ending in 2000 occurred during 1996–2000. Although national and provincial highway networks—that is, expressways and class 1 highways—expanded most rapidly, all classes grew at high rates, including major urban roads and class 2 and other local roads.

Vietnam has assigned priority to piped water distribution in urban areas, with implementation in the hands of provincial water authorities and, in the

TABLE 10.1 Road and Highway Investment in China

Period	Billions of yuan	Share of total (%)
1981–1989	19	2
1990–1995	153	14
1996–2000	881	84

Source: Mitchell Stanfield & Associates, as reported in Bellier and Zhou 2003.

TABLE 10.2 Road and Highway Investment in China, by Type

Road type	1990		2000	
	Billions of yuan	Share	Billions of yuan	Share
Express-ways	0.01	0.1%	56	28%
Class 1	0.02	0.3%	30	15%
Class 2	0.20	4.0%	60	30%
Class 3	0.84	16.5%	12	6%
Class 4	2.60	51%	27	13.5%
Unclassified roads	1.43	28.1%	15	7.5%

Source: Mitchell Stanfield & Associates, as reported in Bellier and Zhou 2003.

TABLE 10.3 Piped Water Coverage within the Urban Population, Vietnam

Year	Region		
	North	Central	South
1997	42.0%	30.4%	40.4%
2000	52.1%	38.9%	42.7%

Source: World Bank 2002b.

largest cities, water enterprises attached to local governments. Despite high rates of urban population growth, coverage rates have expanded remarkably in a short time (see table 10.3). In 2000, 41.5 percent of the average urban water system was five years old or younger.

China's government has recently given especially high priority to urban wastewater collection and treatment, reflecting heightened concern over the condition of urban water bodies. Higher standards imposed on local governments show how the center transmits signals to local authorities in a principal-agent relationship.

In May 2000, China's Development Planning Commission—under the Environment Protection Agency in the Ministry of Construction—circulated "City Dirty Water Treatment," which specified that the wastewater treatment rate in all towns and cities would be at least 50 percent by 2010. The treatment rate for cities would be at least 60 percent, and that for provincial capitals and other major cities at least 70 percent. The circular also defined treatment quality standards for different types of cities (Government of China 2000). Given that the vast majority of China's cities then had no wastewater treatment of any kind, the targets imply a massive infrastructure investment program.[1] Recognizing the need to mobilize capital for such an effort, the Development Planning Commission in October 2002 stated that "cities with existing wastewater and garbage treatment facilities shall start to immediately charge a treatment tariff," and that all other cities should do so by the end of 2003. The tariff "shall cover operations cost and a reasonable investment return" for wastewater treatment plants, to generate revenue for raising commercial investment funds. Cities in better economic conditions were urged to set tariffs high enough to cover the cost of constructing wastewater collection networks.

In a system with strong upward accountability such as China's (and Vietnam's), local authorities take national investment targets seriously.[2] Each municipality incorporates specific targets for infrastructure coverage into its five-year development plan, approved by the provincial government and ultimately by the Development Planning Commission. The political careers of local officials in the Communist Party hinge on meeting or surpassing the goals. As a result of either conscientious planning or competitive zeal, local officials often set targets that exceed national standards. This is true in the wastewater area. Analysis conducted for City Development Strategies has found that the majority of covered cities—although located in the poorer western provinces—are on their way to meeting investment targets that surpass state-mandated levels (Chreod Ltd. 2003). Local development plans emphasize these ambitions throughout urban infrastructure: municipalities have set targets even for square meters of green space per capita, triggering local investment in parks and other green areas.

Although driving higher infrastructure investment levels, standards that emphasize the capacity of capital facilities—whether or not they actually are operating or doing so economically—have often led to significant inefficiencies in operations and maintenance. The next section discusses these impacts.

China's intergovernmental system is gradually moving toward more sophisticated and meaningful measures of infrastructure performance, such as outcome measures. In the wastewater area, for example, the national government now requires localities to test the quality of receiving bodies of water, which are subject to quality standards measured along seven dimensions. Some cities voluntarily sample discharge quality from wastewater treatment plants and have included locally defined targets in their five-year development plans. Thus, the principal-agent relationship has proved to be more than a one-way street. The implementing agent not only incorporates mandated standards into its planning but may also set higher standards that become the basis for upward accountability.

Lessons Learned. The strong investment performance of subnational governments in China reflects many factors. The same national investment priorities communicated to local governments have been transmitted to the state-controlled banking system, clearing the way for lending that has financed much of the expansion in infrastructure coverage. Commercial banks have lent these funds for three- to five-year periods, creating the need for municipalities to roll over short-term debt. Local governments are therefore beginning to face high debt service burdens, which may exacerbate the uncertain creditworthiness of loan portfolios in the banking system. China also has a tradition of strong policy direction from the center, coupled with a high degree of de facto freedom in local budget management not found elsewhere.

One lesson that can be generalized, however, is the power of performance measurement and accountability in China. Measurable performance targets tied to upward accountability have driven China's infrastructure investment. The quantified standards have sometimes proved unduly rigid, upward accountability has substituted for accountability to clients, and national standards have curtailed local investment choice. But the effectiveness of infrastructure performance standards in steering budget choices at the local level is clear.

"Autonomous" Decentralization

Countries such as the Philippines and Indonesia have opted for political decentralization, with local authorities formally recognized as autonomous bodies. Inherent in their powers is setting priorities for local budgets, including capital budgets. Concern has arisen in both countries as to whether this type of decentralization can sustain capital investment and maintenance. In particular, the transfer of large numbers of central government employees—subject to wage protection—to local rolls, and the legal and political difficulties of raising local revenues, subject subnational governments to budget pressures. In the face of such pressures, local governments are thought more likely to maintain employment levels rather than adjust their budgets to sustain investment. Within capital programs, spending on maintenance and repair is believed to be particularly vulnerable. Displacement of local investment has potentially serious consequences. The World Bank has estimated that, in Indonesia for example, some 60 percent of total development expenditures are now a local responsibility (World Bank and Asian Development Bank 2003; World Bank 2003b, 2003c).

The Philippines has the longest experience with local budget allocations following decentralization. The share of capital spending in city and municipal budgets surged in 1993, shortly after new revenue and expenditure assignments took effect (see table 10.4). That occurred because initial revenue allocations exceeded the cost of transferred functions, leading to sizable local surpluses, which were then drawn down by capital investment. Since 1993, however, the share of local budgets devoted to capital spending has fallen steadily, with declines totaling more than 50 percent. These declines accelerated in 1998 with the Asian financial crisis and the consequent loss of public revenues before reviving briefly the following year. Such spending does not tell the entire story, as central line ministries continue to pay for some capital projects at the local level, as do some congressional allocations that are treated off-budget. However, the overall trend in local investment is clear.

TABLE 10.4 Capital Spending as a Share of Local Government Expenditure, Philippines

	1992	1993	1994	1995	1996	1997	1998	1999	2000
Cities	10.7%	17.3%	17.6%	16.4%	11.1%	8.8%	8.7%	8.9%	8.2%
Municipalities	8.7%	9.8%	8.9%	7.5%	6.5%	6.8%	4.2%	5.1%	4.7%

Source: Orial 2002.

Indonesia's decentralization process is too young to draw comparable conclusions about its impact on investment spending. Development spending on roads and mainland transportation fell sharply during the Asian financial crisis—from 15 percent of total development spending in 1994–97 to a little more than 5 percent in 1999–2001—before recovering somewhat. Another potential factor affecting this slowdown is significant deconcentrated spending by line ministries, and the difficulty of adapting the DAK (*dana alokasi khusus,* a conditional equalization grant) and providing funds within a decentralized environment. The World Bank has expressed concern that road maintenance at the *Kabupaten* level has suffered from underfunding, and that decentralization may exacerbate neglect of road maintenance, with consequences that are not immediately visible (World Bank 2003d). Whether local maintenance and repair budgets have actually suffered disproportionately from local budget adjustments under decentralization is unknown. However, protecting maintenance funds may require a greater role for professional planners and engineers, as opposed to local political officials and civic groups, in allocating expenditures.

The apparent decline in local infrastructure spending in the Philippines, and concern over local investment levels in Indonesia, have generated debate about the role of national standards and performance measures. This debate is occurring most vigorously in Indonesia, where decentralization legislation calls for national agencies to develop guidelines rather than mandatory standards promulgated via the provinces, whose capacity for oversight has greatly weakened.

Upward accountability for complying with mandatory infrastructure standards seems fundamentally at odds with strategies that place primary importance on local choice in investment projects and priorities. The challenge is to capture the power of performance measurement and accountability within a framework for political decentralization. The first step is agreement on performance measures in the infrastructure sector. National guidelines can establish a handful of basic measures reported by all local authorities and monitored by central institutions. Such measures would include fundamentals such as:

- Hours per day or week of water provision.
- Coverage of road networks (kilometers per 1,000 persons, kilometers of road per square kilometer of territory); quality of roads (percent in good condition, percent of all-weather roads).
- Wastewater removal rates.
- Expenditure on road maintenance as share of gross domestic product (GDP) or kilometers of roads.
- Affordability of transport services (freight rate per ton per kilometer, average bus fare per passenger per kilometer).

The absence of such measures handicaps both national decisions about infrastructure priorities and local attempts to measure and improve investment efficiency.

Decentralization frameworks now provide ample opportunities for incorporating these measures into an accountability system. At the national level, categorical grants such as Indonesia's DAK already recognize performance measures, although so far they do not actually take them into account. Where national authorities have clear investment priorities not adequately captured by local decision making, they can introduce standards—either absolute levels or improvement from a baseline—as a condition of capital grants. The ratio of matching grants can reflect both national priorities and local performance. Simple benchmarking of infrastructure performance and transparent reporting of performance measures can enhance efficiency. Individual local authorities, for example, can cite the range of actual costs per kilometer of standardized road construction elsewhere in conducting competitive bidding for local construction.[3] Civic groups can compare basic output levels with those of other local authorities in setting up their own reporting systems.

For other types of infrastructure projects and service delivery, formal accountability to the citizenry through contractual agreements and performance monitoring appears to be the most effective way to use standards under autonomous decentralization. Experience with 24 water utilities in Indonesia, known as PDAMs, shows that NGOs can monitor business plans that specify improvements in water coverage, quality, and reliability—established after public debate as part of a social contract. Fulfilling these goals then becomes the basis for raising service tariffs and supporting financial sustainability (Urban Institute 2003). Several local governments in the Philippines have similarly published performance goals and invited monitoring by the nongovernmental sector after public participation in setting priorities for infrastructure services (World Bank and Asian Development Bank 2003).

Lessons Learned. In the politically decentralized systems of East Asia, a lack of standardized performance monitoring severely hampers understanding of local infrastructure. No country now has a routine monitoring and reporting system for the sector. Such systems can be built gradually and improved over time. However, national guidelines should quickly establish a rudimentary system of reporting that can be built into budgeting at all levels. Upward accountability is more difficult to establish in politically decentralized systems than in systems that remain centralized. Decentralized systems need to incorporate performance goals into local budgets, local corporate plans for water utilities, and local development planning—in a form that can be monitored by civil society organizations. Quantitative accountability to informed civic monitors can substitute for traditional upward accountability, but only if public agencies provide specific and verifiable information.

Efficiency Gains from Decentralizing Infrastructure

A fundamental argument in favor of decentralizing infrastructure is that moving decision making on investment and implementation closer to clients will yield efficiency gains. These gains can come from two sources. First, production efficiency implies that local entities can build and operate a given infrastructure package less expensively. Cost savings may derive from cheaper local building materials, less expensive local labor, more efficient project design, fewer layers of bureaucratic oversight, and less corruption, among other sources. Sustainability is an important aspect of production efficiency. Second, allocative efficiency implies that local investment priorities will reflect the preferences of citizens more than those of the central government, and that households will therefore value each unit of infrastructure spending more highly. As this chapter later shows, governments need to balance such efficiencies with possible economies of scale (which for some infrastructure sectors can be significant) and externalities (both negative and positive) across local jurisdictions.

Analysts have made several attempts to test, in East Asia, the hypothesis that decentralization enhances the efficiency of infrastructure services. Rigorously evaluating the gains from production and allocative efficiency is a demanding exercise. Evidence so far suggests efficiency gains, but it is far from conclusive, as it is drawn largely from case studies (this differs from the health and education sectors, where systematic monitoring and household surveys are far more common). As a result, we know a good deal more about how to extract efficiency gains from decentralized infrastructure through well-designed implementation strategies than we do about broad generalizations as to whether decentralized approaches, on average, are more efficient.

Production Efficiency

The World Bank has reported that village infrastructure constructed under Indonesia's *Kecamatan* Development Program, which involves community-level planning and implementation, "cost significantly less—on average about one-third but in many cases more than half less—than equivalent works built through Ministry of Public Works contracts." Maintenance costs were also reportedly lower because communities provided the labor. Unfortunately, the analysis supporting this conclusion has not been published, leaving open the question of how the study compared costs. In particular, such comparisons often do not take into account the social infrastructure costs of supporting local project development (World Bank 2003e).[4]

In collaborating with 24 PDAMs in Indonesia, the Urban Institute reported that the PDAMs believed they could substantially reduce investment costs when they handled construction, land acquisition, project design, and scheduling, as opposed to complying with central specifications. Savings on projects that produced a given increment in the capacity of the daily water supply reportedly run as high as 50 percent. Some PDAMs have expressed reluctance to accept low-cost loans from central sources, should these become available, if they must adopt centrally imposed project standards, believing that the costs of complying with those rules would more than offset the savings from low-cost credit (Urban Institute 2003).

Loehr and Manasan (1999) conducted one of the more ambitious attempts to compare production costs for standardized projects in the Philippines. Drawing on World Bank and other data, the authors found costs in the range of ₱ 180,000–235,000 when local governments built their own schools, compared with ₱ 305,000 per classroom for the central Department of Public Works and Highways. Alonzo (1998) has reported comparable differentials in the costs of locally versus centrally built classrooms in the Philippines, as well as local savings per kilometer of road construction.

Corruption is a major source of cost escalation in infrastructure projects throughout East Asia. Azfar et al. (2000) have estimated that it adds 20–40 percent to the cost of infrastructure projects in the Philippines. Respondents to a 1999 survey conducted by Social Weather Stations ranked the central Department of Public Works and Highways as the most corrupt organization in the Philippines (Azfar et al. 2000).

Because a reduction in corruption costs is an express rationale for decentralizing infrastructure services, the findings of household and other surveys asking respondents to compare the severity of corruption at local and central levels therefore hold special interest. In a survey of 468 respondents in 13 randomly selected *Kabupaten/Kotamadya* in West Java, Indonesia, Azfar (2002) found that 29 percent paid fewer bribes following decentralization, while only 5 percent reported that they paid more. Respondents attested to similar changes in the cost of bribes, or "unofficial payments" (see table 10.5). At least in the eyes of citizens, corruption becomes more widespread and costly the further removed government agencies are from the local level.

Although this evidence supports the hypothesis that decentralization reduces corruption, much depends on how reform is implemented. In the Philippines, infrastructure projects selected by Local Development Councils but built by the Department of Public Works and Highways or other central agencies tended to trigger a cascading effect of unofficial payments at each layer of government (Hofman and Kaiser 2002). Analysts have also reported examples of corruption and rent seeking among local councils, including cases where legislators have voted themselves large salary increases and automobiles, and where a local council has voted to simultaneously approve an investment project and name the party to be awarded the contract. Thus, blanket generalizations about comparative corruption are suspect.

TABLE 10.5 Citizen Perceptions of Corruption in Different Layers of Government in Indonesia

Corruption	Never	Rare/ infrequent	Common	Quite/very common
Local government	17.7%	25.4%	23.3%	11.3%
Kabupaten/*Kotamadya*	1.7%	35.7%	28.2%	18.0%
Provincial government	0%	19.5%	29.9%	33.3%
Central government	0.2%	4.5%	37.0%	48.1%

Source: Azfar 2002, p. 7.
Note: Percentages do not sum to 100 because the figures exclude "don't know" responses.

Probably the strongest evidence for gains in production efficiency from decentralizing infrastructure comes from studies designed to determine whether latrines and small-scale water distribution projects were still functioning and actually used by villagers several years after installation. Studies in Cambodia, Indonesia, Lao People's Democratic Republic, and Vietnam all concluded that projects that relied on community consultation on design, and community organizations for maintenance and oversight, were significantly more likely to be sustained than projects built from a central design without such consultation, or that relied on outside expertise for maintenance and management (Gross 2003; Chanthaphone and Lahiri 2003; World Bank 2002a). Production efficiency overlaps with efficiency in allocative choice and community participation (discussed later in the chapter). Rural Indonesians, for example, were found to have a strong preference for pour-flush latrines, which were far more likely to remain in operation than alternative designs. Women assigned a high priority to small-scale water and sanitation projects, and community-scale water management organizations with strong participation by women proved more sustainable than organizations operated solely or dominated by men.

Such evidence tends to confirm that decentralizing projects to the village or commune level allows community involvement in support of sustainability to emerge. However, simply decentralizing investment and management decisions does little to promote sustainability unless primary users participate in maintenance and management decisions.

On a larger scale, the efficient use of capital in municipal utilities relates directly to performance measures targeted and rewarded under national accountability systems. One of the apparent paradoxes of China's investment in municipal wastewater treatment plants is that local governments are investing heavily in new plants while existing facilities operate at 50 percent or less of designed capacity because of lack of funds for operation and maintenance. This phenomenon has been reported in Hunan province, among other locations (Chreod Ltd. 2002). It reflects the fact that infrastructure targets initially included in local development plans and monitored by higher-level authorities were based on the treatment capacity of completed wastewater treatment plants. Under this yardstick, localities met coverage targets whether or not treatment plants were actually operating, as no one measured the volume of treated discharge or the quality of receiving water bodies. Yet in Changsha, the capital of Hunan province, wastewater treatment plants operated at 50 percent capacity for two years because the city simply shut off intake valves and diverted incoming flows directly into the river. Meanwhile, the municipality was planning large-scale construction of new plants. This experience reveals the power of performance measures tied to accountability procedures: poorly selected performance measures can fail to capture the intended effects. Similarly, centrally imposed cost targets may jeopardize productive efficiency gains if they fail to account for local variations in exogenous costs that are not under the control of municipalities.

When wastewater treatment facilities feed into the same body of water, coordinating projects across local jurisdictions can yield better water quality at lower cost. The top-down system in China, combined with strong decentralized authorities, however, does not provide enough incentives for local governments to consider economies of scale and coordination. In the Guangdong River delta, for instance, each of 51 administrative districts has a wastewater treatment facility, although cooperative agreements based on economies of scale could have yielded significant savings. In Vietnam, in contrast, flexibility in local management and timing of water delivery has resulted in significant drops in water use per hectare, revealing the gains from production efficiency that can result from decentralizing rural irrigation systems (see box 10.1).

Allocative Efficiency

A full argument for gains in allocative efficiency from decentralization would marshal several lines of evidence. First, central and provincial officials fail to correctly identify the spending priorities of local citizens. Second, choices on spending priorities made by local officials, as well as choices made by citizens themselves through participatory procedures, better reflect true local preferences. For example, reliance on central quality standards, as in the Chinese model, may significantly reduce the

BOX 10.1 Vietnam's Red River Delta: Efficiency Gains from Decentralizing Irrigation

The Red River Delta (RRD) in Vietnam has one of the highest-density rural populations in the world. The delta depends on irrigation for crop production. Experience shows the efficiency gains that can be obtained from decentralizing management of an infrastructure network, as well as links between gains from production and allocative efficiency.

Since Vietnam decollectivized its agricultural sector in the 1980s, two types of institutions have provided irrigation in the RRD to farmers. One is state-owned Irrigation and Drainage Management Subsidiary Companies (IDMSCs), which centrally manage pumping stations and irrigation networks. The other is cooperatives, which operate on a smaller scale through joint management and localized pumping stations. Cooperatives entered the irrigation business in response to inflexibilities in water provision from the centrally managed state companies, which scheduled uniform water flows in advance regardless of local conditions or planting patterns. Cooperatives obtain raw water supplies through contracts with regional irrigation management companies. The cooperatives are, in effect, decentralized alternative suppliers of irrigation services to farmers. In the RRD, IDMSCs and cooperatives each serviced about half of the land, facilitating comparisons between the institutions.

Cooperatives have improved allocative efficiency by making water delivery more flexible in response to farmers' demands. Empirical observations over an irrigation season found that, on average, cooperative pumping stations provided water flows within 2 days of a request, compared with 11.5 days for centrally managed systems, which work off a predetermined rotational schedule. The shorter delivery time and greater flexibility of cooperative supply give farmers more choice in cropping patterns, rice varieties, and growing conditions. Production efficiency can be measured in terms of water use per hectare—table 10.1B below shows observed differences in water use for comparable paddy fields.

Part of the observed differential in water use reflects the shorter canal networks of local cooperatives, which reduce water losses and present fewer opportunities for diversion to illegal users. Part of the savings comes from management efficiency motivated by the desire to save on contracted costs for water supply. An important part of the savings, however, comes from reduced corruption. Staff of the state-owned company reportedly made illicit agreements to sell water on the side, adding to the amounts pumped per eligible hectare.

Sources: Fontenelle and Molle 2002; Fontenelle 2000.

TABLE 10.1B Average Volumes of Water Pumped per Hectare, Spring Season 1996, Vietnam
(cubic meters)

Supplier	Water used to prepare land	Water used during growing season	Total
Local station	1,600	2,400	4,000
Centrally managed	3,900	5,900	9,800

Sources: Fontenelle and Molle 2002; Fontenelle 2000.

gains in allocative efficiency from decentralization if it prevents municipalities from adjusting the quality of service to the preferences of their constituencies.

Analysts have collected evidence on parts of this argument. For example, Azfar et al. (2000) found that Filipino households strongly favor spending incremental funds on roads, but that household preferences vary substantially across locations, presumably reflecting differences in both local values and conditions. Municipal officials had a statistically significant ability to identify local preferences, while provincial officials had no ability whatsoever to identify local preferences—with a negative correlation between their predictions and actual household preferences. In particular, provincial officials vastly underestimated local demand for spending on roads and other local infrastructure.

Household surveys in Indonesia and Cambodia have also found strong preferences for road construction as the top investment priority. Internationally funded programs that involve community choice report a significantly higher level of investment in roads than among projects whose outputs are negotiated at the central level. Local development projects that incorporate citizen participation in project selection appear to more accurately reflect both the general preference for roads and variations across communities. For example, during the first two years of the *Kecamatan* Development Program in Indonesia, road projects were by far the most popular local investment choice (62 percent), compared with bridges (10 percent), irrigation (8 percent), and clean water (7 percent). Follow-up surveys found that even given these percentages, households felt that too much had been expended on clean water. Evidence from these and other studies, in short, is that citizens have clear-cut priorities for spending, and that distant representatives and bureaucrats do not grasp these priorities or assign great importance to local priorities. Moreover, local demand for simple infrastructure projects—primarily roads—is high compared with alternatives. Of course, how much deference central governments should pay to household preferences in allocating spending across sectors is an open question, especially when sectors like education and health generate positive externalities not fully captured by local residents. Nonetheless, for spending assigned to local investment choice, evidence supports the conclusion that decentralization is closing the gap between local preferences and project selection.

Lessons Learned

More important than the first-round impacts of decentralization on the efficiency of infrastructure services are the lessons that can be learned to better extract potential gains.

Because the costs of corruption are high in providing infrastructure, countries should take practical steps to reduce corruption and other inefficiencies under decentralized management. In most East Asian countries, central authorities have traditionally handled infrastructure procurement, even for locally selected projects supported by significant local funding. Meanwhile, however, decentralization has given local authorities responsibility for defining their own procurement rules. This situation has not only created confusion and inconsistency across the local government landscape, but has also led to procurement abuses, such as lack of competitive bidding and technical evaluation of proposals, steering of contracts to particular firms by elected officials, and extensive price renegotiation after contracts are awarded. Adoption of a uniform local procurement code should be a top priority for decentralization, to build in competition and transparency. The Government Procurement Reform Act of 2003 in the Philippines offers a model of such support. An oversight and regulatory board empowered to investigate and punish procurement abuses needs to supplement formal procedures.

Best-practice local examples suggest other steps for improving procurement. Naga City in the Philippines, for example, now publishes in the newspaper and on the Internet winning per unit prices for all procurement contracts. This simple action both supports transparency and encourages price competition among suppliers (World Bank and Asian Development Bank 2003). In administering the *Kecamatan* Development Program in Indonesia, the World Bank has found that the simple expedient of requiring that an independent (local) third party as well as contracting principals sign off on all contracts and procurements, however small, saves funds and fosters a culture of transparency.

Excess capacity in infrastructure design is a major source of cost inefficiency. Paradoxically, at a time of large infrastructure backlogs, a number of projects suffer from substantial overcapacity, raising costs unnecessarily. In some cases, excess capacity has resulted from centralized application of standard project designs or per capita use estimates that do not take local conditions into account. Some Indonesian PDAMs are operating at only one-third of designed capacity because abundant groundwater sources are available and households prefer to continue pumping their own water rather than pay for connecting to the piped water system.

Many Chinese cities suffer from overestimated water demand because authorities failed to anticipate the drops in demand that would occur with full-cost water tariffs and the rapid decline in state-owned firms—often the most inefficient water users. This situation has left some local governments with "take or pay" contracts with private companies, which require governments to either purchase more water than consumers will use or displace lower-cost municipal water with higher-cost supplies. As in all countries, grant and low-cost loan financing also promotes excessive scaling of infrastructure facilities. When investment appears to be free to local authorities, they tend to base estimates of future demand on the most optimistic assumptions. Comparable projects financed from own-source funds reflect more realistic growth projections and the time and cost entailed in tying up funds. Again, the practical lessons are straightforward. Wherever possible, major infrastructure projects should occur at the local level *after* reforms in user prices, so officials can estimate the impact on demand more accurately. Uniform per capita projections of use should be scuttled in favor of demand studies based on local conditions. All infrastructure projects of significant scale should require substantial own-source financing, to create incentives for realistic cost projections and savings.

Predicting a country's optimal infrastructure capacity compared with its long-term investment needs is admittedly complex, given the "lumpiness" of investments and the uncertainties associated with long-term planning. Hence, whereas today's use of infrastructure facilities points to overcapacity, the extent to which that overcapacity is likely to persist is difficult to gauge.

Gains from Citizen Participation

For countries pursuing autonomous decentralization, the hallmark of reform has been the promise of greater citizen participation in local budget decisions, investment choices, and development planning. Such participation is supposed to yield greater citizen satisfaction with basic services and more coverage for previously excluded groups—particularly the poor, ethnic minorities, and women—while laying the groundwork for broader democratic participation in national government.

Cambodia's 2003 Poverty Reduction Strategy illustrates the weight of expectations placed on decentralization as a tool for achieving participation:

"*Decentralization has three objectives in Cambodia:*

- Promote pluralist participatory democracy at local level . . . by creation of popularly mandated and autonomous local governments that are responsible to the citizens . . . and make decisions over delivery of public goods and services.
- Promote the culture and practice of participatory development (planning, management, resource mobilization) at local level.
- Contribute to reduction of poverty in the country through improvement of service conditions . . . and [service] improvement to poor and deprived ones" (Royal Government of Cambodia 2003a, p. 108).

Countries have introduced autonomous decentralization primarily through grants to local communities that allow citizens to directly choose small investment projects and provide for community management of the projects once installed. The Seila Program has brought citizen choice over small infrastructure projects to Cambodia; the *Kecamatan* Development Program has done the same for subdistricts in Indonesia; as have *barangay* investment programs in the Philippines for urban subdistricts. Several other programs follow the model of providing communities with investment resources that they can allocate among eligible projects. Such programs have typically won strong support from the World Bank, the Asian Development Bank, the United Nations Development Programme, and other international organizations seeking to imprint local citizen choice as the bedrock support for decentralization.

Experience with citizen participation in East Asia raises two critical questions. First, does participation in fact improve sustainability and coverage of basic infrastructure services at the village, urban subdistrict, and neighborhood scale? Second, can experience in direct participation be successfully scaled up to larger political units and infrastructure networks? As the following evidence reveals, the answer to the first question is yes, while the jury is still out on the second question. Despite some promising local experience, scaling up has proved more difficult than optimistic advocates of participation foresaw.

Community-Scale Participation

A large body of evidence supports the importance of community-scale participation in infrastructure choices and management. This evidence also provides guidelines on specific responsibilities that communities can handle to extract the maximum value from participation. For example, in a study of 88 community-managed water supply projects worldwide, Gross et al. found that:

- Community-based water supply projects which were more demand-responsive—that is, those that involved greater community choice in the type of water supply, households to be covered, and the method for paying for operations and maintenance—were more likely to be sustained and better maintained.
- The more broadly participatory and gender representative the decision-making procedures, the higher the rate of cost recovery.
- Communities that set up water management organizations (WMOs) had better project sustainability records than communities that participated only in initial project selection; the more equitably WMOs represented women and the poor, the greater their sustainability.
- Household contributions to construction were significantly associated with better-sustained water supply services only if the community actively participated in project selection and subsequent management (Gross et al. 2001).

Hopkins' study of 33 sites in Flores in the Philippines found higher rates of sustainability where planning included both women and men, as well as poor households. The World Bank has reported higher rates of sustainability of locally selected infrastructure projects when project choice reflected direct community participation (Hopkins 2003; World Bank 2003d).

Some of the benefits to be reaped from local participation and choice require careful listening by outside experts, whether national officials or international advisors. In 2001 Lao PDR adopted a new policy of allowing communities to choose their hygiene solutions and influence their design. Follow-up work found that villagers primarily valued the "comfort and convenience" of latrines rather than the health benefits, which were foremost in the minds of external experts (Meadley 2003). This finding influenced both the design of the latrines and the strategy for disseminating the program, which relied on "champion families" respected by other families. After the champion families receive latrine facilities, photos showing their convenience and the families' pride in owning them are used to engage the widely dispersed rural community in discussing the benefits of latrines and gain support for their adoption.

The literature on decentralized fiscal choice has emphasized the gains from allowing clients to choose among a wide array of project options, constrained by either a fixed budget or the requirement that users pay for the service they choose. Many East Asian experiments in decentralized project selection have followed this model, offering local residents a broad initial choice of investment priorities. The Seila Program in Cambodia and the *Kecamatan* Development Program in Indonesia are two examples that offer relatively open-ended choice.

However, some national programs have defined community choice and participation differently, particularly those that retain strong roles for governmental planners and service providers. In the poor rural province of Guizhou, China, for example, prospective township clients can choose to receive private water connections at a tariff level that covers operating costs plus some 75 percent of capital costs, including all debt service. Less expensive alternatives, such as public stand posts, are not offered, nor does the community have a voice in tariff policy or technology. Community consultation consists of carefully explaining to residents the kind of water service they will receive, the tariff costs, and the procedures for collecting the tariffs, which entail house-by-house collection (Zhixiong 2003). The community may then embrace the program and its rules or, in principle, express reluctance to pay for it. Village committees identify delivery problems and exert collective pressure on citizens to pay water bills. However, the plant manager remains in control of all aspects of management. A portion of his salary is deducted if tariff collection rates fall below 90 percent.

Scaling Up Participation

The difficulties of scaling up successes in community participation are widely recognized (World Bank 2003b). Ironically, scaling up community and rural village projects has proved easier in some respects in a centralized rather than a decentralized environment, where many levels of government exert authority. Scaling up means multiplying the number of villages and urban subdistrict communities reached using the same implementation principles. Such scaling up is constrained primarily by the resources of a program and the central government's willingness to support it through its own resources or agreement with international donors. If the financial and human resources are replicable, projects can be reproduced throughout the country. Seila in Cambodia is an example of a community participation program that is rapidly scaling up to reach the entire country with direct central support, without much interaction with other levels of government. The *Kecamatan* Development Program in Indonesia is another program that has spread quickly by replicating the same neighborhood approach, with central government and donor support. Only now, in its third generation, is the program attempting the more difficult task of integrating priority setting at the community level with the formal planning procedures of the decentralized system.

Scaling up community-identified priorities within a decentralized government structure requires finding ways to transmit community preferences on infrastructure investments to successively higher levels of government. Community "demand" may include both community-scale projects that need higher-level financial support and community views on the priority of village, district, and municipal investment projects that affect the community. The transmission of community preferences about capital projects to higher levels of government has proved problematic. Part of the difficulty stems from distrust of representative government and suspicion of the willingness of municipal officials to respect community investment priorities. This distrust has been compounded by the difficult interface between top-down national investment planning and bottom-up community and local planning. Both the Philippines and Indonesia have attempted to address this challenge by directly involving community groups in progressively higher levels of decision making.

Indonesia illustrates the complexity of transmitting community preferences.[5] The urban planning process begins with village development meetings attended by the village representative council, NGOs, and a representative of the subdistrict (*Kecamatan*). A major objective is to submit project proposals to the *Kecamatan* subdistrict level. There officials review and weed out community proposals and add new proposals, and then submit a priority list to the next level of government (*Kabupaten/Kota*), which adds proposals from technical officials. The project preferences of the *Kabupaten* parliament also become part of the mix and may override other recommendations. Finally, an umbrella system is supposed to coordinate local investment priorities with provincial and national priorities. As part of this structure, the Indonesian government has promulgated general guidelines for participatory planning at the *Kabubaten* and *Kota* level, including open meetings that bring together representatives of communities, NGOs, and technical bureaus as well as municipal elected officials. The entire process—facilitated by a government-provided scoring sheet—should yield a consensus list of local priorities.

Case studies reveal that this process plays out differently in different locations. Municipal parliaments, technical agencies, and NGOs typically have different priorities (Pratikno 2002; Indonesian Partnership on Local Governance Initiatives 2002). Negotiations leading to final project prioritization at the municipal level depend on the relative clout of these parties and the role the mayor chooses to play. Most case studies have concluded that the preferences of local elites, the municipal parliament, and technical agencies tend to drown out the preferences of community groups. The mandated participation of NGOs has not resolved this issue, because—instead of representing a consensus of lower-level priorities—NGOs have more often proved to be splintered advocacy groups for particular priorities. A similar system of planning and priority setting operates in the Philippines, including the mandated participation of community NGOs in local development councils. Similar difficulties in sustaining grassroots participation in municipal priority setting have been reported.

A realistic reassessment of what community participation in infrastructure decision making means at the municipal scale is in order. Intermediation is plainly required in scaling up from the community level to the municipal level. Elected representatives in the municipal parliament provide one form of intermediation; NGOs provide another. In the most successful examples of public inclusiveness in setting infrastructure priorities, NGOs have played the role of intermediary between community and government. This has required continuous involvement by NGOs, starting with community-level meetings and extending to collaboration with the technical agencies of municipal government. Against this preparatory background, structured meetings on investment priorities and budget allocations, such as citizen forums, can succeed. The conditions for success, however, are demanding: NGOs must be willing to see themselves as partners with local government rather than antagonists, and local officials must be open to input from institutions outside the political and governmental technical sphere. Clear examples of successful implementation of this vision do exist. These include the involvement of the Indonesian Partnership on Local Governance Initiatives with both municipal government and communities in urban forums in Indonesia, and the culture of partnership in all decision making in Naga, the Philippines. Efforts to include community expression under the *Kecamatan* Development Program and ordinary decentralized priority-setting procedures in Indonesia are other examples. Whether scaling up direct community participation in setting investment priorities is widely workable remains to be seen, however. Many communities have reported a public stalemate that gives rise to the older pattern of nontransparent decision making by elites.

Lessons Learned

Community participation is essential to the success of infrastructure projects at the village and subdistrict level. Participation is required at the point of project selection as well as in continued project management. Meaningful participation requires the involvement of a cross-section of project users, especially women and minority groups, who are often excluded from project management.

Scaling up participation in infrastructure choice has proved difficult. Other mechanisms, such as genuinely representative municipal governments, and NGOs willing to serve as intermediaries to both municipal government and local communities, are needed to make the process work.

The most promising approach involves NGO participation from the start of the priority-setting process through the municipal meetings that establish local investment priorities. Only NGO involvement at the last stage—such as through the Local Development Councils prescribed by Filipino law—has proved unsuccessful.

The idea that community participation in setting infrastructure priorities will breed a national culture of democratic decision making has seen a modest amount of empirical support thus far. Just as scaling up infrastructure priorities can be difficult, so can scaling up expectations about democratic participation in governance. The experience of allocating budgets to communities undoubtedly empowers households and raises their expectations about responsive government. Whether such participation helps consolidate national democracy remains to be seen.

Paying for Infrastructure Services

Infrastructure services must be financed at two levels. Capital resources must be mobilized to pay for the initial investment in facilities. Then recurring revenues must cover the annual cost of operations and maintenance, plus contributions to servicing the debt incurred to finance the initial investment. In an economically efficient world, the full cost of infrastructure facilities, including depreciation, would be recognized and recovered through user fees and—given positive externalities—explicit subsidies from government, in the form of capital grants or targeted subsidies.

Much of the institutional unbundling of large infrastructure utilities in East Asia has been motivated by a desire to generate more reliable financing streams, and to make infrastructure services more attractive candidates for commercial investment or lending. The latter goal has sometimes conflicted with the goal of making monopoly utilities more directly accountable to local governments.

Asia faced a formidable infrastructure pricing challenge at the beginning of this decade, as it had the lowest water and sanitation tariffs—both in absolute terms and as a percentage of the costs of production—of any other region (see annex 10.1). The median urban tariff for water supply reportedly covered less than 85 percent of operating and maintenance costs, with no contribution to the cost of capital. The median tariff for sanitation covered an even lower portion of operating and maintenance costs. If anything, the tariff ratios reported by governments are likely to underestimate the true cost gap.

In examining financing approaches, we can extend the distinction introduced at the beginning of this chapter between China and (in incipient terms) Vietnam, on the one hand, and the Philippines, Indonesia, and (in incipient and less clear-cut terms) Cambodia, on the other. Aided by strong economic growth, China has devised a broad model for self-financed infrastructure investment and market-based capital financing. Both the Philippines and Indonesia have been handicapped by a stronger impact from the Asian financial crisis and less robust economic growth. However, they have compounded the difficulty by retaining central control of lending to local authorities for infrastructure investment—an anomaly in their otherwise sweeping embrace of decentralization.

China's Infrastructure Financing Strategy

China has pursued a clearly defined sequential strategy for financing local infrastructure. Although the model has important weaknesses, it contains lessons for the rest of the region. To finance the first wave of investment in local infrastructure networks, the government relied primarily on local taxes and fees, supplemented by borrowing from international donor agencies and capital grants and budget assignments from central government. Starting in 1998, the government began to borrow heavily from the domestic market to finance infrastructure. Between 1998 and 2002 it issued ¥ 660 billion (US$79.5 billion) in infrastructure bonds—some 30 percent of which was then transferred to local governments, half as subloans and half as grants. Along with this use of the domestic bond market, the government communicated the priority of local infrastructure lending to China's banks, all of which are publicly owned. Short- to intermediate-term loans from banks have been a principal source of capital financing for local governments investing in infrastructure.

One undesirable effect of the surge in local borrowing to finance infrastructure investment has been a high and rising level of municipal indebtedness. Under existing arrangements, municipalities had to repay outstanding debt from their general budgets, placing a high degree of strain on their finances. This was especially true in light of the inadequate structure for service fees, which did not recover operating and maintenance costs, much less the costs of debt service. Further squeezing municipal budgets was the short maturity of infrastructure bank loans—typically three years, sometimes five years.

In response, the central government took three important steps designed to ready local governments to further finance local infrastructure within a fiscally responsible framework. First, it announced that most local governments would be responsible for obtaining capital financing for infrastructure investment from the market. State onlending and grants from the proceeds of state infrastructure bonds would be limited to the economically laggard western provinces—other local governments had to be self-financing. Second, to support this self-sufficiency, the government decreed that municipalities should adopt full-cost tariffs for water supply, solid waste, and wastewater treatment, on a highly accelerated timetable. Full-cost pricing was defined to include all operating and maintenance costs plus debt service and a competitive return on newly invested capital. Better-off municipalities were supposed to set tariffs to allow for full recovery of systemwide capital costs. This regime was designed to provide adequate revenue streams to cover debt service and attract private-sector capital into the local infrastructure sector, via either direct investment or lending.

In a third—and in some respects most interesting—initiative, the government decreed that local government should be restructured to separate the ownership of infrastructure and other assets from operating responsibilities. This last initiative had two goals. First, it was intended to yield more efficient management of municipal assets, following so-called New Government trends established in Australia, New Zealand, and other countries, in which the asset-owning institution levies a capital charge on users to allocate costs more efficiently. In China's case, however, a more important motivation was to place under a single institutional umbrella assets used as collateral for municipal loans. As part of governmental restructuring, only the asset-holding institutions, known as Urban Development Investment Corporations (UDICs), may now borrow on behalf of municipal government. The restructuring was supposed to ensure that municipal borrowing did not exceed the collateral capacity of the municipality's asset base. Moreover, as only UDICs are legally authorized to borrow, the restructuring was supposed to insulate the general municipal budget from debt service claims while providing a powerful incentive to

UDICs to implement fees that would cover the cost of capital.

In some respects, China's infrastructure finance reforms are less sweeping than they may at first appear. Although municipalities are prohibited from direct borrowing, they continue to provide comfort letters to local UDICs. These in effect commit a municipal government to use general budget revenues or income from municipally owned property to help meet the UDIC's debt service obligations, should such support become necessary. Although UDICs tap the general corporate debt market, their debt instruments are a form of municipal borrowing. The change in the institutional name of the borrower does not relieve local public institutions of the debt service burden created by short-term borrowing to finance long-term infrastructure projects. From the banking sector's perspective, the large amount of local assets held in the form of loans to local governments represents a credit risk of unknown magnitude. No defaults on municipal borrowing from banks have been reported. However, banks routinely roll over short-term loans as they come due. Questions remain as to whether banks will continue this policy as foreign competition enters the banking sector under WTO rules, how much of their outstanding debt municipalities could actually pay under existing schedules, and how politically feasible and economically rewarding it would be for banks to foreclose on assets offered as collateral.

One finding of potential significance to other East Asian countries has emerged from UDIC restructuring, however, especially for periods of strong economic performance. Municipal governments in China possess undeveloped or redevelopable land with great market value, which could finance a substantial proportion of the local infrastructure investment burden. Changsha, the capital of Hunan province in China's interior, illustrates this situation. The municipality holds title to some 1.33 million hectares of land, valued at the municipality's minimum long-term leasing price in 2001 at some ¥ 105 billion. Of this total, about ¥ 85 billion (more than US$10 billion) corresponds to land not occupied by the municipality itself that could be leased. Changsha officials estimate that some 60 percent of the gross price of leased land represents costs for land that must be set aside as matching open space under planning regulations, resettlement costs, and revenues that must be shared with higher levels of government. Still, with 40 percent of the gross value representing net profit, the net value of Changsha's land inventory is some ¥ 34 billion, which could finance a large part of the municipality's 10-year capital investment plan.

The potential for converting Chinese land values into infrastructure assets is even greater if one considers that a large share of local infrastructure investment is capitalized into the value of municipally owned land, and that municipalities' landholdings are far from static. As population growth pushes the urban boundary outward, more and more land reverts from collective rural ownership to municipal ownership, providing a continuing basis for capturing land value. Rural land at the edge of urban centers is indeed seriously underpriced, as the replacement cost of rural land is based on its agricultural use without the premium reflecting proximity to urban centers. This gives municipalities strong incentives to convert land from rural to municipal ownership. And municipalities are in fact converting land values into infrastructure investment throughout China. In some municipalities studied under the City Development Strategies (Cities Alliance), land has financed as much as 70 percent of local infrastructure investment, either directly through proceeds from leases or indirectly by serving as collateral for infrastructure loans.[6] However, concerns are growing that reliance on revenues from periurban land may lead to unsustainable urban planning and degrade the quality of urban life, calling for the development of and integrated approach to land use and urban planning at the municipality level.

The combination of full-cost tariffs for water supply, sanitation, and solid waste, coupled with increments in land value created by road construction and expansion of urban boundaries, provides a potentially sound basis for financing municipal infrastructure.

Infrastructure Financing in the Philippines and Indonesia

The structure of lending to local governments for financing infrastructure has become an important bottleneck to decentralization in both the Philippines and Indonesia. Despite plans to graduate creditworthy municipalities and local utilities to the competitive credit market, the central government remains in control of credit channels in both countries, acting as a monopoly intermediary between loans provided by international financial institutions and local governments. This position has frustrated development of sustainable sources of domestic financing while allowing central government institutions to restore—through loan conditions and discretionary loan approvals—some control over the local infrastructure sector formally relinquished in the decentralization process.

The local credit market in the Philippines illustrates the unequal playing field established by the government. The Development Bank of the Philippines and the Land Bank of the Philippines obtain financing from international organizations and from the National Bank at below-market rates. Their onlending to local governments is secured by the authority to intercept intergovernmental revenue-sharing allotments—authority that is not available to private lenders. Reliable local loan repayment to government financial institutions was intended to introduce commercial banks to municipal lending as a creditworthy activity. However, commercial banks cannot match the cost of funds of the government financial institutions, as they are prohibited from serving as depository institutions for municipalities, which would strengthen their ties to municipal budgets and provide a lower-cost source of financing. As a result, commercial bank lending to municipalities for infrastructure has yet to get off the ground, despite the formal policy of promoting creditworthy municipalities to the private credit market.

Indonesia illustrates the legacy power of bad loans in thwarting development of a local credit market. As of March 31, 2000, 63 percent of the borrowing accounts of water utilities through subsidiary loan agreements and the Regional Development Account were reportedly in arrears (World Bank 2003b). Although the country has launched a program of debt restructuring, it has made little headway in straightening out legacy borrowing. Resolution of the inherited debt runs straight to the fundamental issues raised by political decentralization. If central authorities made past investment decisions and mandated loan agreements, should a decentralized water utility be required to honor that debt, and, if so, how will it recover the debt if municipal governments are unwilling to impose the required tariff increases? On the other hand, writing off these loans implies a substantial fiscal loss to the central government as well as an undesirable precedent for future onlending. These conditions seem to lay the groundwork for loan restructuring, but reaching comprehensive agreement has proved difficult.

Lessons Learned

A self-sustaining local credit market is essential for successfully decentralizing the infrastructure sector. National government, as the original onlender to municipal governments and utilities, needs to have a strategy for developing a domestic local credit market from the outset. This strategy requires three components:

- *Establishing a track record of timely debt repayment by local authorities.* The injection of political considerations into debt repayment to government financial institutions creates a credit risk in local lending that can set back market development for decades. The institutional weight of bad loans deters entry by private financial institutions into the subnational credit market.
- *A policy that promotes replacement of government lending by private lending as quickly as feasible.* This, in turn, requires a level playing field regarding revenue intercepts, depository functions, and other regulations. In other regions, internationally sponsored municipal development funds have proved successful by onlending to municipalities through commercial banks, which fully accept the credit risk. This strategy introduces commercial banks to municipal lending while giving them access to longer-term, lower-cost funds than are available on the domestic market. This approach requires a willingness on the part of government financial institutions to introduce decentralization to the financial sector by eliminating their monopolistic role as sole municipal lenders.
- *A policy of substantial capital cost recovery through service tariffs.* For services such as water supply and wastewater removal, which cannot directly generate gains in land value, the only reliable recurring source of revenue is service fees. One of the most useful standards that

national government can set in the infrastructure sector is model tariff agreements between municipal authorities and water utilities. Under these, the municipality agrees to sanction cost-recovery tariffs if the water utility meets performance targets for service delivery and coverage.

How Far to Decentralize?

Decentralization requires unbundling the functions associated with providing infrastructure services and allocating them among different tiers of government. The optimal level of decentralization will vary with government's policy goals and the types of infrastructure. This section discusses the mandate of higher tiers of government in the context of decentralized services.

The Role of Higher Tiers of Government

Even with aspects of infrastructure that are essentially local, an argument can be made for allocating specific functions to tiers of government higher than the municipal level given one of the following conditions:

Spillover effects. Interjurisdictional spillovers—or externalities—arise when the activities of one jurisdiction affect the welfare of people in surrounding jurisdictions. If municipal services produce spillover benefits or costs, service provision will be inefficient without intervention by higher-level government, as local governments would ignore these impacts. For example, local decisions on regulating effluent discharges into rivers have implications for users in other jurisdictions that are part of the same catchment area. Similarly, spillover effects occur when municipalities are responsible for managing feeder roads whose benefits accrue to more than one jurisdiction.

To correct for such spillover effects, the tier of government whose jurisdiction encompasses all the users benefiting from such services should decide on investment priorities and allocate resources. For example, managing environmental resources according to water basins is becoming more common to correct for externalities in shared water resources. The functions entrusted to water basin authorities include managing and conserving watersheds, controlling floods, reducing pollution, and licensing water extraction. On the other hand, overuse and degradation of natural resources may occur when an intermediate tier of government does not take responsibility for integrated water resource management (see box 10.2). Spillover effects similarly call for devolving management of secondary road networks to intermediate tiers of government.

Economies of scale. A municipality responsible for providing basic infrastructure services may be smaller than the minimum scale required to ensure

BOX 10.2 Vietnam: Watershed Management

In Dak Lak, Vietnam, groundwater is in high demand to feed the expanding cultivation of coffee plantations. Groundwater resources in the Ea Tul and Quang Phu catchments have so far been freely accessible, leading to overuse and degradation of the natural resource base. Growing competition in water use has led to conflicts between upstream and downstream users.

Local agencies have failed to mediate these conflicts. For example, attempts by irrigation officers to introduce irrigation calendars failed because communes could not consolidate their cropping calendars to fit the desired schedule. Under the new Water Law, Water Users Associations have emerged to make decisions and coordinate water resources. At the provincial level, the Province People's Committee established a Participatory Irrigation Management Steering Committee to provide guidance to the Water Users Associations, along with supporting committees at the district level. The water associations, which cooperate with local line agencies, have encouraged farmers to view watershed problems more holistically and mobilized new forms of collective action to address overuse and erosion.

The focus on participatory irrigation management is seen as a starting point for a more environmentally integrated approach to managing water resources. However, even in the new institutional landscape, no effective regional institutions regulate access to and use of groundwater.

Source: Dupar and Badenoch 2002.

technical efficiency, especially for services that are local in nature but require large capital investments, such as water supply, electricity distribution, and public transport.[7] When excessive fragmentation of service provision is a concern, clustering municipalities to provide regional services can boost efficiency.[8] However, regional utilities require an institutional interface at a higher level of government in charge of setting investment priorities and regulating services. Spontaneous coordination across municipalities is indeed difficult to achieve and may be unsustainable when no higher tiers play a coordinating role. As an example, in Caracas, 23 municipalities agreed to cooperate to award a single water concession. However, the resulting agreement lacked credibility to investors, and the group received no responsive bids from private operators (Triche et al. 1993).

Scarcity of human resources. A scarcity of specific skills may also make multiplying the number of service providers undesirable. In such a context, fewer larger entities may be in a better position to attract the minimum required skills than more numerous, smaller service providers. A similar argument can be made for limiting the number of regulatory entities to enhance their capacity when human resources are scarce (see, for example, Smith 2000).

Equity considerations. Fiscal decentralization may conflict with equity goals if the poorest regions have limited leeway to mobilize financing and raise own-source revenues to meet their infrastructure needs, such as through local taxation, user fees, and access to capital markets. This may argue for limiting fiscal decentralization to allow higher tiers of government to redistribute resources to areas lagging behind in economic development. In this context, intergovernmental transfers are instrumental in ensuring that all localities can afford to invest in infrastructure. As an example, the government (or regulatory authority) may impose a levy on all firms operating in a market, and redistribute the revenues to companies connecting new users in poor regions that cannot afford steep user charges. Higher tiers of government may also need to retain some discretion in setting investment priorities to ensure that local projects contribute to national and regional strategies for reducing poverty.

Distortion of interjurisdictional trade. Local regulation of basic infrastructure services may affect interjurisdictional trade, adding transaction costs for operators. For instance, local regulations governing transportation safety may conflict and thus limit or distort opportunities for trade. When local regulations impede trade across jurisdictions, there is an economic argument for setting homogeneous quality standards throughout the area. As an example, in catchment areas cutting across several municipalities, water basin authorities may play a role in harmonizing environmental standards and regulating inland waterways. Higher tiers of government could similarly be entrusted with responsibility for setting quality standards for secondary road networks (see box 10.3).

Destructive competition. Decentralization may increase efficiency by promoting competition among local governments. However, devolution of decision-making powers to the lowest tiers of government may turn the potential for competition into a "race to the bottom," where competition among local governments to attract foreign investment in

BOX 10.3 Indonesia: When Transport Regulations Distort Trade

One area where transport regulations may discriminate against outsiders is the introduction of licenses for use of roads within a certain region. The *Izin Trayek* rule in South Sulawesi, Indonesia, for example, requires that all transport trucks carry one of three specific licenses: for interprovincial transport, for intraprovincial transport, and for entering the regencies (*Kecamatan*). The first two licenses are issued at the provincial level in accordance with gubernatorial decree (*Keputusan*) No. 10 1996, while local governments issue the third type of license. Trucks not carrying licenses are typically fined Rp 35,000. This regulation clearly discriminates against trucks from other areas, particularly because licenses are not available outside South Sulawesi.

Source: Goodpaster and Ray 2000.

infrastructure can prompt municipalities to bid down taxes or other regulatory obligations (or bid up subsidies or regulated rates of return).[9] Excessive competition may induce inefficient allocation of resources and overinvestment, with municipalities building or upgrading ports or other infrastructure facilities in their own areas to enhance their prestige, rather than relying on facilities in adjacent regions.

Efficiency of revenue collection. The scope for decentralizing financial powers may be limited when the central level can collect budgetary revenues more efficiently, and when there is little opportunity for collecting cost-covering charges at the point of service. This is often the case in the road sector, for example, where financing comes largely from fuel taxes and vehicle operating fees, which are more efficiently collected by higher tiers of government. Higher levels need to redistribute those revenues to lower tiers where services are provided. An example is dedicated road maintenance funds financed by user charges collected at the national level (mainly through fuel taxes). Sophisticated cost-sharing formulas can allocate these funds among different road networks (and corresponding levels of government), and robust accountability mechanisms can oversee use of the funds.

Interjurisdictional Coordination in China

In China, sustained economic growth is spurring a few major cities to develop into metropolitan areas that cut across more than one jurisdiction. These areas include the Pearl River Delta region (centered around Guangzhou, Shenzhen, and Hong Kong), the Lower Yangzi Delta region (centered around Shanghai), and the Beijing-Tianjin region. Coordinated development has started to emerge, as municipalities have begun to see the benefits of regional integration. For example, a pilot exercise in the Pearl River Delta region, led by the Ministry of Construction, aims to establish a metropolitan planning model to be replicated in other regions. An even more ambitious project is the plan to develop a Pan-Pearl River Delta Regional Cooperation and Development Area, which would encompass almost one-fourth of China's territory, including nine provinces, Hong Kong, and Macau. The main goal of this regional initiative is to facilitate the management of highway and railway projects, which are expected to generate significant externalities. The trend toward regional integration is therefore an important step toward more efficient infrastructure service provision.

On the other hand, examples of interjurisdictional management of shared water resources, where spillover effects also call for the involvement of higher tiers of government, are still rare in China. The main exception is the recent attempt to promote shared environmental infrastructure in the Pearl River Delta (PRD), one of the most complex urban systems in Asia. Many sections of the PRD have extremely poor water quality. The municipalities of the Guangdong province are the highest contributors to PRD pollution, and the provincial government—through its Environmental Protection Bureau—has recently announced an eight-year, US$5 billion program to invest in wastewater treatment facilities. The plan is based on the recognition that investment in environmental infrastructure should be guided by a regional development strategy that reflects sound environmental management and fiscal sustainability. A pilot project will promote development of environmental infrastructure for three groups of two or more municipalities, districts, and towns. A key parallel activity is the PRD Cleanup Campaign, which has set phased targets for meeting water quality standards. One of the goals of the campaign is to enhance intermunicipal collaboration.

In China, more effective regional coordination in setting investment priorities and allocating resources is also needed to help avoid excessive competition among municipalities in the provision of infrastructure services. Amid economic transition and decentralization, local investment policies are indeed driven primarily by a growth and competitiveness agenda. As a result, municipalities tend to compete excessively to attract outside investment in businesses and infrastructure projects. Their competitive tools are mainly preferential policies such as tax holidays, free land, and discounted land concessions. In this context, lacking coordination at higher tiers of government, such ad hoc policies may unduly distort resource allocation between municipalities, as well as between stakeholders within a municipality.

The Missing Middle: The Case of Indonesia

In Indonesia, Law 22 of 1999 accords provinces two roles: as deconcentrated representatives of the center, and as autonomous regions. While provinces can officially coordinate regional policies and perform joint tasks on behalf of local governments, the legislative framework provides no hierarchical relationship between provinces and local governments. This has jeopardized the ability of provinces to facilitate cooperation among local governments and establish their authority in regional functions. As a result, sectors with large externalities and significant economies of scale, such as watershed management, have consistently underperformed. Moreover, decentralization has resulted in a multiplicity of standards at the municipal level, which may distort trade across jurisdictions (see box 10.3).

The resulting efficiency losses from the "missing middle" are compounded by the small size of some local entities, which suggests diseconomies of scale and points to consolidation of regions.[10] The narrow administrative boundaries of local governments, combined with the limited role of provinces, have led to suboptimal investment decisions from a regional and national perspective. The argument for strengthening the role of provinces in managing road networks, whose benefits accrue to more than one local jurisdiction, is especially compelling. Secondary road networks have been largely underfunded compared with the need (the country confronted an estimated 15–20 percent funding shortfall in 2000) (World Bank 2004). In this context, giving provinces greater financial authority can broaden their influence on local governments and thus increase investment efficiency. One approach is to link provincial and national road funds, and assign the provincial government strategic oversight of all roads (provincial and *kapubaten*) in the province, as well as responsibility for assessing investment needs and allocating resources. The provincial road funds would finance maintenance and rehabilitation of local networks, provided that the *kapubaten* adopt sound road management practices.

In Indonesia, the central government retains significant control in allocating resources between jurisdictions. Limited decentralization of revenue-raising powers can help reduce regional inequality, given redistributive mechanisms. The intergovernmental transfer system includes two equalization grants (the DAK and the DAU, or *dana alokasi umum*) to fund investment in infrastructure, especially services that generate externalities. However, in practice, these grants have tended to exacerbate rather than reduce regional inequality.[11]

The Philippines: Another Example of the Missing Middle

In the Philippines, the national government is responsible for providing primary infrastructure, including backbone transmission grids in the power sector and primary road networks, while cities and municipalities are responsible for tertiary infrastructure such as roads and water. However, it is unclear which tier of government is responsible for planning investment and coordinating development of secondary networks that serve more than one local government and involve common resources such as river basins. While in principle provinces play a coordinating role among cities and municipalities, they lack the technical and financial resources to do so.

As a result, no intermediate tier is capable of managing water resources shared by several local governments. Without a regional body to coordinate investment, local governments often argue over river basin planning and management, allocation of water rights, and pollution control, and water-stressed municipalities have had trouble negotiating water rights outside administrative boundaries. For example, Cebu City reportedly had great difficulty convincing Bohol province to supply the water-starved city even though the marginal value of water consumption in the city was high.

A similar situation arises in managing secondary road networks. While road density in the Philippines is among the highest in the region, only 20 percent of the road network is paved. Provincial roads account for only 13 percent of total roads, with more than 70 percent consisting of city, municipal, or *barangay* roads. Moreover, in 2000, only 21 percent of provincial roads were paved—a rate much lower than that for national roads (62 percent), city roads (77 percent) and even municipal roads (34 percent) (Department of Public Work and Highways 2003). Under the institutional framework, volunteer cooperation among local governments is the only mechanism for coordinating management of the secondary road network (see box 10.4).

Provinces also suffer from an acute lack of financial resources. This is due largely to the fact that decentralization has significantly shifted own-source revenue from provinces to cities and municipalities.

BOX 10.4 The Philippines: Toll Road Management

The construction of a circumferential road across Cabanatuan City and adjacent municipalities is a good example of cooperation in planning investment and implementing a project. Cabanatuan City signed a memorandum of agreement with the municipalities of San Leonardo and Sta. Rosa that defined their contributions and obligations to this project. The toll road, financed by contributions from the local governments, is expected to raise revenues once it is operating. The cooperation reflected strong leadership from the chief executives of the three local governments and their understanding of the benefits of a joint approach to combating rising urban congestion.

Source: Gilbert Llanto, mayor of Cabanatuan City, field interview.

Not only are the taxing powers of provincial governments inferior to those of city and municipal governments, but cities do not have to share their tax revenues with provinces. As a result, provinces depend mostly on the Internal Revenue Allotment (IRA)—a mechanism for transferring funds from the center.

Regional Development Councils (RDCs) could play a role in integrating regional and local infrastructure plans with the country's overall infrastructure plans.[12] However, the majority of RDCs are weak and ineffective in planning and coordinating infrastructure projects. The perception is that RDCs merely act as endorsers of projects initiated by regional offices of line ministries or local governments, which require international funding or a guarantee from the national government. Thus, rather than playing a coordinating role, RDCs are seen as more concerned with monitoring national projects implemented at the local level (Llanto and Lasam 2003).

In the Philippines, as in Indonesia, the IRA is supposed to correct the mismatch between revenue and expenditure assignments across different levels of government. Although local governments have become more and more dependent on the IRA, the transfer system has not contributed to increase equity. On the contrary, the IRA formula favors bigger and richer local governments at the expense of poorer and smaller ones, as it is based on land area and population. Hence, cities and municipalities that are more populous and have larger land areas enjoy a strong advantage, and richer local governments with larger tax bases receive a bigger share of the IRA.

Lessons Learned

This section has discussed the role of higher tiers of government in decentralized infrastructure by drawing on the experiences of China, Indonesia, and the Philippines. The need to strengthen the role of higher levels of government in providing infrastructure services appears particularly compelling in Indonesia and the Philippines, where there is clear evidence of a missing middle in the architecture of decentralization. The experiences of all three countries suggest the following lessons on how far to decentralize infrastructure services:

Partnership between national, provincial, and municipal governments is crucial to maximizing the efficiency gains from decentralization. Infrastructure services entail a broad set of functions. The extent to which higher levels of government perform some of these functions often depends on the characteristics of a particular industry. For example, when the main economic argument for involving provincial authorities is the presence of spillover effects, higher levels of government need to retain a planning and coordinating role, while municipalities may be better positioned to build and operate facilities. When the main concern is excessive fragmentation, decentralization of service provision only to the regional level can retain economies of scale. Clearly defining responsibilities and providing mechanisms for coordinating all tiers of government are essential to maximizing the benefits of decentralization.

A progressive approach to decentralization has merit. Developing countries may need to build or strengthen institutions at intermediate and lower levels of government to coordinate responsibilities—institutions that are often the norm in mature infrastructure industries. This implies that countries may need to phase in decentralization while building capacity. Another argument in favor of a progressive approach is that once functions are decentralized to the lowest tiers, creating a role for higher tiers of government can be very difficult, as municipalities may be reluctant to relinquish decision-making and revenue-raising powers. However, political considerations often play a critical role in designing a decentralization strategy. For example, while a more gradual phasing-in may have been warranted in the Philippines and Indonesia, political imperatives called for a Big Bang approach, under which local governments assumed responsibility for providing basic infrastructure services almost overnight.

Given economies of scale, decentralizing infrastructure to the lowest tiers of government may lead to excessive fragmentation. The risk of excessive fragmentation is particularly high when decentralization is not conceived as a response to specific problems but rather as a byproduct of wider reform. The result could be an industry structure that is far from optimal from an economic point of view.

Careful design of intergovernmental transfer mechanisms is needed to meet equity objectives. While central intervention may be warranted to redress regional inequalities, experiences in Indonesia and the Philippines show that limiting fiscal decentralization has not produced the expected results in terms of income redistribution. On the contrary, intergovernmental transfers have exacerbated regional difference in income, jeopardizing the ability of the poorest regions to finance their infrastructure needs. Countries need to improve the efficiency of their equalization mechanisms to address fiscal imbalances across regions.

Key Issues for Policy Makers

Several key issues stand out from this review of East Asia's experience in decentralizing infrastructure. Perhaps the most important is the coherence and alignment of administrative, financing, performance measurement, and incentive policies and programs. Where alignment exists, anticipated results will be forthcoming, as in the case of the principal-agent arrangements of China and Vietnam. Of course, this can be a doubled-edged benefit. If the goals make sense, performance will yield desirable outcomes. On the other hand, doing the wrong thing well is also a possibility. Thus, it is as important to ensure that coherence and alignment favor appropriate local decision making, control of results, and accountability for results. This lesson is elaborated in detail below.

Performance measurement opens the door to efficiency gains from decentralized infrastructure because it permits meaningful accountability. At the local level, standardized cost comparisons, such as cost per kilometer of road construction, can immediately translate into savings when used as a guide for competitive procurement. Performance contracting—in which a municipality commits to authorizing tariff increases if a utility meets well-defined performance goals—can upgrade performance while breaking the deadlock over setting tariffs high enough to recover service costs, which has handicapped local investment. NGOs and citizens gain the power of accountable oversight only if they can measure performance against quantified targets.

The power of upward accountability is evident in the case of China, where measurable performance against state-determined investment targets has driven the infrastructure sector. On the other hand, in politically decentralized systems, performance measures are almost totally lacking in the infrastructure sector. This is in striking contrast to the health and education sectors, where client surveys and output measures are far more common. Simple, transparently reported measures of infrastructure performance tracked locally and used for local management would enable countries to go far in realizing the potential of decentralization.

Community participation at the project level is critical. A large body of evidence supports the importance of community-scale participation in infrastructure choices and management. Community water supply and latrine projects have proven more sustainable—longer lasting, more fully used, and more financially self-sufficient—when designed in partnership with the community and managed by community organizations. The participation of a cross-section of users in management has been found to be particularly important. Women and the poor are most likely to be excluded from management, undermining project sustainability.

The economic literature on decentralized fiscal choice has emphasized the gains from allowing clients to choose among an array of project options. On the other hand, some East Asian countries offer communities a much smaller range of choices. Rural water projects in China, for example, give communities the opportunity to sign on to standardized arrangements. Community consultation consists of explaining to residents the services they will receive and the tariff costs they will be responsible for, if they participate. Such projects have high sustainability in China despite the closed nature of the initial choice.

Scaling up community participation in municipal-level capital planning is difficult. Decentralization in the infrastructure sector has been premised on the value of community choice. Both Indonesia and the Philippines have attempted to incorporate community participation in higher-level choices by including NGOs in efforts to set municipal investment priorities. The results of this experiment have been mixed, at best. The presumption that NGOs represent community consensus rather than advocate particular points of view has often broken down in practice. Urban forums open to all have proved valuable in stimulating public debate over investment priorities, but a difficult vehicle for actually establishing capital budgets. Whether direct community participation in investment decision making overcomes skepticism about local representative democracy remains to be seen. Substantial differences in the information available to stakeholders remain a significant problem, as such asymmetry contributes to the greater influence of elites in decision making.

Efficiency in capital investment is important. Paradoxically, at a time of great pressure on infrastructure investment budgets, large portions of existing capital remain unused. In China, wastewater treatment plants in some provinces are not functioning for lack of operating and maintenance funds while expensive new treatment plants are being built. In Indonesia, some water utilities have much excess capacity because they failed to take into account ample free water from household wells. In politically decentralized systems, community participation in initial project design and required local cost sharing can reduce excess capacity. In upwardly accountable systems, performance targets need to measure relevant outputs rather than merely the capacity of capital facilities.

A well-functioning local credit market is an essential ingredient of a decentralized infrastructure sector. The supply of credit for local investment has become a bottleneck to decentralizing infrastructure. In both Indonesia and the Philippines, central authorities retain control over the channels for local credit, frustrating development of a self-sustaining domestic credit market that meets municipal needs for financing infrastructure. Government financial institutions can encourage the emergence of a municipal credit market by removing regulations that give them preference over commercial banks and other lenders. Onlending of international funds to municipalities via commercial banks, rather than government financial monopolies, would likely speed development of such a market.

Higher tiers of government play a critical role in the architecture of decentralization. A partnership between national, provincial, and municipal governments is crucial to maximizing the benefits of decentralization, even in infrastructure industries that are essentially local. For example, empowering provincial governments to perform a planning role is essential to correct for interjurisdictional spillovers, while limiting fiscal decentralization may be warranted on equity grounds to allow for cross-subsidies between geographic groups. The need to strengthen the role of intermediate tiers of government is compelling in Indonesia and the Philippines, where the missing middle has resulted in poor coordination between jurisdictions. The consequences are particularly evident in the transport sector, where secondary road networks have suffered from severe maintenance backlogs as a result of poor interjurisdictional coordination.

Annex: Comparing Water Coverage in Different Countries and Regions

Truly comparable data across countries on infrastructure coverage, investment levels, and tariffs are difficult to produce and generally not available. *Global Water Supply and Sanitation Assessment 2000,* prepared by the World Health Organization and the United Nations Children's Fund, provides probably the most standardized reporting, but even the data in that volume are imperfect. Coverage rates reflect access to "improved" water and wastewater systems. Tariff and investment ratios are reported as averages for the decade 1990–2000 and therefore do not take into account recent changes. Nonetheless, the data do provide a general comparative baseline for East Asian countries:

TABLE 10A.1 Water Supply Coverage Rates
(percent of population covered)

Country	Year	Urban coverage	Rural coverage	Total
Cambodia	1990	—	—	—
	2000	53%	25%	30%
China	1990	99%	60%	71%
	2000	94%	66%	75%
Indonesia	1990	90%	60%	76%
	2000	91%	65%	87%
Philippines	1990	94%	81%	87%
	2000	92%	80%	87%
Vietnam	1990	81%	40%	48%
	2000	81%	50%	56%

Source: WHO and UNICEF 2000.
Note: Rapid rates of urban population growth mean that even where urban coverage rates declined, large numbers of households gained access to a municipal water supply. (—) = not available.

TABLE 10A.2 Sanitation Coverage Rates
(percentage of population covered)

Country	Year	Urban coverage	Rural coverage	Total
Cambodia	1990	—	—	—
	2000	58%	10%	18%
China	1990	57%	18%	29%
	2000	68%	24%	38%
Indonesia	1990	76%	44%	54%
	2000	87%	52%	66%
Philippines	1990	85%	64%	74%
	2000	92%	71%	83%
Vietnam	1990	—	—	—
	2000	86%	70%	73%

Source: WHO and UNICEF 2000.
Note: Given the high differentials in coverage between urban and rural areas, one of the most statistically significant ways of expanding national coverage is through rural to urban migration and other sources of urban population growth. (—) = not available.

Through the Millennium Development Goals, all the East Asian countries have set far more ambitious targets for coverage during the period 2000–5. Because of decentralization, local governments will be the primary instruments for implementing and financing this accelerated coverage.

Investing in the Water Supply and Sanitation Sector

During the decade 1990–2000, Asia lagged behind other developing regions in the share of governmental investment devoted to water supply and sanitation. This probably implies, as *Global Water Supply and Sanitation Assessment 2000* concludes, that Asian countries gave the water and sanitation sector lower priority, but the situation also reflects the higher shares of public sector budgets devoted to investment in Asia.

Investment shares in East Asia in this sector have climbed recently as countries have focused on meeting their coverage targets. China has also set ambitious targets for treating wastewater before discharge.

TABLE 10A.3 Median Investment in Water Supply and Sanitation, 1990–2000
(percentage of overall government investment)

Region	Percentage
Africa	5.3%
Asia	3.5%
Latin America and Caribbean	8.3%

Source: WHO and UNICEF 2000.

TABLE 10A.4 Median Urban Tariff Rate
(US$ per cubic meter)

Region	Water	Sewerage
Africa	0.35	0.12
Asia	0.22	0.14
Europe	0.67	0.59
Latin America	0.44	0.21
North America	0.48	0.41

Source: WHO and UNICEF 2000.

Tariff Rates

Median urban tariffs for water and sewerage from 1990–2000 were lower in Asia than in other regions, although Asia's lower rates partly reflect lower production costs. Asia faces a particularly challenging task in raising tariffs to commercial levels.

Endnotes

1. As of 2001, only 200 of China's 667 cities treated any wastewater before discharge (Murray 2003).
2. Local officials are evaluated based on their contribution to economic growth, which is often interpreted as reaching investment targets.
3. The city of Naga in the Philippines makes similar use of comparative disclosure at the local level. The city publishes all per unit costs from different bidders for local construction contracts on its website.
4. In the case of the *Kecamatan* Development Program, 30,000 villagers were hired and trained in project development and 2,000 community facilitators were also hired and trained.
5. This discussion follows Usui and Alisjahbana 2003.
6. A city development strategy is an action plan for equitable growth in cities and their surrounding regions, developed and sustained through participation, to improve the quality of life for all citizens. See Chreod Ltd. 2002.
7. For example, Tynan and Kingdom 2004 proved econometrically that smaller water utilities, particularly those serving a population of 125,000 or less, could reduce per customer operating costs by increasing their scale of operation.
8. However, there is often a trade-off between efficiency gains and loss of local accountability, which efforts to identify the optimal area of service provision would need to take into account.
9. This argument is made, for example, in Smith 2000.
10. Local governments range in population from 24,000 to 4.1 million. The per capita wage bill of local governments seems to suggest that efficiency falls sharply at the level of about 500,000 people.
11. In Indonesia, revenue disparities are significant at all levels of government. These inequalities are most extreme at the local level, where the richest region accounts for 46 times the revenues of the poorest region. The richest province also has 32 times the per capita revenues of the poorest province.
12. There are nine RDCs, including those in the Cordillera Administrative Region and the Autonomous Region of Muslim Mindanao.

Bibliography

Alonzo, Ruperto P. 1998. "Local Governance and Poverty Alleviation." In *Growth, Poverty, and Income Inequality in the Philippines,* eds. A.M. Balisacan and S. Fujisaki. Tokyo: Institute of Developing Economies.

Azfar, Omar. 2002. "Decentralization in Indonesia: A Report from a Household Survey in West Java." Paper presented at the Regional University Consortium Conference on Regional Economic Development in a Decentralizing Indonesia.

Azfar, Omar, Tugrul Gurgur, Satu Kahkonen, Anthony Lanyi, and Patrick Meagher. 2000. *Decentralization and Governance: An Empirical Investigation of Public Service Delivery in the Philippines.* College Park, MD: University of Maryland, Department of Economics, Center for Institutional Reform and the Informal Sector.

Bellier, Michel, and Yue Maggie Zhou. 2003. "Private Participation in Infrastructure in China." Working Paper No. 2. Washington, DC: World Bank.

Chanthaphone, Soutsakhone, and Santanu Lahiri. 2003. "Looking Backward to See Forward." In *Sustainability Planning and Monitoring in Community Water Supply and Sanitation,* eds. Mukherjee and van Wijk Washington, DC: World Bank.

Chreod Ltd., with the Urban Institute. 2002. *China City Development Strategies: Changsha, Zhuzhou, Xiangtan.* Ottawa: Chreod Ltd.

———. 2003. *China City Development Strategies II: Inception Missions—Lanzhou, Chengdu, Zhengzhou, Xinxiang, Erdos.* Ottawa.

Department of Public Work and Highways, Philippines. 2003. "Roads in the Philippines." Manila: Department of Public Work and Highways.

Dupar, Mairi, and Nathan Badenoch. 2002. "Environment, Livelihoods, and Local Institutions: Decentralization in Mainland Southeast Asia." Washington, DC: World Resources Institute.

Fontanelle, Jean-Philippe. 2000. "Water Management Decentralization in the Red River Delta, Vietnam: An Uncompleted Transition Process toward Local Governance." Paper presented to the eighth biennial conference of the International Association for the Study of Common Property, Bloomington, Indiana.

Fontanelle, Jean-Philippe, and François Molle. 2002. "The Intricacies of Water Pricing in the Red River Delta, Vietnam."

Paper presented to International Conference on Irrigation Water Policies, Agadir, Morocco.

Goodpaster, Gary, and David Ray. 2000. "Trade and Citizenship Barriers and Decentralization." *Indonesian Quarterly* 3.

Government of China. 2000. *City Dirty Water Treatment and Pollution Prevention and Treatment Policy.* Beijing: Ministry of Science and Technology, Ministry of Construction, State Environment Protection Administration.

Gross, Bruce. 2003. "Do Project Rules Promote Sustainability and Equity?" In *Sustainability Planning and Monitoring in Community Water Supply and Sanitation*, eds. Mukherjee and van Wijk. Washington, DC: World Bank, International Water and Sanitation Centre.

Gross, Bruce, Christine van Wijk, and Nilanjana Mukherjee. 2001. "Linking Sustainability with Demand, Gender, and Poverty: A Study in Community-Managed Water Supply Projects in 15 Countries." Delft, Netherlands: Water and Sanitation Program and IRC International Water and Sanitation Centre.

Hofman, Bert, and Kai Kaiser. 2002. "The Making of the Big Bang and Its Aftermath: A Political Economy Perspective." Paper presented at conference on Can Decentralization Help Rebuild Indonesia?, Atlanta, GA.

Hopkins, Richard. 2003. "How Well Did Those Development Projects in Flores Work?" In *Sustainability Planning and Monitoring in Community Water Supply and Sanitation*, eds. Mukherjee and van Wijk. Washington, DC: World Bank, International Water and Sanitation Centre.

Indonesian Partnership on Local Governance Initiatives. 2002. Various papers for the International Workshop on Participatory Planning Approaches for Local Governance, Bandung, Indonesia.

Llanto, Gilberto M., and Joel Lasam. 2003. "Report on the Forum on Planning, Programming, and Monitoring." Submitted to National Economic and Development Agency and Deutsche Gesellschaft für Technische Zusammenarbeit.

Loehr, William, and Rosario Manasan. 1999. "Fiscal Decentralization and Economic Efficiency: Measurement and Evaluation." Cambridge, MA: Harvard Institute for International Development.

Meadley, Thomas. 2003. "Community Design of Hygiene Promotion IEC Materials." Presentation to World Bank Water Week. World Bank, Washington, DC.

Murray, Bruce. 2003. Presentation to Workshop on National Guidelines for Urban Wastewater Tariffs and Management. Manila: Asian Development Bank.

Orial, Lydia N. 2002. "Local Government Finance and LGU Bond Market Development: Philippines." Manila: Asian Development Bank.

Pratikno. 2002. "Initiating Citizen Participation in Local Policy Making in Indonesia: The Case of Surakata Municipality in the Post Authoritarian Regime, 1999–2002." Gadjah Mada University.

Royal Government of Cambodia. 2003a. *National Poverty Reduction Strategy 2003–2005.* Phnom Penh: Council for Social Development.

———. 2003b. *Water and Sanitation Resources: Sector Overview and Market Structure.* Phnom Penh: Ministry of Commerce.

Smith, Warrick. 2000. "Regulating Utilities: Thinking about Location Questions." World Bank Summer Workshop on Market Institutions, Washington, DC.

Triche, Thelma, Abel Mejia, and Emanueal Idelovitch. 1993. "Arranging Concessions for Water Supply and Sewerage Services: Lessons from Buenos Aires and Caracas." WS-10. Washington, DC: World Bank, Transportation, Water, and Urban Development Department.

Tynan, Nicola, and Bill Kingdom. 2004. "Optimal Size for Utilities? Returns to Scale in Water—Evidence from Benchmarking." Viewpoint note. rru.worldbank.org/documents/publicpolicyjournal/283tynan.pdf.

Urban Institute. 2003. "Local Government Water Services Project Final Report." Washington, DC: Urban Institute.

Usui, Norio, and Armida Alisjahbana. 2003. "Local Development Planning and Budgeting in Indonesia: Update." Prepared for the international symposium on Indonesia's Decentralization Policy: Problems and Policy Directions. Jakarta.

World Bank. 2002a. "Selling Sanitation in Vietnam: What Works?" Vietnam Country Report, WSP-EAP. Washington, DC: World Bank, Water and Sanitation Programme.

———. 2002b. "Benchmarking the Urban Water Sector Vietnam." Hanoi.

———. 2003a. "China Country Assistance Strategy." Washington, DC: World Bank.

———. 2003b. "Cities in Transition: Urban Sector Review in an Era of Decentralization in Indonesia." Working Paper No. 7. Washington, DC: World Bank.

———. 2003c. "Decentralizing Indonesia: Regional Public Expenditure Review." Report 26191-IND. Washington, DC: World Bank.

———. 2003d. "Indonesia: Selected Fiscal Issues in a New Era." Report 25437-IND. Washington, DC: World Bank.

———. 2003e. "Project Appraisal Document for a Third Kecamatan Development Project." Washington, DC: World Bank.

———. 2004. "Indonesia: Averting an Infrastructure Crisis—A Framework for Policy and Action." Washington, DC: World Bank, Recent Economic Development in Infrastructure.

World Bank and Asian Development Bank. 2003. "Philippines: Decentralization and Service Delivery—From Promise to Performance." Manila: World Bank and Asian Development Bank.

WHO (World Health Organization) and UNICEF (United Nations Children's Fund). 2000. *Global Water Supply and Sanitation Assessment 2000.* www.wssinfo.org/pdf/GWSSA_2000_report.pdf.

Zhixiong, Luo. 2003. "Financing Arrangements for Rural Water Supply and Sanitation Project in China: Experiences from Guizhou Province." Presentation to World Bank, Washington, DC.

11

GOVERNANCE GONE LOCAL: DOES DECENTRALIZATION IMPROVE ACCOUNTABILITY?

Jose Edgardo Campos and Joel S. Hellman

The case for decentralization is fundamentally an argument about governance. The case is rooted in two powerful intellectual traditions: the critique of economic centralism (especially central planning), and the perceived economic advantages of federalism. The first tradition posits that decentralization aligns government decision making more closely with local preferences, largely because of the information advantages associated with smaller jurisdictions.[1] The second tradition emphasizes the competition among regions sparked by decentralization, as local governments have incentives to engage in a "race to the top" to attract capital and labor, or simply to build their political reputations.[2] Both strands argue that decentralization will make local officials more accountable to constituents for their performance.

Though these arguments are deeply rooted in theory, surprisingly few empirical studies have examined the direct relationship between decentralization and governance. And the majority of studies that have been done tend to dispute the expected governance gains from decentralization.[3] Though case studies often trumpet the successes of particularly innovative local governments, we hear much less about the impact of decentralization on governance in the median region, beyond these shining stars. As attractive as the theoretical foundations of decentralization may be, the relationship between decentralization and governance in practice is still very much a matter of debate.

Moreover, the decision to pursue decentralization is largely political, with the underlying economic rationale secondary, if not marginal. In many cases, the decision to decentralize is sparked by strong reactions to a prolonged period of highly authoritarian rule. This has certainly been the case for the two countries on which this chapter focuses—Indonesia and the Philippines.

Nevertheless, the development community has generally welcomed decentralization with some enthusiasm, and has responded by shifting a significant share of development assistance to local governments, and to support for the decentralization framework.[4] As decentralization projects in East Asia are still under way or in the early stages of implementation, an assessment of lessons from the region on the relationship between decentralization and governance is not yet available. Yet there is a certain urgency for learning more about the impacts of decentralization. Experience so far has highlighted a range of governance risks that appear to threaten the promised accountability gains from decentralization.

This chapter describes five key governance risks that could mitigate the posited advantages of decentralization: capture, clientelism, capacity constraints, competition over the balance of power between levels of government, and weaknesses in the interregional information flows that are critical for effective competition. To be sure, some of these risks can affect all levels of government. But this chapter argues that they may be more prevalent at the local level than at the national level. The chapter also argues that decentralization itself—if poorly designed—could exacerbate these governance distortions, undermining any positive gains in accountability. This is not to suggest that the conventional arguments about decentralization and governance are wrong. Rather, these experiences raise challenges that need to be addressed in designing decentralization, assessing its appropriateness in different political contexts, and assisting the process.

The chapter is organized in four parts. First, to help guide the analysis, we present a conceptual framework for governance building on the World Bank's *World Development Report 2004*. Second, we discuss the implications of decentralization for governance. Third, within this framework, we analyze the limited experience of East Asian countries with decentralization, given the above-mentioned risks. And fourth, we suggest possible avenues for minimizing these risks, given the numerous constraints that these countries face.

The Foundations of Governance

The *World Development Report 2004* presents a simple triad to illustrate the multiple relationships that constitute a framework for thinking about accountability in delivering public services. The triad focuses on three basic relationships: between citizens and policy makers, between policy makers and the bureaucracy (those responsible for providing public goods and services), and between the bureaucracy as delivery agents and the citizenry as clients.[5] The first leg of the triad deals primarily with how policy makers acquire authority and thus power.

FIGURE 11.1 The Accountability Framework

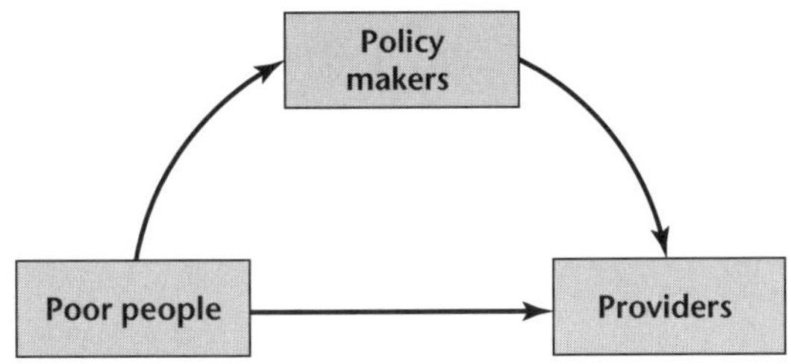

Source: World Bank 2004c.

The second and third legs address how they exercise that authority, such as by formulating policies, programs, and projects (see figure 11.1), and by delegating implementation to the public bureaucracy, civil society organizations, or the private sector.

The key idea of the triad is to show that citizens—as clients of public services—have two routes by which they hold providers accountable for service quality. The first is a "long route," whereby citizens give feedback to policy makers about their preferences, who then control the providers of public services. The second is a "short route," whereby users give direct feedback to service providers, creating pressure and providing information that helps policy makers hold them accountable for their performance.

Decentralization adds an alternative route to this accountability framework by shortening the link between policy makers on the one hand and citizens and public service providers on the other. Decentralization, proponents argue, brings politicians closer to the people, by giving them better information about constituents' preferences and making it easier for constituents to monitor politicians' performance. At the local level, citizens can more easily learn of the activities and programs that their local leaders have promoted and supported, discern how much effort they have devoted to improving public services, and confirm whether they have delivered on campaign promises. In other words, the information that citizens need to make judgments is more readily accessible under decentralization. Hence, it strengthens political accountability (see figure 11.2).[6]

Similarly, local politicians, being much closer to the action and having more direct interactions with the local bureaucracy, are potentially better able to monitor the performance of local agencies. Local leaders can more easily find out whether doctors are arriving at work at local health clinics and whether

FIGURE 11.2 Decentralization and the Accountability Framework

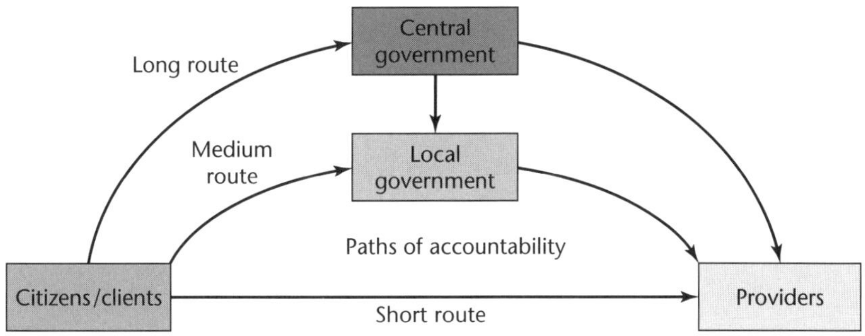

Source: Author.

teachers are showing up at community elementary schools. Leaders can also more quickly receive alerts on security problems that arise in different parts of the locality. In other words, decentralization improves bureaucratic accountability as well.

Finally, local communities are potentially better endowed with social capital, and thus face lower costs in organizing into groups. Client power at the local level is therefore likely to be much greater, and citizens are better able to communicate the nature and location of problems to local politicians. This induces improvements in the compact between local politicians and the local bureaucracy.

However, this simple approach includes some important untested assumptions. First, it assumes that proximity breeds accountability, and that accountability is largely a function of information. Yet a range of other political factors also determines accountability—factors that may not necessarily be more prevalent at the local level. Second, the standard approach assumes a frictionless relationship between levels of government, and thus that local governments can respond effectively to the concerns of their constituents and exercise effective authority over service providers. Yet competition between policy makers at the center and in the localities could constrain the responsiveness of local governments to constituent pressures and weaken their capacity to control service providers. And third, the simple model does not incorporate interregional dynamics and asymmetries that could alter the responsiveness of local governments to their own constituencies and influence their control over service providers.

Even more importantly, this approach ignores the importance of capacity constraints. Government officials need to have enough training, experience, and professional skills to competently make and execute responsive public policies. If officials do not have adequate capacity, then they cannot implement their designated tasks effectively. *Capacity* in this context refers to the skills public officials need to deliver on various mandates, the resources (capital and financial) they require to support their efforts, and the systems (such as budgeting systems) that enable large numbers of bureaucrats to work together effectively. Obviously, the same considerations hold for members and staff of civil society organizations.

Accountable government generally requires a certain degree of institutional capacity. In particular, participants need information for auditing, evaluation, reporting, investigations, and prosecution. They also need processes, skills, and resources to provide the infrastructure and create the incentives to produce the right information. Accountability is thus circumscribed by both institutional and individual capacity.

The Risks of Decentralization

In practice, decentralization does not occur in a vacuum. Many factors—including historical trends, institutional inertia, and class cleavages—may undermine the simple links between decentralization and improved governance. The next section examines some of these risks.

State Capture at the Local Level

At every level of government, state capture may distort political accountability between citizens and policy makers. State capture refers to "actions of individuals, groups, or firms either in the public and/or private sectors to influence the formation of laws, regulations, decrees and other government policies to their advantage through the illicit and nontransparent provision of private benefits to politicians and/or civil servants" (World Bank 2000: xv).[7] State capture distorts the chain of accountability between politicians, service providers, and constituents through asymmetries of political influence. Analysts have only recently studied the dynamics of state capture at the local level (Bardhan and Mookherjee 2000; Zhuravskaya 2000). The question is: are local governments more susceptible to state capture than their national counterparts? The limited empirical studies suggest that they are.

First, state capture thrives in an environment where highly concentrated interest groups—especially powerful firms and families—dominate the market for political influence, and where political competition is weak. Local economies tend to be more homogeneous, more concentrated, and less competitive than the national economy, creating fertile ground for dominant economic actors to engage in state capture. This is particularly true in resource-rich regions in developing countries, where local economies depend on a particular state monopoly or powerful firm. In such cases, the boundary separating the interests of the region and the firm can be murky at best, and local political and economic elites are closely intertwined in promoting state capture.

Second, many of the institutions normally expected to serve as checks on state capture are weaker at the local level than at the national level, especially in developing countries. Local legislatures in most East Asian countries typically do not yet serve as a significant countervailing force on the executive. Even more than their national counterparts, these legislatures lack technical and support staff, resources, experience, and training.

For the same reasons, local judicial systems tend to be less effective (and more incompetent and corrupt) in rendering fair judgments in the face of substantial asymmetries of power among contesting parties.[8] As a result, the executive branch tends to dominate local polities in decentralized countries, with local representative and judicial institutions offering weak constraints.

Third, countervailing powers representing a broader range of public interests, such as the media and nongovernmental organizations (NGOs), are generally less developed in local jurisdictions. Even in large, geographically and linguistically diverse countries such as Indonesia, the main media outlets are highly concentrated in the capital city. At best, an emerging but still loose network of local newspapers and television stations resorts to "selling news for cash" to survive, regardless of its veracity.

In most East Asian countries, years of authoritarian rule have systematically weakened the development of an NGO sector. Though the number of NGOs is growing, they still tend to not only concentrate in the capital city but also depend on donor support. Some are even government-sponsored and thus cannot conduct their activities at arms length. Local NGO networks in most East Asian countries—while expanding—therefore remain quite weak. With limited resources, low capacity, weak links to national networks, and significant government interference in their activities, local NGOs still tend to play a restricted role in holding local governments accountable.

In many East Asian countries, the question of who captures whom at the local level is less straightforward than in other parts of the world, where the private sector is more autonomous. The problem of local state actors using their power to capture ownership of local businesses or de facto cash flow rights is particularly serious. This has been a longstanding issue in China. In Indonesia, a preliminary study of regional legislation (known as *perdas*) showed surprisingly frequent references to local *pemda* companies—those wholly owned by district governments, with control exercised by local executive officials. Whether local governments are seizing opportunities to expand their control over local businesses, or businesses themselves are using their influence to capture local officials, the impact is generally the same: the exercise of state power favors particular firms, often at the expense of the region's broader welfare.

Expanding Clientelist Roots

Clientelism—in which politicians distribute publicly funded goods to selected members of the electorate in return for votes and political support—systematically weakens political accountability in a variety of ways.[9] It narrows the range of constituents to whom politicians are responsive. Through the distribution of "reversible" goods—those that can be withdrawn—to exclusive networks, clientelism also gives politicians a mechanism to punish voters who do not provide continuous support. Clientelism also creates disincentives for groups to develop collective forms of representation and therefore weakens interest group competition. Like state capture, clientelism is common to many different types of political systems and at all levels of government. However, it might be more pervasive at the local level, for several reasons.

With smaller jurisdictions, local politicians are more likely to engage in clientelist forms of "retail" politics to win elections and maintain political support networks. In such jurisdictions, politicians can more effectively identify individual voters for clientelist networks and more easily monitor their political support, making clientelist "contracts" more feasible and enforceable.[10] Local clientelism redirects the arrows linking policy makers, providers, and clients. Rather than citizens holding local officials accountable, clientelist politics allows politicians to shape constituencies to their own advantage by selectively providing public services and other benefits. For example, discretionary distribution of front-line service jobs to political supporters systematically weakens the potential links between clients and service providers, as job recruitment and promotion have little to do with performance.

Moreover, local elites in more homogeneous communities tend to be bound together by a dense network of familial, ethnic, social, and cultural ties that encourage clientelist behavior and, more generally, corruption (Tanzi 1995; Prud'homme 1995). The continued presence of aristocratic lineages in the sugar-producing provinces in Central Luzon and Western Visayas in the Philippines; the network of tribal leaders in Papua New Guinea; and the system of *ulama* in East Java, Indonesia, are all ready-made local clientelist networks that build on predemocratic legacies. These legacies have proven quite adaptable to new modes of political competition. Such exclusive patron-client networks are far more difficult to build and maintain in a more diverse and competitive national playing field. As a result, clientelism is generally a phenomenon of local politics.

Where clientelism is prevalent, decentralization can seriously exacerbate inefficiencies and inequalities in public services. Clientelist governments tend to favor investments that generate jobs, which they can then distribute to build patronage networks. In a common example, newly empowered local governments may favor investing in new schools as opposed to improving existing schools. As a result, each school is underresourced, undermining any positive impact on educational levels. Indeed, clientelism can distort a range of decisions about public services—from the service mix, to the location of facilities, to standards discriminating in favor of particular constituent groups at the expense of more overall community welfare.

Amplifying Capacity Constraints

Decentralization shifts the responsibilities of local government from purely implementing policy to both formulating and implementing policy. This requires a wider range of skills and experience, which local politicians and bureaucrats may have to develop. Hence, at least in the initial stages of decentralization, local skill levels and policy-making processes are likely to lag behind those at the national level.[11]

Besides skills and processes, capacity also implies appropriate management systems—accounting, budgeting, procurement, tax administration, auditing, reporting, and personnel management. In many developing countries, national governments continue to struggle with reforming these systems. Given their relative inexperience and more modest resources, local governments are likely to find establishing such systems and processes even more challenging.[12] (See chapter 7 for more on the problems East Asian countries face in creating personnel management systems.)

Resources are often a forgotten or underestimated aspect of capacity. To train personnel, develop systems and processes, strengthen accountability, and ultimately deliver public goods and services, local governments need funds. Other chapters discuss funding issues—in particular, intergovernmental transfers and local taxation—in more detail. Suffice it to say that efforts to fund local government present complex considerations and challenges with which newly decentralizing countries—including most East Asian countries—are only starting to grapple.

Capacity problems are not limited to institutions and processes within the executive branch; the same constraints affect other actors in the accountability framework. The accountability of local governments—like that of the national government—depends largely on the strength of countervailing institutions, such as the legislature and judiciary and civil society groups, to provide effective inputs and monitor policies. Here again are reasons for concern that capacity among these actors is not as strong at the local level as at the national level. As suggested, local legislatures in East Asia generally have limited access to independent policy expertise and analysis and therefore are much more dependent on local executives. Local courts generally remain embedded in centralized hierarchies even in the most decentralized countries. As a result, patterns of career advancement draw court officials to the center, leaving local courts with less capacity.

Comparing the capacity of civil society between the center and the regions is more difficult but also essential to determine the foundation for local accountability. As mentioned, the local civil society institutions regarded as key checks to prevent state capture and clientelism are not well developed in many East Asian countries, especially those in transition from previously authoritarian systems, where the legacy of public participation is particularly weak. With a few exceptions, NGO penetration at the local level is also lower than at the national level. Though no systematic quality comparisons exist, it is widely agreed that the quality of the media beyond the national level drops substantially in most developing countries. In sum, it is not only local governments that face capacity constraints relative to their national counterparts, but also the other institutions and actors whose participation is essential to holding local governments accountable.

Creating Intergovernmental Tension

Regardless of the initial enthusiasm with which many countries have embraced decentralization, when it comes to actual dividing power and authority across different levels of government, decentralization generally remains contested terrain for a prolonged period. While the initial impetus for decentralizing power in East Asia has been broader political transitions from highly centralized regimes or within such regimes, implementation has confronted a variety of fiscal and administrative challenges. These challenges often generate conflicting incentives at different levels and within different branches of government. The result is that the shape of decentralization is constantly evolving, reflecting changing political and economic realities, conflicting interests, and shifting priorities.

This changing landscape has a number of potentially serious implications for the impact of decentralization on local governance. First, contests over the extent and contours of decentralization between levels of government tend to constrain local autonomy. The shifting relationship between local politicians and service providers and their national counterparts blurs lines of accountability. This can reduce the responsiveness of local governments and weaken their authority over service providers, who may be responding to incentives from national hierarchies.

Second, contests across levels of government often lead to what might be called imbalanced decentralization—especially between power and financial responsibility, distorting incentives at lower levels. In Indonesia, for example, local governments have considerable control over expenditures for basic public services but little control over the civil servants that provide those services. Thus, these governments cannot downsize the workforce, alter remuneration packages, or introduce new (and perhaps more meritocratic) recruitment and promotion to coincide with changing expenditure priorities.

In many countries local governments also face strong constraints on raising revenues, limiting any autonomy they receive over local services. Such imbalances might not only constrain local governments but also create incentives for them to make inefficient investment decisions, especially if they can shift costs to central budgets (see chapters 5 and 6).

Both of these factors generate substantial uncertainty regarding the distribution of functions and responsibilities, the extent of autonomy, and the balance of power between levels of government. Such uncertainty can weaken accountability at every leg of the triad, as it affects the expectations of all actors in the framework. Such uncertainty can also stifle investment and thus interregional competition.

Stifling Rather Than Promoting Interregional Competition

The view that competition among jurisdictions can enhance governance has been an important justification for decentralization. The basic foundation of this idea is simple: officials who steal or waste resources, or fail to provide essential public goods relative to other regions, will lose residents and businesses, thus reducing the tax base. This argument has taken on greater weight with the growing focus on the investment climate. Given mobility of capital among countries as well as within countries, businesses can seek out jurisdictions where regulation is not overly onerous, infrastructure is sound, and trust relationships can be forged with local officials. This kind of competition for investment is seen to discipline local governments, strengthening their incentives for delivering transparent and accountable governance.

Recent literature has stressed that competition among regions could also have a host of negative implications for governance. Competition for capital and residents could become too intense, pushing governments to overshoot in cutting tax rates and expenditures and providing public goods (Keen and Marchand 1997). Such competition could also have negative spillover effects, such as exporting taxes or pollution to neighboring regions (Gordon 1983; Oates and Schwab 1988). More generally, competition for investment could lead regional governments to distort the investment climate to favor particular firms through preferential regulations and protectionism, or, even worse, by sheltering firms from tax policies and regulations of the central government. In the latter event, competition among regions could weaken the capacity of the central government to collect revenue, enforce law, and regulate interregional competition to ensure welfare-enhancing outcomes. This scenario has been called "state-corroding" decentralization (Cai and Treisman 2002).

The risks of state-corroding decentralization are particularly high in countries where central law enforcement and respect for the constitution are still quite weak. In such contexts, regional governments can undermine national laws and regulations without likelihood that these actions will be subject to central review and potential revocation. This allows regional governments to entice firms with tax evasion strategies, legal exemptions, regional protectionism, and even shelter from court actions, further undermining the center's regulatory and enforcement capacity. Interregional competition thus becomes not a race to the top but an escape route by which firms avoid the reach of national authorities. In East Asia, we see this particularly in the justice sector, where complex and high-profile legal challenges are often deliberately shifted to remote regional courts, where the opportunities for undue influence may be greater. Such a phenomenon is also evident in regional regulations that provide preferential tax and regulatory regimes for specific firms in contradiction to national legislation.

The Early Experience in East Asia

Few empirical studies of the impact of decentralization on governance in East Asian countries exist so far. This is partly because most countries in the region began the decentralization process only recently: the Philippines and Vietnam in the early 1990s, Thailand and Indonesia in the late 1990s, and Cambodia at the turn of the century. Of these, Indonesia and the Philippines have gone the furthest in implementing comprehensive programs, and thus offer modest empirical evidence on the impact of decentralization on governance. While the experiences of each country are undoubtedly unique, these two nations can provide a glimpse of the potential benefits, risks, problems, and challenges to governance as a country decentralizes.

Empirical evidence on these two countries comes from perception-based surveys; no systematic analysis based on objective indicators is yet available, at least for East Asia.

Indonesia

Because Indonesia implemented its Big Bang decentralization only in 2001, it is still quite early to expect reliable estimates of the impact of complex and slow-moving institutional changes on perceptions of governance. Though the reform did rapidly transfer control over a significant share of public resources and direct authority over nearly 2 million civil servants to the local level, the institutional changes are still in flux and the lines of authority are unclear in many areas. Moreover, the country has recently revised the basic laws defining decentralization, so considerable uncertainty remains about its ultimate extent and shape. To expect this fluid environment to exert a clear impact on perceptions of governance—which generally lag behind institutional changes—is premature.

A number of empirical studies have attempted to measure governance trends across districts in Indonesia, but few provide a benchmark for comparing governance indicators before and after decentralization. As a second best—one that focuses on how the perceptions of firms change over time—the World Bank's Productivity and Investment Climate Survey (PICS) explicitly asked firms to identify the direction of change on a variety of governance dimensions before and after decentralization. Though these data are preliminary, they provide some basis for exploring these issues.

The PICS survey asked firms directly about the impact of decentralization on key aspects of governance and the investment climate. Firms perceived decentralization as having a negative impact in four areas: labor regulations, licenses, policy uncertainty, and corruption (see figure 11.3). While just under 30 percent of the firms felt that decentralization has made licensing and labor regulations worse, nearly 50 percent think policy uncertainty and corruption—two broad indicators of accountability—have worsened.

FIGURE 11.3 The Negative Impact of Decentralization, as Cited by Firms in Indonesia

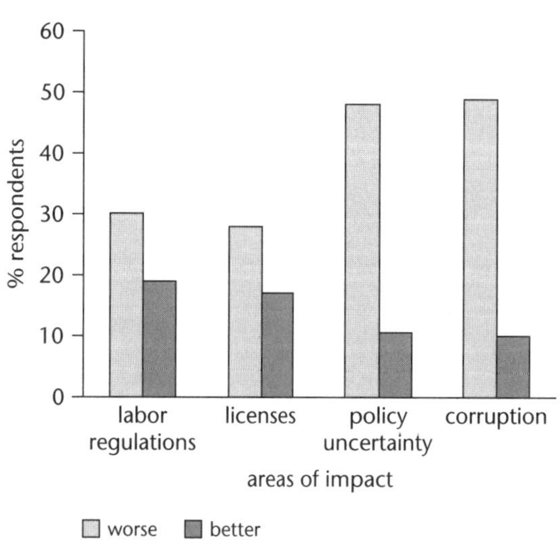

Source: PICS.

FIGURE 11.4 Obstacles to Business, as Cited by Firms in Indonesia

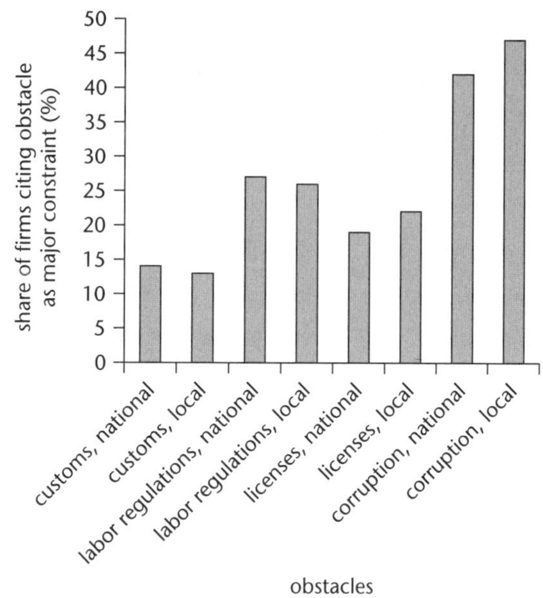

Source: PICS.

The survey results suggest that greater proximity to the client—in this case, in the business arena—does not necessarily lead to perceptions of greater accountability. The survey also asked firms to rate the extent to which a number of standard problems affect their business. In customs, labor regulations, licenses, and corruption, firms see little difference between the constraints imposed by national governments and those imposed by regional governments (see figure 11.4). Indeed, in some areas such as licenses and corruption, firms rate local governments worse than the national government, despite the greater proximity of the former.

Corruption appears to be a particular problem under decentralization in Indonesia. Over one-third of firms stated that informal payments had grown under decentralization, while less than 15 percent cited some improvement (see figure 11.5). Moreover, firms pay 64 percent more in informal payments as a share of annual revenues to local governments than they do to national level officials, on average (see table 11.1). Firms also spend 15 percent more of their time dealing with local regulations than with national regulations. Together,

FIGURE 11.5 Informal Payments after Decentralization, as Cited by Firms in Indonesia

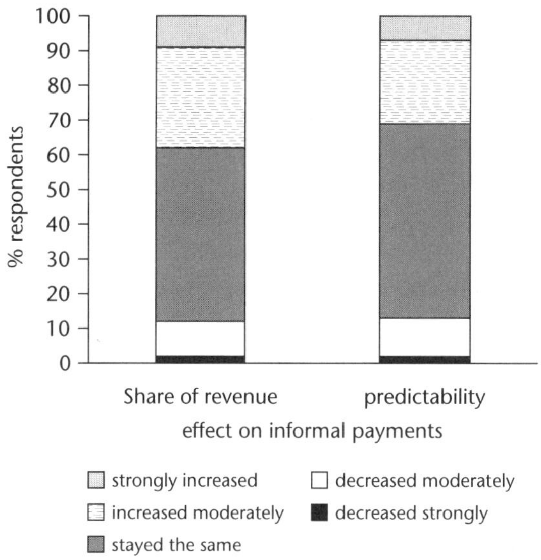

Source: World Bank 2005.

TABLE 11.1 Regulatory Burdens on Firms in Indonesia

	National government	Local government
Time spent dealing with regulations *(percent of total time)*	7.1%	8.2%
Informal payments *(percent of total sales)*	1.35%	2.1%

Source: World Bank 2005.

these results suggest that bringing government closer to clients—at least those in the business community—has not led to greater accountability compared with the national government. Instead, decentralization is linked with a general decline in perceptions of government accountability at the local level.

These perceptions are consistent with analyses of the fiscal performance of local governments under decentralization. Several recent studies have pointed to a widespread trend in which regional governments have imposed numerous nuisance taxes and charges—levies that cost more to administer than they reap in revenues—on small-scale economic activity. Many of these levies contradict national guidelines on the tax authority of local governments. Annual studies by the Jakarta-based monitoring organization Regional Autonomy Watch have emphasized the negative impact of these nuisance taxes and charges on regional investment climates. Studies of the legislative processes under which the taxes and charges have been formulated show little citizen consultation or participation (Lewis 2003; Regional Autonomy Watch 2004). Moreover, they tend to be poorly designed, with no clear links between service delivery and charges. Despite a requirement that national authorities review all regional legislation authorizing new taxes and charges within 30 days, a recent estimate suggests that some 60 percent of these regulations have not been reviewed, and that regions never sent a large share to the center for review (Lewis 2003). Though many regional governments have indeed introduced innovative programs to improve public service delivery and strengthen the transparency of local processes, little empirical evidence so far reveals a race to the top to improve regional investment climates.

In conjunction with World Bank projects that aim to invest in communities committed to governance reform, detailed case studies have examined governance dynamics at the district level (World Bank 2004b). These studies point to common factors distorting the potentially beneficial impact of decentralization on governance. First, these studies emphasize weak development of local "accountability infrastructure": institutions that constrain the authority of the executive branch. The heads of districts in Indonesia—*bupatis* and *walikotas*—are still appointed by local legislatures, rather than elected, with a strong role played by national parties. Removing district heads requires the approval of national authorities. The local legislatures themselves are extremely weak and ineffective: they have virtually no technical expertise, and rely entirely on the executive branch in key areas such as legal drafting, budget analysis, and public accounting. Moreover, case studies of elections for local legislatures have shown that the chosen candidates have weak accountability ties to their constituents. Candidates routinely pay national party organizations for ballot slots, and their selection is closely linked to elite village networks. Voters are also strongly influenced by direct payments and other transfers. As a result, the local governance environment is highly susceptible to clientelism and capture.

Local legal and judicial institutions play only a minor role in the accountability infrastructure. A detailed study of 37 cases where public officials stole or misused local development funds concluded that most communities could not overcome local power structures and elite networks to gain access to justice through formal and informal dispute resolution mechanisms. Only in cases where external actors such as national civil society groups, outside media, and representatives of a national project management structure intervened were corrupt local officials successfully prosecuted.

Civil society groups and other external constraints on government such as the media remain weak in most districts. Efforts to promote local plans to address poverty have been hampered by low levels of participation, except in districts near major universities or technical institutes. Though community radio is developing rapidly, print media do not penetrate far beyond the provincial capital. According to a recent poll, more than 85 percent of Indonesians obtain their political information from television (International Foundation for Electoral Studies 2004). Provincial and national media devote minimal attention to district news. Interviews also suggest that it is standard practice for local governments to pay provincial and national journalists for positive stories on a per story basis.

As mentioned, a major factor weakening the impact of decentralization on governance is uncertainty about the proper role of different levels of government and the resulting conflicts. In Indonesia, despite recent revisions to the main decentralization laws (formerly Laws 22 and 25 of 1999; now Laws 32 and 33 of 2004), the roles and responsibilities of district governments have not been fully clarified. The role of provincial governments in decentralization is also poorly defined. Moreover, the oversight functions of different central ministries—especially the ministries of Home Affairs and Finance—remain unclear. This has led to constant conflict, as different levels of government and competing agencies stake their claims over vaguely defined roles and powers. This conflict is reaching a crescendo with recent proposals to further revise the main decentralization laws. The boundaries of decentralization in Indonesia have thus been in a permanent state of renegotiation since Big Bang decentralization began in 2001. Not surprisingly, decentralization has exerted its most negative impact on policy uncertainty.

The World Bank's engagement in decentralization has highlighted the lack of information on regional performance, which is essential to promoting a race to the top among regions. Decentralization—especially the initial shift of control over civil servants to local governments—has undermined Indonesia's regional information systems. The problem is particularly severe in key decentralized public service sectors such as health and education. Minimum service standards mandated in the decentralization laws have not yet been developed. Only a small minority of districts have submitted the required performance self-assessments based on annual and five-year plans. Districts send only a small share of laws and decrees to the center for official review, and the Ministry of Home Affairs does not have a system for analyzing and cataloging this material. While several civil society groups have begun to develop systems for comparing performance across districts, especially regarding the investment climate, these efforts do not yet serve as a reliable basis for monitoring districts. As a result, little information about regional performance is available to stimulate competition and disseminate good and bad practices.[13]

The Philippines

In contrast to Indonesia, which is still in the very early stages of decentralization, the Philippines has several years more experience, having launched its major reform in 1992–93 under the mandate of its post-Marcos democratic Constitution of 1987.[14] Given more than a decade of experience, analyzing the long-term impact of decentralization on governance outcomes might indeed be possible. However, empirical analysis in the Philippines is nearly as sparse as in Indonesia, and no direct survey measures have explicitly examined the impact on perceptions of governance or related indicators. Existing evidence comes from an extensive study by the Center for Institutional Reform and the Informal Sector (IRIS) at the University of Maryland and the World Bank, based on surveys of households and public officials at different levels of

TABLE 11.2 Perceptions of Corruption in the Philippines
(mean statistics, scaled from 0 to 100)

	Type of respondent				
Survey questions	Municipal health official	Municipal administrative official	Municipal official at DECS	Teachers at public schools	Teachers at private schools
Corruption in the national government	74.00	69.23	62.77	66.35	80.85
Corruption in the provincial government	59.43	43.86	37.96	50.65	69.57
Corruption in the municipal government	43.42	29.32	24.79	36.86	62.32
Corruption in the *barangay* government	38.96	28.85	22.22	24.76	48.89

Source: Azfar et al. 2000.
Note: DECS = Department of Education, Culture, and Sports.

government.[15] The study presents a mixed picture of the impact of decentralization on governance and concludes that "the results do not match the most optimistic theoretical expectations." The authors find that while perceptions of corruption are much lower at lower levels of government, local governments are no more accountable to local preferences than the central government, given a variety of constraints on responsiveness.

Perception-based measures of corruption in the Philippines have shown significant and consistent improvement since decentralization, though establishing a clear causal connection is difficult. According to most international rankings of corruption, the Philippines began to show progress in the early 1990s and maintained this progress throughout the decade. Moreover, surveys of public officials revealed that respondents in every category saw corruption as more prevalent at the national level than at lower levels of government (see table 11.2). While municipal officials have obvious biases, the pattern is the same among teachers at private schools, suggesting that the responses may in fact reflect reality in the ground.

These differences in perceptions of corruption may reflect different sources of information about local and national levels that may be even more important in explaining the dynamics of accountability. The IRIS–World Bank survey asked respondents whether they had seen or heard reports of local and national officials engaged in corruption. Among the sample of over 1,100 households, 49 percent had seen or heard reports of national officials engaged in corruption, while only 27 percent had seen or heard reports of local officials engaged in corruption (Azfar et al. 2000).

A deeper probe into the sources of information on politics among Philippines respondents led to an interesting result (see table 11.3). While nearly 98 percent of respondents rely on the media—especially radio and TV—for their information on national politics, these sources are far less prominent with regard to local politics. Instead, 42 percent of the respondents used personal networks as their primary source of information on local politics and corruption, relying on community leaders or local officials rather than the media. This reflects the weak penetration of local media and their generally weak capacity to cover local politics. Thus, the media may play a much weaker role in monitoring local officials for corruption, and information on local politics could be more susceptible to manipulation through clientelist networks and state capture.

The IRIS–World Bank survey also explored local accountability by asking both households and officials to identify their funding priorities. Except for infrastructure (roads, canals, bridges), the professed preferences of municipal officials failed to match those of households. In the critical area of health, the correlation is in fact negative (see table 11.4).[16]

To supplement this finding, the survey asked public officials how they learned of household preferences. All the officials attested to making some effort to understand such preferences. About

TABLE 11.3 Sources of Information on Politics, as Cited by Households in the Philippines

	Local politics	National politics	T-test for difference between the two results[a]
Television	0.221	0.635	−16.12
Radio	0.332	0.307	0.91
Newspaper	0.030	0.037	−0.67
Officials	0.181	0.008	10.50
Civic associations	0.014	0.003	2.04
People/neighbor/friends/family	0.195	0.009	10.91
Inside information	0.018	0.002	2.80
Other	0.105	0	2.46
Total media	0.583	0.979	−16.94
No source	0.491	0.416	3.57

Source: Azfar et al. 2000.
Note: Table indicates the percentage of people using each source (given that a source is used, scale 0 to 1).
a. Numbers greater than 3 indicate that the difference is statistically significant at the 1 percent level.

TABLE 11.4 Correlation between Funding Priorities of Public Officials and Households in the Philippines

Priorities	Municipal officials (municipal average; number of officials = 78)
Roads, bridges, canals	0.495 (2.14)[a]
Education	0.015 (0.08)
Health	−0.703 (−2.14)[a]
Agriculture/irrigation	−0.090 (−0.34)
Garbage collection	−0.099 (−0.22)
New jobs	−0.030 (−0.08)
Aid to poor	−0.068 (−0.68)
Water, drainage	0.339 (1.08)

Source: Azfar et al. 2000.
Note: Public officials' preferences are regressed on household preferences for each priority type where variables are differences from the national mean. The first number in column two is the OLS regression coefficient, with t-statistics in parentheses.
a. Significant at the 1 percent level.

30 percent consult with community leaders and local civic organizations, while 15 percent also conduct surveys and make other inquiries (Azfar et al. 2000). However, neither method significantly strengthened the relationship between the funding priorities of households and municipal officials.

Despite this apparent mismatch, assessments of decentralization's impact on public service provision in the Philippines are mixed. For example, experts express concern about the deteriorating quality and administration of public health programs, but most people express more positive views. According to a June 1999 survey by Social Weather Station (a nonprofit organization specializing in survey-based research), 58 percent of respondents said health care had improved with decentralization, while only 8 percent said it had worsened (USAID 1999). A more quantitative measure of service quality is administrative delays in hiring and paying staff, which are significantly more severe in education than in health (see table 11.5). This is revealing, as the education sector has seen far less decentralization than the health sector, even though the Local Government Code requires devolution of basic education to local governments. Although performance measures before and after decentralization are not available, devolved services seem to work better on some dimensions.

TABLE 11.5 Responses from Facilities on Administrative Delays in the Philippines

Health facility	Index
How often has there been a delay of more than one month in getting a new health worker on a payroll?	3
In the last year, were there any nonpayments or delay of more than two weeks in the payment of your salary?	17
In the last year, were there any nonpayments or delay of more than two weeks in the payment of your allowances?	7
Primary school	
How often has there been a delay of more than one month in getting a new teacher on a payroll?	26
In the last year, were there any nonpayments or delay of more than two weeks in the payment of your salary?	20
In the last year, were there any nonpayments or delay of more than two weeks in the payment of your allowances?	17

Source: Azfar et al. 2000.
Note: The higher the index, the worse the problem. The index, which is scaled from 0 to 100, is constructed as follows: {(0*% responded never) + (1*% responded sometimes) + (2*% responded most of the time) + (3*% responded always)}/3.

Some aspects of governance and service delivery standards have improved under decentralization, although whether these changes are due to enhanced accountability at the local level is much less clear. Surveys have shown that, as in Indonesia, key institutions in the local accountability framework—such as an independent media, and legislative and judicial branches to check the power of local executives—are weak. However, unlike Indonesia, the Philippines has seen civil society groups mushroom at the local level. A number of studies reveal that NGOs have indeed become actively involved in the decision making of the local government.[17] In 1986, when the country restored democracy, 27,100 NGOs had registered with the Securities and Exchange Commission. After passage of the Local Government Code, this number quickly doubled to 50,800 in 1992. Today more than 95,000 NGOs exist, with some 7,000 operating at the grassroots level (Alonzo 2003). One study concluded that "NGOs operating at the local level often found themselves in direct confrontations with local elites who, understandably, feel threatened when NGO members build alliances, muster funds and other resources for use by local people outside the control of traditional patrons, and gain the moral high ground in the process" (Alonzo 2003: 17).[18]

However, these surveys suggest that the responsiveness of local governments to the new layer of NGOs has been limited, owing to legal and procedural constraints on decentralization and fears among central officials that they will lose control over the regions. While boosting local taxing authority, the Local Government Code also constrains local revenue collection through rules on rates, assessments, appeals, and administrative responsibilities (USAID 1999). The code also regulates earmarked funds such as the Special Education Fund, specifying the property levies through which these funds are raised and the rules for distributing the proceeds. These requirements significantly compromise local revenue autonomy. In fact, whenever fiscal (deficit) problems have become serious, the central government has conjured up schemes to reduce mandated, formula-based transfers, further limiting the flexibility and responsiveness of local governments (Azfar et al. 2000; Alonzo 2003).

Not surprisingly, as in Indonesia, the hypothesized race to the top among local governments has not emerged. But unlike in Indonesia, and perhaps because of longer experience, reliable information on performance is beginning to develop, spurring some competition among local governments. The power of information in fostering competition is perhaps best illustrated by the success of the Galing Pook Awards. These awards, first introduced in 1993 in response to the Local Government Code, were patterned after awards to U.S. local governments for notable achievements in improving service delivery and public welfare. Since their inception, a total of 2,339 programs have competed for these awards, with just 175 selected and 8 consistently cited for excellence and elevated to the Hall of Fame. The awards carry no monetary compensation; they simply provide a credible signal to local—and potentially higher-level constituencies—that a mayor or governor is doing a good job.[19]

Conclusions

Though decentralization is, fundamentally, a strategy for improving governance, its impact on governance outcomes is still largely unknown. A strong body of theory posits governance gains from decentralization, but recognition of how decentralization can go wrong has grown. The expected gains are based on assumptions about the politics of accountability at the local level and the nature of interjurisdictional competition that need to be examined closely, especially in developing countries. Using an accountability framework that links citizens, policy makers, and service providers, this chapter examined the potential risks in each link that threaten to undermine the expected governance gains from decentralization. The chapter then applied that framework to the two East Asian countries with the most significant decentralization programs: Indonesia and the Philippines.

Not surprisingly, in neither country has decentralization fulfilled the governance goals predicted by the most optimistic theories. In Indonesia, which is still in the early stages of its reform, the initial impact on perceptions of governance and selected outcomes has not been positive. There is a widely held view that decentralization has exacerbated corruption and significantly increased policy uncertainty across different levels of government. Decentralization has also led to a greater regulatory burden on firms and questionable financial management practices. These problems have contributed to a general weakening of the investment climate, which has harmed Indonesia's growth prospects. In the Philippines, which has a longer record of decentralization, the picture is more mixed. Overall, perceptions of corruption have declined, and service delivery standards have improved somewhat. However, the link between these outcomes and improvements in the accountability of local politicians is weak.

In both countries, surveys and case study research suggest that the most serious problem is the weakness of local institutions intended to play a major role in the accountability framework, including local legislatures, judicial institutions, and the media. Local officials—even more than their national counterparts—are subject to the risks of capture and clientelism. Countervailing institutions at the local level generally lack the independence and capacity to check these risks. This does not suggest that decentralization in such contexts should be avoided. Indeed, experience in the Philippines shows that decentralization can encourage the development of a vibrant local civil society network. Yet more needs to be done to support the other key institutions in the accountability framework that guarantee and sustain the expected governance gains from decentralization.

The case studies also reveal the risks associated with sustained uncertainty about the division of roles and responsibilities across levels of governments. In Indonesia, in particular, decentralization is hotly contested terrain. The enabling legislation is often inconsistent and leaves many issues unresolved. These inconsistencies have set the stage for serious political conflicts across levels of government and among agencies, further exacerbating these uncertainties. Even after a decade of decentralization, the Philippines suffers from similar problems. Such an environment constrains the ability of local officials to respond to the demands of their constituents, and shifts their focus to bureaucratic struggles to preserve their powers. Uncertainty blunts the impact of decentralization on accountability at the local level.

Finally, the case studies emphasize the critical role of information in spurring interregional competition, yet these systems have largely been overlooked in the context of decentralization. The decentralization process itself tends to fragment and weaken information flows from the local level over the short term. Significant efforts are needed to preserve these channels and develop new standards and instruments for measuring and disseminating information on regional performance. These flows expand the range of information available to local voters, who surveys have shown still largely depend on social networks for information, which can encourage clientelism and capture. These flows are also essential to enabling investors, donors, and others to compare the performance of different regions, and to widely disseminate good and bad practices to maximize their impact.

The analysis in this chapter suggests a strategy for enhancing the impact of decentralization on governance. Such a strategy should rest on three pillars:

- *Frame decentralization within national rules that weaken the ability of local governments to engage in capture or clientelism.* To combat local capture, national authorities need to enforce strong restrictions on the ability of local governments to offer tax and regulatory privileges to specific firms and groups. Local legislation often codifies such privileges, and needs to be subject to some form of central administrative review. To combat clientelism, countries also need to link decentralization to national civil service reform, stipulating meritocratic recruitment and advancement with appropriate central oversight and appeals. The political and economic incentives for the center to enforce such standards in regions may be stronger than the incentives for the center to adhere to the same standards.
- *Focus on strengthening local countervailing institutions and collective associations, not only through bottom-up participation but by linking them to national networks, which can help these institutions counterbalance entrenched local elites.* To enhance local accountability, countervailing institutions and collective associations may need to marshal resources outside their localities to enhance their power and influence. Capacity-building programs should therefore focus on forging closer links between local institutions and national networks. Local legislatures may be more effective at checking the executive branch if they are allied more closely with a national legislative network. Local civil society groups may be more effective in promoting accountability if they can rely on the capacity and power deriving from their national networks.
- *Strengthen a national framework for encouraging competition among regions, so local capture and clientelism entail reputational costs and lower external investment.* Providing information on regional performance measures and the quality of governance is particularly important, as such information can counterbalance the powerful local pressures supporting capture and clientelism.

Overall, this strategy entails using national structures and networks to enhance the ability of local organizations to promote greater political accountability under decentralization. This approach complements community-driven development (see chapter 12) by strengthening countervailing institutions and building local demand for good governance.

Endnotes

1. The main proponent of this view was Freidrich Hayek 1948.
2. The classic statement of this view is Tiebout 1956.
3. For a review of the literature, see Bardhan 2002. See also Bardhan and Mookherjee (2000) for a discussion of decentralizing infrastructure services that questions received wisdom on the impact of decentralization on governance.
4. The World Bank has been particularly active in this area, especially in East Asia. In Indonesia, for example, 40 percent of the Bank's lending program for 2004–7 will focus on local governments and support decentralization.
5. The *World Development Report 2004* characterizes these bilateral relationships between agents and principals as fostering accountability (World Bank 2004c).
6. This argument dates from the classic works of Rousseau 1986.
7. More specifically, the possibility of obtaining rents drives influential groups and individuals to bribe politicians and high-ranking civil servants, who introduce and maintain bad laws, policies, and regulations to perpetuate their illicit earnings. Note that in this context, corruption causes bad governance.
8. See, for example, World Bank 2004b.
9. For a review of the literature on clientelism, see Keefer and Khemani 2003.
10. Illustrating the contrast with the national political arena, a popular song on the eve of Indonesia's first democratic national elections exhorted voters to "take Golkar's money, but vote for someone else." See Friend 2003.
11. While no systematic studies have compared skills and experience across levels of government, greater prestige and higher stakes and living conditions at central levels are likely to attract more competent individuals.
12. John Stuart Mill raised a related argument in *On Representative Government.* He worried that in a decentralized state, "the local representative bodies and their officers are almost certain to be of a much lower grade of intelligence and knowledge, than Parliament and the national executive."
13. The World Bank has introduced a local government reform platform within its Country Assistance Strategy for 2004–7 to address these information gaps and help develop a system for monitoring and evaluating regional performance.
14. Ferdinand Marcos ruled the country as a virtual dictator from 1964 to 1985.
15. The study was based on nine separate surveys covering 1,100 households; 80 municipal administrators, health officials, and education officials; 20 provincial administrators, health officials, and education officials; 160 workers at government health facilities; and 160 school principals (Azfar et al. 2000).
16. Unfortunately, the survey did not include national officials, so we cannot determine if the correlation is stronger than at the national level.

17. See especially Rood 1998; Alonzo 2003; and USAID 1999.
18. For an extended discussion, see Racelis 2000.
19. *Galing Pook* means means "place of excellence." The Ford Foundation provided seed funding for the awards; today the Galing Pook Foundation raises money from private sources, both local and international.

    "The Galing Pook winners have become models of good practices in local governance. Their programs have been documented, published, studied and visited by countless local and national government personnel, academics, students, media practitioners, civil society leaders, and ordinary citizens from the Philippines and abroad. Local chief executives and program managers of these programs have become sought-after resource persons in conferences and have served as mentors to other LGU's that have adopted their programs. Schools of public administration and other institutions have used the Galing Pook case studies in their academic courses and training programs. The awards *have* served as a seal of good housekeeping on program excellence and *have* opened many windows of opportunity in terms of accessing funds, *particularly* from donors." See www.inq7.net/globalnation/galingpook/about_gp.php.

Bibliography

Alonzo, Ruperto. 2003. "The Political Economy of Decentralization in the Philippines." Washington, DC: World Bank, East Asia and Pacific Region.

Azfar, Omar, Tugrul Gurgur, Satu Kähkönen, Anthony Lanyi, and Patrick Meagher. 2000. "Decentralization and Governance: An Empirical Investigation of Public Service Delivery in the Philippines." College Park, MD: University of Maryland, Department of Economics, Center for Institutional Reform and the Informal Sector.

Bardhan, Pranab. 2002. "Decentralization of Governance and Development." *Journal of Economic Perspectives* 16 (4): 185–205.

Bardhan, Pranab, and Dilip Mookherjee. 2000. "Capture and Governance at Local and National Levels." *American Economic Review* 90 (2): 135–9.

Cai, Hongbin, and Daniel Treisman. 2002. "State-Corroding Federalism." Los Angeles: University of California Los Angeles (UCLA), Department of Political Science.

Friend, Theodore. 2003. *Indonesian Destinies.* Cambridge, MA: Belknap Press.

Gordon, Roger H. 1983. "An Optimal Taxation Approach to Fiscal Federalism." *Quarterly Journal of Economics* 98 (4): 567–86.

Hayek, Friedrich von. 1948. "The Economic Conditions of Interstate Federalism." In *Individualism and Economic Order.* Chicago, IL: University of Chicago Press.

Hoffman, Bert, and Kai Kaiser. 2003. "Decentralization, Democratic Governance, and Local Governance in Indonesia." Washington, DC: World Bank, East Asia and Pacific Region.

International Foundation for Electoral Studies. 2004. *Presidential Election Survey.* Jakarta: International Foundation for Electoral Studies.

Keefer, Philip, and Stuti Khemani. 2003. "Clientelism." Background Paper for *World Development Report.* Washington, DC: World Bank.

Keen, Michael, and Maurice Marchand. 1997. "Fiscal Competition and the Pattern of Public Spending." *Journal of Public Economics* 66: 33–53.

Lewis, Blane D. 2003. "Tax and Charge Creation by Regional Governments under Fiscal Decentralization: Estimates and Explanations." *Bulletin of Indonesian Economic Studies* 39 (2).

Mutebi, Alex. 2003. "Challenges of Participatory Local Management under Decentralization: Lessons from Chiangrai Municipality." INDES workshop. Bangkok: Asia Development Bank.

Oates, Wallace E., and Robert M. Schwab. 1988. "Economic Competition among Jurisdictions: Efficiency Enhancing or Distortion Inducing?" *Journal of Public Economics* 35: 333–54.

Porter, Doug, and Clay Wescott. 2002. "Decentralization and Citizen Participation in East Asia." INDES workshop. Bangkok: Asian Development Bank.

Prud'homme, Rémy. 1995. "The Dangers of Decentralization." *World Bank Research Observer* 10 (2): 201–20.

Racelis, Mary. 2000. "New Visions and Strong Actions: Civil Society in the Philippines." In *Funding Virtue: Civil Society, Aid, and Democracy Promotion*, eds. M. Ottaway and T. Carothers. Washington, DC: Carnegie Endowment for International Peace, pp. 159–87.

Regional Autonomy Watch. 2004. *Regional Investment Attractiveness: A Survey of Business Perception, 2004.* Jakarta: Asia Foundation.

Rood, Steve. 1998. "Decentralization, Democracy, and Development." In *The Philippines: New Directions in Domestic Policy and Foreign Relations,* ed. D. Timberman. New York: Asia Society.

Rousseau, Jean Jacques. 1986. "The Social Contract." In *Political Writings,* translated and edited by Frederick Watkins. Madison, WI: University of Wisconsin Press.

Tanzi, Vito. 1995. "Fiscal Federalism and Decentralization: A Review of Some Efficiency and Macroeconomic Aspects." In *Annual World Bank Conference on Development Economics 1995.* Washington, DC: World Bank.

Tiebout, Charles. 1956. "A Pure Theory of Local Expenditures." *Journal of Political Economy* 64: 416–24.

USAID (U.S. Agency for International Development). 1996. "Issues in Local Government Finance: Local Taxation and Other Revenue Generation." Report No. 96–02. Manila: USAID.

———. 1999. *The Governance and Local Democracy Project (GOLD): Summary Assessment.* Manila: USAID.

World Bank. 2000. "Anticorruption in Transition: A Contribution to the Policy Debate." Washington, DC: World Bank, Europe and Central Asia.

———. 2004a. "Kabupaten Reform Dynamics Study." Jakarta: World Bank Indonesia Resident Mission.

———. 2004b. "Village Justice in Indonesia." Jakarta: World Bank Indonesia Resident Mission.

———. 2004c. *World Development Report 2004: Making Services Work for Poor People.* Washington, DC: World Bank; and New York: Oxford University Press.

———. 2005. "Raising Investment in Indonesia." Washington, DC: World Bank, East Asia Poverty Reduction and Economic Management Network.

Zhuravskaya, Ekaterina V. 2000. "Incentives to Provide Local Public Goods: Fiscal Federalism, Russian Style." *Journal of Public Economics* 76 (3): 337–68.

12

COMMUNITY-DRIVEN DEVELOPMENT: DECENTRALIZATION'S ACCOUNTABILITY CHALLENGE

Susan Wong and Scott Guggenheim

Decentralization is often hailed for moving government closer to its citizens and providing opportunities for participation in decision making. Achieving this goal, however, depends on a variety of conditions, including establishing mechanisms to promote broad civic participation and more responsive and accountable local governments. These goals are especially relevant for East Asian countries pursuing large-scale decentralization programs. One mechanism intended to make development planning and management more responsive and accountable arises from what the World Bank has called community-driven development (CDD).

A great deal of empirical evidence reveals that decentralization will not always achieve the goal of making local governments more responsive and accountable. They are often susceptible to elite capture: that is, public decision making often reflects disproportionate influence by well-off and well-connected groups. In many countries, officials exploit the opportunities offered by decentralization to promote their own commercial activities. Standard mechanisms for accountability, such as elections, audits, and performance benchmarking, often do not work well in environments where information is scarce, open elections are unfamiliar or rare, and clarity about performance standards is lacking. Decentralization can also aggravate existing social problems. Polarized local environments can erupt into open conflict when decentralization leads to the exclusion of one group from government. Marginalized groups, particularly the poor, often fare worse under decentralization when local governments do not see redistributive or highly targeted social programs as priorities—particularly if the primary beneficiaries of such programs are people least likely to vote. A great deal of work is needed to introduce transparency, consultation, participation, and accountability mechanisms that can link public administrations with their surrounding communities and give the poor a greater voice.

Decentralization and CDD are inherently political reform processes. Nevertheless, because development programs channel significant resources into the existing administrative structure, donor choices can help determine to what extent decentralization promotes healthier links between communities and governments.

The challenge of finding mechanisms to promote more responsive and accountable local governments is especially relevant in East Asian countries undergoing large-scale decentralization. China, for example, has quietly but effectively pursued a national program for village elections, and is developing a package of programs that provide new village governments with investment resources. Indonesia, as this chapter will show, is similarly concerned with fostering more effective, adequately funded local governments that can pursue a range of investments, and with encouraging communities to feel they have a stake in local government and the means to change it.

CDD programs are one mechanism for making development planning and management more accountable. Although community development is a well-established idea in the literature, large development agencies such as the World Bank first became involved with significant CDD programs in the late 1990s.

This chapter defines CDD as an approach that gives communities or locally elected bodies control over the decision making, management, and use of development funds.[1] CDD differs significantly from an earlier generation of community-based rural development projects in emphasizing the role that communities play in driving the development process rather than acting as passive beneficiaries.

The long-term goal of CDD projects, especially in East Asia, has been to reduce poverty by improving local governance and empowering local people. While varying somewhat in design, CDD programs generally consist of a participatory planning process at village and commune or subdistrict levels, leading to funding and implementation of priority activities. CDD programs emphasize giving communities and locally elected bodies the power, information, and skills to determine the best use of development resources.

CDD approaches are especially relevant in countries where the priorities of central and local governments with respect to poverty are weak, and where governments will respond more readily to poverty if there is strong demand emanating from society. The demand side is as important and fundamental in politics as in the realm of economics. CDD hypothesizes that the community demand-side approach—if well designed and implemented—will exert multiplier effects in broader decision-making processes at the local level.

The growth of CDD programs has occurred in parallel with a general trend toward decentralization and democratization in countries within the region over the last decade or so, driven by varying political motivations. Given these trends, what has been the relationship between the portfolio of CDD programs and decentralization reforms? How have these programs worked within evolving decentralization frameworks? This chapter describes some of the dynamics behind these two trends and focuses on three main issues:

- CDD's role in *improving the quality* of decentralization by promoting greater civic participation, voice, and accountability in local governance.
- CDD's role in *delivering cost-effective and timely services* within a decentralized context.
- CDD's role in *informing and formulating* decentralization regulations.

Based on the above analysis, this chapter argues that in a decentralized environment, CDD programs can improve the quality of the decentralization framework by promoting greater civic participation, voice, and accountability in local governance; providing an effective means of delivering much-needed services in a decentralized context in a cost-effective and time-efficient manner; and directly informing and shaping decentralization regulations. While CDD projects are too new to allow definitive statements about their overall success or failure, preliminary evaluations point to tangible contributions in these areas. The chapter also discusses challenges that lie ahead for CDD in decentralized environments.

CDD as Public Sector Heresy: CDD Works in Practice but Does It Work in Theory?

Specialists in public administration are often wary of CDD for understandable reasons. CDD financial flows bypass formal intergovernmental transfer systems, and CDD sits outside integrated government planning. But are there persuasive counterarguments as well?

One is that CDD can improve the way local governments function and thus help them work better for their citizens. The decentralization literature says little about the role of nonstate actors in making local governments work in transparent and accountable ways. CDD aims to strengthen that role. By promoting demand, competitive pressure, and the flow of information between governors and the governed, CDD programs introduce a range of accountability mechanisms and participatory processes that improve local governance, especially in a decentralized environment. CDD encourages the creation and strengthening of community groups, and forges new norms regarding civic behavior and expectations regarding the relationship between government and the people.

Whereas reforms of public administration tend to focus on the government side of the governance equation, CDD emphasizes the other half of the equation: strengthening citizen participation and demand. These two efforts are not mutually exclusive, but the starting points are quite different. CDD approaches governance from the bottom up by helping poorer communities make their demands more audible and visible, thus influencing local planning and decision making.

CDD also responds to an efficiency problem. East Asian subnational bureaucracies are already overburdened trying to meet routine district-level requirements. All too often, faced with limited time and resources, these governments simply delay new efforts to meet the development needs of villages, or collapse them into existing programs that may or may not reflect local development priorities. Thus, for example, a 1997 review of 48 villages in Indonesia found that fewer than 3 percent of village development requests proposed through the government's development planning system ever received funding (Evers 1998).

CDD programs have the potential to eliminate some of these problems. CDD projects do not have to follow cumbersome or leaky procedures for transferring funds or develop complicated mechanisms for coordinating and delivering services. Community groups can fulfill many of these functions instead. And, for certain types of infrastructure and services, preliminary evidence suggests that delivering funds directly to communities complements investments of district governments with no loss of quality, and allows large-scale provision of productive investments that would otherwise not have occurred.

This chapter examines how CDD approaches have been designed to operate in different decentralized environments. As other chapters explain, the forms, dimensions, and degrees of decentralization—political, administrative, and fiscal—vary across the region. CDD programs also show wide variation in design, management, and closeness to local governments. These variations relate to historical and structural factors within specific country contexts, as well as to different strategic approaches to CDD.

A note of methodological caution is needed. Large-scale CDD programs at the World Bank are relatively new, with the large majority having been in effect for less than three years. Within such a limited time frame, it is premature to draw conclusions, whether positive or negative, about critical aspects of CDD, such as their impacts on poverty and local government, evolution, and sustainability. Furthermore, CDD projects have proved no more immune to the general lack of rigorous evaluation than other development projects. Such rigorous evaluation is rare in all contexts, and some studies indicate that the CDD community devotes

"There have been spectacular successes and miserable failures in the efforts by developing countries to make services work. The main difference between success and failure is the degree to which poor people themselves are involved in determining the quality and the quantity of the services which they receive."

World Development Report 2004: Making Services Work for Poor People

"The core message from poor people is a plea for direct assistance to them, without exploitative and corrupt 'middlemen' and free of well-intended but often wasteful development programs. They call for systemic change."

"They [poor people] want to develop their own organizations so they can effectively negotiate fair partnerships with governments, with traders, and with NGOs; they want direct assistance and local ownership of funds through community-driven programs, with governments and NGOs accountable to them."

Voices of the Poor, World Bank, 2000

(Personal accounts from over 60,000 men and women in 60 countries of the realities of living with poverty, and what they need to improve their lives)

substantial if not more effort than other sectors to such evaluations (Wassenich and Whiteside 2003). That being said, funders are now making concerted efforts to install comparable measurement systems across the CDD portfolio.

The lack of comparable evaluations precludes any conclusive statements about the overall impacts of CDD. Yet it is possible to draw some preliminary conclusions about CDD performance. Projects already under way collect a great deal of useful information, and several older projects are yielding a growing body of evidence, including evaluations of their technical quality, audits, cost-benefit analyses, case studies, and information on types and levels of participation. This chapter draws on that information while noting that a full assessment of CDD will have to wait several years.

Given the diversity of CDD, this chapter addresses general approaches while honing in on three countries where specific large-scale CDD programs intertwine with significant decentralization reforms: Indonesia, Cambodia, and the Philippines. While all these CDD programs are housed within government ministries or interministerial committees, they differ somewhat in terms of their design, links with local government entities, and historical evolution.

The Indonesian *Kecamatan* Development Program (KDP) gives communities planning and decision-making power over development resources. KDP initially built on the government's bottom-up planning structure while introducing a broad range of reforms to make that system more participatory and efficient. KDP channels funds outside the usual government disbursement mechanisms, allowing financing to flow directly from the national level to *kecamatan* and village-level bank accounts controlled by communities. Since Indonesia's decentralization in 2001, the second and third phases (2002–7) of KDP have emphasized greater oversight from district parliaments, government monitoring, links with sectoral agencies such as education and health, district matching grants, and local involvement in drafting formal decentralization regulations on village autonomy.

The *Kapit Bisig Laban sa Kahirapan*-Comprehensive Integrated Delivery of Social Services (KALALHI-CIDSS) in the Philippines began in 2002. Its design is similar to that of KDP, except that community-funded plans are more closely integrated with municipal development plans. This partly reflects the country's more evolved decentralization process, in which local governments play a more significant role than in Indonesia.

The Seila Program in Cambodia is rather different.[2] It began as a postconflict government experiment in alleviating poverty through decentralized systems for planning, financing, and implementing development at the province, commune, and village levels. The program has evolved considerably, and in its second phase (2001–5) has supported further design and implementation of deconcentration and decentralization reforms and worked more closely with locally elected bodies, with funds flowing through official intergovernmental fiscal transfer systems.

This chapter also highlights a sectoral CDD project to show how they operate. Sectoral CDD projects generally work within line ministries and provide block grants to community organizations such as school committees, health management councils, and farmer or irrigation organizations, which decide how to use the grant funds. The Cambodia Education Quality Improvement Project (EQIP) provides block grants directly to school cluster committees for use as they see fit to improve educational quality (see box 12.1).

We chose these case studies for two reasons. First, they represent the latest thinking on CDD design and approaches in the East Asia region and are considered the most successful of the CDD portfolio. While not without significant problems and challenges, they afford a glimpse of some of the trends and issues facing CDD. Second, the CDD projects in these three countries are intricately linked to their national decentralization reforms. Thus, they illustrate concrete ways in which CDD projects can interact with and influence reforms within a decentralized framework.

How Does CDD Strengthen the Decentralization Framework?

Promoting Civic Participation in Local Planning and Decision Making

In theory, decentralization facilitates participation by local populations. In actuality, the legacy of decades of authoritarian rule and embedded hierarchical structures and behavior in many countries subvert

BOX 12.1 CDD Projects in Three East Asian Countries

Indonesia: The Kecamatan Development Program (1998–2007)
Begun in 1998, the government's KDP aims to alleviate poverty by raising rural incomes, strengthen local government, and community institutions, and improve governance. KDP recently completed its first phase, funding more than 50,000 infrastructure and economic activities and benefiting some 35 million poor people. Field studies and audits show that KDP projects delivered a broad range of services at lower-than-normal cost with greater community involvement. KDP is now entering its second and third phases, which emphasize building villagers' technical skills and strengthening local government institutions as part of the country's overall decentralization process. The program encompasses some 28,000 villages—almost 40 percent of the country's total.

Cambodia: Seila/Rural Investment and Local Governance (RILG) Project
RILG Project aims to contribute to rural development and reduce poverty by supporting the provision of priority public goods and services at the commune level, and to promote good governance by enhancing participation at the commune and provincial levels. RILG works through Cambodia's Seila Program, a mechanism for mobilizing and coordinating aid that supports the government's decentralization and deconcentration reforms. Together, RILG and Seila provide grants for rural infrastructure and related public goods identified through the planning process. The two programs also provide technical assistance for strategic studies to inform deconcentration reforms, and to review and strengthen the regulatory framework for decentralization.

While the RILG Project began only recently, Seila started in 1996. The first phase (1996–2000) enabled the government to formulate and fully test in five provinces provincial and commune systems for budgeting, planning, financing, and implementing development. Seila initially supported elected commune and village development councils and emphasized participatory local planning and financing. The program has since evolved with the country's deconcentration and local election process to work with the 2002 elected Commune/*Sangkat* Councils. The second phase (2001–5) supports the implementation and further design of decentralization and deconcentration reforms.

Cambodia: Education Quality Improvement Program (1999–2004)
EQIP aims to develop a model for a participatory approach to improving school quality and pursuing performance-based management of resources. The project has two main components. The first finances grants to provincial committees, quality improvement grants to school clusters, and monitoring and evaluation activities. The second component supports the National Committee on Effective Schooling, policy studies, and provincial and district education offices.

Philippines: KALAHI-CIDSS Project (2002–6)
This project aims to strengthen participation in village governance and develop communities' capacity to design, implement, and manage development activities that reduce poverty. The project was influenced by Comprehensive Integrated Delivery of Social Services, the country's previous poverty alleviation program, as well as by Indonesia's KDP. The project will encompass some 5,300 villages in the country's 40 poorest provinces.

broad-based participation and the idea that people can hold local government officials accountable. In such contexts, CDD projects can provide mechanisms to accelerate participation and accountability through broad-based planning, decision making, and implementation. CDD can help design the planning cycle to engage the poor and other marginalized groups, thus moving toward more inclusive governance. In most cases, the CDD community planning process begins with participatory appraisals that include social mapping, wealth-ranking exercises, and, in Indonesia, separate meetings for women. The local planning process varies from country to country. In Indonesia and the Philippines, it takes the form of a list of development priorities. In the Philippines, local governments agree to include the CDD list of projects in municipal development plans. Activities that appear in those plans qualify for funding through donor assistance or other sources.

Under CDD, decisions on allocating resources occur in a decentralized, participatory manner—in contrast with the first generation of social funds, which typically relied on external parties at the national level to make such decisions. Forums composed of elected community representatives make decisions at intervillage and subdistrict levels. In Indonesia, quotas ensure that women participate in the decision-making process, thus broadening the scope of civic participation.

Cambodia's Rural Investment and Local Governance (RILG) Project under the Seila Program illustrates the link between decentralization reforms and CDD. Begun in 1996, Seila piloted a model for decentralized planning, financing, and managing development activities at the province and commune levels. At the time, the country had no formal decentralization policy. In its early stages, Seila supported participatory planning and decision making through community, village, and commune development councils, with local plans funded outside normal government channels. As decentralization reforms slowly evolved and commune elections were held in 2002, the program was integrated into local government institutions and processes.

Scaled up from an initial five provinces to a nationwide program, the Seila pilot experience on participatory planning and decision making fed directly into the country's deconcentration and decentralization reforms. The Inter-Ministerial Administrative Proclamation (*Prakas*) on Commune/*Sangkat* Development Planning—the regulation governing the preparation and implementation of a commune development plan—incorporates lessons from Seila on how to prepare a commune development plan, a commune investment plan, and an annual budget. The regulation and accompanying guideline encourage local governments to open budget discussions to the public. These guidelines also highlight the need to set up appropriate mechanisms to facilitate the direct involvement of beneficiaries in the detailed design and supervision of all projects in the commune development plans.[3]

In the Philippines, the KALAHI-CIDSS Project is designed to promote community participation and development within existing government structures.[4] Communities and local governments engage in a demand-driven, bottom-up process of planning and problem solving that leads to grants for community investment programs. The emphasis is on ensuring that decision making and management of public resources are participatory and demand-driven. Local governments play an important role by providing technical services for planning projects, to ensure their feasibility. Municipal development plans automatically include all the activities selected under this process, and therefore so do the annual budgets of local governments, safeguarding the sustainability of these investments.

These CDD processes are not without their challenges and limitations. First, many struggle to integrate village and subdistrict planning with planning at the district and provincial levels. The subvillage or village level may not be appropriate for choosing the location of certain public facilities or forms of service delivery, such as health clinics and schools. "Supralocal" or interjurisdictional cooperation is needed to achieve economies of scale and pool limited resources. Local planning cannot supplant the need for improved regional and integrated multisector planning. Countries need to better link small, dispersed investments occurring at community levels with larger investment projects to achieve technological sophistication and economies of scale.

As a second challenge, a community-driven planning process may overlook some needs. Efforts to address violence against women and assist widows and female heads of household, respond to health needs, and conserve the environment often do not survive a participatory, competitive community planning process. Greater advocacy is needed to highlight concerns such as immunization programs, accompanied by special funding windows, quotas, and vertical programming so the local planning and budgeting process can address them.

Giving Citizens a Voice

One of the main apprehensions regarding decentralization has been the extent to which local elites may dominate local decision making just as easily as—if not more easily than—central authorities. Particularly in highly stratified societies, local elites may capture the benefits arising from a decentralized planning and financing system. Dropping funding to provincial or local levels where, for decades, people have not been allowed to develop broad civic decision-making institutions or accountability mechanisms hardly seems wise.

What can be done to counter these inequalities? Decentralization needs to be accompanied by reforms that increase the transparency and accountability of local government. CDD programs build on the premise that gradually broadening participation in policy making and resource allocation can enhance accountability and transparency and improve equity in service delivery.

CDD programs encourage citizens to exercise voice and demand accountability and transparency through several mechanisms:

- A strong emphasis on *information disclosure and transparency,* especially related to project budgets, financing, contracting, and procurement. Financial and contract information is discussed publicly and displayed on village information boards. In Indonesia's KDP, village committees must report back to the general village assembly at least twice during subproject implementation to discuss progress and financial status.
- A *grievance mechanism* (Indonesia and the Philippines) that channels anonymous complaints to project authorities and encourages efforts to address grievances.
- *Strong community monitoring* mechanisms. In Indonesia and the Philippines, each village forms an independent committee responsible for overseeing contracts, procurement, finances, and implementation of development projects. These committees must report on financial status and physical progress at various stages. Provincial journalists and NGOs are also invited to act as watchdogs over the proper use of public development funds. Together these mechanisms provide a system of checks and balances to help keep local governments accountable.

Studies and preliminary evidence highlight two other features of the CDD process. First, CDD projects generally include a decentralized financing mechanism that operates more quickly than comparable disbursements from line agencies. Second, the services delivered are cost-effective compared with the delivery of small-scale works by public agencies.

Decentralized Financing Mechanisms

The pitfall of many decentralized planning processes worldwide has been a lack of resources to implement the resulting plans. CDD projects tackle this problem by providing finances directly from the national level to local levels to implement community-identified priority projects. Several CDD case studies, in the region as well as globally, show that one of the main reasons for the popularity of CDD projects is that they do in fact disburse funds quickly. Why did the governments of Indonesia and the Philippines initially choose a CDD model when they had traditional line agency programs to combat poverty at their disposal? Those programs were not disbursing funds fast enough and were not reaching the poor.

In Indonesia, for example, KDP's ability to provide quick, high-volume disbursements of development funds from the national level straight down to the local level was the main reason that the government chose to launch the program in 1997–98. The traditional methods for disbursing funds through line ministries had failed, as shown by the poor track record of the $1.2 billion national social safety net program, which was canceled halfway through implementation because of poor targeting, leaks, and limited effectiveness.

Moreover, the direct financing mechanism cleared up decision-making bottlenecks caused by central efforts to plan and control activities. KDP's disbursement system takes an average of two weeks between the time when a village places a request and when funds arrive in the village account. Even during the East Asian financial crisis, KDP disbursed funds nearly twice as fast, on average, as agriculture, health, and education projects implemented through line departments (see figure 12.1). Bypassing intermediate levels of government enabled KDP to move quickly to respond to village-level demands.

Furthermore, as these CDD programs evolved, they opened windows of opportunity for additional financing from government and private sources as well as communities. Under KDP, communities contribute 17 percent of project costs, on average, and these contributions often equal or surpass the grant amount. Among participating districts, 40 percent provide matching grants from their own resources to contribute to capital costs.

Community-identified projects do not have to be financed by CDD: officials can establish links with many potential sources of financing. For example, in the Philippines, all projects identified through the CDD process are included under municipal development funds, so the local budget covers recurrent costs. This also helps attract funding from other government and nongovernmental

BOX 12.2 Funds Arriving in Cambodian Schools

The Cambodian Educational Quality Improvement Project (EQIP) is a CDD sectoral project that is modeling a participatory approach to improving school quality and using performance-based management. Cambodia's Ministry of Education, Youth, and Sports (MoEYS) has emphasized decentralization in its Education Strategic Plan 2001–2005. Projects such as EQIP, as well as several other donor-funded school grants and cluster programs, show what can happen when governments devolve responsibilities and funding to local schools and communities.

Funded in part by a World Bank credit of US$5 million, EQIP began in 1999 and supports clusters of schools in three provinces. The project allocates grants based on priorities identified through school committees composed of representatives from communities and each member school. The project is highly popular with participating schools and communities. According to one evaluation:

There was widespread enthusiasm for EQIP among those interviewed, and a desire to build on the progress already made. Decentralization issues featured prominently. Stakeholders welcomed the opportunity EQIP provided for making decisions at local levels. Being able to decide what to purchase for a cluster through a cooperative process at that level was greatly appreciated. It was recognized that the actual process of making decisions at provincial, district and cluster levels was developing skills in prioritizing, planning, budgeting and reporting . . . When asked what was the most important achievement of EQIP, the most popular answer was that it gave finances for priority needs in a timely and predictable manner. Enormous value was placed in this achievement. Previously there had been no resource flow from the MoEYS to schools and little if any to the provinces.

Source: Turner 2002.

FIGURE 12.1 Project Disbursement in Indonesia by Ratio, Fiscal Years 2000–2

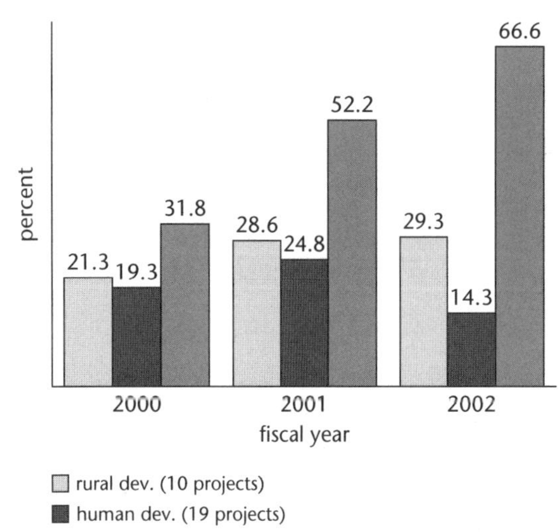

Source: World Bank Indonesia disbursement reports.

sources. In Cambodia, under the RILG Project, district integration workshops provide a forum for other government and nongovernmental actors to fund projects identified through the local planning process.

Cost-Effective Service Delivery

Studies of Indonesia's KDP and the Urban Poverty Project, its urban counterpart, as well as preliminary estimates from KALAHI in the Philippines, show that infrastructure projects cost some 25 to 56 percent less than similar small-scale works delivered by other public agencies. These cost savings are consistent with estimated savings from CDD projects in other regions. For instance, a case study of CDD projects in Brazil cites savings of 30 to 50 percent.

All these CDD programs have delivered demand-responsive public investments in infrastructure and economic and social activities. Because CDD planning and financing is decentralized, small-scale infrastructure projects are usually funded and implemented within three to four months. Under the first stage of KDP, villages completed more than 50,000 infrastructure, economic, and social subprojects. Technical reviews and external evaluations show that these projects were popular with communities and government officials alike. A sample of infrastructure projects showed that they yielded high internal rates of return ranging from 33 to 83 percent. These projects generated 25 million workdays, with 2.8 million villagers gaining short-term employment through labor-intensive works (World Bank 1998).

The national size and scope of these CDD programs have allowed governments to deliver essential public goods and services in a demand-responsive way while relieving overburdened national and subnational bureaucracies of the need to manage thousands of small village projects and byzantine financial sign-offs at multiple levels.

Technical Assistance in Formulating Decentralization Procedures

Increasing Public Engagement with Local Governments

In both Indonesia and Cambodia, CDD programs evolved as national decentralization reforms began to play out at local levels. In Indonesia, KDP incorporated greater roles for district parliaments, monitoring and supervision by local governments, and cost-sharing arrangements with district governments. In Cambodia, the Seila Program was adapted to work through the newly elected Commune/*Sangkat* Councils in place of the early Commune Development Councils. Financial transfers now flow to Commune/*Sangkat* Funds as well as provincial investment funds.

The CDD programs in both countries have built on lessons from participatory, decentralized planning and financing to shape decentralization regulations. The institutionalization of participatory, transparent mechanisms in decentralization procedures and frameworks has been a key aim. Both governments had passed legislation and decrees outlining decentralization frameworks but were still formulating implementation guidelines, making them amenable to community contributions.

A further benefit is that national ministries responsible for creating decentralization guidelines have implemented CDD programs. In Indonesia, the Ministry of Home Affairs, with guidance from Bappenas, the national planning agency, is responsible for issuing the implementing guidelines for decentralization. In Cambodia, the Ministry of Interior and the Ministry of Economy and Finance are key members of the Seila Task Force, and the Seila Program has provided financial and technical resources to new departments in these two ministries that regulate and support subnational authorities.

Drawing on lessons from the first and second phases, the third phase of KDP will assist district and village authorities in crafting 13 regulations (*perdas*) for village autonomy under Decentralization Law 22. Building on the KDP platform, the Initiatives for Local Governance Reform Project is designed to support district policies related to information disclosure, procurement, revenue generation, budget planning, and allocation, leading to higher pro-poor expenditures (World Bank 2004a).

Similarly, the Seila Program in Cambodia has channeled five years of experience with participatory planning and financing into helping government working groups complete the country's decentralized regulatory framework, draft supporting guidelines, and revise and strengthen regulations. For example, technical advisors from Seila have advised the government in developing the manual of financial management and procurement procedures for commune funds.

In contrast to Indonesia and Cambodia, where central governments are still formulating decentralization reforms and regulations, the Philippines has had a Local Government Code for some 12 years, and local governments are already well established. From the outset, the KALAHI-CIDSS project has worked within the decentralization law and engaged with formal institutions such as the *Barangay* Development Council and the Municipal Development Council to make the process for planning and allocating local development resources more participatory. Furthermore, to strengthen coordination with local governments and enhance sustainability, the Philippines project works with municipal committees chaired by the mayor and composed of the heads of all local departments. Local representatives of national agencies, NGOs, and donor institutions also participate. These multiagency committees meet every two weeks to discuss progress and determine needed contributions to KALAHI projects, including staff, salaries, and other recurrent costs (World Bank 2002).

Conclusions and the Challenges Ahead for CDD

Community-driven development projects aim to influence and strengthen local governance, with the intention that the participatory approach will spill over into broader decision-making processes at the community level. For CDD sectoral programs, such as those in health, education, and water and sanitation, the aim is to institutionalize mechanisms whereby users of services can engage in decision making and monitor investments and services.

TABLE 12.1 Points of Local Government Engagement in CDD Projects

	Indonesia	Philippines	Cambodia	
	KDP	KALAHI-CIDSS	Seila	EQIP
Project implementing agency	Ministry of Home Affairs and National Coordination Team.	Department of Social Welfare and Development (DSWD).	Seila Task Force (composed of 5 ministries) provides overall policy and program guidance. Implementation rests with ministries, provinces, and communes.	Ministry of Education, Youth and Sports (MoEYS).
Laws and regulations	KDP3 will help to draft the 13 village autonomy regulations.		Seila's pilot experience directly influenced the laws and regulations on commune/*sangkat* planning. Program provides technical assistance.	
Local planning	*Kecamatan* and village officials join in local planning process.	Municipal and village officials join in local planning process. DSWD staff facilitate planning.	Planning has become part of formal government at the commune/ *sangkat* levels.	MoEYS staff and school administrators join with community and school reps. in planning.
Financing	Ministry of Finance (MoF) transfers funds directly to village and intervillage accounts.	MoF transfers funds directly to village and intervillage accounts.	MoF transfers funds directly to commune/*sangkat* and provincial levels.	Funds flow from MoEYS directly to school clusters for school grants.
Cofinancing	By 2004, under KDP3, local governments will be paying all or partial capital costs.	Local governments and communities must contribute a minimum of 25%.		
Monitoring and oversight	District parliaments and local officials provide oversight and monitoring.	DSWD staff at different levels, as well as local governments.	Close monitoring and oversight provided by Seila staff at all levels.	MoEYS staff and local school cluster committees.
Capacity building	Training for *kecamatan* project managers, village councils, district parliaments.	DSWD staff and local governments.	Seila supports training of local government staff and local commune councils.	MoEYS line staff; school administrators.

Source: Various World Bank project appraisal documents, project reports, and discussions with task teams.

CDD has improved decentralization frameworks by:

- Promoting greater civic participation, voice, and accountability in local governance. CDD introduces mechanisms for participatory planning and decision making, as well for monitoring and transparency, into the local governance equation.
- Providing an effective means of service delivery within a decentralized context by delivering needed services in a cost-effective and time-efficient manner.

- Informing and shaping decentralization regulations.

CDD entails challenges, too. As noted, CDD projects are too new to allow definitive statements about their overall success or failure. Nevertheless, preliminary evaluations point to some challenges ahead, especially in decentralized environments.

First, can CDD become an overall development strategy, or will CDD projects provide a relatively narrow way to fulfill numerous small, discrete development investments? Existing reviews show that communities can build village roads, water supplies, schools, and clinics. However, such reviews do not reveal how village projects will tie in with efforts to plan road networks, protect watersheds, train teachers, and supply needed drugs. Experiences in Cambodia and the Philippines suggest how to coordinate local government input into discrete CDD investments and address recurrent and operational costs, but this area needs more exploration.

Expansion to this higher level requires that CDD programs engage more effectively with sectoral agencies to help them become more demand-driven and responsive. As CDD projects such as Seila and KDP become better established, techniques for integrating the CDD platform with higher-level planning and sectoral agencies become clear. As the Cambodia EQIP Project has shown, helping the Ministry of Education, Youth, and Sports move responsibilities for planning and financing down to school clusters can yield significant benefits for schools and communities. The challenge will be to strengthen accountability and participation in service delivery.

Second, can CDD improve links with private sector service providers? CDD projects tap such suppliers for construction materials and some forms of specialized technical assistance, but few have explored the use of private markets to procure books and teachers, qualified health services, and specialized training. Local procurement of goods and services sacrifices economies of scale, and identifying qualified service providers in poorly regulated professional environments is difficult. Nevertheless, some scope for promoting private sector service supply may exist.

Third, can governments better integrate CDD projects into their budgeting and planning process to address recurrent costs, operations and maintenance, and sustainability? As countries gradually integrate CDD capital and operating costs into intergovernmental fiscal systems, they need to ensure that these systems and financial flows remain transparent and easily tracked by the public.

When Is CDD Appropriate and When Is It Not?

Community-driven development programs are not always appropriate. Large-scale CDD operations such as KDP, Seila, and KALAHI presume fairly sophisticated management structures, conducive local social environments, and mechanisms that allow direct fiscal transfers to reach communities and be accounted for with reasonable accuracy. CDD projects in postconflict areas, where few of these conditions apply, seem to work reasonably well within limits, but involve significant quality tradeoffs.

Other conditions for success relate to the specific design of each CDD program. KDP assumes that private markets can provide qualified technical assistance. Seila assumes that local markets for contractors are reasonably competitive and can provide quality services. KALAHI relies on the competence of municipal governments. Programs that cannot assume that such conditions exist must adjust their design accordingly.

A subtle but important risk is that CDD projects may be asked to do more than their design can sustain. A good example is the challenge of linking CDD operations to district planning and budgeting. The solution lies in complementing CDD approaches with projects and strategies directed toward district- and province-level reform, not in transforming CDD operations into two-headed beasts that must perform both local and district planning and budgeting.

The need to supplement CDD with a broader reform strategy for local government is fundamental. CDD can be seen solely as a low-cost way to provide basic infrastructure and services. In certain environments, particularly postconflict and transitional countries, where virtually all standard systems and normal activities have been disrupted, CDD projects may be the only way to operate. But for most countries, CDD will work best if it is one part of a broader reform strategy intended to improve the quality and efficiency of government services.

Annex: CDD Portfolio Breakdown

Global Trends

For fiscal years 2001 to 2003, World Bank lending in support of CDD has totaled nearly $2 billion annually, and averaged approximately 11 percent of all Bank investments. The following tables and figures reveal the contours of this lending worldwide and in East Asia.

TABLE 12A.1 World Bank Lending in Support of CDD, Fiscal Years 2000–3

	No. of CDD projects	Total World Bank lending[a] (US$ billions)	Total World Bank CDD lending[b] (US$ billions)	CDD as % of Bank lending (percent)
FY00	55	15.3	1.0	7
FY01	78	17.3	2.3	14
FY02	78	19.5	1.9	10
FY03	83	18.5	2.0	11
Total	**294**	**70.6**	**7.2**	**11**

Source: World Bank CDD briefing note for Mr. Shengman Zhang, July 14, 2003, SDV.
a. Includes the International Bank for Reconstruction and Development and the International Development Association.
b. Excludes enabling environment.

FIGURE 12A.2 Regional Trends—CDD Investments by Fiscal Year

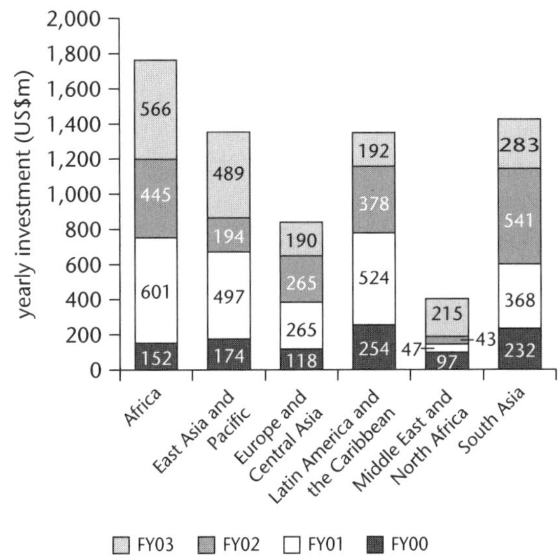

Source: World Bank CDD briefing note for Mr. Shengman Zhang, July 14, 2003, SDV.

FIGURE 12A.1 Bankwide CDD Lending for Fiscal Years 2000–3

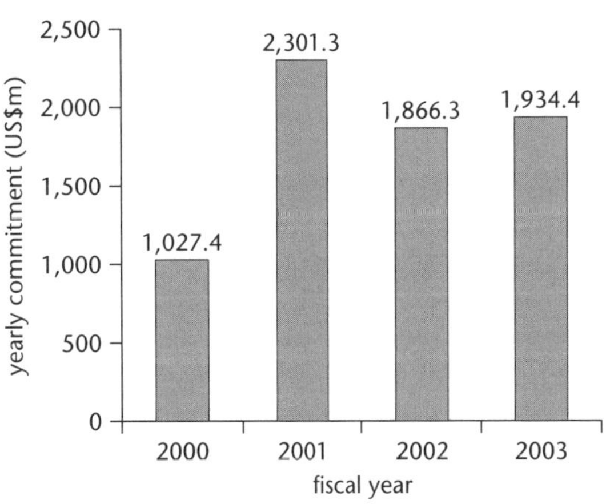

Source: World Bank CDD briefing note for Mr. Shengman Zhang, July 14, 2003, SDV.

CDD Trends in the East Asia and Pacific Region

FIGURE 12A.3 CDD Project Breakdown by Country

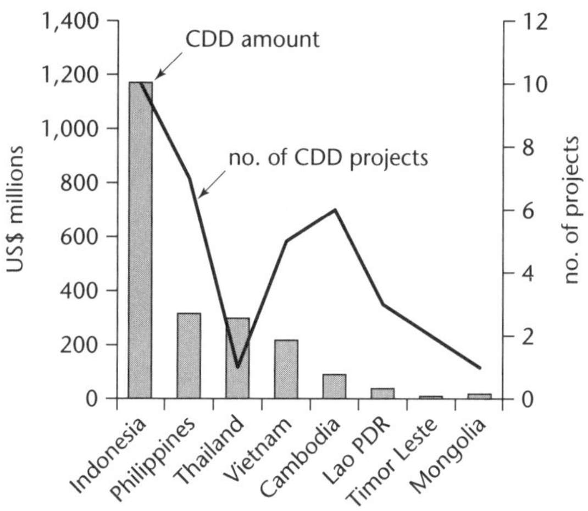

Source: Authors' calculations and desk review research.

FIGURE 12A.4 CDD Project Breakdown by Sector

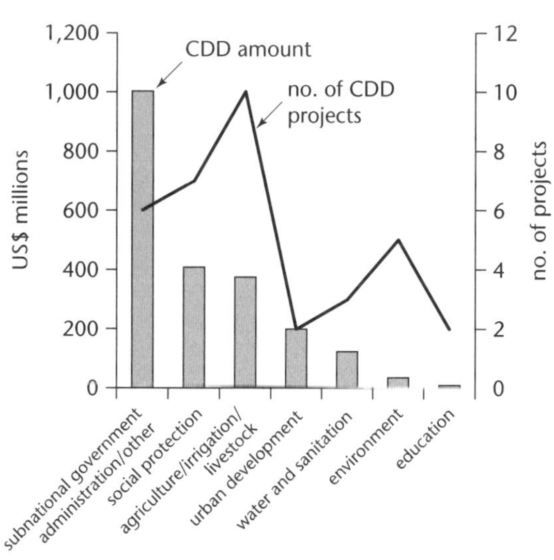

Source: Authors' calculations.

FIGURE 12A.5 Sectoral Breakdown of CDD Projects by Country

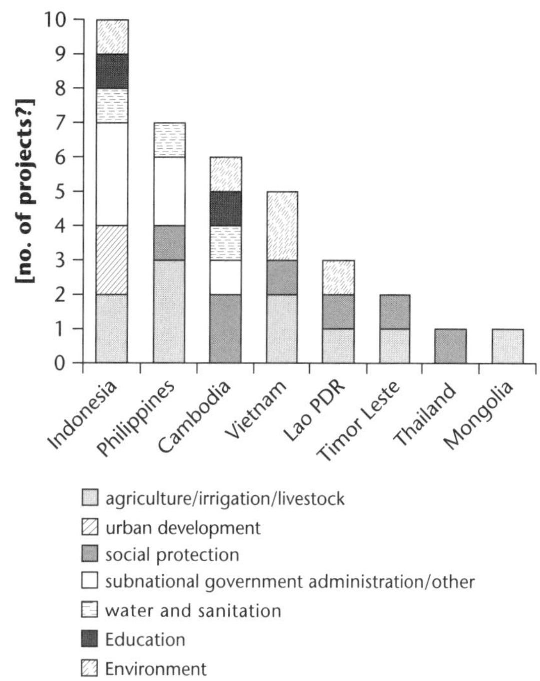

Source: Authors' calculations.

TABLE 12A.2 World Bank–Funded CDD Projects Open in the East Asia Pacific Region, as of June 30 2003

	Country	Number of CDD projects	World Bank[a] amounts (US$ millions)	CDD amounts (US$ millions)
1	Indonesia	10	1,220	1,170
2	Philippines	7	341	316
3	Vietnam	5	333	217
4	Thailand	1	300	298
5	Cambodia	6	89	89
6	Lao PDR	3	38	38
7	Mongolia	1	19	17
8	Timor-Leste	2	9	9
	Total	**35**	**2,349**	**2,153**

Source: Authors' research and calculations.
a. Includes the International Bank for Reconstruction and Development and the International Development Association.

Endnotes

1. The content of the CDD portfolio has been the subject of wide debate within social and human development circles. This chapter adheres to the broad definition used by the World Bank's social development network: "Community-driven development (CDD) gives control of decisions and resources to community groups. These groups often work in partnership with demand-responsive private sector, NGOs, and central government agencies."

   This definition raises two issues. First, who decides how to allocate resources? CDD projects are distinguished from earlier Social Funds by the fact that local communities or local elected bodies make such decisions. The earlier generation of Social Funds—and even many to this day—involve communities in planning, preparing proposals, and implementing projects. However, Social Fund staff at national or regional levels actually make decisions on proposals.

   CDD projects, on the other hand, retain decision making within communities through village-elected forums or elected local government. Thus, for the last several years, Social Funds that do not involve communities in decision making on resources have been considered separate from the CDD portfolio.

   The second issue relates to the role of locally elected governments. Traditionally, CDD projects have focused on community organizations and forums that are not part of the formal government decision-making structure. Over the last two years, however, the World Bank has defined CDD to include both locally elected community organizations and democratically elected government bodies working in partnership with community groups. Thus, debates about whether CDD is outside or inside the usual political channels have blurred.
2. Seila is a Khmer word meaning "foundation stone."
3. For a fuller description, see World Bank 2003b, annexes 11 and 12.
4. Interview with Cyprian Fisiy, former World Bank task team leader for the KALAHI-CIDSS Project.

Bibliography

Asian Resource Center for Decentralization. 2002. *Decentralization and Power Shift: An Imperative for Good Governance.* Quezon City, Philippines: University of the Philippines, National College of Public Administration, Center for Local and Regional Governance.

Evers, P. 1998. "Village Government: Does the Current System Enhance Good Government?" Washington, DC: World Bank, Social Development Department.

Ministry of Home Affairs, Community Development Agency, and National Management Consultants, Indonesia. 2002. "Kecamatan Development Program: Phase One—Final Report, 1998–2002." Jakarta: Ministry of Home Affairs.

OECD (Organisation for Economic Co-operation and Development). 1997. "Final Report of the Ad Hoc Working Group on Participatory Development and Good Governance." Paris: OECD, Development Assistance Committee.

Turner, M. 2002. "Whatever Happened to Deconcentration? Recent Initiatives in Cambodia." *Public Administration and Development* 22: 353–64.

Wassenich, Paul, and Katherine Whiteside. 2003. "CDD Impact Assessments Study: Optimizing Evaluation Design under Constraints." World Bank, Washington, DC.

Wescott, Clay, and Doug Porter. 2002. "Fiscal Decentralization and Citizen Participation in East Asia." Paper for conference on Citizen Participation in the Context of Fiscal Decentralization: Best Practices in Municipal Management in Latin America and Asia.

World Bank. 1998. Project Appraisal Document, Kecamatan Development Project. Internal draft document. World Bank, Washington, DC.

———. 1999. Project Appraisal Document, Education Quality Improvement Project. Internal draft document. World Bank, Washington, DC.

———. 2000. *Voices of the Poor,* vols. I, II, III. Washington, DC: World Bank.

———. 2001a. "Promoting Good Governance with Social Funds and Decentralization." *PREM Notes,* Public Sector No. 51. Washington, DC: World Bank.

———. 2001b. "Decentralization and Governance: Does Decentralization Improve Service Delivery?" *PREM Notes*, Public Sector No. 55. Washington, DC: World Bank.

———. 2001c. Project Appraisal Document, Second Kecamatan Development Project. Internal draft document. World Bank, Washington, DC.

———. 2002. Project Appraisal Document, Kapitbisig Laban Sa Kahirapan/Comprehensive and Integrated Delivery of Social Services (KALAHI-CIDSS) Project. Internal draft document. World Bank, Washington, DC.

———. 2003a. "Decentralizing Indonesia: Regional Public Expenditure Review: Overview Report." Washington, DC: World Bank, East Asia Poverty Reduction and Economic Management Unit.

———. 2003b. Project Appraisal Document, Rural Investment and Local Governance Project. Internal draft document. World Bank, Washington, DC.

———. 2004a. Project Appraisal Document, Initiatives for Local Governance Reform Project. Internal draft document. World Bank, Washington, DC.

———. 2004b. *World Development Report 2004: Making Services Work for Poor People.* Washington, DC: World Bank; and New York: Oxford University Press.